AF660010

BEYOND NORMS:
MARKETING FOR EXCELLENCE

BEYOND NORMS: MARKETING FOR EXCELLENCE

Editors

SANDEEP PURI
JAYANTHI RANJAN
RAKESH CHOPRA

BLOOMSBURY

LONDON • NEW DELHI • NEW YORK • SYDNEY

© *Bloomsbury Publishing India Pvt. Ltd., 2013*

First Published, 2013

All rights reserved. No part of this publication may be reproduced or transmitted in any form or by any means, electronic or mechanical, including photocopying, recording, or any information storage or retrieval system, without prior permission in writing from the publishers.

No responsibility for loss caused to any individual or organization acting on or refraining from action as result of the material in this publication can be accepted by Bloomsbury India or the author/editor.

BLOOMSBURY PUBLISHING INDIA PVT. LTD.
London New Delhi New York Sydney

ISBN: 978-93-82563-46-4

Published by Bloomsbury Publishing India Pvt. Ltd.
VISHRUT Building, DDA Complex, Building No. 3, Pocket C-6 & 7
Vasant Kunj, New Delhi 110 070

Laser Typeset by FORTUNE GRAPHICS
WZ-911/2, Shankarlal Street, Naraina, New Delhi

Printed at Anvi Composers
1 DDA Market, Block A-1B, Paschim Vihar, New Delhi 110 063

This book is meant for educational and learning purposes. The authors of the book have taken all reasonable care to ensure that the contents of the book do not violate any existing copyright or other intellectual property rights of any person in any manner whatsoever. However, the editors are not responsible for the authors' plagiarism if any. In the event the author(s) has/have been unable to track any source and if any copyright has been inadvertently infringed, please notify the Publisher in writing for corrective action.

Acknowledgements

The editors are grateful to the management and Dr. Bibek Banerjee (Director) of IMT, Ghaziabad, India without whose support it would not have been possible to bring out this volume. We would like to thank Dr. Rajendra Nargundkar (Sr. Dean) and Dr. Suresh Bedi (Dean) for their guidance and help in numerous activities to organize FOBE 2012. We specially thank our knowledge partners Mazagon Dock Limited, for their support in making FOBE 2012 a big success.

Research is a painstaking business and we cannot overemphasize the importance of carefully researched papers in contributing to a volume of this type. A large number of distinguished authors from academia and practicing managers from industry have shown a keen interest in the subject area and have contributed well researched papers. Thanks to their interest that this volume has been possible. We would like to thank our colleagues from academia for their valuable time, support and guidance. The support came in many forms: review and re-review, suggestions and modifications and observations to make this volume more focused and relevant.

Our thanks are also due to Bloomsbury Publishing, their editors, production experts and their entire staff for their cooperation in bringing out this volume. We would also like to thank all the faculty colleagues, officers and staff members at IMT, Ghaziabad in extending their support for FOBE 2012. Special thanks are due to Mr. Krishna Murari Sinha for his contribution in the progress of this volume.

We value your feedback and suggestions on this volume. We look forward to your comments on emails: jranjan@imt.edu; rchopra@imt.edu; spuri@imt.edu in order to bring out a better innovative volume in future.

Finally, deep thanks go to our family members for their understanding, patience and support for this endeavor.

Sandeep Puri
Jayanthi Ranjan
Rakesh Chopra

Preface

In this changing business world, where the old ways of marketing a business are quickly becoming obsolete, it is more imperative than ever for any size company to think out of the box in promoting and delivering its products or services. "Thinking beyond Norms Marketing" provides an authoritative review of the concepts of new approaches in the areas of Marketing Management.

FOBE 2012 – International Conference Facets of Business Excellence – Thinking beyond the Box is organized by IMT Ghaziabad after the successful FOBE 2011 – International Conference Facets of Business Excellence – Leveraging Information Technology for Strategic Advantage.

The primary goal of the FOBE 2012 is to bring together creative academic and industrial experts in the field of Business Administration to discuss, exchange views and experiences on thinking beyond the box to help today's business organizations to exceed their goals and expectations while pursuing their full growth and earning potential. This conference is a platform for discussing contemporary issues in Strategy, IT, Management and Marketing and for exchanging views and experiences on various issues related to out of box thinking in business management.

It contains rich resources from the vast experiences of researchers, academicians and practitioners in the industry. This premier reference source contains a very comprehensive knowledge on this changing paradigm and provides an all-encompassing perspective on the importance of out of box thinking in these functional areas of business.

Hope this volume finds space in the minds of the practicing world of business and IT and draws new landscapes in future.

Sandeep Puri
Jayanthi Ranjan
Rakesh Chopra

The Editors

PROF. SANDEEP PURI

Sandeep Puri is working as a faculty in Marketing at IMT, Ghaziabad. He is pursuing his Ph. D on Private labels. He is Gold Medalist during B. Pharmacy. He has over 19 years of experience in Industry & academics. He has held senior level positions in Marketing and Sales Management in Trident & Novartis. He has 24 publications till date. He has 5 publications in various International Journals and 9 in magazines and newspapers. He is also having 2 publications in International conference proceedings and 2 in national conference proceedings. He is also a visiting faculty at prestigious business schools like S P Jain, Singapore, Fachhochschule Vorarlberg, Austria and Great Lakes His teaching, research and training interests include Customer Relationship Management, Sales Management & Service Marketing. He has published six edited books He can be reached at spuri@imt.edu.

DR. JAYANTHI RANJAN

Jayanthi Ranjan is a Professor in IT Management area at IMT, Ghaziabad. She is also Associate Dean-International Relations, IMT Ghaziabad. She has more than 19 years of teaching experience. She has published various papers on Data clustering, Data Mining, Database security, business intelligence, educational technologies that appeared in various international refereed journals. She has over 110 publications till date. She has over 53 publications in various International Journals, 15 national conference proceedings and 10 International conference Proceedings till date. She has published 14 edited books. She has published research papers with refereed publications like in World Scientific, Emerald, Indersceince, ANSINET, GIFT society. She is the recipient of 'Best Teacher Award' from AIMA-Ghaziabad Management Association, India for her contribution to teaching and research. She is also the recipient of Best Management Researcher award, from Association of Management Scholars AIMS.

She is serving on the editorial board for the international journal "Information Technology Journal", Asian Network for Scientific Information. She is also the editorial member of "Indersceince-International Journal of E-CRM". She is the Editorial member of "Inter disciplinary journal of information knowledge and management", Informing Science Institute, UK. She is the associate editor of "Journal of Applied and Theoretical

Information Technology". Her Teaching and Research interests include Data Mining & Building Data Warehouses, Information Systems Design, Information Agents Building and Business Intelligence. She can be reached at jranjan@imt.edu

PROF. RAKESH CHOPRA

Dr. Rakesh Chopra is a professor in the area of Economic Environment & Strategy. He is a Ph. D and M.Phil from Mumbai University in Strategic Studies & International Relations focusing on Energy Security, M.Sc. from Madras University, and an MBA from JBIMS, Mumbai. He was Senior Visiting Research Fellow with the "Oxford Leverhulme Programme on the Changing Character of War" at Oxford University. He is an alumnus of the Harvard Kennedy School. Prior to joining IMT, he was a Professor of Strategy at XLRI Jamshedpur. He served in the Indian Navy for 38 years. He has commanded three ships including a ship in the 1971 Indo Pak war in the Eastern Theatre, and has held various operational appointments. He is an alumnus of the National Defense Academy, and the Defense Services Staff College, Wellington, where he has been on the Directing Staff. He was the Chief Instructor and Dean of the College of Naval Warfare at Karanja, Mumbai, and Chief Instructor of the Navigation & Direction School where officers specialize in the planning and conduct of maritime operations. He was mentioned in 'Mention in Dispatches' for gallantry during military operations in Sri Lanka and was awarded the Vishisht Seva Medal by the President of India for exemplary service.

Contents

A Comparative Study of CRM in Telecom and Banking Sector

Sandeep Puri, Aashish Kumar and Manish Kumar

Institute of Management Technology, Ghaziabad

ABSTRACT

A well implemented CRM strategy can lead to – more suitable products and services to customers, higher availability of services, higher level of satisfaction of customers, better customer classification and more effective marketing campaigns. Also in today's world the voice of the customer has amplified due to the increased use of social media and thus brand communication which used to be one directional earlier has now become bidirectional. Thus there lies a great opportunity of leveraging social media to build stronger relationship with customers.The objective of this research paper is to analyse the scope of CRM in the Banking and the Telecom sector. The study explores how CRM is being applied in the Banking and the Telecom industry and what are their unique requirements. Owing to the unique characteristics of services i.e. - intangibility, perishability, heterogeneity and inseparability, it becomes even more critical for Banking and Telecom companies to manage relationship with their customers. Effective CRM makes it possible for the organisations to provide customers better products and services while maximizing their lifetime value due to the increased satisfaction.

INTRODUCTION

The fact that retaining a customer is considerably cheaper than acquiring new customers is well understood by businesses world over. Thus, high importance is given to maintaining relationship with the customers and improving their satisfaction level. Customer relationship management can be defined as (Parvatiyar&Sheth, 2001) - a comprehensive strategyand process of acquiring, retaining, and partnering with selective customers to create superior value for the company and the customer. It involves the integration of marketing, sales, customer service, and the supply-chain functions of the organization to achieve greater efficiencies and effectiveness in delivering customer value.

Thus customer relationship management is a cross functional activity and not limited to the marketing or sales department. CRM should not be looked at as a tool because it can only be beneficial if customer relationship management is integrated in the corporate strategy. Thus

CRM is not just a tool or a process, it is a philosophy.

In the service industry the importance of customer relationship management becomes even more important owing to the nature of the business. CRM tools can be very beneficial as they allow better handling of the characteristics of services i.e. - intangibility, perishability, heterogeneity and inseparability ((Parasuraman et al., 1985).In the banking sector CRM leads to effective management of the three S of the banking industry: speed, size, service (V.P. Gulati and M.V. SivaKumaran (2003)). While in the telecom sector CRM helps in identifying the needs of different consumer segments (Haridasan and Venkatesh, 2011).

CRM enables the banking companies to know the customer better. In addition it helps uncover potential customers and improves overall customer service. It helps build an advantage over competitors as firms are enabled to increase their intelligence about the customer. CRM manages to provide this information to almost every employee. CRM in banking industryenables to improve and encourage relationship building with existing and potential customers, the various departments within the organization, management etc.

CRM in today's world is also important due to the amplified voice of the customer owing to the increasing use of Social Media. Social Media has changed communications by brands from unidirectional to bidirectional. A customer can now leverage social media to communicate directly with brands, thanks to their increased presence on social media. This also means that consumer views can go viral on social media thus making major impact on the reputation of the brand. Therefore businesses need to monitor what people are talking about them on social media and be able to respond in real time. Considering this requirement, the CRM providers have now adapted their product to include social media management tools. Thus businesses can now generate leads, take customer feedback and promote their brand on social media with the help of Social CRM.

LITERATURE REVIEW

Researchers have observed that CRM is more than a set of management tools; it is a management philosophy, a way of running the business. CRM has revealed many aspects that closely resemble the total quality management (TQM) approach (Adrienne Curry, Elena Kkolou, (2004)). The core principles of total quality outline those of the CRM system, which are a focus on the customer, participation and teamwork and continuous improvement and learning. Owing to the characteristics of the service industry i.e. intangibility, perishability, heterogeneity and inseparability ((Parasuraman et al., 1985) the need to maintain better customer relationship becomes even more important. More so in case of Banks since the lifetime value of customers is considerably higher compared to other industries like Telecom for whom the customer volumes are the main business drivers.

For the telecom sector some of the relevant questions (Haridasan and Venkatesh, 2011) that need to be answered for better customer relationship are-

- What products and services does the customer need?
- Which consumer segment should be offered a given set of scheme and offers?
- Who are most profitable customers and how can their value to the company be increased?
- Using a CRM tool can help the Company answer these questions better sinceeffective CRM implementation makes it possible for the organisations to leverage the historical data of the customeras well as unifies the communication through multiple channel which in today's world also includes Social Media.

In the banking sector, customer relationship management is given high importance owing to the nature of the service. When it comes to banking services, customers want to be reassured that they can trust the bank for providing a high level of safety and convenience. High relevance is given to the value added by CRM in banking (V.P. Gulati and M.V. SivaKumaran (2003)). For banks a well implemented CRM strategy can lead to – more suitable products and services to customers, higher availability of services, higher level of satisfaction of customers, better customer classification and more effective marketing campaigns. Thus CRM leads to effective management of the three S of the banking industry: speed, size and service.

TELECOM SECTOR

Players in Indian Telecom Industry are facing enormous pressure because of rapidly changing market and stiff competition. They have to innovate continuously their product and service offerings as per changing market dynamics. Margin from voice is squeezing because large number of local players entering into market with reduced call rates. With the advent of smartphones (iPhones and Galaxy) in the Indian market, the future lies in effectively tapping the growing demand of data and video. Companies have to adapt to changing need of customers and follow customer centric practices such as Customer Relationship Management for increasing customer retention and loyalty in this volatile market.

Telecom industry has special CRM needs. New technologies, such as DSL and UMTS, are driving the convergence of voice, data, and media content, and they are forming the basis of new products, services, and service bundles. Growing competition is leading to shorter product life cycles. CRM system should enable to launch new products quickly and to bundle new and existing services flexibly. It has to support both contracts and one-time sales, and, because of the increasing focus on customer profitability, it must recognize the importance of cross- and up-selling.

According to Newell (2000) there are often three different types of customers: the top, middle and lower groups. The top group (top 10 %) consists of customers with excellent loyalty higher customer satisfaction and profitability for the organization. CRM is essential to retain and offer them the best possible services in order to avoid them going to competitors. Middle group customers (next 40% to 50%) are ones delivering good profits and having good potential for future growth and loyalty. These customers are susceptible to moving to competitors.

The focus should be to use CRM to target middle group customers effectively as they are the greatest source of potential revenue. Lower group relational (bottom 40 to 50 %) customers are those who are only marginally profitable. Thus least attention should be given to these types of customers. Otherwise it can hinder the effectiveness of servicing top and middle group customers.

Telecom operators can use data such as order and contract data, channel data, billing data, information on customer devices, tariffs and combine with basic data on names, addresses, gender and age to form an operational database for each type of customer groups (top, middle and lower groups). A new class of data is generated in social networks by customers themselves. On Facebook, Twitter and in other communities, users can provide information to and about the operators. Telecom operators can cooperate with social communities to access this contextual data.

Operational customer data could be used for campaigns, loyalty programs and analysis while contextual data for evaluating customer satisfaction with the operators services, tariffs, network quality etc. CRM can help in tapping customer information at every touch points in its life cycle and bring many insights into individual customer behaviour. Telecom operators could provide customised services for top group customers in their entire life cycle to make them a loyal customer prohibiting them from moving to competitors.

BANKING SECTOR

Obtaining, maintaining and utilizing customer database in an effort to maximize or improve customer relationships will go a long way in increasing overall productivity for the banking industry. A failure to focus on the different aspects of relationship marketing can prove detrimental while knowing and indulging your customer preferences can go a long way in securing and raising profitability.For the banking sector high relevance is given to the value added by CRM (Gulati and Sivakumaran (2003)). For banks a well implemented CRM strategy will provide following advantages:

- Identification of potential customers
- More suitable products and services to customers
- Higher availability of services
- Provision of data regarding history and preferences of investors
- Encouraging customer relationships
- Increasing and improving financial productivity
- Storage and provision of financial data of customers
- Higher level of satisfaction of customers
- Better customer classification and
- Easy access to collated financial data

- Investment selling
- Tracking and monitoring financial deals
- Aiding the sales team in the provision of customers' needs
- Encouraging and assisting the increase of cross selling and upselling
- More effective marketing campaigns

In the banking industry the three S: speed, size, service plays a very important role in deciding the fate of customer relationship. With the proper application of CRM, improvement can be made in all the three domains. Due to availability of customer data, it is easier to predict their needs and thus provide higher quality service in time. Also the customer data can help to segment the customers according to the size of their transactions.

MOBILE CRM IN BANKING

Mobile CRM can be defined as "Customer relationship management of any kind including interactive communication between an organisation and a customer using a mobile device" (Liljander et al., 2007).

For developing countries like India where the rate of mobile adoption is far greater than the internet adoptions, mobile CRM can be highly promising. With the present technology banks now offer services like viewing account details, fund transfer, balance enquiry, loan details, bill payments, enquiry about credit card and demat account and add value to existing ones by disseminating the information at user defined time and place. For the consumers intention to adopt a mobile banking application is governed by eight factors namely perceived utility value, perceived ease of use, compatibility, context, perceived cost, perceived risk, negative attitude and personal innovativeness. Among this perceived utility value is the most prominent factor as far as adoption of mobile CRM services is concerned (Purnimaet al, 2011). In the short- to medium-term, the mobile channel can be expected to become a key part of multi-channel strategies emerging for the banking sector, establishing the need for more research in the field (Peevers et al, 2011).

MANAGERIAL IMPLICATIONS

From our work we observe that owing to the unique characteristics of services i.e. - intangibility, perishability, heterogeneity and inseparability, it becomes even more critical for business to manage relationship with their customers. Thus CRM can be beneficial for both Banking and Telecom sector by helping them leverage historical data of the customers, better classifying their customers, increasing effectiveness of their marketing campaigns, responding faster and better understanding and satisfying customer needs.

TELECOM

Telecom operators have difficulties understanding their customers because they are facing following data challenges:

- They generate huge volumes of very valuable data from telephony and data services in their fixed and mobile day-to-day business.
- Their internal setup makes it difficult to transform all this data into knowledge.

Companies such as Apple, Google and eBay define the benchmark for customer understanding (Klaus-Ulrich Feiler, Klaus Fuest, Dr. Marcus Steiner). They identify customer needs and design goods and services based on innovative preference profiles. Telecom operators are fighting with their complex data systems. But the future of business does not lie just in more sophisticated databases and algorithms. A rethinking in management is required, going far beyond the question of how to manage and handle data. The philosophy should be to understand what does our customer wants and how can we deliver it?

The process starts at the very top, where senior management has to develop a passion for the customer and lead the way towards the corporate philosophy. They need a vision and then have to define a customer-centric strategy that is anchored in the overall mid to long-term business strategy based on this vision. Every aspect and every strategic move should be considered from the customer's point of view

BANKING

Unlike the telecom sector there is need for more detailed data base regarding the customer. Better classification of customers can help in deciding the target segment for a given scheme. For example, if a loan scheme of high amount is launched, it can be beneficial if the Bank has a classified list of HNI's who would be the right target group for such a scheme. Thus, it becomes easier to target the right customer base. However as in case of Telecom, a Bank may want to have highly detailed data regarding the top 10% of their customers by account size.

4P MODEL IMPLICATION

We now take a look at the implications of adopting Customer Relationship Management using the 4P model-

Product

For the service sector since the product is intangible so it becomes even more relevant to gather customer feedback and adapt the offering to better meet the customer needs. CRM can help leveraging the customer data to better understand the customer needs and thus respond accordingly. CRM assures for both the Banking and Telecom sector that Voice of Customer plays an important role in product development.

Price

A Company involved in CRM monitors customer transaction data on a regular basis. Thus impact of any price increase or decrease on the customer usage can be analysed in case of Telecom sector. Hencethe price elasticity is better determined. In case of Banking sector also the impact of interest rate variation can be analysed similarly.

Promotions

A Company adopting CRM strategy can classify the customer base and determine which marketing campaigns are effective for any particular market segment. Thus the impact of marketing campaign can be amplified while decreasing the cost of campaign.

Place

For nationwide Telecom operators, it can help in analysing the pattern of usage and popularity of the different services in different regions. Thus they distinguish between the requirements in different states.

CONCLUSION

We conclude that customer relationship management is critical to both the Banking as well as Telecom Sector. This is due to the unique characteristics of services i.e. - intangibility, perishability, heterogeneity and inseparability. However the approach towards customer relationship may differ due to the different needs of the two sectors. In case of Banks, due to the considerably higher lifetime value of customer the focus of CRM should be to allow leveraging detailed database of customers which in turn can help in understanding and predicting their needs better.In Telecom, the focus of CRM should be on better classification of the large user base and predicting suitable schemes and offerings for them.

Adopting an effective CRM strategy would enable both these segments to better understand the consumer needs, respond faster to consumer demand and increase effectiveness of their marketing campaigns by directing it to the right segment.

REFERENCES

[1] V.P. Gulati and M.V. Sivakumaran, "CRM in Banking and Financial Services CRM for Banks in India" Book on Customer Relationship Management by Excel Books Publications, 2003 Edition

[2] Parasuraman, A., Zeithaml, V.A. and Berry, L.L. (1985), "A conceptual model of service quality and its implications for further research", Journal of Marketing, Vol. 49, pp. 41-50.

[3] Haridasan and Venkatesh, "Assessing the Effectiveness of CRM Practices by Mobile Service Providers Using Data Envelopment Analysis", 2011

[4] Adrienne Curry, Elena Kkolou, (2004),"Evaluating CRM to contribute to TQM improvement - a cross-case comparison", The TQM Magazine, Vol. 16, No.5 pp. 314 – 324

[5] Parvatiyar, Atul and Jagdish N. Sheth (2001). "Customer Relationship Management: Emerging Practice, Process, and Discipline". Journal of Economic and Social Research, Volume 3, Number 2, 1-34

[6] Purnima S. Sangle, PreetyAwasthi, (2011),"Consumer's expectations from mobile CRM services: a banking context", Business Process Management Journal, Vol. 17 Iss: 6 pp. 898 – 918

[7] Liljander, V., Polsa, P. and Forsberg, K. (2007), "Do mobile CRM services appeal to loyalty program customer", International Journal of E-business Research, Vol. 3 No. 2, pp. 24-40

[8] Newell, F (2000) „Loyalty.com: CRM in the new era of internet marketing McGraw-Hill Professional, New York.

[9] Klaus-Ulrich Feiler, Klaus Fuest, Dr. Marcus Steiner,"What customers really want-A customer-centric strategy for telecom"

[10] SergiosDimitriadis and Eric Stevens,"Integrated customer relationship management for service activities An internal/external gap model"

[11] Bruhn, M. (2003), Relationship Marketing, Management of Customer Relationship, Prentice-Hall,Harlow.

[12] Crosby, L., Kenneth, E. and Cowles, D. (1990), "Relationship quality in services selling: an interpersonal influence perspective", Journal of Marketing, Vol. 54, pp. 68-81.

[13] G. Peevers, G. Douglas, D. Marshall, M.A. Jack, (2011),"On the role of SMS for transaction confirmation with IVR telephone banking", International Journal of Bank Marketing, Vol. 29, No.3, pp. 206 – 223

Brand Customer Centricity Association Maps for Developing Stronger Brands

Nidhi Sinha

Jaypee Institute of Information Technology, Noida

ABSTRACT

Customer-based brand equity is seen as particularly important and scholars propose that the concept incorporates several different dimensions. Included among these dimensions are the various associations that consumers attribute to a brand. Such associations can be intentional or unintentional and serve to generate brand image and meaning for consumers. Managers are able to position and differentiate the brand using these associations, which may also provide a logical basis for brand extensions. It is therefore accepted that management of brand equity demands associations that need to be carefully selected, created and maintained in order to positive influence consumer attitudes and purchase intention. Extant literature acknowledges the existence of "associative networks". However, analysts have not yet been able to devise techniques that allow marketers to compare a brand with others through the mapping of their respective associations. Achieving such an aim is consequently the main purpose of the current study.

Brand managers focus on strategically positioning their brands and influencing the brands' associative networks in consumers' memory. Among different alternatives, brand managers can at least choose from two fundamentally different alternatives in building their brands: Firstly, focus on many *favorable associations, pursuing a* broad brand strategy *or focus on strengthening some* few *diagnostic associations, pursuing a* narrow brand strategy.

The primary purpose of this paper is to illustrate a methodology for gaining actionable, strategic insight into a brand's associations and its competitive uniqueness against its competitors. The authors integrate free association protocols and response latency techniques to draw the associative brand maps for the five product brands of Pepsico, to develop a overview of the brand's associations and to depict brand's strategic meaning in a visual representation across the six major brand functions.

The present techniques used in this research paper effectively uncover associations that the consumers have for the brand and how strong, unique, relevant and favorable those associations can be for the practicing managers. The strategic brand association maps demonstrate an excellent and a clear consumer-driven strategic view of the associations that the brand has in the minds of the consumers, thus providing the organizations actionable insights for understating the grey areas with respect to the positioning of the brand in the minds of the consumers.

INTRODUCTION

The current literature in brand management offers no guidance on which of these alternatives will most likely influence brand performance. However, according to the theory of the fan effect (Anderson, 1974), brands built using few associations should have stronger associations in consumers' memory and these associations should be activated faster from memory in judgment situations.

Innovation. It's a word that appears in just about every annual report of consumer products companies. Although everyone talks about it, very few companies think innovatively about the concept, especially when it comes to new product development. Instead, many consumer-facing organizations remain focused on risk-averse activities aimed at slow-but-steady growth.

To be successful, companies will need to engage consumers in dialogue and leverage their insights to create nationally recognized brands that are worthy of their price. Consumer-Centric Innovation (CCI) can often be the path to this outcome as it can help create products that capture the customer's imagination, provide entertaining brand experiences, or offer solutions to previously unmet needs.

One of the most fundamental tasks of brand managers is to understand and manage the set of associations around their brand. These associations (both intended and unintended) give meaning to the brand are an important component of brand equity. Here we present a methodology designed to give managers a strategic, comprehensive and consumer-driven view of their brand and how their brand is differentiated vis-a' -vis key competitors. Brand equity is one of the core concepts in marketing and has been the focus of much research over the last 30 years (Aaker, 1991; Keller, 1993). The concept is traditionally defined as the "marketing effects uniquely attributable to the brand" (Keller, 1993).

This competitive advantage is based on the price premium attained, increased efficiency and effectiveness of marketing programs, increased margins, increased customer demand and satisfaction, brand extension facilitation, negotiation leverage, and lower vulnerability to competitors (Aaker, 1992; Bendixen et al., 2004). Research on brand equity has supported these claims by linking it to a variety of performance measures such as profit and market performance (Baldauf and Cravens, 2003) as well as stock market performance (Aaker and Jacobson, 2001). One key component of brand equity is the associations consumers have with the brand (Aaker, 1991; Keller, 1993). For example, consumers may associate "refreshing," "youth," and "caffeine" with the brand Pepsi, and these associations then may drive their choice of this brand (Keller, 1993).

Brand associations have been called "the heart and soul of the brand" (Aaker, 1996), and "fundamental to the understanding of customer-based brand equity" (Hsieh, 2004). The central role of brand associations in the creation and maintenance of brand equity is widely accepted (Chaudhuri, 1999; Hart and Murphy, 1998; Hsieh, 2004; Maltz, 1991; Walvis, 2008; Wansink, 2003).

Brand associations are important to practitioners for a variety of reasons. First, they help consumers process and retrieve information and can help differentiate or position the brand. Second, if the associations are positive, they will create beneficial attitudes and feelings and provide a reason to buy. Lastly, brand associations may be exploited to create effective brand extensions (Aaker, 1991). Overall, the selection, creation, and maintenance of brand associations are among the most important steps in the management of brand equity (Aaker, 1991).

Due to their fundamental importance, measurement of brand associations is at the center of brand management. One of the most important tasks for brand managers is to understand and manage the set of associations around their brand. Moreover, recent academic work on brand equity has called for the development of "brand maps" and "richer, more comprehensive, and actionable models of brand equity" (Keller, 2001).

The present study is an attempt to fill this gap in the literature by presenting a methodology designed to map brand meaning. These maps present managers with a strategic, comprehensive and consumer driven view of their brand, and how their brand is differentiated from key competitors.

BRAND ASSOCIATIONS

Both Aaker and Keller emphasize the important role of brand associations. Aaker (1991), in his book, Managing Brand Equity, conceptualizes brand equity in terms of five dimensions: brand loyalty, brand awareness, perceived quality, brand associations, and other proprietary brand assets. Aaker (1991) defines brand associations as "anything linked in memory to a brand", and states that the core role of brand associations is to create meaning for consumers. Keller (1993) breaks brand equity down into brand awareness (recall and recognition) and brand image (measured in terms of the favorability, strength, and uniqueness of the brand associations). Together, both of these writers focus on measuring brand equity in terms of consumer perceptions of the brand, and emphasize the importance of consumer knowledge and brand associations as fundamental building blocks of brand image.

Drawing the roots from the associative network theory, Keller (1993) posits that brand associations differ in three important ways. First, associations have different strengths, that is, they have stronger or weaker links to the brand's node in memory. Second, associations differ in terms of favorability, i.e. have differences in how their associations are evaluated, positively or negatively. Lastly, some associations are more unique than others. In addition to Keller's (1993) focus on favorability, strength, and uniqueness, two other brand association features are important. The first of these is number of associations. While it is not a key feature of a single brand association, the number of associations for a brand is potentially relevant for practitioners (Krishnan, 1996). Number of brand associations has been found to influence brand awareness, and may also influence the effectiveness of advertising activities (Krishnan, 1996, Meyers-Levy, 1989). The final brand association feature is relevance. Campbell (2002) mentions that the brand associations that practitioners should focus on are those that are "meaningful and relevant to customers" and Hart and Murphy (1998) state the successful branding is founded on creating distinctiveness in a consumer relevant way.

BRAND ASSOCIATIONS USED FOR THE PURPOSE OF THIS STUDY

Based on the theoretical perspective of memory as a network of interconnected nodes, the methodology of this study is designed to reveal the associations that are directly part of a brand's immediate network, and also provide a detailed analysis of those associations. Based on a review of past work on brand

The study focuses on five features of brand associations:

1. Strength.
2. Trust
3. Uniqueness.
4. Relevance.
5. Emotional Connection.

Strength

Strength of association is defined as the intensity of the connection between the association and the brand node. Associations have different strengths, i.e. they have stronger or weaker connections to the node. The stronger the association, the more accessible the association will be via spreading activation. One of the central goals of any marketing campaign is to influence the strength of consumers' associations with the brand and exposure to marketing messages should increase association strength (Henderson et al., 1998). Research has linked strength of association to brand evaluations (Dillon et al., 2001) and has suggested the topic as a potential area for future research (Krishnan, 1996).

Trust

Brand choice could be considered as the central problem of consumer behavior, while the perceived risk associated to buying decisions is a pivotal aspect of brand choice. Risk is often perceived to be painful in that it may produce anxiety, in which case it must be dealt in some manner by the consumer. Among the main functions of a brand from the consumers' perspective is considered to be the minimization of perceived purchasing risk, which in turn helps cultivate a trust-based relationship (Keller, 1993).Trust is defined as the willingness to rely on an exchange partner in whom one has confidence. It exists when a party has confidence in an exchange partner's reliability and integrity and when they share common goals and values. It is a consequence of interdependence due to stable customer experience of expectations being exceeded and of being provided the best value by the existing firm.

Emotional Connection

A brand differentiates a product in several forms and it can be broadly divided into two categories- the tangibles (rational), and the intangibles (emotional and symbolic). Either way, while the product performs its basic functions, the brand contributes to the differentiation of a product (Keller, 2003). These dimensions distinguish a brand from its unbranded commodity counterpart and give it equity, which is the sum total of consumers' perceptions and feelings about the product's attributes and how they perform, about the brand name and what it stands for, and about the company associated with the brand (Achenaum, 1993). A strong brand provides consumers multiple access points towards the brand, by attracting them through both functional and emotional attributes (Keller, 2003). Emotional attachment to brands has attracted recent research attention (e.g. Thomson et al., 2005). Researchers have long considered attitudes to be insufficient predictors of brand commitment (e.g. loyalty), and suggest that true loyalty requires the customer to form an emotional bond with the brand (Park et al., 2009; Oliver, 1999).

Uniqueness

Association uniqueness is defined as the degree to which the association is perceived as a distinct and different brand feature within the product category. Some associations are more unique than others. This means that some associations may be shared with many competing brands and be typical for a product category while others may be unique to just one or a smaller number of brands. Marketers often use brand positioning strategies in an attempt to differentiate via unique associations, and this differentiation is often a source of competitive advantage (Farquhar, 1989; Chaudhuri, 2002; Lu et al., 2008). Many discussions of branding strategy put differentiation based on uniqueness front and center (Hart and Murphy, 1998).

Relevance

The relevance of the association is defined as how much people perceive the association as a valuable, important, and purchase decision driving feature for a brand within the product category. Some brand associations are more relevant to consumers than others. For example, the color red is typically strongly associated with Coca-Cola, but it is not so clear how motivating this association is for consumers.

DEVELOPING ASSOCIATION

The second step is to generate the set of brand associations to include in the main study. To generate these associations, participants are cued with each brand name and asked to give the first four associations that come to mind. This method was chosen because it represents a compromise between a discrete association task (participants give just one response for each cue) and a continuous association task (participants give an exhaustive list of associations) (for a discussion of the strengths and weaknesses of each approach Nelson et al. (2000) and McEvoy and Nelson (1982)). One of the potential problems with a continuous association task is chaining, the elicitation of a cluster of primary associations linked to each other, but not to the focal node (brand). To help control this problem, participants were instructed to think about the brand name after each response (this method is taken from Krishnan, 1996). Also, to control for possible order effects, the order brands were presented was systematically rotated. Requesting four associations balances limiting the number of idiosyncratic associations while ensuring a good number and breadth of associations solicited.

RESPONSE LATENCY AND STRENGTH OF ASSOCIATION

At this point, I have chosen five brands of Pepsi for the study (Lays, Uncle Chips, Aliva, Kurkure and Lehar) as well as a large list of associations generated using those brand names as prompts. Participants then engage in a response latency task in which they will simply respond "yes" or "no" to each brand/association pair. Their response (yes or no) as well as their speed of response (response latency) is recorded.

The response latency task is based on previous research on attitudes using an associative network perspective (e.g. Fazio and Williams, 1986; Powell and Fazio, 1984). This response latency method has been applied to a variety of research questions including basic attitude research (e.g. Powell and Fazio, 1984), presidential choice (Fazio and Williams, 1986), and product choice (Fazio et al., 1989). The procedure of this study is strongly based on the method used in Fazio et al. (1992), and is used to measure the strength of the association between each brand association and its focal brand. For this measure, participants are first exposed to one of the brands (such as

Lays) for few seconds. The brand is then replaced with one of the associations from the free association task (such as "innovative" or "tasty"). Participants are instructed to say, "yes" if the association describes innovative or say "no" if the association does not describe innovative. Order of presentation of the brands and associations is randomized to reduce any bias from order effects or association chaining.

For strength of association, only the "yes" responses (the brand and association belong together) are analyzed. Each brand/association pair has an average response time (averaged across all participants who responded "yes").

Subsequently, I categorized each brand/association pair as either "strong" (top 25 percent of response times), "medium" (middle 50 percent of response times) or "weak" (bottom 25 percent of response times).

After the response latency task participants rated each association on trust, emotional connection, relevance, and uniqueness using a seven-point Likert type scale. Each of these scales used items previously employed in the literature. The eight items measuring relevance were based on Berens et al. (2005), Zaichkowsky (1985), and discussion between the researchers. Lastly, the five uniqueness items were based on Netemeyer et al. (2004) and Chaudhuri (2002). Also, following the method in Cobb-Walgren et al. (1995), for each association subjects completed a simple categorization of the association (not favorable, neutral, or favorable; not relevant, neutral, or relevant). The association scores on trust, emotional connection, relevance, uniqueness, and strength scales were then categorized into one of three groups (low, medium, or high) based on a quartile analysis of the mean score for each association. The highest 25 percent of the means were categorized as high, the lowest 25 percent were categorized as low, and the remaining fifty percent were categorized as medium.

CONSTRUCTION OF BRAND MAPS

One of the key features of this process is the visual presentation of the results in a way that is informative, intuitive, and strategic. Each brand is presented as the center of a constellation of associations. In order to determine which associations actually appear on a particular brand's map, I have used the response latency task and focus on the percentage of participants who said "yes" that association belongs with that brand.

Each of the features of brand associations is represented in this brand map. The factors on which the Association maps are constructed:

- Trust
    1. Green color for high trust
    2. Yellow color for medium trust
    3. Red color for low trust
- Relevance
    1. Larger the size, more is the relevance
    2. Smaller the size, lower is the relevance
- Uniqueness
    1. Smaller the distance, more is the uniqueness
    2. Larger the distance, less is the uniqueness
- Strength
    1. More the thickness, more is the strength
    2. Less the thickness, less is the strength
- Emotional Connection
    1. ---- → For high emotional connection
    2. **** → For medium emotional connection
    3. — → For low emotional connection

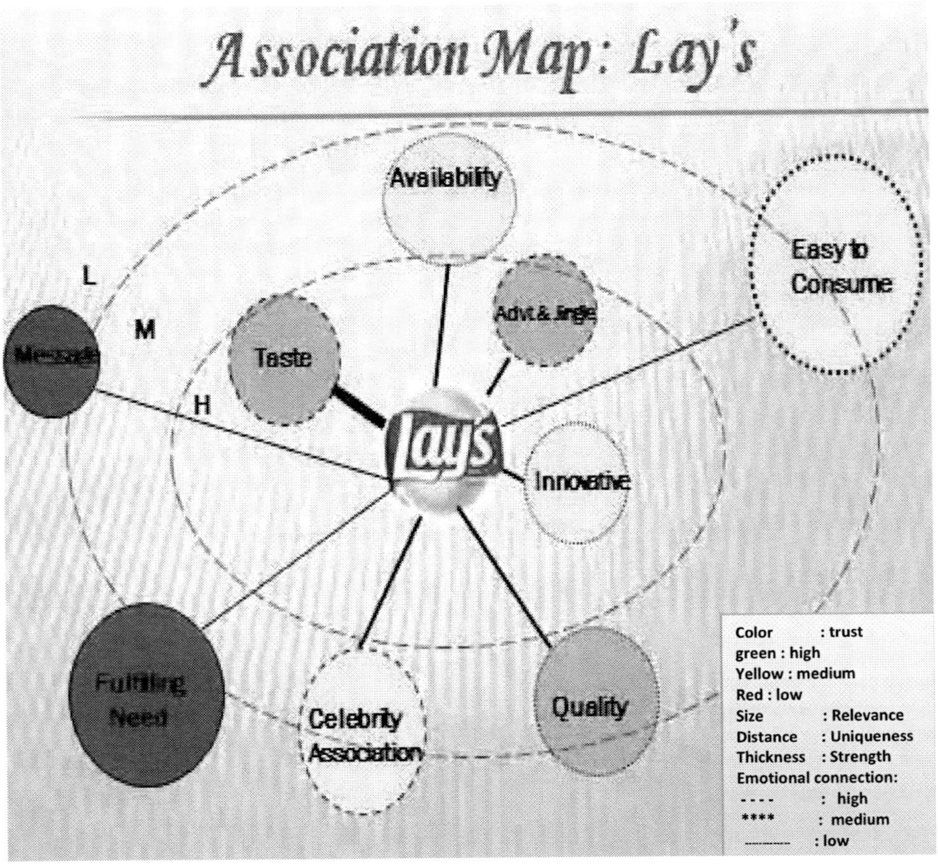

Fig. 1. Strategic Brand Association Map for Lay's

Similar maps were created for the remaining four brands. Based on this, I could develop for each brand a "core brand essence" map. This map shows the brand and associations for all the five product brands of Pepsi in the minds of the consumers. See Figure 2 for the core brand essence map for Pepsi.

CONCLUSION AND MANAGERIAL IMPLICATIONS

The strategic brand association map methodology presented here is a strategic, comprehensive framework designed to give marketing and brand managers actionable insight into the meaning their brand has vis-a'-vis key competitors. These maps depict a brand and its associations along with an assessment of the strength, relevance, uniqueness, trust and emotional connection of each association.

This strategic brand map process provides strategic insight into how a brand is viewed in the marketplace and how that brand is (or is not) differentiated from key competitors through the associations the brand has developed. This work can serve to reinforce the strategic direction of a brand, or help point the way to a change in strategy that will enhance the brand's attractiveness to its target audience. Strategic brand association maps can also serve as a diagnostic tool for brands that may be struggling or otherwise be underperforming vis-a'-vis management expectations.

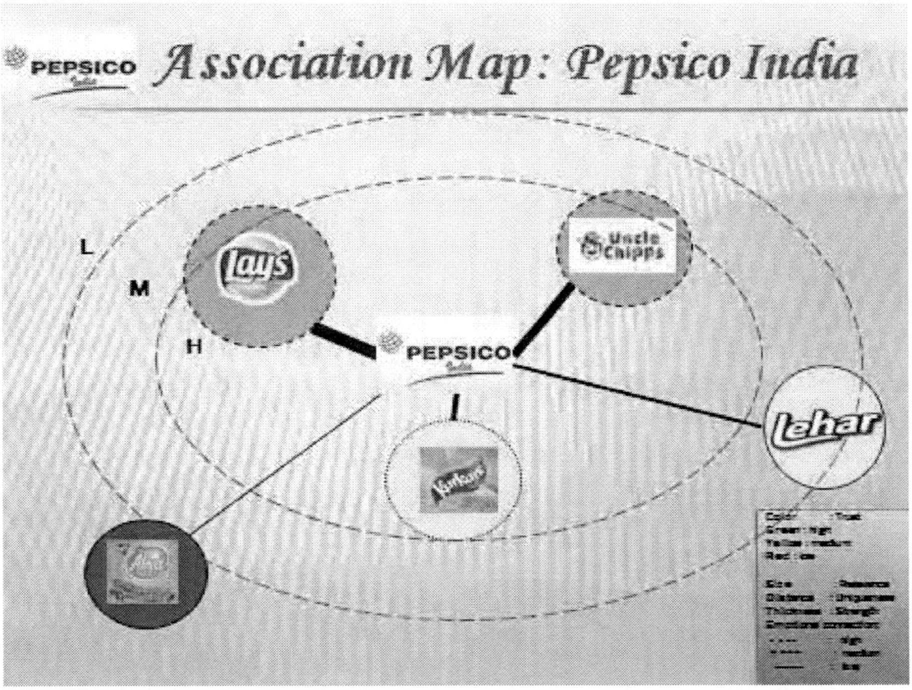

Core Brand Essence Map for the Five Product Brands of Pepsico

REFERENCES

[1] Aaker, D.A. (1991), Managing Brand Equity, The Free Press, New York, NY.

[2] Aaker, D.A. (1992), "Managing the most important asset: brand equity", Planning Review, Vol. 20 No. 5, pp. 56-9.

[3] Aaker, D.A. (1996), Building Strong Brands, Free Press, New York, NY.

[4] Aaker, D.A. and Jacobson, R. (2001), "The value relevance of brand attitude in high-technology markets", Journal of Marketing Research, Vol. 38 No. 4, pp. 485-93.

[5] Baldauf, A. and Cravens, K.S. (2003), "Performance consequences of brand equity management: evidence from organizations in the value chain", Journal of Product&Brand Management, Vol. 12 No. 4, pp. 220-36.

[7] Bendixen, M., Bukasa, K.A. and Abratt, R. (2004), "Brand equity in the business-to-business market", Industrial

[8] Marketing Management, Vol. 33 No. 5, pp. 371-80.

[9] Berens, G., Riel, C.B.M. and Bruggen, G.H. (2005), "Corporate associations and consumer product responses: the moderating role of corporate brand dominance", Journal of Marketing, Vol. 69 No. 3, pp. 35-48.

[10] Brin˜ ol, P., Petty, R.E. and Tormala, Z.L. (2004), "Selfvalidation of cognitive responses to advertising", Journal of Consumer Research, Vol. 30, March, pp. 559-73.

[11] Campbell, M.C. (2002), "Building brand equity", International Journal of Medical Marketing, Vol. 2 No. 3, pp. 208-18.

[12] Campbell, M.C. and Keller, K. (2003), "Brand familiarity and advertising repetition effects", Journal of Consumer Research, Vol. 30 No. 2, pp. 292-304.

[13] Chaudhuri, A. (1999), "Does brand loyalty mediate brand equity outcomes?", Journal of Marketing Theory and Practice, Vol. 7 No. 2, pp. 136-46.

[14] Chaudhuri, A. (2002), "How brand reputation affects the advertising-brand equity link", Journal of Advertising Research, Vol. 42 No. 3, pp. 33-42.

[15] Cobb-Walgren, C.J., Ruble, C.A. and Donthu, N. (1995), "Brand equity, brand preference, and purchase intent", Journal of Advertising, Vol. 24 No. 3, pp. 25-40.

[16] Collins, A.M. and Loftus, E.F. (1975), "A spreadingactivation theory of semantic processing", Psychological Review, Vol. 82 No. 6, pp. 407-28.

[17] Dacin, P.A. and Smith, D.C. (1994), "The effect of brand portfolio characteristics on consumer evaluations of brand extensions", Journal of Marketing Research, Vol. 31 No. 2, pp. 229-42.

[18] Dillon, W.R., Madden, T.J., Kirmani, A. and Mukherjee, S. (2001), "Understanding what's in a brand rating: a model for assessing brand and attribute effects and their relationship to brand equity", Journal of Marketing Research, Vol. 38, November, pp. 415-29.

[19] Farquhar, P.H. (1989), "Managing brand equity", Marketing Research, Vol. 1 No. 3, pp. 24-33.

[20] Fazio, R.H. (1990), "A practical guide to the use of response latency in social psychology research", in Hendrick, C. and Clark, M.S. (Eds), Review of Personality and Social Psychology, Vol. 11, Sage Publications, Newbury Park, CA, pp. 74-97.

[21] Fazio, R.H. and Williams, C.J. (1986), "Attitude accessibility as a moderator of the attitude-perception and attitudebehavior relations: an investigation of the 1984 presidential election", Journal of Personality and Social Psychology, Vol. 51, pp. 505-14.

[22] Fazio, R.H., Herr, P.M. and Powell, M.C. (1992), "On the development and strength of category-based associations in memory: the case of mystery ads", Journal of Consumer Psychology, Vol. 1 No. 1, pp. 1-13.

[23] Fazio, R.H., Powell, M.C. and Williams, C.J. (1989), "The role of attitude accessibility in the attitude-to-behavior process", Journal of Consumer Research, Vol. 16 No. 3, pp. 280-8.

[24] Hart, S. and Murphy, J. (Eds) (1998), Brands: The New Wealth Creators, New York University Press, New York, NY. Henderson, G.R., Iacobucci, D. and Calder, B.J. (1998),

"Brand diagnostics: mapping branding effects using consumer associative networks", European Journal of Operational Research, Vol. 111 No. 2, pp. 306-27.

[25] Hsieh, M.-H. (2004), "Measuring global brand equity using cross-national survey data", Journal of International Marketing, Vol. 12 No. 2, pp. 28-57.

[26] Janiszewksi, C. and Van Osselaer, S.M.J.V. (2000), "A connectionist model of brand-quality associations", Journal of Marketing Research, Vol. 37 No. 3, pp. 331-50.

[27] John, D.R., Loken, B., Kyeongheui, K. and Monga, A.B. (2006), "Brand concept maps: a methodology for identifying brand associations", Journal of Marketing Research, Vol. 43 No. 4, pp. 549-63.

[28] Keller, K.L. (1993), "Conceptualizing, measuring, and managing customer-based brand equity", Journal of Marketing, Vol. 57 No. 1, pp. 1-28.

[29] Keller, K.L. (2001), "Editorial: brand research imperative", Brand Management, Vol. 9 No. 1, pp. 4-6.

[30] Krishnan, H.S. (1996), "Characteristics of memory associations: a consumer-based brand equity perspective", International Journal of Research in Marketing, Vol. 13 No. 4, pp. 389-405.

[31] Lu, J., Kadane, J.B. and Boatwright, P. (2008), "The dirt on bikes: an illustration of CART models for brand differentiation", Journal of Product & Brand Management, Vol. 17 No. 5, pp. 317-26.

[32] McEvoy, C.L. and Nelson, D.L. (1982), "Category name and instance norms for 106 categories of various sizes", American Journal of Psychology, Vol. 95 No. 4, pp. 581-634.

[33] Maltz, E. (1991), "Managing brand equity", paper presented at The Marketing Science Institute Conference, Austin, TX.

[34] Meyers-Levy, J. (1989), "The influence of a brand name's association set size and word frequency on brand memory", Journal of Consumer Research, Vol. 16, September, pp. 197-207.

[35] Nelson, D.L., McEvoy, C.L. and Dennis, S. (2000), "What is free association and what does it measure?", Memory and Cognition, Vol. 28 No. 6, pp. 887-99.

[36] Netemeyer, R.G., Krishnet, B., Pullig, C., Wang, G., Yagei, M. and Dean, D. (2004), "Developing and validating measures of facets of customer-based brand equity", Journal of Business Research, Vol. 57, pp. 209-24.

[37] Powell, M.C. and Fazio, R.H. (1984), "Attitude accessibility as a function of repeated attitudinal expression", Personality and Social Psychology Bulletin, Vol. 10 No. 1, pp. 139-48.

[38] Raaijmakers, J.G.W. and Shiffrin, R.M. (1981), "Search of associative memory", Psychological Review, Vol. 88 No. 2, pp. 93-134.

[39] Tong, X. and Hawley, J.M. (2009), "Measuring customerbased brand equity: empirical evidence from the sportswear market in China", Journal of Product & Brand Management, Vol. 18 No. 4, pp. 262-71.

[40] Van Osselaer, S.M.J. and Janiszewski, C. (2001), "Two ways of learning brand associations", Journal of Consumer Research, Vol. 28 No. 2, pp. 202-23.

[41] Walvis, T.H. (2008), "Three laws of branding: neuroscientific foundations of effective brand building", Journal of Brand Management, Vol. 16 No. 3, pp. 176-94.

[42] Wansink, B. (2003), "Using laddering to understand and leverage a brand's equity", Qualitative Market Research, Vol. 6 No. 2, pp. 111-8.

[43] Zaichkowsky, J.L. (1985), "Measuring the involvement construct", Journal of Consumer Research, Vol. 12 No. 3, pp. 341-52.

Branding in Hotels: A Value Driver More than Logo Visualization

Nidhi Chowdhry and J.K.Tandon

Jaipur National University, Jaipur

ABSTRACT

The process of building a brand begins with a clear understanding of what consumer desire from a particular product or service. This understanding is then translated into a promise, which is the basis of the brand and tells consumers what they will receive. Hotel industry is a form of an intense interaction between employee and consumer. As a single brand cannot meet the demands of all travelers, hotel organizations have turned to brand segmentation. Brand can be the most valuable asset of a company. A hotel can develop its market size and build consumer loyalty by proper branding. This paper explains the importance of a balance between brand-building and promoting through marketing, operational understanding and creating brand asset value in hotel industry. The paper used strategic analysis methodology for evaluating the importance of Brand building to generate revenues and will also identify various challenges faced in this path.

INTRODUCTION

A brand is an interesting and popular topic in global hotel industry. When there is a question about the importance of a brand for a hotel, then the brand position will automatically represent the hotel directly as a brand used for non-service product. In other word, brand existence is important.

Over the past three years a number of National and Internationalbrands have materializedin India with particularly heavy supply being added in Pune, the National Capital region (NCR), Bangalore and Hyderabad. There are announcement by several global hotel majors like Marriott, Accor, Best Western and Carlson to significantly increase their portfolio of hotels by 2015/16.

The last year has proved to be one of the most challenging sales environments in decades, not only for hotels and resorts but for all industries. In such a competitive environment, it is those organizations that can develop (or retain) a strong brand identity and reputation that will perform most strongly, ensuring not only their survival but setting themselves to benefit most from the resulting upturn.

Strong brands will secure guest loyalty, and with existing customers up to 7 times more profitable to deal with than new customers this is vital in efficiently utilizing the organization's resources and keeping costs down. Strong brands will also have a clear position when economic conditions improve, enabling them to attract new customers quickly due to their clear message and offering.

There was a time when such venerable brand names as Hilton, Sheraton, and Marriott were all a consumer needed to know to make a decision about where to stay. That changed dramatically with the era of consumer choice and market segmentation. Just as cola and toothpaste brands have proliferated, so have lodging brands.

During the 1980s, the hotel industry saw an explosion of new brands. Market segmentation has served as one of the most powerful drivers in the creation of more and more branded products a trend that became a popular marketing concept in the 198Os and remains so today. Seen as a vehicle for growth by a number of hotel companies that tapped a virtually limitless supply of capital in those years. Large hotel chains assumed that they could create new markets by establishing niche products in a variety of segments. With the benefit of hindsight, however, some hotel chains that started out in a mid-market segment have tried to move up-market by creating new brand concepts to do so. As hotel companies fine-tune their identities, reposition their products and promote growth through aggressive franchising programs.

This is similar to Marriott's brand strategy, an illustration of the proliferation of brands within a single company. In fact, Marriott has been one of the more successful chains at introducing meaningful brands. Courtyard, for example, Marriott's innovative brand for business travelers, was introduced in 1983. Today, Courtyard has more than 700 hotels in 25 countries and is the world's 13th-largest lodging brand, according to Marriott. Courtyard will be introduced to the Japanese market in April 2007.Wyndham Worldwide franchises the Super 8, Days Inn, Travelodge, and Ramada brands. Choice's portfolio includes the Econo Lodge, Comfort Inn, Quality, and Sleep Inn brands.

Various chains take different approaches to logos and identifying information for their various product brands. Choice Hotels International, for example, uses similar and consistent sign designs for its Comfort Inn, Comfort Suites, Quality Inn, Sleep Inn, and Clarion brands.

BRAND SEGMENTATION

A variety of brands have now been developed in the lodging industry, tailored to serve diverse consumers who have certain demands based on budget, expectations, and travel needs. As a single brand cannot meet the demands of all travelers, hotel organizations have turned to brand segmentation. Brand segmentation refers to developing separate brands based upon certain standards and regulations while still maintaining to represent an entity of their parent organization.

VARIOUS BRAND SEGMENTS

The economy brand has been developed for the budget traveler in which the market segment does not rely on producing luxury accommodations but rather focuses on producing quality rooms at a low price. The customer in this market segment is not requesting exclusive services or accommodations but is looking for a low rate. Hoteliers experience low costs per room because they are not offering certain amenities such as complimentary continental breakfast, wireless internet, or a fitness center. Instead they are offering a quality guest room at a low, affordable price. This accommodation is appropriate for the traveler whose stay will be for a short period of time, and is not in need of many amenities or additional services. Brands such as RedFox, Ibis (Accor), Ginger are few of the names in this category.

The **midscale market** provides travelers with quality accommodations and amenities while paying a reasonable price. The rooms are most often interior corridor and spacious. This market offers many complimentary amenities and services such as breakfast, Internet access, food and beverage accommodations, and access to business and fitness centers. Such brands in this market include Lemon Tree Hotels, Citrus hotels, Country Inn & Suites and Park Plaza (Carlson Hotels) etc. This particular market segment is the most prevalent as these brands best serve the common needs of consumers, but is still not too pricy. In addition, it is more available for franchisees to build and develop because costs of construction often are at a reasonable level, which can be covered by the room revenue of this market level.

The **extended stay market** is a new market segment that has experienced large growth over the past few years. Each major hospitality organization has released a brand that features guest rooms for the purpose of extended stay. These guest rooms usually comprise of bedroom, sitting area, and kitchenette or bar. Marriott has released Residence Inn, Towne Place Suites, and Spring Hill Suites. Intercontinental has released Candlewood Suites and Staybridge Suites, while Choice Hotels International has released Mainstay Suites, Comfort Suites, and Suburban Extended Stay Hotels. Extended stay brands are further being developed to provide a home-like atmosphere for travelers looking to stay for an extended period of time and who are in need of more suitable accommodations.

The **upscale market** segment generally includes hotels that provide full service and rooms which contain more ergonomic furniture and modern design. The room rates are much higher than that of the economy and midscale brands as this market segment offers more in terms of services. Some services, such as food and beverage or Internet access, are not usually found to be complimentary; however they are higher in quality than that of the midscale segment. Travelers that are looking to stay in more attractive accommodations with higher levels of service and plenty of amenities are sure to choose an upscale hotel such as Radisson, Wyndham, Crowne Plaza, Hyatt, Marriott International, or Hilton.

The **luxury market** includes hotels that are luxurious and feature the best accommodations in the lodging industry. The guest rooms are designed to be very spacious and comfortable with a modern upscale design. All hotels are full service and have amenities and accommodations that are quite lavish. Services found in this market level that are not found in others are concierge services, spa, recreational activities, and entertainment. This segment is intended for travelers willing to pay premium prices for first-class accommodations and service. Well-known brands in this segment include Taj Group of Hotels, Oberoi Hotel, Maurya by ITC, Ritz Carlton, Conrad, and Four Seasons.

LITERATURE REVIEW

Brand is an un-separate part of world market nowadays. American Marketing Associations gives definitions of brand as a name, term, sign, picture or symbol or the combination of those mentioned before which propose to identify a single or group of seller's product or service and to differentiate their product or service from its competitor. Giribaldi (2003) defines brand as a combination of attributes which is communicated through name or symbol which can influence consumer' mind in buying decision process. Actually, brand's role is more than this. A brand is actually a promise given by the company to its consumer about what the product can give to the consumer. That's what make a brand has important role for a company in their effort to satisfy its consumer (Campbell, 2002). A research is needed to know a company's brand position in their consumer's mind. Perception, consumer's feeling and their experience with the brand is something that differentiates a brand of a product from its non-brand competitor. Berry (2000) claimed that branding is regarded as the cornerstone in 21st century while taking service marketing domain in to consideration. Today's researchers declared the brand as the most influential character in services because of its innate distinctiveness like perishability, inseparability, tangibility and heterogeneity (Kapferer, 2004).

The hotel industry, in particular, and all businesses whose service depend on building long term relationship need to concentrate on maintaining customer's loyalty. Prasad and Dev (2000) are of the opinion that branding is an effective method for hotels and hotel chains to identify and distinguish themselves from competitors in the mind of the customer. Bailey and Ball (2006) defined hotel based brand equity as "the value that consumers and hotel property owners associate with a hotel brand and the impacts of these associations on their behavior". Prasad and Dev (2000) and later on, Forgacs (2003) found that extensive strategies have been applied for the development and prolific growth of new branded hotels over the last five years, worldwide. This overabundance of hotel brands has given rise to severe confusion among customers according to the arguments of Gibson (2003), Olsen et al. (1998) and Kim (2008). Now it clearly demanded efforts to enhance and enrich the specific knowledge related to hotel brand management, so that improved and better decision making related to marketing activities could be recognized and practiced to stand high in the crowd.

In the past twenty-five years, the hotel industry has firmly embraced and accepted the value of branding as an essential component of its marketing strategy, especially given extensive hotel brand segmentation. This segmentation strategy is based on the idea that a brand name is part of the process of giving tangibility to what is essentially intangible, providing a "shorthand" method of establishing a particular property's quality by giving the customer important information about its product and service, sight unseen (Brucks, Zeithaml, and Naylor 2000). In this regard, the brand's value is based on potential guests' awareness of the brand, their perception of its quality, and overall customer satisfaction (O'Neill and Mattila 2004).The remarkable growth of hotel branding rests on the concept that brands provide added value to both guests and hotel companies, in large part because they foster brand loyalty (O'Neill and Xiao 2006). From a corporate strategy viewpoint, well-managed hotel brands tend to gain increasing market share (O'Neill and Mattila 2004), even though different parent companies take diverse approaches to managing their individual brand identity. Marriott International, for instance, is careful to include its corporate name on most of its brands. One exception to this approach is Ritz-Carlton, which was a well-established brand before being acquired by Marriott. Other firms, such as Starwood and Choice Hotels International, employ a house-of-brands strategy.

This family approach to design simultaneously distinguishes the brands from each other, identifies them as all being part of a unified organization, and differentiates them from their competition. As a brand represents the company itself, its presentation generally should be consistent. Though there are cases where companies have changed their positioning or strategies, their corporate colors, and even their logos, few have abandoned an established brand name for a new one (Vaid 2003). Indeed, long-established brand names continue in operation after being reinvented and reinvigorated, including Holiday Inn, Ramada Inn, and Howard Johnson.

Gobé (2001) has posited that the biggest misconception in branding strategies is that people focus on branding in the context of market share, when a brand really involves the mind and emotion "share." This does not negate the superficial aspects of branding that we have already touched on, including ubiquity, visibility, and function, but the brand's major significance is to establish in a consumer's mind an emotional connection. This emotional connection to a brand arises in part from the promise that we mentioned above. Hotel guests rely on brand names to reduce the risks associated with staying at an otherwise unknown property (O'Neill and Xiao 2006). Beyond that, brands are supposed to be intense and vibrant, to connect on multiple levels of the senses, and to be a reminder of a pleasant experience. Brands consistently interact with consumers and should not disappoint them, since that constitutes a broken promise. Thus, a brand is something for consumers to feel good about (Vaid 2003), and successful brand organizations promote themselves as such. This relationship is built as consumers get to know a brand (even if they initially choose their accommodation at random), use its facilities, evaluate their experience, and begin the relationship; and it becomes cemented as guests continue using its services. Ultimately, the brand represents the consumer's experience with its organization. The intense competitive landscape has forced hotel brands to focus on providing memorable experiences to their guests rather than simply selling services (Gilmore and Pine 2002). Thus, even though Hilton operates both the Waldorf-Astoria and the New York Hilton, and both are first-class hotels, staying at one should be a different experience from staying at the other.

The perception of customers about quality was predicted to be linked with their loyalty with brand because favorable perception about the brand quality leads to more and more brand loyal customers. That's why Bolton and Drew (1991) suggested "service quality has significant effects on customer loyalty". In general, perceived service quality seems to be positively related to customers' likelihood of remaining a loyal customer and their attitudes toward the service provider i.e. brand loyalty (Anton, Camarero, & Carrero, 2007; Bell, Auh & Smalley, 2005; Aydin & Ozer, 2005). Among others, Jones et al. (2002) found a significant relationship between perceived quality and customer loyalty. To report the direct relation between perceived service quality and brand loyalty, existence of a significant and positive relationship between the perceptions of customers related to service quality and their intentions to buy and, subsequently, willingness to recommend the company (positive word of mouth) is very much evident in various studies (Parasuraman 1988; 1991).

Conflicting findings regarding the relationships between service quality and brand loyalty are also found in empirical studies in the hotel context. Kandampully and Hu (2007) and Kim et al. (2008) did not find a significant relationship between service quality and brand loyalty. Lai et al. (2009) found indirect relationships between service quality and brand loyalty through perceived value. Kayaman and Arasli (2007) reported that only tangible and responsiveness dimension has significant effect on brand loyalty. Others report indirect relationship between service quality and brand loyalty through perceived value and customer satisfaction (Chitty et al., 2007). Suhartanto (2011) reported that there are a number of studies examining service quality as the determinant of brand loyalty in the hotel industry, mostly conducted in developed countries.

BUILDING 'THE BRAND'

An effort to build brand identity needs several decision considered the name, color, tagline, and symbol. A brand is more than just marketing tools and tactics. Essentially, a brand is a marketer's promise to deliver several product feature, benefit and consistent service to the buyer. A marketer has to determine a mission for that brand and a vision about what that brand will become and what that brand can do. Marketer has to think that a contract is being offered today to the consumer about how that brand will perform. That brand contract has to be an honest one. Maximally, a brand campaign will only create a name recognition, brand knowledge, and even brand tendency. But no matter how much a company allocate campaign budget, an advertising campaign will not create a brand bonding. Brand bonding or brand attachment will only happen if a consumer experiences a direct benefit which has been promised by the company. The fact is that a brand is not build by advertising but by experience with that brand. Many companies create promises considering their brand but fail to train its employees to understand and give what has been promised in their brand. Companies can internally create branding among its employees in order to make its employees understand, wishing, and giving the promise that has been delivered by the brand. (Kotler, 2003).

The table below helps to illustrate the Path to Brand strategy:

Internal Discovery	*External Discovery*	*Brand Strategy*	*Communications Plan*	*Creative Development*
• Strategy session • Individual interviews • Focus groups • Communications • audit	PRIMARY • Visitor/Gues t interviews • Partner interviews SECONDARY • Competitive audit • Secondary literature • review	• Master brand messaging • Product/service brand hierarchy • Audience message matrix	Recommended communications strategies: • Brand maintenance • Awareness tactics • Lead gen tactics • Relationship management tactics • Communications calendar •Budget Measurementand evaluation	• Visual identity • Collateral • Web site • Advertising • Signage • Direct mail, etc

MAINTAINING THE BRAND POSITIONING

An image is a color, symbol, words and tagline that deliver a clear message, consistent, and not just a name (Berry et al, 1988). In some brand literature, an image is also frequently mentioned as brand image. Consumer differentiates between two brands by the different images /logos (Schiffman & Kanuk, 1991). Having a good image and perception in eyes of customer will increase selling, attract new consumer by word of mouth activities and reduce unsatisfied customer (Rogerson, 1983). A recognized brand will help the consumer to accept its new product (Aaker, 1991). A hotel that has an established brand can sell it service with premium price (Tepeci, 1999).

Based on the information from Express & Travel Tourism (www.expresstraveltourism.com) about hotel industry, an event was held to measure hotel brand performance by giving an award named Best Premier Hotel Brands. This was won by Taj Hotels, Resorts & Palaces. This hotel has 56 properties, 39 are located in India and the rest are scattered at Maldives, Mauritius, Malaysia, Seychelles, England, America, Bhutan, Srilanka, Africa, and Middle East. Taj is the first hotel in India that has a dining package in India by introducing several international meals such as Sichuan, Thai, Italy, Mexican, and California. In fact, since 1972, Taj is the first hotel which has 24 hours coffee shop.

The Hotels Were Judged on Objective Criterion and Subjective Criterion

Objective criterion consists several factors such as:- Number of properties, Operational revenue (rooms, F&B), Online reservation, Room inventory, Number of rooms sold across all properties, Revenue per available room, Average room rate, Number of employees, Gross operating profit.

Subjective criterion consists factors such as:- World class cuisine, In-house-service, Front office interaction, Back office interaction, Guest facilities, Value for money promotion, Loyalty schemes, Marketing & communications,

Therefore it can be inferred, that Brand building in hotels means integrating a lot of factors in hotel operational procedures.

However, independent hoteliers believe that separating themselves from the norms of branding and positioning themselves as a unique hotel is a more effective strategy than building a hotel to specific brand standards and regulations. The idea is to position the hotel as one that can fulfill the same quality and demands of its franchised competition while portraying an exceptional distinctiveness. This strategy allows them to be creative and go outside the box in business development. The independent market segment appeals to many consumers who are willing to experience unique accommodations and recognize that quality and service does not need to be supported by franchise standards and regulations.

PROMOTING THE BRAND

Hotels should use their brand as a platform for creating fresh, distinctive ways of creating a personalized experience that makes each guest feel special.

1. **Logo visualization:** Focus on specific interactions (e.g., check-in, room entry) and using the brand as a foundation for orchestrating memorable moments that leave a distinct impression in the customer's mind. As Four Seasons Hotels and Resorts entered a period of unprecedented growth, the company realized that rapid expansion would present a challenge of maintaining a consistent yet personal experience across many more properties around the world. Recently, they created a thoughtful way to determine which aspects of the hotel experience should be branded and which should not.Rather than putting logos on every last sugar packet and shampoo bottle, Four Seasons brands the entire experience as a distinctive, local, and individualized expression of the brand through each of its locations and each of its highly trained staff members.
2. **Getting back to basics:**As hotel groups around the world continue to expand, one basic truth is overlooked: Strong brands clearly communicate what makes a hotel distinctive and relevant to its customers. By returning to branding basics this problem can be simplified. Hotel companies can develop a distinctive promise that captures the essence of each brand in simple terms and provides a platform for true differentiation and a distinctive customer experience.Getting back to basics and being clear about what distinguishes each hotel brand will the hotel in a much better position to grow its base of loyal customers and attract new ones.
3. **Young at heart:** A general review of research conducted on younger audiences– generation Y in particular– reveals that these groups have specific needs and preferences that must be addressed. This includes a demand for real-time information and the expectation that the web will be a delivery tool of any product or service that they buy. Using simple, straightforward messaging is critical to reaching younger customers.
4. **Prefer Preferences:** Catering to each guest's preferences on a one-off basis can be expensive and complicated. How can a hotel develop guest interactions that are simple,

cost-effective, and have an impact? A handwritten note or a phone call from a hotel manager can make a big difference. But a hotel's strategy for making guests feel special shouldn't stop there. Hotels should use their brand as a platform for creating fresh, distinctive ways of creating a personalized experience that makes each guest feel special.

A better experience for guests is closely aligned with the brand, so it works overtime at strengthening the brand associations that you desire. By tapping into what the hotel stands for and what makes it unique, there are countless ways to create a customer experience that stands out from the pack.

5. **Localized Freedom:** As hotel groups continue to expand, they're challenged by balancing the need for brand consistency across all their properties with the need to express some degree of individual personality and character at each location.Individual hotels need the freedom to bring out the spirit and flavor of the local surroundings and the personalities of the staff. Freedom of expression should be encouraged.However, individual properties should also be encouraged to maintain some "family ties." In the end, guests often choose one hotel over another because they have a sense of comfort and familiarity with the name and the special, shared characteristics of that hotel family that transcend any one individual location.The result is an experience that guests can rely on, balanced with a localized flavor that they can look forward to discovering.
6. **Online Marketing / promotions:** Innovative means are adopted by hoteliers for online hotel marketing that keep them ahead in the race. A website with rich and detailed information about services and offers get effective and attractive web presence. To stand out from the competition, online hotel marketing requires website optimization web promotions with campaigns and most importantly online/GDS booking engines. Spreading reach in the market requires a multichannel marketing medium including social media, mobile campaigning. With smarter customers, smarter marketing techniques are required. These should be successful in persuading customers to opt for a certain facility of hotel.

Promotions, last-minute deals and photos have a strong impact on the visitor that beholds them. Information and things appealing emotions make for a perfect marketing strategy. Giving clients what they want marks the success of the marketing campaign. This kind of persuasion is an integral part of marketing strategy in travel and leisure business.

The traditional model would view this is outward communication, 'pushing' your controlled brand message to relevant audiences, and this is still important. Ensuring all your communications are on brand, focusing on what is important and differentiates you, and that you utilize cost-effective channels such as a branded interactive website, targeted PR and electronic communications, will grow awareness of your brand and what it stands for, and encourage trial.Ensure a robust guest feedback system is in place, monitor social media and review websites to identify any common issues that need to be addressed, and respond when appropriate so browsers see you take guest opinions seriously. Reputation can take years to establish, and days to lose, so constant monitoring is essential.

BRANDING AS A FUNCTION OF OPERATIONAL MANAGEMENT & MARKETING

A brand is not only a name for that product or for a hotel. A brand will always be connected to company identity.

Some of the performance measure indicators for large brands are:

1. Average price.
2. Level of occupancy.
3. Revenue per available room.
4. Return on investment.

Brand performance actually can be linked with marketing and operations. In operations side, brand which is well managed can integrate maximally giving better training to its employees, and create a consistency in delivering their service.

On marketing side, the hotel can build brand with existing resources in segmented market more effectively, broader and more coordinate promotion, and developing a more advance product. In this case a brand can reach penetrated market stronger and offering a higher or premium price.

A hotel name can represent an image and status of the hotel as well as explains the characteristics and attraction of hotel. This concept is known as brand personality. It will be unfair when we compare the advantage of hotels with different facility. For example, comparing 3 stars hotel with 5 star hotel. Of course in this case there is a difference degree of facility availability which is being offered by the hotel to its consumer whereas completely different one to another.

Hotel management has 2 important elements in hotels which are marketing and operational. The balancing between those 2 elements is required in the course of maintaining asset value in form of maintaining the economic value of brand.

Marketing and operations is balanced by management to make sure that role and function is range as it should be. Both of it has to run equally because in this case marketing is a promise to the consumer whereas operations is the evidence to make sure that the promise has been fulfilled. Unbalance of those 2 elements will create a negative impact to the brand indirectly and directly. A brand image will fall and the consumer perception about the hotel brand will no longer strong. If a hotel markets with ideal concept about its facility, service and attributes which make that hotel has advantage and attraction but obviously in operations to serve its consumer or giving promise in marketing phase is unsatisfied then the image of the hotel become negative. This effect is actually give bigger effect for the company externally which are the consumers. It could be that in this condition consumer see that the hotel is over-promised but not well managed and failed to satisfy its visitors. An overpriced hotel happens because the consumer feels that what has been promoted is failed to be fulfilled. Promise is different with operations because service is not as good as it's been promoted. Consumer will feel that the price they pay is to high compare to its competitor because the consumer is unsatisfied.

Marketing side will offer the specialty of the hotel good and service and the operations side will make sure that the offer will be fulfilled. The achievement of hotel's consumer expectation with the service is the satisfying hotel operations. Therefore, hotel's image will positively move and influence the consumer view of the hotel brand. Nevertheless, the most important thing to be remembered as the distinguish identification of a hotel is not its location, facility, price nor other technical elements but the brand itself as the basic. Image for a company is as important as having good name to individually or business consumer. But actually, there is a higher demand or expectation for a hotel. Especially hotels with strong brand such as Taj Hotels and resorts, Maurya, Leela Kempsiki, Oberio, Sheraton, JW. Marriot, Mandarin Oriental, Hilton etc.

BRAND PROMOTION LEADS TO REVENUE GENERATION

Few dispute the value that a brand brings to a hotel property, but questions remain regarding exactly how the brand creates guest loyalty and how it generates value. Over the past twenty-five years, a brand flag has become an essential element of arranging a hotel development deal. Because of this, researchers have examined how brands influence top- and bottom-line revenues and overall asset value.

A hotel's brand drives the operating ratios that are correlated with a hotel property's market value. Some brands consistently have stronger net operating incomes (NOIs) than do others (O'Neill and Mattila 2006), while other brands report consistently stronger average daily rates (ADRs) than others do.

A study found that a positive brand effect occurs only in the middle chain scale categories (upper upscale, upscale, and midscale), but not in the top (luxury) and bottom (economy) categories.A concurrent study found that brand affiliation, name recognition, and reputation for highquality service together can contribute as much as 20 to 25 percent of the goingconcern value of a successfully operating hotel (O'Neill and Xiao 2006). In addition, a well-managed brand can discourage competition.

The four known components of Brand Equity are: brand awareness, brand loyalty, perceived quality, and brand image (Kim and Kim 2004). In the hotel industry, the level of brand equity may be related to the brand's ability to geographically expand, to expand via franchising, and to develop sub-brands. These issues are particularly salient for global lodging organizations such as Marriott or Accor.Well-established brands are intangible assets that serve as a source of strategic advantage and create financial value due to their ability to generate cash flows via relatively higher margins (O'Neill and Mattila 2006). Hotel brands first create value for guests by helping to assure them of a uniform level of quality (O'Neill and Xiao 2006). As customers' loyalty grows, the brand owner can capitalize on the brand's value through price premiums, decreased price elasticity, increased market share, and more rapid brand expansion.

PROBLEMS & CHALLENGES IN HOTEL BRANDING

1. Brand is not an entirely Marketing function: A brand is much more than a logo and a brochure put together by your Marketing department. If we take the case of a hotel, all the sales and marketing tools, whether they are offline or online is only a part of a larger picture. For the brand to come to life, the core values and essence of your brand must be led by all the departments and functions within the organization: Human Resources, Guest Relations, Front Office, Food and Beverage, Housekeeping, Ambiance, Interior Design, Architecture, Payable, Receivable, Car fleet, Sales, Marketing, Communication etc..
2. Brand is an Operational Management tool:A Brand is not what you say it is but what your guests say it is.The responsibility of shaping a brand must be placed as high as possible within the company structure. In the case of a hotel, the responsibility should not go lower than the Resident Manager. He or she only has the general overview over all touch points and can ensure that the brand is being brought to life strategically and consistently. Ideally the General Manager must take charge.
3. Brand maintains Consistency: Consistent quality may be one of the biggest challenges facing hotel brands. Consistency has been one of the most important aspect of successful branding. In many cases, hotels are franchised or managed by companies independent of the hotel chain's parent company.This means the quality from one hotel to another, even within the same brand name, can be inconsistent. That is downright dangerous to a brand's credibility.
4. Big Brands (Chain of hotels) Vs Individual brands: The problems of the big brands haven't escaped the attention of a newer breed of hotel: the independent brand. Individual hotels are capitalizing on the lack of brand differentiation by creating unique personalities and targeting niche segments that larger chains may be unable to efficiently service. These Boutique hotels tend to serve targeted markets and be very trendy—resulting in a hotel room with an exorbitant price tag.

CONCLUSION

The idea of brand segmentation is for the hotelier to develop a great brand and offer that same brand quality and service in different destinations, which in turn will encourage customer loyalty. Having many different brands that represent various levels of service and accommodations allows travelers to choose a brand that is perfect for them. Regardless of their destination, vacationers are sure to find a brand that suits them best.Although the value of hotel brands is widely accepted, one frequently sees the complaint that brands are often being mismanaged. Commonly service is described in 4 unique attributes which are intangibility (not concrete), heterogeneous (many variations), inseperability (unable to separate), perishability (unable to store), and lack of ownership. Consumer or customer has absolute need to be fulfilled in a good way and that demand will get higher following how good a company serve and offer a solution to their need. The level of consumer appreciation to the brand is a result of brand popularity and quality perception offered by the brand. An advantage value which makes the hotel perceived as "more" than other hotels. Brand stature shows other facet of the hotel where consumer see a favorable specific characteristic apart of its prime power which is brand name. A clear, compelling brand represents a rich, proprietary source for developing a distinctive guest experience that will drive loyalty. Loyalty means repeat customers, more revenue and, ultimately, growth and stability for your hotels.

REFERENCES

[1] India Hotel Business Management Guide 2009

[2] India Tourism Market & Future Forecast, 2009 – 2015

[3] Industry insight: Indian Hotel Industry 2007

[4] Indian Hotel Industry analysis, 2005

[5] Kotler, Philip (1996). Marketing Management. The millennium ed. US Prentice Hall

[6] Jones, Peter and Pizam, Abraham (1993). The International Hospital Industry. John Wiley and Sons Inc.

[7] Lovelock H Christopher, (2007). Services Marketing, 6th edition. Prentice Hall. By website: *http://www.prenhall.com/lovelock/*

[8] Starkov, Max (2006) e-CRM Strategy in Hospitality, from *http://www.hospitalityebusiness.com/hr/hr102104121407.html*

[9] CRM: How to keep your travel customers? from *http://www.hotelmarketing.com/index.php/content/article/061101_crm_how_to_keep_your_travel_customers*

[10] Building Strong Brands, the Free Press, New York, NY. ASHE Higher Education Report, 2005, 31(2), 27-37. Akbaba, A. (2006).

[11] Business Week (2001) 'World's most valuable brands', league table, Business Week, 6th August. Also see Interbrand (2001) 'Leveraging Brand Value in a Downturn', Interbrand, February.

[12] Klein, N. (2000) 'No Logo', Flamingo (HarperCollins Publishers Ltd).

[13] The Economist (2001) "Pro Logo". Why brands are good for you', The Economist, 8th September.

[14] Aaker, D.A. (1996). Building Strong Brands, the Free Press, New York, NY. ASHE HigherEducation Report, 2005, 31(2), 27-37.

[15] Akbaba, A. (2006). Measuring service quality in the hotel industry: A study in a businesshotel in Turkey. International Journal of Hospitality Management, 25(2), 170-192.

[16] Alexandris, K., Dimitriadis, N., & Markata, D. (2002). Can perceptions of service qualitypredict behavioural intentions? An exploratory study in the hotel section in Greece. Managing Service Quality, 12(4), 224-232.

[17] Al-Rousan, M. Ramzi, Badaruddin Mohamed (2010), "Customer Loyalty and the Impacts ofService Quality: The Case of Five Star Hotels in Jordan", International Journal ofHuman and Social Sciences 5:13 2010

[18] Anton , C. , Camarero , C. , &Carrero , M. (2007). Analysing firms' failures asdeterminants of consumer switching intentions: The effect of moderating factors. European Journal of Marketing, 41 (1/2), 135 -158

[19] Aydin, S., & Ozer, G. (2005). The analysis of antecedents of customer loyalty in the Turkishmobile telecommunication market. European Journal of Marketing, 39(7/8), 910-925.

[20] Bailey, R. and Ball, S. (2006), "An exploration of the meanings of hotel brand equity", TheService Industries Journal, Vol. 26 No. 1, pp. 15-38.

[21] Bell, S. J., Auh, S., & Smalley, K. (2005). Customer relationship dynamics: Service qualityand customer loyalty in the context of varying levels of customer expertise and switching costs. Journal of the Academy of Marketing Science, 33, 169–183.

[22] Chitty, B., Ward, S., Chua, C. (2007), "An application of the ESCI model as a predictor ofsatisfaction and loyalty for packpacker hostels", Marketing Intelligence & Planning,Vol. 25 No.6, pp.563-80.

[23] Cobb-Walgren, C.J., Ruble, C.A., & Donthu, N., (1995). Brand equity, brand preference, andpurchase intent. Journal of Advertising, 24, 25-40.

[24] Cretu, A. E., & Brodie, R. J. (2007). The influence of brand image and company reputationwhere manufacturers market to small firms: a customer value perspective. IndustrialMarketing Management, 36(2), 230–240.

[25] Campbell, Margaret, C. (2002). "Building Brand Equity". International Journal of Medical Marketing : Henry Stewart Publications.

[26] Dyson, P., Farr, A., & Hollis, N.S., (1996). Understanding, measuring, and using brandequity. Journal of Advertising Research, 36(6), 9-21.

[27] Damonte, T., Rompf, P., Bahl, R.,&Domke, D. (1997). Brand affiliation and property size effects on measures of performance in lodging properties, Journal of HospitalityResearch, 20(3), 1-16.

[28] Forgacs, G. (2003), "Brand asset equilibrium in hotel management", International Journal ofContemporary Hospitality Management, Vol. 15 No.6, pp. 340-342.

[29] Gronroos, C., (1988). Service quality: The six criteria of good perceived service quality.Review of Business, 9(3), 10–13.

[30] Giribaldi, V. (2003). "The Fundamentals of Branding". Website BrandchannelHtttp://www.brandchannel.com

[31] Jones, M.A., Beatty, S.E., & Mothersbaugh, D.V., (2002). Why customers stay: measuringthe underlining dimensions of services switching costs and managing their differentialstrategic outcomes. Journal of Business Research, 55,441-50.

[32] Jiang,W.,Dev, C.,&Rao,V. (2002). Brand extension and customer loyalty: Evidence fromthe lodging industry, The Cornell Hotel and Restaurant Administration Quarterly,43(4), 5-16.

[33] Kandampully, J., & Hu, H. H. (2007). Do hoteliers need to manage image to retain loyalcustomers? International Journal of Contemporary Hospitality Management, 19(6),435-443.

[34] Kapferer, J.N. (2004), The New Strategic Brand Management, Kogan Page, London.

[35] Kayaman, R., & Arasli, H. (2007). Customer based brand equity: Evidence from thehotelindustry. Managing Service Quality, 17(1), 92-109.

[36] Keller, K. L. (2003). Strategic brand management: Building, measuring, and managing brand equity. Upper Saddle River, NJ: Prentice-Hall.

[37] Keller, K.L. and Lehmann, D.R. (2006), "Brands and branding: research findings and future priorities", Marketing Science, Vol. 25 No. 6, pp. 740-59.

[38] Keller, K.L., (1993). Conceptualizing, measuring and managing customer-based brandequity. Journal of Marketing, 57, 1-22.

[39] Khan, M., (2003). ECOSERV: eco-tourists' quality expectations. Annals of TourismResearch, 30(1), 109-24.

[40] Kim, H., & Kim, W.G., (2005). The relationship between brand equity and firms'performance in luxury hotels and restaurants. Tourism Management, 26, 549-60.

[41] Kim, H., Kim, W., & An, J. (2003). The effect of customer-based brand equity on firms'financial performance. Journal of Customer Marketing. 20(4), 335-351.

[42] Kim, W.G., Jin-Sun, B. and Kim, H.J. (2008), "Multidimensional customer-based brandequity and its consequences in midpriced hotels", Journal of Hospitality and TourismResearch, Vol. 32 No. 2, pp. 235-54.

[43] Landrum, H., Prybutok, V.R., Zhang, X. (2007), "A comparison of Magal's service qualityinstrument with SERVPERF", Information & Management, Vol. 44 No.1, pp.104-13.

[44] Michell, P., King, J., & Reast, J. (2001). Brand values related to industrial products.Industrial Marketing Management, 30(5), 415–425.

[45] Prasad, K., & Dev, C.S., (2000). Managing hotel brand equity. Cornell Hotel and RestaurantAdministration Quarterly, 41(3), 22-31.

[46] Roses, L.K., Hoppen, N. & Henriqu, J.L., (2009). Management of perceptions of informationtechnology service quality. Journal of Business Research, 62 (9), 876-82.

[47] Suhartanto, D. (2011), "An Examination of Brand Loyalty in the Indonesian Hotel Industry", Lincoln University Digital Thesis, Christchurch New Zealand

[48] Shocker, S., Srivastava, R., & Ruekert, R. (1994, May). Challenges and opportunities facingbrand management: An introduction to the special issue. Journal of MarketingResearch, 31, 149-158.

[49] Suite dreams. (2001, July). Consumer Reports, 12-18.

[50] Tepeci, Mustafa. (1999). "Increasing brand loyalty in the hospitality industry",International Journal of Contemporary Hospitality Management, Vol. 11 No. 5, pp. 223 –230.

[51] Wilkins, H., Merrilees, B., & Herington, C. (2007). Towards an understanding of total servicequality in hotels. Hospitality Management, 26(4), 840-853.

Consumer Preference for Laptops in India

Gunjan Malhotra, Varun Manglik and Apaar Gupta

Institute of Management Technology, Ghaziabad

ABSTRACT

The recent growth of a new breed of technology conscious Information Technology (IT) users the sales of Laptops in India have tremendously increased. There has been a drastic shift in Indian working population and the environments where they work, coupled with a new lifestyle that is always 'on the move'. In this paper we analyze the Indian consumer preferences for the brand of laptop they prefer to buy. Also we aim to find the market leader of laptops in India. We have empirically tested our results by using analysis of variance (ANOVA) to see if there is any difference among the different features of the laptop brands used. The results show that Dell is the major market player in the laptop industry in India, followed by Hewlett-Packard (HP) laptops and Compaq. We find that the features of laptop brands like price, reliability, looks, and battery backup do not have much importance when the consumer buys a particular laptop brand. Moreover the sales of a brand of laptop are independent of its region and language.

INTRODUCTION

The laptop industry is an extremely competitive industry, and a firm's survival depends on its efficiency. Consequently, the continuous search for improvement in operating and production efficiency is crucial for laptop manufacturers (Chang, Lin & Kao, 2003). India is one of the largest and the fastest growing economies of the modern world. It is an emerging market with a huge scope of expansion. It is regarded as a paradise for the sale of electronic goods due to the rising population and the demand for goods that make life easier. People today want all gadgets to be portable and want to work on things while they are 'on the move'. Besides the work-related market, various other segments are capitalizing on these handy portable computers. A large number of households and students are using these portable Personal computers (PC) for entertainment and study purposes respectively.

In the Indian markets, Laptops are more popularly used for their portability rather than mobility. Portability has become the number one factor as to why more Indians are buying these PCs. The laptop market in 2007 saw a significant growth of 84.8 per cent. Laptops are considered as being just the right size to fit on someone's lap; they are taking the Indian market by storm and are certainly giving the desktop computers a run for their money. If staying within a budget is more important to you than sleekness or screen size, you're not alone. The best selling notebooks are workhorses with slightly slower processors and fewer cutting-edge features like DVD brilliant 15 inch screens (Fortune, 2001).

Convenience and flexibility could be other reasons why laptops are selling out fast in the Indian markets.The drive in Indian markets over the use of laptops can finally be compared to the global sales of laptops. So the overall scenario has given thumbs up to laptops and they are certainly not going out of popularity for many more years to come. It's not far that it becomes a basic necessity of every home.

LITERATURE REVIEW

To analyze the Indian consumer preferences on the brand of laptop that they buy on the basis of parameters like price, reliability, looks, battery backup, etc. we have gone through the following literature material. It has been really helpful for our research and has given us some great insight that we share by presenting this paper.

Prior Research

Hewlett-Packard (HP) and Dell retained their status as the world's two largest suppliers of desktops and notebooks despite the global economic downturn and increased competition from Acer and other low cost laptop vendors (Insight). HP has focused on delivering on customer needs and requirements; we are geared to both drive growth and excel in our own performance in the desktop and notebook markets, bolstered by a powerful product line, value solutions and a committed partner network (Swaminathan, 2003).Aggressive PC pricing has helped improve PC penetration among small businesses, homes and in small towns. PC sales are expected to reach 7.5 million units by the end of this year, with desktop sales accounting for 6.25 million units, up from 5.43 million units a year ago. (Mehta, 2007) The local operations have grown 12-fold over the last seven years; so we are very happy with this growth (Dell, 2008).

The Indian market is red hot. According to data from computer hardware industry body, Manufacturers'Association for Information Technology(MAIT), it has grown over 16 per cent from 6,431,640 units (including desktops, notebooks and servers) in 2006-07 to 7,466,484 units in 2007-08. While desktop sales have actually declined by 2 per cent, that loss has been more than offset by a 114 per cent jump in laptop sales. "It has been a phenomenal story until now and we're poised to grow even further, Dell India's government business has grown six-fold over the last six quarters (Garde, 2008). We are witnessing rapid pick-up of business in new categories of consumer and SME and segments of government, banking, financial services and insurance and education. We grew 99 per cent year-on-year by units in Q1 calendar 2008. This is 10 times the industry growth rate. We are overall now at third position in the market with a 7.6 per cent market share and we continue to be number one in large corporate segments (Ahuja, 2008).

The July-September 2009 quarter experienced a strong boost from newfound consumer confidence that reflected in increased demand during the festive season. Overall Consumer PC sales recorded a 28 percent growth quarter-on-quarter (3Q CY09 over 2Q CY09). This performance underlines the recovery in the India PC market (KD Singh, 2009). Dell's ascent in the India notebook PC market in 4Q CY09 can be attributed to their consistent marketing efforts over the previous quarters. Availability of a wide product portfolio with appealing aesthetics and branding helped Dell connect with 'Gen X' buyers – students as well as young executives" (Mukherjee, 2010).

Dell did well across all market segments in the second quarter, including consumer, commercial, and small and medium businesses, Dell may have also been helped by disruptions in HP's consumer business as HP moved from a national distribution model to a network of regional distributors. HP has been traditionally strong in the consumer market. HP however held its number one position in desktops in the second quarter with a 10.2 percent share, followed by HCL Infosystems, and Acer. Dell did not focus enough on the consumer desktop, and is expected to do so in the next quarters. IDC India's figures for the second quarter also reflect a strong turnaround for the PC market in India. PC market sales in the country touched 2.4 million during the April-June 2010 quarter, up by 34 percent from the same quarter last year. Government spending and improved buying by consumers and small and medium businesses aided the recovery of the PC market last year. With large businesses also now buying, the PC market in India is set to grow by about 20 percent by units this year (Mukherjee, 2010).

Dell's momentum picked up ever since it set up a factory in India four years ago. Asked whether the company would need to expand capacity in India, growth in India was now coming from the consumer and SMB segments. "We have been consistently No. 1 in market share in the large enterprise segment" (Felice, 2010).

Our customer-centric focus and strategy have paid rich dividends, validated by our becoming the number one PC vendor in India (Garde, 2010).

OBJECTIVES

The following are the objectives for the study:

- To collect the primary data through survey and find out the current consumer preference.
- Consumer preference trending with the help of the secondary data.
- To analyze how various features are affecting the overall preference of the consumers with the help of statistical tools.
- To analyze the effect of demographics on the overall sales of the laptops.
- To give recommendations about the various future policies of these companies.

HYPOTHESIS FORMATION

The null hypothesis is a hypothesis about a population parameter. The purpose of hypothesis testing is to test the viability of the null hypothesis in the light of experimental data. Depending on the data, the null hypothesis either will or will not be rejected as a viable possibility. The null hypothesis is often the reverse of what the experimenter actually believes; it is put forward to allow the data to contradict it.

When a one-tailed test is conducted, the null hypothesis includes the direction of the effect. A one-tailed test of the differences between means might test the null hypothesis that $\mu_1 - \mu_2 \geq 0$. If M_1 - M_2 were much less than 0 then the null hypothesis would be rejected in favour of the alternative hypothesis: $\mu_1 - \mu_2 < 0$.

A null hypothesis is not accepted just because it is not rejected. Data not sufficient to show convincingly that a difference between means is not zero; do not prove that the difference is zero. Such data may even suggest that the null hypothesis is false but not be strong enough to make a convincing case that the null hypothesis is false.

AlternateHypothesis 1: The effect of all the independent variables (features) is not equal to the dependent variable (rating), i.e., mean rating values of all the features of dell are not equal ($\mu_1 \neq \mu_2$‘‘‘ $\mu_3 \neq \mu_4 \neq \mu_5 \neq \mu_6$; where: $\mu_1$is mean Rating of the price, μ_2 isfor the reliability, μ_3 isfor the looks, μ_4 isfor the battery backup, μ_5 isfor the extended features and μ_6 isfor the overall satisfaction for Dell.

Alternate Hypothesis 2: The effect of all the independent variables (features) is not equal to the dependent variable (rating), i.e., mean rating values of all the features of HP are not equal ($\mu_1 \neq \mu_2 \neq \mu_3 \neq \mu_4 \neq \mu_5 \neq \mu_6$; where: $\mu_1$is mean Rating of the price, μ_2 isfor the reliability, μ_3 isfor the looks, μ_4 isfor the battery backup, μ_5 isfor the extended features and μ_6 isfor the overall satisfaction for HP & Compaq.

Alternate Hypothesis 3: The effect of all the independent variables (location) is not equal to the dependent variable (sales), i.e., mean sales values of all the locations for Dell and HP & Compaq are not equal ($\mu_1 \neq \mu_2 \neq \mu_3 \neq \mu_4 \neq \mu_5$; where: population mean of sales for north region is μ_1, for south region is μ_2, for east region is μ_3, for west region is μ_4, for central region is μ_5.

Alternate Hypothesis 4: The effect of all the independent variables (usage level) is not equal to the dependent variable (sales), i.e., mean sales values for all types of users for dell and HP & Compaq are not equal ($\mu_1 \neq \mu_2 \neq \mu_3$; where: population mean of sales for novice users is μ_1, for mediocre users is μ_2, for expert users is μ_3.

METHODOLOGY

The laptop industry is increasing at a very high pace in India. Significant changes were observed over the past decade in the competition trending. The secondary data is compared with the primary data through survey. An attempt will be made to reason out the factors for the shift in the consumer preference. Internet research primarily focuses on the shift of consumer preference with the help of comparison between the historical sales figures of both Dell and HP. It formed the base of our research and supported the survey with actual facts and figures. The sampling technique used in our survey was "simple random sampling". It was most suitable for the project as its objective was to survey the consumer preference for laptops for all groups.We have used Microsoft Excel and SPSS Software for analyzing.

ANOVA

In statistics, analysis of variance (ANOVA) is a collection of statistical models and their associated procedures, in which the observed variance is partitioned into components due to different sources of variation. In its simplest form ANOVA provides a statistical test of whether or not the means of several groups are all equal, and therefore generalizes Student's two-sample *t*-test to more than two groups. ANOVAs are helpful because they possess a certain advantage over a two-sample t-test. Doing multiple two-sample t-tests would result in a largely increased chance of committing a type I error. For this reason, ANOVAs are useful in comparing three or more means.

The null hypothesis in a one-factor, between-subjects ANOVA is that all the population means are equal: H_0: $\mu_1 = \mu_2 = \ldots = \mu_a$. Unfortunately, when the analysis of variance is significant and the null hypothesis is rejected, the only valid inference that can be made is that at least one population mean is different from at least one other population mean. The analysis of variance does not reveal which population means differ from which others. Experimenters usually are interested in more information. They want to know precisely where the differences lie. Consequently, further analyses are usually conducted after a significant analysis of variance. These further analyses almost always involve conducting a series of significance tests. This causes a very serious problem: the more significance tests that are conducted, the greater the chance that at least one of them will produce a Type I error.

DATA ANALYSIS

- One-way ANOVA is applied to the features and ratings for Dell. The significance came out to be 0.003. This means that the null hypothesis is rejected and that all the features are not contributing equally.

Table depicting one-way ANOVA between features and ratings for Dell

	Sum of Squares	*df*	*Mean Square*	*F*	*Sig.*
Between Groups	7.387	5	1.477	3.657	.003
Within Groups	147.871	366	.404		
Total	155.258	371			

- One-way ANOVA is applied to the features and ratings for HP & Compaq. The significance came out to be 0.000. This means that the null hypothesis is rejected and that all the features are not contributing equally.

  Table depicting one-way ANOVA between features and ratings for HP & Compaq

	Sum of Squares	*df*	*Mean Square*	*F*	*Sig.*
Between Groups	13.353	5	2.671	6.462	.000
Within Groups	81.824	198	.413		
Total	95.176	203			

- One-way ANOVA is applied to the different geographic divisions and sales. The significance came out to be 0.682, which is greater than 0.05. Hence, the null hypothesis is not rejected and it means that sales of Dell and HP & Compaq laptops are not affected by the different locations.

Table depicting one-way ANOVA between geographic divisions and sales of Dell and HP & Compaq

	Sum of Squares	*df*	*Mean Square*	*F*	*Sig.*
Between Groups	.541	4	.135	.574	.682
Within Groups	21.418	91	.235		
Total	21.958	95			

- One-way ANOVA is applied to the different level of usage and sales. The significance came out to be 0.423 which is greater than 0.05. Hence, the null hypothesis is not rejected. It means that sales of Dell and HP & Compaq laptops are not affected by users' level of usage.

Table depicting one-way ANOVA between different level of usage and sales of Dell and HP & Compaq

	Sum of Squares	*df*	*Mean Square*	*F*	*Sig.*
Between Groups	.403	2	.201	.869	.423
Within Groups	21.555	93	.232		
Total	21.958	95			

POLICY IMPLICATIONS

The government has contributed to the development of computer software industry by formulating an appropriate policy framework and providing necessary infrastructure facilities. The government's commitment to software development is stated in its policy document of

November 1986. Firstly, it wants to promote software exports to achieve a quantum leap and obtain a sizeable proportion of global markets in software. Secondly, the government aims for an integrated development of software for national and export markets. Thirdly, it wants the simplification of present procedures to accelerate the rate of growth in the industry. Following the crisis of 1991, computer industry policy was subject to a familiar set of liberalizations. Government/public sector purchasing also continued to form the major part of demand, with a number of very large investments from 1993-94. Hardware exports were also promoted through the initiation of the Electronics and Hardware Technology Park (EHTP) scheme.

Government spending and improved buying by consumers and small and medium businesses aided the recovery of the PC market last year. With large businesses also now buying, the PC market in India is set to grow by about 20 percent by units this year. Stronger projects, like the national ID project, will unleash a huge demand for an entire ecosystem of big and small solution providers. The government is in effect increasing the entire landscape by stimulating its investments, spending and by the greater participation from states for IT infrastructure.The Government has identified growth of Electronics Hardware Manufacturing Sector as a thrust area. National Manufacturing Competitiveness Council (NMCC) has been set up to provide a continuing forum for policy dialogue to energize and sustain the growth of manufacturing industries in India and this includes IT Hardware. Besides, a slew of measures like liberalization of foreign trade policy for Electronics and IT products, simplified customs and excise procedures, customs duty on specified capital goods and raw materials for electronics hardware brought down to 0%., setting up of Electronics Hardware Technology Parks (EHTP) and Special Economic Zones (SEZ) are set to boost manufacturing in the country.

CONCLUSION AND RECOMMENDATIONS

From the Internet research, we can conclude that Dell has become number one in laptop industry in India leaving behind HP & Compaq over the past few years. The secondary data through internet research is supported by the primary data through survey that Dell is preferred over HP in each region and also for each type of user. Consumers are considering price factor over the battery backup for both Dell and as well as HP. Similarly, consumers prefer overall performance to battery backup for both Dell and HP. Consumers are considering some factors viz. price, looks, extended features and overall performance equally for Dell. Consumers are considering looks over price in case of HP & Compaq laptops.

As consumers prefer price factor to battery backup feature, we can recommend the lowering of R&D expenses and cutting down the cost in case of both Dell and HP & COMPAQ. While purchasing a laptop, since the consumers are considering price as the defining factor, HP should work on its pricing strategies for increasing its market share. Since the sales of Dell and HP are not affected by region, they should channelize their distribution equally among all the regions. HP should not compromise on overall performance so as to reduce the price to capture the market because both the factors are playing significant roles. As a particular type of user does not dominate sales, all user categories should be given equal importance.

BIBLIOGRAPHY

[1] http://en.wikipedia.org/wiki/Hewlett-Packard_Company

[2] http://en.wikipedia.org/wiki/Dell

[3] http://www.pcworld.com/article/203545/dell_dislodges hpindia_for_first place in_pc_market.html

[4] Silicon india :http://www.siliconindia.com/shownews/HP_leads_notebook_ market_ in_India IDC-nid-19670.html

[5] http://businesstoday.intoday.in/index.php?option=com_content&task= view&id= 7479&issueid=86

[6] http://businesstoday.intoday.in/index.php?option=com_content&task= view&id= 12100&issueid=86

[7] http://businesstoday.intoday.in/index.php?option=com_content&task= view&id=1974 &issueid=86

[8] http://in.reuters.com/article/idINIndia-50952220100819

[9] http://www.idcindia.com/press/19Feb2010.asp

[10] http://www.channelworld.in/news/idc-india-pc-sales-register-33-yoy-growth-jfm-2010

[11] http://www.topnews.in/node/269938

[12] http://www.laptopindia.co.in/

[13] "Laptop Market Overview ", http://www.naukrihub.com/india/fmcg/overview/laptop/, November 2012

[14] http://www.scribd.com/doc/25432804/Laptop-Industry-in-India-Jan-2010

[15] http://www.business-standard.com/india/news/dell-beats-hp-to-become-top-pc-seller-in-india/405059/

[16] "Introduction to Between-Subjects Analysis of Variance: Preliminaries", http:// davidmlane.com/hyperstat/B119234.html. (2012)

[17] The Little PCs That Could, Fortune Winter (2001), Technology Guide Vol 142 Issue 12 p78

Consumer's Preference of Personal Care Products in India

Gunjan Malhotra, Kunal Arora and Kartikeya Sharma

Institute of Management Technology, Ghaziabad

ABSTRACT

The number of people living in rural India has decreased. Indian urban poor have been moving to cities and towns to get employment thereby increasing their income level. FMCG companies believe that these people buy personal care segment (PCS) products to compete with the urban population and self awareness. Thus we study different brands of PCS in terms of soap, shampoo, hair oil and toothpaste that compete in the market. We also emphasise on the factors that are responsible behind the purchase decision of urban poor and find that price and offer/discounts are the most popular.

INTRODUCTION

With liberalisation and globalisation of the Asian economies the number of people living in rural sector has decreased. India is not an exception. India becoming increasingly globalized and urban, there has also been an increase in the number of poor people living here. As the fruits of development have not reached the 'real India' or 'Bharat', people from villages have been moving to cities and towns in order to get employment and make a livelihood for themselves. Not only India but whole of Asia has been experiencing simultaneous growth, urbanisation and growing poverty.

Economic development and urbanisation go hand in hand as over 55% of the GDP comes from cities and towns (Urban poverty report, 2009). With urbanisation, there is also increase in the slums in the urban areas. The number of people living in slums in India has more than doubled in the past two decades and now exceeds the entire population of Britain, the Indian Government has announced. The number of people living in slums in India was around 93 million in 2011 or 7.75 percent of the total population almost double the population of Britain. It is interesting to note that the ratio of urban poverty in some of the larger states in India (Urban poverty report, 2009) is higher than that of rural poverty leading to the phenomenon of 'Urbanisation of Poverty'.

Urban poor in India have been working in diverse job areas like electricians, daily wage labourers, construction workers, rikshaw pullers, factory workers, servants, maids, security gaurds, cook, waiters etc and have been earning sufficient amount to meet their daily needs. But in last few years there has been an increase in spending of the urban poor. And here lies a big opportunity for Fast Moving Consumer Goods (FMCG) companies to cater to these untapped markets. Marketing expert Jagdeep Kapoor, who advises FMCG companies catering to this market, estimates that Indian slums account for Rs 30,000 crore of spending. This is growing at 20-25% a year. Of the total consumption in India urban poor has a 10% share (Kamath, et al., 2011).

In this paper, we examine how different demographics of the urban poor influence consumption of selected personal care segment (PCS) products namely soaps, shampoos, oil and toothpaste in India and whether this relationship is attenuated, i.e. to lessen the amount, force, magnitude, or value of: weaken/ to make thin in consistency, by product type and personal care brands available in Indian markets.

Our research makes five important contributions. First, we show the demographic profile and socio-economic status of urban poor consumers in Delhi and national capital region (NCR). Second, we observe the consumption pattern of preferred brands in PCS among urban poor. Third, we establish the empirical framework using factors influencing purchase decisions. Fourth, we offer useful implications for public policy officials, market researchers, businessmen and consumers who are interested in establishing PCS products in Indian markets. In turn these findings become relevant to brand managers who are increasingly being held accountable for contributing to the variety of PCS products to urban poor.

We organise the rest of the article as follows: we first summarize prior findings, introduce PCS products and brands in the Indian rural markets, and develop our hypothesis. Next, we describe the factor analysis test measures. Then, we specify and report the findings. In the final section, we offer implications for mangers and researchers.

LITERATURE REVIEW

Urbanization has been taking place around the globe and at a very fast pace in the developing countries. Over the next 30 years (i.e. 2000–2030), the world's population is projected to grow at an annual rate of 1.8 per cent, or nearly double the rate expected for the total population of the world (almost one per cent per year). By 2030, demographers predict that around 61 per cent of the world's population will be living in urban areas. Compared against the rapid rise in the urban population, the growth of the world's rural population has been relatively slow. Thus, all future population growth for the foreseeable future is expected to be absorbed in urban areas (Cohen, 2006).

The urban expansion that is projected in Asia will be nearly 30 times as large as the urbanization that unfolded over half a century ago in the United States—and will take place in less than 20 years. By 2025, nearly 2.6 billion Asians will live in cities, accounting for 55 per cent of the world's urban population. India and China alone will account for more than 64 per cent of the overall growth of urban populations in Asia and a 42 per cent share of global urban population growth from 2005 to 2025. China will have the world's largest urban population at triple the size of that of the United States; India's urban population will be double that of the United States (Sankhe et.al., 2011).

This urbanisation along with the large rural market has one big advantage for the Indian FMCG companies. Indian cities are expected to add 379 million people to the consumer base for FMCG companies, as the urbanisation rate is expected to increase from the current 30 to 45 per cent in the next 40 years. With the widespread distribution reach, FMCG companies earned US$ 18 billion from rural areas in 2010. Rural India accounts for close to one-third of the total consumption pie. Robust consumption in the rural economy is a key driver of India's sustained growth. The penetration of companies into rural north India increased from 9.5 per cent in 2000 to 46 per cent in 2008, due to companies selling their products in small packets or sachets (IBEF 2010).

Along with introducing smaller variants, packaging also has been changing with times. Packaging is a key component of marketing, according to studies by the Point of Purchase and Advertisement Institute (POPAI), which indicate that 70% of consumers' buying decisions are made at the point of sale (Parker, 1997). Pandey (2005) also claims that impulse purchase is increasing rapidly. The package is a very effective tool for influencing impulse purchasing (Sehrawet, 2002; Sehrawet and Kundu, 2003). Further, Kundu and Sehrawet (2002) showed that consumers feel that the package is very helpful in identifying and distinguishing products.

Therefore, in order to develop guidelines that address the outlined gap, we begin by identifying factors that are important to and are used by urban poor customers in differentiating one packaged PCS product brand with other in NCR markets. Further the consumption (taste, price, convenience, availability) and reasons for the purchase decision of the urban poor consumers towards PCS products market are being studied. Moreover the research evaluates the factors influencing brand preference of PCS. We anticipate the availability of these products is mostly attracted by the young population. This study will help us to understand the type of most preferred PCS brands.This will also highlight the choice of brand with respect to demographic profile of the consumer.

METHOD

Design and Procedure

In this study, descriptive research technique was adopted. Main objective of the survey is to know the consumers' preference of a particular brand of personal care segment items in Indian markets. A non-probability convenient sampling technique was used to collect primary data keeping in view the subject matter of research, ease accessibility and convenience of the researcher. The study period was 4 months (September 2011 – November 2011). Sample units i.e. the urban poor were approached personally and were asked to complete the questionnaire.

The questionnaire was spread across Delhi NCR region, as it is the fastest developing region in India and the urban poor population has more purchasing power and exposure as compared to other urban poor in Indian States. The target population was people living in slums of Jal Vihar in delhi, slums of Ghazibad near vijaynagar, Badarpur and noida and other slums in the NCR region. A survey design was employed, and a sample of four Indian PCS products were selected namely shampoo, soaps, toothpaste and hair oil. A total of 168 responses were gathered and after editing questionnaire, the unsuitable or partial responses were discarded and the final analysis included only 130 responses.

The questionnaire probed three areas of the urban poor consumer profile/psyche: the consumer's demographic information, generic factors related to PCS products and factors specific to the brands selected for our study in Indian market. Collected data were categorized, tabulated and interpreted on the basis of different dimensions mentioned in the questionnaire.

Estimating Measures

Factor analysis –In order to determine the minimum number of factors that would account for the maximum variance in the data collected, we used multivariate techniques – factor analysis. Factor analysis is a general name denoting a class of procedures used for data-reduction and summarizing. It is employed in our study for the purpose of analyzing the data. The Principal Component Method is considered appropriate and the data is analyzed by using SPSS, version – 17. For this reason the results of the factor analysis using Principal Component Method are found out. Results of four factors being extracted from the data collected. Only factors with Eigen value(s) greater than 1 were retained and others were ignored. By comparing the Varimax Rotated Factor Matrix with Un-rotated Factor Matrix (entitled as component matrix), rotation has provided simplicity and has enhanced interpretability. From the rotated factor matrix the factors have been extracted and listed.

DISCUSSION AND RESULTS

Urban Poor Consumer's Preference for PCS Products

Over the years PCS products have gained their popularity in Indian markets. Urban poor have gained from the opening up of the Indian economy in terms of their higher income and earning ability which has changed their outlook to buy different variety of products available. Compared to rural consumers, the urban poor are more aware and more discerning (Kamath et.al., 2011). Since they are reliant on daily or sporadic cash flows, products and brands with a lower per purchase price appeal to them (Roosevelt D'Souza, executive director of Nielsen, a market research company, 2011). Two factors are spurring this shift. One, higher earnings. The daily wage rate has increased from Rs 100-150 to Rs 300-350 in the past three years. This is possible because of more members of the family being employed and thus urban poor are earning and spending more (Rama Bijapurkar, expert on market strategy and consumer related issues, 2011). Further due to social exposure, as urban poor go to urban houses or plush offices, the exposure has increased their aspirations and consumption (Damodar Mall, director of food strategy at future group, 2011). Moreover television advertisements are hugely influencing purchases by youngsters in categories like shampoos, deodorants, razors and body wash (Jayesh Trivedi, owner of a general store in Dharavi, 2011).

With rising prices of food and commodity products forcing India's huge middle class market to lap up low-unit packs of soaps and detergents, shampoos, biscuits and snack foods more than ever before, companies such as Hindustan Unilever (HUL), ITC, Britannia, Frito-Lay, Godrej, CavinKare, Dabur and Nestle are banking on these 'magic price points' to push volumes. Last year, such packs accounted for 25-30% of their sales. India continues to provide affordable and accessible variety of goods in the range of Rs 5- Rs 10 points (Vinita Bali, CEO of Britannia Industries, 2011). Britannia Industries have introduced 'Good Day' biscuits in Rs 5 packs. GlaxoSmithKline (GSK) has launched Asha, a low-cost variant (40 per cent lower cost) of Horlicks for rural markets only. The product is priced at US$ 1.8 for a 500-gm pouch pack. In January 2010, Nestlé launched Maggi Masala-ae-Magic and Maggi Rasile Chow priced at INR 2 and INR 4, respectively, for rural consumers with low purchasing power. Maggie Rasile Chow has been developed especially to provide a low-cost, light meal fortified with iron. Masala-ae-Magic is a taste enhancer containing iron, iodine and vitamin A. These products have been developed to address the widespread concern around micro-nutrient malnutrition in India (IBEF 2010).

Demographic Profile of the Urban Poor Consumers for Using PCS Products

The results of the demographic profile of the lower income group living in urban slums and villages are presented in table 1.

Table 1: Demographics Characteristics of the Respondents (in percentages)

Gender		*Age (in years)*		*Marital Status*		*Education*		*Monthly income*		*Place of residence*	
Male	76.92	< 20	7.692	Married	83.85	< 5th standard	21.54	<3000	13.85	Urban village	26.15
Female	23.08	20-30	43.08	Single	16.15	5th -10th Standard	40.77	3000-5000	40.77	Slums	33.07
		30-40	27.69			12th pass	11.54	5000-10000	36.15	Village	36.92
		40-50	10			Graduate	9.23	10000-15000	4.62	City	3.07
		> 50	10.78			No Education	16.92	>15000	4.62	Work place	0.769

Other than this, 32.3 % of the respondents had a cycle, 19.23 % had a 2 wheeler, 3.8 % had a 4 wheeler and the remaining 43.8 % had no transport. In case of sources of media at their home, 23 % read newspaper, 56.15 % had a TV, 16.92 % had a radio, 1.54 % read magazine, 6.15 had a computer and 73.84 % i.e. 96 out of 130 of the respondents had a mobile. The percentage of mobile shows the penetration of mobile handsets in the lower income groups.

Utility and Preference of Urban Poor Consumers' Choice of PCS Products

Table 2: Respondents usage Pattern of Personal care Product - Soap

Brand of Soap Used		*Purpose for using Soap*		*Frequency of Usage*		*Money Willing to Spend on Buying soap*		*Willing to Change Brand of Soap*	
Lux	32.3	Bathing	40.63	Twice a day	16.4	<10	49.23	Yes	50.77
Lifebuoy	16.92	Hand washing	23.44	Once a day	77.34	10-20	38.46	No	49.23
Godrej No. 1	10	Hair wash	3.125	Once in 2 days	5.46	20-30	6.15		
Dettol	11.53	All of the above	60.94	Once in 3 days	0.78	>30	5.38		
Vivel	0.769								
Local	0								
Dove	1.54								
Malik	0.769								
Don't know	10								
Breeze	0.769								
Nirma	6.15								
Rexona	0.769								
Godrej	0.769								
Sinhola	0.769								
Margo	0.769								
Pears	1.54								
Sinhola	1.54								
Hamam	1.54								
Liril	0.769								
Don't use	1.56								

Urban poor market in terms of usage of the personal care product soap (table 2) is dominated by the brand Lux, around 32.3% of the respondents use this soap. This is followed by lifebuoy (16.92%), Dettol (11.53%) and Godrej No. 1(10%). The respondents (60.94%) mainly use soap for bathing, hand washing and hair wash while around 40% use it only for bathing. It was interesting to find that the urban poor people are willing to spend less than Rs.10 (49.23%) on the brand of soap they buy which is used once a day (77.34%). Almost half of the urban poor respondents were willing to change the brand of the soap they buy. This indicates that urban poor people tend to adapt the life style of the people living in the cities.

Table 3: Respondents Usage Pattern of Personal Care Product - Shampoo

Brand of shampoo used		*Purpose for using Shampoo*		*Frequency of usage*		*Money Willing to spend on Buying Shampoo*		*Willing to Change Brand of Shampoo*	
Clinic Plus	20	Dandruff	12.35	Twice a day	3.7	<5	74.1	Yes	43.75
Head and		Dryness	6.17	Once a day	25.9	10-20	2.46	No	56.25
Shoulders	9.23	Silkiness	37.04	Once in 2 days	25.9	20-30	1.23		
Vatika	3.46	Clean	64.19	Once in 3 days	30.8	30-50	6.17		
Sunsilk	3.08	Shine	2.46	Once in a week	12.3	>50	16.05		
Rejoice	0	Hair fall	2.46	Occasionally	1.23				
Almond	0.769	Quality	7.41						
Local brand	0	Breakage	1.23						
Dove	3.46								
Pantene	3.08								
Chick	12.31								
Don't Know	6.15								

In case of shampoo the urban poor market (table 3) is dominated by clinic plus with 20 percent of the respondents using it. This is followed by Chick (12.31%) and Head and Shoulders (9.23%) shampoo. The urban poor respondents mainly use shampoo for cleaning their hair (64.19%) and making it silky (37.04). During the survey we observed that these respondents prefer to buy sachets of shampoos available rather than bottles. It was noted that 30.8% of the respondents use shampoo once in three days though they are willing to spend less than Rs.5 on the shampoo's they buy and mainly prefer to the brand once used by them. This is because these urban poor people are becoming aware of health and hygiene and are able to understand the need to be clean and presentable. This may be again because of their movement in the middle and upper middle class of urban cities.

Table 4: Respondents Usage Pattern of Personal Care Product – Hair Oil

Brand of Hair oil used		*Purpose for using Hair oil*		*Frequency of usage*		*Money willing to spend on buying Hair oil*		*Willing to change brand of Hair oil*	
Parachute	8.46	Dryness	22.3	Twice a day	4.62	<10	5.38	Yes	45.16
Dabur amla	19.23	Healthy hair	39.23	Once a day	67.69	10-20	8.46	No	54.84
Baba ji	0	Shine	8.46	Once in 2 days	12.31	20-30	18.46		
Dabur Vatika	0.769	Silkiness	13.36	Once in 3 days	6.15	30-40	10		
Navaratan Cool	5.38	Freshness	2.31	Once a week	2.31	40-50	46.15		
Local	0	Long hair	0.769	Occasionally	1.54	>50	6.92		
Sarso	28.46	Head ache	0.769			Don't know	4.61		
Bajaj Amla	10.77	To set	13.07						
Hair and Care	2.31	Clean	0.769						
Kiokarpin	6.923	Itching	0.769						
Don't know	5.38	To keep them black	1.54						
Himganga	3.85	Cool	0.769						
Almond Drops	0.769	Smell	0.769						
Clinic plus	0.769	Don't know	5.38						
Shalimaar	0.769								

Table 4 shows that in case of hair oil the majority of the respondents prefer to use "Sarso" oil (28%) and Dabur Amla (19%) for healthy hair (39.23%), silkiness (13.36%) and also for setting their hair (13.07%). These respondents are willing to spend between Rs.40-50 (46.15%) in one buy and most of them (67.69%) apply it once a day. They are fully content with the hair oil they use and do not prefer to switch to the new brand of hair oil available and believe in using the traditional oil. Only 43.75% of the respondents said they are willing to change. Also there is a misconception among the urban poor people that hair oil is helpful in setting the hair.

The urban poor respondents mainly use Colgate (49%) toothpaste (table 5) and are not willing to change (56.25%) to any other brand of toothpaste. The second most preferred product is Dabur Lal Dant Manjan, which is used by 18 percent of the respondents. It is surprising to know that some of the respondents preferred to use "Gul" instead of toothpaste majorly because of its intoxicating content. Majority of the respondents use toothpaste daily to clean their teeth and they are not willing to spend more than 20 rupees on this product.

Table 5: Respondents Usage Pattern of Personal Care Product – Toothpaste

Brand of Toothpaste used		*Purpose for using Toothpaste*		*Frequency of usage*		*Money willing to spend on buying Toothpaste*		*Willing to change brand of Toothpaste*	
Colgate	49.23	Cleaning	94.53	Twice a day	14.28	<20	54.76	Yes	43.75
Pepsodent	9.23	Diseases	6.25	Once a day	84.12	20-30	19.84	No	56.25
Close-up	2.31	Mouth freshness	15.63	Once in 2 days	0.793	30-40	11.11		
Miswak	0	Getting high	4.68	Once in 3 days	0.793	40-50	5.55		
Neem	0					50-60	3.17		
Babool	4.62					>60	3.96		
Vicco	0.769					Don't know	1.58		
Promise	0								
Sensodyne	0								
Red	0								
Dabur lal dant manjan	18.46								
Datun	3.07								
Colgate herbal	0.769								
Don't know	2.31								
Gul	6.15								
Don't use	3.07								

PCS Brand Preference in Delhi NCR Region

Companies like hero Honda, Piramal healthcare and FMCG companies like Nestle, Dabur, have already launched specific plans and operations targeted towards urban poor. Some FMCG companies are tweaking their distribution chain to include the urban slums in their business plans. To tap the limited purchasing power of urban poor FMCG companies have been introducing small sachets and packets of their products. Lux soap at Rs 10, Good Day biscuit packet at Rs 5, Nestea premix ice tea pack at Rs 2. These are some of the most popular offers in the consumer products market where companies expect low-priced units to account for more than 40% of their total sales this year (drypen.in, 2010).

From the above table 1-4 we can infer that majority of the urban poor respondents prefer Lux soap and Clinic Plus shampoo, which are the brands of Hindustan Unilever Ltd. (HUL). This is in consensus with the claim made by HUL that every two out of three Indians use its products. In case of toothpaste and oil respondents prefer Colgate by Colgate Pamolive and and "sarso" oil and Dabur Amla, which is a brand of Dabur India Ltd. respectively. This shows that among the personal care products manufacturing companies, HUL has the highest penetration and the most effective distribution in the urban poor market.

Empirical Analysis

In order to find the most important factors that influence the purchase decision of PCS products among urban poor consumer's in NCR region we have used factor analysis test. Cronbach alpha indicated that the scale was reliable (a = .681). Factor analysis is a statistical method used to describe variability among observed variables in terms of fewer unobserved variables called factors. The information gained about the interdependencies can be used later to reduce the set of variables in a dataset. The respondents result for factor analysis (table 6) was extracted by the Principal component method. The total of 69.96% of variations has been explained by the model. After looking at the rotated component method we reduce the number of variables and group them into three prominent factors. We name the four factors as below:

Influential factors – word of mouth and employer usage

Promotional factors – Advertisement and brand ambassador

Cost factors – price and packaging

Sales factor - Offer discount and availability

Table 6: Factor Analysis

KMO and Bartllett's Test				
Kaiser-Meyer-Olkin Measure of Sampling Adequacy: 0.549				
Bartlett's Test of Sphericity Approx. Chi-square: 186.310				
Sig: 0.000				
Total Variance Explained				
Initial Eigen values				
Total	% of Variance	Cumulative %		
2.104	26.301	26.301		
1.299	16.233	42.534		
1.181	14.759	57.293		
1.014	12.673	69.965		
Rotated Component Matrix				
	1	2	3	4
Price	-1.71	.129	.778	-.023
Advertisement	.132	.799	.078	-.235
Package	.243	.039	.654	.090
Availability	-.206	.423	-.417	.475
Offer discount	.114	-.037	.102	.888
Word of mouth	.933	.133	.044	.031
Employer usage	.928	.085	.046	.045
Brand ambassador	.114	.677	.103	.231

MANAGERIAL IMPLICATIONS

Based on our research, we found that urban poor is not much influenced by the brand ambassadors of the PC products they use. Around 80% of the respondents said brand ambassadors are not important to them. For long, FMCG companies have been relying on brand ambassadors to boost sales or for the purpose of brand recall and have been paying hefty amounts to the brand ambassadors for endorsing their products. Thus some amount of spending can be put into some investment. Also the respondents have been price conscious as around 68% said that price is a very important criteria in their purchase decision. While around 18% said price is not important as for them it's the product quality which matters. Thus even in the urban poor segment, there are quality conscious consumers and are not totally driven by price. Also, around 57% of the respondents said that offers/discount plays an important role in their purchase decision.

Thus based on the above findings, we suggest that rather than spending exorbitant amounts on brand ambassadors, companies can use the financial resources to develop superior products, offer low price products or introduce offers/discounts.

Among the 4 products in our research, the usage of shampoo was the least as only 62.3% of the respondents used shampoos. Thus companies with shampoos in their portfolios can emphasize on the usage part while advertising their products.

Also we found that electronic media was more popular among urban poor than print media. While only 23% read news paper, 56% had televisions at their homes, almost 17% had radios and almost 14% had both. Thus in orders to reach the urban poor, companies need to advertise their products more on electronic media rather than print media.

CONCLUSIONS AND FUTURE WORK

According to the research, majority of the respondents had income in the range of Rs. 3000-5000 (40.77 %) and Rs. 5000-10000 (36.15 %). Among the urban poor, electronic media was found to be more popular than the print media. A whopping 73.84 % had a mobile phone. Most popular brands among the urban poor are lux and lifebuouy in the soap category. Clinic plus and chik among shampoos, dabur amla and bajaj amla in the oil category and colgate in the toothpaste category. The major factors responsible behind the purchase decision of urban poor are price and offer/discounts. Also, majority of the respondents were found to be loyal towards the brands they are using.

Although our research provides valuable findings and sufficiently explains the demographics, consumption pattern and factors responsible for purchase among the urban poor, it may raise further questions like- the effect of proximity of a developed urban area to a rural/urban villages on the usage and awareness of various brands, the differences in the consumption pattern between urban poor and rural poor etc.

In summary, this research examined speaks widely to the diverse urban poor community's purchasing habits in Delhi NCR region in India. Although our findings might raise a new set of questions, we believe that future marketer in the urban rural sector can elaborate this research by adding few more empirical analysis namely chi-square test, ANOVA, cluster analysis, etc.

BIBLIOGRAPHY

[1] Cohen. B (2006) 'Urbanization in developing countries: Current trends, future projections, and key challenges for sustainability', *Technology in Society,* vol.28, pp. 63-80. http://www7.nationalacademies.org/dbasse/cities_transformed_world_technologyinsociety_article.pdf

[2] Drypen.in/articles (2010), 'Big FMCG sales come in small packages', http://drypen.in/featured-articles/big-fmcg-sales-come-in-small-packages.html (last assessed on December 20, 2011).

[3] Kamath, G.; Philip, L.; Chumbhale, A.; and Gokhale, N. (2011), 'What cos like Future Group, Piramal Healthcare, Dabur, PepsiCo, Nestle and others are doing to tap the Rs 30,000 crore slum economy', Economic Times Newspaper, 23 October 2011. http://articles.economictimes.indiatimes.com/2011-10-11/news/30266755_1_largest-slum-dharavi-rural-markets/3

[4] Lipton, M., Ravallion, M. (1995) 'Poverty and policy'In: Behrman, J., Srinivasan, T.N. (Eds.), Handbook of Development Economics, Vol. 3. North-Holland, Amsterdam.

[5] Pandey, D.P. (2005) 'Education in rural marketing', *University News*, Vol. 43, pp. 7–8.

[6] Parker, R. (1997) 'Counting down the top 10 US packaging trends', *Packaging India*, August–September, 79–82.

[7] Sankhe, S.; Vittal, I. And Mohan, A. (2011) 'Urban Giants: India and China, and their Urbanization Paths Environment and Urbanization Asia, March 2011, Vol. 2, No.1, pp 1-12.

[8] Sehrawet, M. (2002) 'Impact of packaging on consumer buying behaviour: a comparative study of rural and urban consumers in Haryana', Unpublished PhD Thesis.

[9] Sehrawet, M. & Kundu, S.C. (2003) 'Packaging as a marketing tool: a study. In *International Business and Financial Services in WTO Regime* (ed. by M.S. Turan & S.C. Kundu)', pp. 287–298. Excel Books, New Delhi.

[10] Urban Poverty Report (2009) 'India: Urban Poverty Report 2009', *India Development Gateway*, http://www.indg.in/social-sector/urban-poverty-alleviation/india_urban_poverty_report_ 2009.pdf , last accessed on December 5, 2011.

[11] Indian Brand Equity Foundation (2010) 'Fast moving consumer goods'. http://www.ibef.org/download/FMCG_270111.pdf, November 2010 (last assessed on December 14, 2011).

Contemporary Retailing: An Insight into Challenges to Innovate to Achieve Competitiveness

Pardeep Bawa, Zara Ehsan, Irshad Ahmad, Shivam Mishra and Tawseef Farook

Lovely Professional University, Jalandhar, Punjab

ABSTRACT

Retailing has been getting into more & more competition as more corporates are venturing into retailing. India as a case isn't an exception. Raising the limit of FDI in multi brand retailing would only increase the competition where only fittest will survive. To be as fittest retailers have to get into what is called innovative retailing. Innovative retailing has to do with integrated execution of strategies which would not only influence shoppers but to push them to stay longer with them as more no. of retailers would increase defection levels. Apart from retailer the two parties which are primary stakeholders in retailing phenomenon are manufacturers & customers. Only those innovative practices would lead to competitive advantage that would ensure a win-win-win situation for these three more significant stakeholders than others. Paper examined the challenges being faced to innovative by retailers in a questto stay competitive and developing sustainable competitive advantage over a period of time. Study found that link among manufacturer, retailer & consumer lacks integrated learning.Shopper-centric store layout and design, customized sensory experiences, online navigational path design, virtual shop testing, rationalisation of in-store instruments/vehicles are some of the innovative practices being followed by reatilers to take on these challenges.

INTRODUCTION

Innovation is no more an option or an alternative but a primary requirement to achieve competitiveness & stay competitive. Innovations can be in the form of new products or services, or cost-reducing process improvements, or innovative business models and methods. The benefits of innovation occur in all aspects of the profit/loss statement: innovators drive additional sales volume, achieve price premiums and reduce costs through process improvements. In addition to the financial benefits, innovation goes hand-in-hand with sustainable development initiatives, as both require progressive leadership and an appetite for change, combined with a tolerance of experimentation and some risk. It must be acknowledged that no firm is always successful with its innovations, including the global 'innovation masters' such as Intel, Samsung and Sony, due to the challenging and uncertain factors in introducing new products, services, processes etc. However, it is reasonably assumed that those with a robust and systematic innovation capability are more likely to have higher probabilities of success on any single new innovation activity, and significantly more such successes overall. Hence in these successfully innovative firms, such as Sony and Apple, Samsung and HP, there is a sustainable capability for the successes to more than fund the failures. Everybody is familiar with Sony's Walkman, Discman and series of PlayStations more than making up for its product failures and similar is so with Apple's Macintosh, iPod, iPhone, iTunes and Apple retail stores. Both these companies have had spectacular product flops, even once launched on to global markets, but the successes in their portfolio of innovations have given an overall business advantage which is substantial.

RETAILER-CUSTOMER CHANGING RELATIONSHIP

Retailers are currently confronted with several challenges in regard to their relationship with their customers. Shoppers expect retailers to sell quality products and to provide them with good service levels within their stores. However, they also expect the retailers' prices to be as low as possible. The last several years have seen fierce price competition, which has forced retailers to cut costs wherever possible. Apart from the optimization of supply chain activities, through initiatives such as Efficient Consumer Response (ECR), retailers have also reduced the number of employees in their outlets. This cutback has led to a lower employee to customer ratio in retail stores, which in turn created new problems like longer waiting lines at the point-of-sale (POS) and difficulty for customers in finding store personnel for assistance. And this is not all as there are other challenges as well being faced by retailers. Solution can be innovative approach in every link in retail process like a value delivery chain. Stiff competition in retailing has made the job of retail managers even tougher. Innovation requires resources but resources incur a lot of money upon & that in turns decreases competitiveness. Quite a few studies analysed challenges & most of those studies found the link among manufacturer, retailer & consumer lacks integrated learning.

CHALLENGES

There are manychallengesfor managers impeding progress in shopper marketing innovations (Gallagher 2008). The future of shopper marketing and related innovations depends critically on overcoming these challenges. Below we discuss some of the key challenges at three levels.Closing the collaboration gap between manufacturers and retailers Shopper marketing is inherently a joint effort of retailers and manufacturers. Cooperation among retailers and manufacturers is essential for the success of shopper marketing. Understanding shoppers' needs without retailers' cooperation and willingness to share detailed data to create customized insights and provide sufficient access to their shoppers is difficult for the manufacturers. Conversely, retailers cannot benefit from manufacturers' shopper marketing resources, insights, and programs until retailers work symbiotically with their channel members and dedicate attention to manufacturers' brands. However, despite the enthusiastic reception and endorsement of shopper marketing by key retailers and manufacturers, the outlook on retailer–manufacturer collaboration is murky (Abens 2009). The key barriers to collaboration in shopper marketing include:

I. Misaligned primary objectives and planning

II. Differing key performance indicators (KPIs) and incentives

III. Lack of strategic alignment

IV. Poor pre-existing relationships and lack of trust

Misaligned primary objectives and planning Annual surveys on "Managing and Measuring Shopper Marketing" by Promotion Marketing Association (PMA) Shopper Marketing Center of Excellence with Nielsen Business Media (2008, 2009) reveal the extent of misalignment between the objectives of manufacturers and retailers. The PMA surveyed 318 retailers, manufacturers and agencies. Although sales growth is the prime stated objective for retailers as well as manufacturers, these entities are not aligned on other key objectives. Specifically, retailers' second priority for shopper marketing is strengthening shopper relationships. In contrast, manufacturers focus more on developing brand equity and fortify relationships with the retailers. That is, manufacturers stress on creating shopper insights and marketing programs that are persuasive to retailers, on the other hand retailers want shopper insights and programs that please their shoppers. Moreover, unsurprisingly, retailers tend to focus on increasing store sales and profits while manufacturers stress their brands' sales. Apart from that, one-third of the retailers participating in the survey mentioned that their planning cycles do not synchronize with those of their vendors. As a consequence, only 40 percent of retailers in the survey were satisfied with manufacturer support for their shopper marketing efforts while the corresponding figure for manufacturers is even lower (32 percent). Dissimilar key performance indicators (KPI) and incentives Different objectives mostly lead to the use of different metrics, and shopper marketing is no exclusion. The PMA surveys unveil that neither the retailer nor manufacturer significantly focuses on the other's KPIs. Only one-third of retailers and manufacturers report that they agree on the metrics for evaluating programs "most of the time," nearly two-thirds of manufacturers say that they only "occasionally" or "never" reach agreement with retailers on howto measure programs, and no retailers agree regularly with their vendors. The indifference and lack of respect for each other's KPIs prevent effective collaboration.

LACK OF STRATEGIC ALIGNMENT

More often Retailers and manufacturers do not follow a common vision on the foundations of shopper marketing components such as shopper segmentation. The PMA surveys disclose that the majority of retailers feel that manufacturers are aware but are not well versed in their views of consumer segments. Likewise, the majority of manufacturers admit that their programs do not revolve around their retailers' segmentation. These contradictions have led to considerable dissatisfaction with the quality of shopper insights delivered by shopper marketing programs and disagreement on who is responsible for improvements. Interestingly, retailers' segmentations are usually shopper-based, while manufacturers' segmentation strategies are user-based. Manufacturers who truly seek to adopt a shopper marketing focus will have to conform their segmentation strategies in order to succeed in the realm of shopper marketing. More specifically, while manufacturers as well as retailers say that bringing shopper insights to the planning table, is primarily the manufacturers' responsibility, a good proportion of manufacturers want retailers to generate more shopper insights. Either way, the misalignment across retailers and manufacturers as to the appropriate shopper segmentation models is proving to be a major obstacle. Collecting knowledge and developing meaningful insights with respect to each retailer's own segmentationmodel and segments impels the manufacturers to collect shopper data for each retailer separately, to allocate significant time and money, and to make elusive decisions with respect to the allocation of shopper insight generation resources to each account. In some cases, the data do not exist to probe the insights at the level the retailer desires.

LITERATURE REVIEW

Some studies related to innovative practices are being followed by retailers are as below.

Shopper-centric Store Layout and Design

How can retailers gear their stores more toward shoppers' needs and preferences than before? In the offline channels, retailers normally segment the market and follow different formats that cater to diverse segments. Nevertheless, even within a storeformat, retailers may want to create stores within stores to address different sub-segments of shoppers. For example, a retailer CVS has created 'Beauty 360' a new store within store selling a wide range of beauty products with professionally trained sales associates to attract high-end shoppers (Boyle 2009).

Online Navigational Path Design

Most of the shoppers make both brand and purchase channel choices based on the quality of their experiences online. Internet is often used as a channel of search by the buyers. They often visit the websites of manufacturers and retailers before they make any purchase decision (Verhoef, Neslin, and Vroomen 2007). Online navigation is a strong driver of shopper trust (Bart, Shankar, Sultan, and Urban, 2005). When the economy is in the downswing, more shoppers look for such offerings on the Internet which are within their means. Such shoppers trust those websites that are backed by intuitive and convenient paths to purchase. Thus, to influence the attitudes and behaviors of buyers, innovations in online navigation are essential.

Customized Sensory Experiences

Since sensory influences play a major role in shopping behavior (Mitchell, Kahn, and Knasko, 1995), marketers need to understand how shoppers respond to different sensory stimuli at both traditional and online channels in a better way. Retailers can employ new thoughts to enhance various elements such as background music, colors, odor, and lighting. For example, a shopper solution display for the CoverGirl Wetslicks Fruit Spritzers product line drew shoppers to a set of multisensory shopper engagement elements about singer Rihanna: a "push and play" trigger to hear Rihanna's hit single, a scratch-and-sniff tear pad to experience the flavors associated with her lip gloss, and a sweepstakes entry for achance to visit Barbados, Rihanna's home country (Neff 2008).

Virtual Shop Testing

Retailers must appreciate technology. They can analyze the result of atmospherics and design elements bycarrying out experiments in virtual stores. Manufacturers such as P&G, Kimberly Clark, ConAgra, PepsiCo and Goodyear, and retailers such as Eddie Bauer have tested store layouts and designs off and on over the past decade. Even though no systematic insights are available as yet, it has been predicted by In-Store Marketing Institute that virtual store testing will turn out to be a standard practice among manufacturers and retailers. As shoppers are becoming more interconnectedacross the world through email and social media, good store design practices can be transported to numerous locations across the globe.

Innovations in In-store Merchandising

Economy wide fluctuations and technological opportunities are changing the approachability of shoppers for shopping, chiefly when they are inside a store. Shoppers tend to have mental budgets that they adjust while they are in the store (Stilley, Inman, andWakefield, 2010). They examined that shoppers have an "in-store slack" that they mentally neglect for making unplanned purchases and resist from making unplanned purchases once this in-store slack is exhausted. Although a model of in-store decision-making exists (Inman and Winer 1998), technology, aisle placement, shelf space positioning, and displays can help to improve in-store merchandising to a large extent. The key innovations are as follows.Retailers employing technology have growing opportunities to influence shopper decisions in store using technologies such as RFID, mobile technology, TV network, holograms, and virtual reality (e.g., Kalyanam, Lal, and Wolfram, 2008). To understand the effectiveness of technologies and the usage situation , manufacturers and retailers may need to go for experimentation. For example, an augmented reality system developed at the Massachusetts Institute of Technology (MIT) media lab and named SixthSense provides shoppers the facility to read packages and make informed choices at the stores using only hand gestures Manufacturers and retailers can test such a system using pilot projects.

Rationalization of In-store Instruments/Vehicles

In-store promotional instruments or vehicles are being used in excess these days in retail stores. These instruments vary from shopping carts, to shelf-talkers, to in-store TV. It is still not clear as to which of these instruments are more effective under different conditions. Manufacturers are making decisions on the extent of allowances to provide to the retailers for the use of each of these instruments. When marketing budgets are tightened in weak economic conditions, such decisions can be improved if holistic data on the separate and combined effectiveness of these instruments are collected and analyzed on a periodic basis.

Aisle Placements and Shelf Positions

Innovations in aisle placements and shelf-space management also play a significant role. Bezawada et al. (2009) show that by placing different categories in different aisles aptly, retailers can enhance overall sales. In particular, the impact of aisle adjacency is substantial (comparable to that of price, feature and display) and asymmetric across categories (Bezawada et al. 2009). Based on insights generated from analysis of shoppers' in-store navigation retailers can also make sound decisions on shelf facings (Chandon et al. 2009). Electronic tracking, eye-tracking, and shopping path recording are some of the means in which elaborate data on shopper navigational behavior can be gathered. The effectiveness of different aisle placements and shelf positions can be better ascertained by undertaking controlled experiments.

Pay-for-performance Displays

In-store promotions such as display promotions can improve the possibility of buying of unplanned things at the store (Stilley, Inman, and Wakefield, 2010). Displays always have a strong effect on shopper decisions in store. The most important challenge for retailers in managing displays is deciding which brand should get what type of display and at what cost. A system in which the manufacturer pays the retailer for displaysbased on the sales of the displayed products is an effective innovation as it is justified for both the manufacturer and the retailer. However, attributing sales to displays is not an easy task as there are challenges in measurement and implementation.

Innovations in Shopper Marketing Metrics

Economy transformations give rise to technological improvements, and due to this appropriate regulations come into force, a critical issue confronting shopper marketing is the lack of generally accepted metrics. The traditional metrics of store traffic, conversion, and sales lift are insufficient and need to be augmented. For online shopping, the issue of browsing versus buying is important. Metrics such as visits, queries, clickthroughs, and conversions need to be linked in an efficient manner. Possible candidates are metrics capturing attention and consideration (e.g., proximity to the target, dwell time, and brands touched), nature of the decision (e.g., planned vs. unplanned, frequent vs. infrequent, and hedonic vs. functional), and cross-effects (e.g., category adjacencies). Promising new methodologies include biometrics (e.g., heart rate monitoring, and ambulatory EEG), RFID-based path tracking, eye cams, handheld scanners, and infrared cameras.

OBJECTIVES

To study the challenges faced by organised retailers that keeping them away from being competitive and have a competitive edge.

To study the innovative practices being followed by organised retailers to stay competitive & develop a competitive edge over others.

RESEARCH METHODOLOGY

Literature of challenges being faced by retailers world over has been reviewed & cases of innovative practices being followed to take on these challenges were analysed taking into consideration specific sets of issues.

FINDINGS

Majority of the problems being faced by retailers is due to a liaison gap among manufacturer, retailers & customers. They are lacking a joint effort called shopper marketing wherein all there components of this phenomenon are equally required.

There is a non uniformity approach as far as key performance indicators of these three components are concerned. As a result an overall performance can't be figured out.

Very few retailers as well as manufacturers lack a mechanism wherein they can measure performance. They don't get themselves involved in any kind of agreement sort of thing for the same mostly.

As far as innovative mechanism is concerned they are trying to create stores within stores to address different sub-segments of shoppers to be more specific to their problems.

Now they are not only customizing websites for different types of customers but them very simple to understand & use rather than complicated path with unnecessary information. In many cases there are micro sites as well.

Retailers are employing new thoughts to enhance various elements such as background music, colors, odor, and lighting to enhance shopping experience.

They are using augmented reality system that provides customers the facility to go through packages and make smart choices at the stores using hand and eye gestures.Many more manufacturers & retailers have started testing such systems using pilot projects.

CONCLUSION & MANAGERIAL IMPLICATIONS

Innovation is not only confined to developing innovative products & services but a firm's business strategy must be centered on finding innovative solutions to its clients'/customers' problems/challenges. From proactively solving these problems, one creates business opportunities. Strategies need to include looking for new and different ways to solve problems for clients and new and different ways to conduct your own business processes. Systematic innovation needs to be properly resourced, and processes must allow for some experimentation, thinking outside the square, and taking carefully judged and calculated risks when needed. This includes stimulating creativity in all staff, which is a training and skilling-up opportunity. Knowledge management is an opportunity here too, requiring systems capabilities and forums for exchanging ideas between staff. Competitiveness can't be always created through some revolutionary thinking but something that provides a solution to the problems being faced by consumers by just changing sometimes the way you deliver quality if not crating quality. A job of retail manager becomes very challenging as he has not only to take on competition efforts but to innovate smartly as well. But quite a few retailers have done that just by changing how they respond to consumers & they were able to increase not only footfall but retention levels as well.

REFERENCES

[1] Abens, Rick (2009), "Exploring the Collaboration Gap: Are Shopper MarketingObjectives at Odds?," Adweek, 50 (19).

[2] Bart,Yakov,Venkatesh Shankar, Fareena Sultan and Glen L. Urban (2005), "Arethe Drivers and Role of Online Trust the Same for All Web Sites and Consumers?A Large Scale Exploratory Empirical Study," Journal of Marketing,69 (4), 133–52.

[3] Bezawada, Ram, Subramanian Balachander, P.K. Kannan and VenkateshShankar (2009), "Cross-Category Effects of Aisle and Display Placements:A Spatial Modeling Approach and Insights," Journal of Marketing, 73 (3),99–117.

[4] Boyle (2009), "CVS Goes Upmarket," Businessweek, February 13, *http://www*.businessweek .com/managing/content/feb2009/ca20090213 670826.htm.

[5] Chandon, Pierre, J. Wesley Hutchinson, Eric T. Bradlow and Scott H. Young(2009), "Does In-Store MarketingWork? Effects of the Number and Positionof Shelf Facings on Brand Attention and Evaluation at the Point of Purchase,"Journal of Marketing, 73 (November), 1–17.

[6] Gallagher, Julie (2008), "Shopper Marketing Programs Fall Short: Study,"Supermarket News, 56 (39), 30–1.

[7] Inman, J., Russell S. Winer and Rosellina Ferraro (2009), "The Interplayamong Category Characteristics, Customer Characteristics, and CustomerActivities on In-Store Decision Making," Journal of Marketing, 73 (5),19–2.

[8] Kalyanam S Kirthi, Rajiv Lal and Gerd Wolfram (2008), "Future StoreTechnologies and their Impact on Grocery Retailing," in Retailing inthe 21st Century: Current and Future Trends, Krafft and Mantrala ,eds. Berlin: Springer.

[9] Mitchell, Deborah J., Barbara E. Kahn and Susan C. Knasko (1995), "There'sSomething in the Air: Effects of Ambient Odor on Consumer DecisionMaking," Journal of Consumer Research, 22 (September), 229–38.

[10] Neff, Jack (2008), "For Caruso, Branded Content Has to Think Small to GetBig," Advertising Age, April 3.

[11] Stilley, K., Jeffrey J. Inman and Kirk L. Wakefield (2010a), "Spending onthe Fly: Mental Budgets, Promotions, and Spending Behavior," Journal ofMarketing, 74 (3), 34–47.

[12] Verhoef, Peter C., Scott A. Neslin and Bjorn Vroomen (2007), "MultichannelCustomer Management: Understanding the Research ShopperPhenomenon," International Journal of Research in Marketing, 24 (2),129–48.

Destination Branding and Role of FDI in UAE Economy

Harvinder Singh, A.N.C. Natarajan and Sreeramula Rajeev

[1]*Institute of Management Technology, Ghaziabad*

ABSTRACT

This paper aims to analyse the potential and performance of Foreign Direct Investments (FDI) in the economic growth of United Arab Emirates (UAE). The research is exploratory. FDI, which is the major source of non-debt financial resources, has been an important driver to the growth of UAE Economy. Faster exploitation of its oil resources for national progress put a serious threat on UAE from being deprived of such resources in the long run. So, UAE decided to open up to the world and enter globalization with the dream of growing into a powerful economy. The branding involved in developing a powerful and unique value proposition for the nation to urge the foreign investors to select UAE over numerous alternatives is studied. The strategies of UAE saw a great success with the FDI inflow reaching US $14.1bn in 2007 thereby UAE emerged as the most attractive FDI destination in the Middle East. The paper has identified the following as the important determinants that attract FDI in the UAE: Market growth, Economic Development, Trade Openness and Human Capital. Statistical techniques and FDI Indices are used to empirically test for the association between FDI and economic growth in UAE from 2002 to 2011. The role of FDI in the UAE Economy from 2002 to 2011 is indicated by the performance index while the potential index indicates the FDI trend for the coming years. These findings have important policy implications for the investors probing lucrative countries to invest. Economists can prepare economic and social development plans based on the indicators suggested by the research and implement them in other nations.

INTRODUCTION

Destination branding, an emerging research area that deserves more attention, gives a holistic view model of destination brand identity and value system that illustrates main concepts of brand identity, brand image, brand value and brand equity in the same gure, incorporating different level actors to the value creation processes (Saraniemi, 2010). The reputations of countries are rather like the brand images of companies and products, and equally important (Anholt, 2007). Whereas the application of branding techniques in the business sphere is well established, it is only in recent years that an upsurge of interest has occurred with regard to the potential benets of applying such techniques to destinations which gave birth to the term destination branding.

The research discusses the performance and potential of FDI in UAE by proposing economic indicators and variables. The effect FDI contributes to the development and progress of the economy. The research aims at aiding the economists to prepare economic and social development plans based on the indicators suggested by the research and implement them in other economies. Total foreign direct investment inflow into the UAE is expected to nearly double from $59.2bn in 2007 to $108bn in 2011, according to a report by Barclays Wealth. It also said the UAE's inflows are high and rising. The value of foreign investment in UAE increased from 7.75% to 10.8% from 2003 to 2007. This increase indicates the success of the policy to attract FDI and the position of UAE as an attractive centre for this investment.

UAE ranks 11th (top Middle East destination) in the AT Kearney FDI Confidence Index which tracks investors' likelihood of investing in countries for a set of three years, thus assessing the future of FDI flows.The UAE government encouraged its Emirates to create free zones to increase the inflow of foreign trade and investments in the country. Free zones provide vibrant networking atmosphere for foreign investors where new relationships and opportunities present themselves with refreshing regularity. It's in these surroundings of entrepreneurship and historical richness that many investors including 120 of the Fortune Global 500 Enterprises. The advantages for investors on investing in a free zone are •100% foreign ownership •No minimum capital investment requirements •No corporate or personal income tax •Low tariffs (around 5% for virtually all goods).

The FDI inflows in the Gulf Cooperation Council Countries (Bahrain, Kuwait, Oman, Qatar, Saudi Arabia, and United Arab Emirates) are represented in the Figure 1 to compare the FDI performance of the member nations from 2003 to 2010. UAE had the highest FDI inflows in the nation till 2004 after which the dominance of Kingdom of Saudi Arabia began. Figure 2 shows the FDI investments made in various industries of UAE.

The evidence data of UAE used throughout the research paper was obtained from Dubai Statistics Centre (DSC) and through secondary research in internet, journals and research papers.

LITERATURE REVIEW

An analysis of 217 research studies(1988-2009) referring to destination branding and related domain categorises the various academic disciplines to threeperspectives based on research interests: producing, consuming and criticizing (Andrea Lucarelli, 2011).A survey of these reviewsreveals that they have three common fallacies; theygenerally analyse a relatively small number of studies which are mainly based on aqualitative analysis and lack a systematic account for the variables studied.

The analysis extracted six factors reecting sixpersonality dimensions for places were from

87 personality traits in the following: excitement, malignancy, peacefulness, competence, conservatism and ruggedness.(Saraniemi, 2010).

The other theme of empirical research of FDI-growth relationship concentrated on identifying determinants of FDI flow and analyzing the effects of these determinants on the attractiveness of the host country to, and the volume and type, of such flows. This includes institutional factors such as degree of openness and trade policies, legislative environment and law enforcement (Lee and Mansfield, 1996), and the degree of economic and political stability (Bajorubio and Sosvilla-Rivero, 1994; Lipsey, 1999). Recognizing the importance of FDI to their growth, many countries are using specific incentives to attract FDI to flow in. Tax breaks and rebates are examples of such incentives (Tung and Cho, 2001). The factors that determine foreign direct investment include growth of GDP (Addison and Hesmati, 2003; Hisarciklilar et al, 2006), population (Hisarciklilar et al, 2006), degree of openness (Onyeiwu, 2003) political stability (Mellahi 2003) infrastructure (Onyeiwu, 2003; Mellahi, 2003; Hisarciklilar et al, 2006).Other determinants include education, research and development, country risk and domestic investment (Moosa, 2006), and risk instability (Chan and Gemayel, 2004). The recipient market, relative factor prices, and balance of payments constraints (Bhasin et al., 1994; Love and Lage-Hidalgo, 2000; Lipsey, 2000) also contribute to the FDI.

It is interesting to note that there are a number of factors that determine both the growth of GDP in a country as well as the growth of FDI. Research has shown that the amount of FDI depends on a number of other factors. Emphasizing the size of the domestic market a study by Hesmati& Addison 2003, shows that FDI seeking a base to produce for the domestic market in the host country is attracted to a country in which real income and therefore domestic purchasing power is growing. However, when analyzing location drivers, Hisarciklilar et al (2006) concluded that the market does not comprise of the host economy but also regional trade and trade with the rest of the world.

SIGNIFICANCE OF THE STUDY

Destination branding brings together a range of existing attributes that a city/nation may hold in terms of its brand management strategies anddevelopmental policies, in particular, with an aim to create a new construct, bringingtogether visionary strategies with hands-on implementation.(Place Branding) It alsoassists in developing a new image of a place that is more appealing and exciting, therebymaking it a critically important phenomenon. UAE had an image of Trucial states ruled by warring tribes in 1971, when British left (Krane, 2009). The steps taken by the government in changing its brand perception to one of the world's safest havens to invest are analysed.

From the references to all the above literature, it was identified that there is research gap in analysing destination branding in the perceptive of a FDI Investor. The examination is restricted to one, rather heterogeneous country, UAE. It would be of interest to conduct comparable analyses with other heterogeneous countries. The research focuses on the choosing the optimum variables and indicators to analyse the trend of FDI in an economically fast growing nation like UAE. There is no such research specific to UAE.

OBJECTIVES OF THE STUDY

The main objective of the study is to choose the appropriate indicators to analyse the potential and performance of FDI in UAE. The research attempts in designing an empirical model for the same. The first step in the empirical model is to identify the stylized determinants of FDI flowsto United Arab Emirates, and discuss how these explanatory variables are measured in thisstudy. Although there is no microeconomic theory of FDI, analysts have used a pragmaticapproach to identify a number of variables as critical for FDI flows to developingcountries, which the research considers for UAE.

RESEARCH METHODOLOGY

For Calculating the Performance of FDI, Proposed model in functional form is as follows

$$FDI = f(FI, FIS, CFG)$$

Where FDI is the net foreign capital inflow, FI is the FDI Inflows, FIS is the FDI inflows controlling for Size of the Country and CFG is the Contribution of FDI in Growth of the Country.

For the Variable FI, FDI Inflows in US$ Millions is used an indicator. For the Variable FIS, Percapita FDI Inflows in US$ Millions is used an indicator. For the Variable CFG, FDI as a Percentage of GDP is used as an indicator.

For Calculating the Potential of FDI, Proposed model in functional form is as follows

$$FDI = f(MG, ED, HC, TO)$$

Where FDI is the net foreign capital inflow, MG is the Market Growth, ED is the Economic Development, HC is the Human Capital and TO is the Trade Openness.

For the Variable MG, GDP Growth Rate is used an indicator. For the Variable ED, Per capita GDP in PPP in US$ is used an indicator. For the Variable HC, Secondary School Enrollment Ratio is used as an indicator. For the Variable TO, Ratio of Total Trade (Imports + Exports) to GDP is used as an indicator.

In the first step, we identified the appropriate indicators under each head (potential & performance). The selection of the indicator was done to best represent the macroeconomic and socio economic fundamentals and policy aspect of reforms carried out in terms of attracting FDI inflows. In the next step, the values under each indicator were converted into an index, namely individual indicator indices. For this purpose, the paper used the methodology of Physical Quality of Life Index (PQLI). Accordingly, the worst and best values of each indicator during the period of 2002 to 2011 were identified. For each indicator the performance of each indicator in each year was put on a 0.1 to 1.00 scale where, 0.1 represents an absolutely defined worst performance and 1.00 represents an absolutely defined best performance and to aid the calculations, one unit point was added to the best values of the indicators. Thus

$$\text{Indicator Scores} = \frac{1}{m} * \frac{1}{n} * \sum_{j}^{m} \sum_{t}^{n} \frac{(\text{Actual value } j - \text{Minimum value } j)}{(\text{Maximum Value } j * \text{Minimum Value } j)} * 100$$

Where, Indicator scores is a value of jth variable of in time t, n stands for the number of the years and m for the number of variables. One mainadvantage of such transformation is that it allows the reform index to be measured overthe same scale. This is an easy method to find out the performance of the Reforms, as anincrease in the value of an indicator index would necessarily mean improvement in theeconomic reforms process and vice versa. Once the indicator indices are formed, the comprehensive Composite Index is then calculated as a simple average of the indicatorindices.

Potential

The market growth is a clear indicator of the Economic growth of a country and it is the most attracting feature of the Foreign Direct Investments. Investors always wish to invest in economies which have fast and consistent growing markets. The GDP of a country can be used to measure the Market growth of a country. The Economic development of a Country is of primary interest to foreign investors (UNCTAD, 1999, p.17). The decision to invest in a host economy, therefore, depends on the risk and return on investment in the economy. Portfolio theory contends that capital tends to flow to economies with low risks and high rates of return. These countries also tend to have low per capita GDP. UAE is the most dominant nation in terms of GDP based on PPP in the Middle East.

The presence of workforce populations that are educated and trained to work in modern business organizations which is indicated as Human Capital has been recognized as an important determinant of FDI flows (Rivlin, 2001). In this study, human capital is measured by secondary school enrollment as a percentage of the population in the secondary school age category. This indicator is expected to be positively correlated with FDI flows. Trade Openness refers to the ease by which goods and services are imported and exported. The sum of imports and exports are considered as a percentage of GDP to measure trade openness. While a positive sign is the norm, a negative sign would suggest that FDI in a country is tariff-jumping, as foreign investors seek to locate in the host economy to avoid high tariffs.

Determinants for Potential of FDI

Performance

FDI inflow is an absolute indicator of performance of FDI in the past decade. It resembles the outcome of all the factors that influence the FDI. FDI inflow controlling the size of the country indicates the influence of FDI on each citizen of UAE and Contribution of FDI in Growth of the Country indicates the share of role played by FDI in overall growth of the country. These are the three indicators that will help in gauging the historical performance of FDI of a country.

Determinants for Performance of FDI

Variables	*Indicators*
FDI Inflows	FDI Inflows in US$ Millions
FDI Inflows controlling for Size of theCountry	Per capita FDI Inflows (US$)
Contribution of FDI in Growth of the Country	FDI as a percentage of GDP

FINDINGS

Potential Index

The index scores of UAE are measured by the PQLI Model (Physical Quality Life Index Model). The scores were evaluated substituting the indicators in the model. The index indicates that in the years 2004 to 2007 UAE had maximum potential for FDI.

Years	2002	2003	2004	2005	2006	2007	2008	2009	2010	2011
Scores	40	47.5	47.5	45	55	42.5	55	25	32.5	57.5

Performance Index

The index scores of FDI in UAE are measured by the PQLI Model (Physical Quality Life Index Model). The scores were evaluated substituting the indicators in the model. The index indicates that the performance of FDI is the lowest in the years and 2010 and 2011.

MANAGERIAL IMPLICATIONS

The performance of FDI is clearly indicating a cyclical nature. There was a continuous increase from 2002 – 2007 and a continuous decrease from 2007 – 2011. Optimistic performance of FDI can be expected from 2012 taking the potential index score of 2012 into consideration. But the upward trend of the performance may last for a shorter span of half a decade taking into consideration the historical cyclical nature of FDI performance in the previous decade. The other implication that can be deduced is UAE's sharp vulnerability of FDI in relation with the world economic movements indicating that its economy is less of independent in nature.

CONCLUSION

The destination branding involved in developing a powerful and unique value proposition for UAE saw a great success with the FDI inflow reaching US $14.1bn in 2007 thereby UAE emerged as the most attractive FDI destination in the Middle East.By this research paper we have analyzed the performance and potential of FDI in UAE over the past decade. By the indices of performance and potential, we can conclude that the present performance of UAE's FDI is less than the potential of FDI which indicates that UAE's FDI may increase in the coming years at least for a short term.

BIBLIOGRAPHY

Anholt, S. (2007). *Competitive Identity: The New Brand Management for Nations, Cities and Regions.* Basingstoke: Palgrave Macmillan.

Krane, J. (2009). *City of Gold.* New York: Picador.

Place Branding. (n.d.). Retrieved November 1, 2012, from placebrands.net: http://www.placebrands.net/placebranding/placebranding.html

Saraniemi, S. (2010). Destination brand identity development and value system. *Emerald* , Vol. 65.

REFERENCES

[1] Addison, T, and Hesmati, A 2003. "The New Global Determinants of FDI Flows to Developing Countries*: WIDER United Nations University*. Discussion Paper"No.2003/45

[2] Agosin, M. and R. Mayer (2000). "Foreign investment in Developing Countries: Does it Crowd in Domestic Investment?" Discussion Paper No.146, UNCTAD, Geneva.

[3] Asiedu E. 2002. "On the Determinants of Foreign Direct Investment to Developing Countries: Is Africa Different?" World Development, Vol.30 (1): 107-119

[4] Athreye, S. and S. Kapur (2001). "Private Foreign Investment in India: Pain or Panacea?" The World Economy, 24, pp.399-424.

[5] Batra G., D. Kaufmann and A. Stone. 2000. "The Investment Climate Around the World: Voices of Firms from the World Business Environment Survey." Technical Report. The World Bank.Washington, DC:

[6] Bengoa, M. and Blanca Sanchez-Robles 2003, "Foreign direct investment, economic freedom and growth: new evidence from Latin America, European Journal ofPolitical Economy", Vol. 19 (2003) 529–545

[7] Bennett A. 2003. "Failed Legacies." Finance and Development, Vol. 40 (1): 4-8

[8] Bhasin, A., Jun, K. and P. Economu, 1994, "Assessing the Sustainability of Foreign Direct Investment Flows", World Bank, International Economics Department

[9] Bisat A. 1996. Building on Progress –Reform and Growth In the Middle East and North Africa.Washington, DC: International Monetary Fund.

[10] Borensztein, E., J. De Gregorio and J. Lee (1995). "How does Foreign Direct Investment Affect Growth", Journal of International Economics, 45, pp.115-135

[11] Buckley, P. J., J. Clegg, and C. Wang 2002. "The impact of inward FDI on the performance of Chinese manufacturing firms, Journal of International Business Studies", 33(4), 637–655.

[12] Chakrabarti A. 2001. "The Determinants of Foreign Direct Investment: Sensitivity Analyses of Cross-Country Regressions." KYKLOS, Vol. 54: 89-112.

[13] Collier P. and J.W. Gunning. 1999. "Explaining African Economic Performance." Journal Of Economic Literature, Vol. XXXVII (1): 64-111.

[14] Culem C. G. 1988. "The Locational Determinants of Direct Investments Among Industrialized Countries." European Economic Review Vol.32: 885-904

[15] DeMello, L.R., Jr. 1999. Foreign direct investment-led growth: Evidence from time series and panel data. Oxford Economic Papers, 51(1), 133–151.

[16] Drucker, P.F. (1994), "The age of social transformation", Atlantic Monthly, November, pp. 53-80.

[17] Dunning J.H. 1981. International Production and the Multinational Enterprise. London: George Allen &Unwin.

APPENDIX

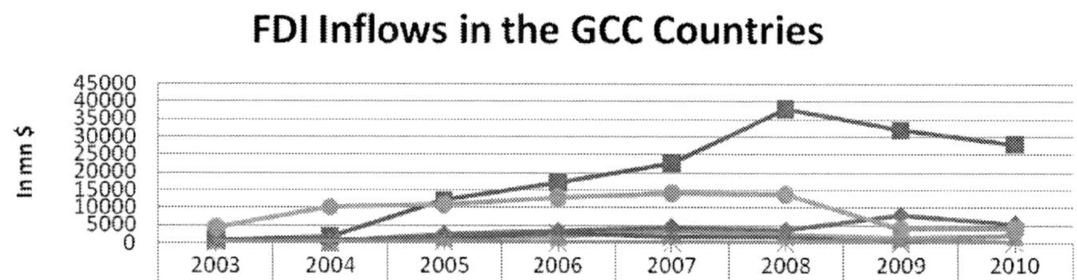

	2003	2004	2005	2006	2007	2008	2009	2010
KSA	778	1867	12097	17140	22821	38151	32100	28105
Oman	528	18	1538	1588	3431	2528	1471	2045
Qatar	625	679	2500	3500	4700	3779	8125	5534
Bahrain	517	865	1049	2915	1756	1794	257	156
Kuwait	67	20	234	121	112	116	1114	81
UAE	4292	10089	10900	12806	14187	13724	4003	3948

Fig. 1. FDI Inflows in the GCC

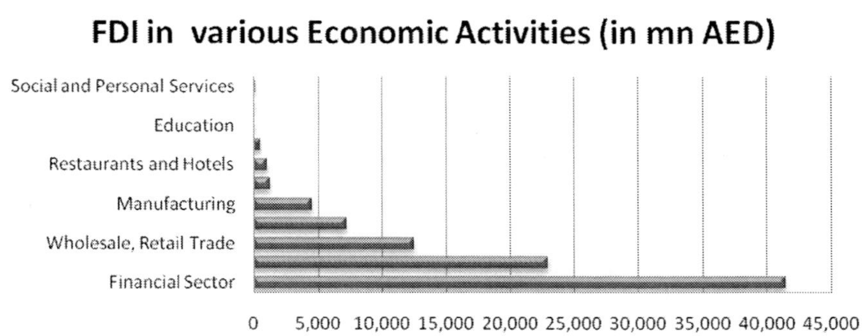

Fig. 2. FDI in various Economic Activities

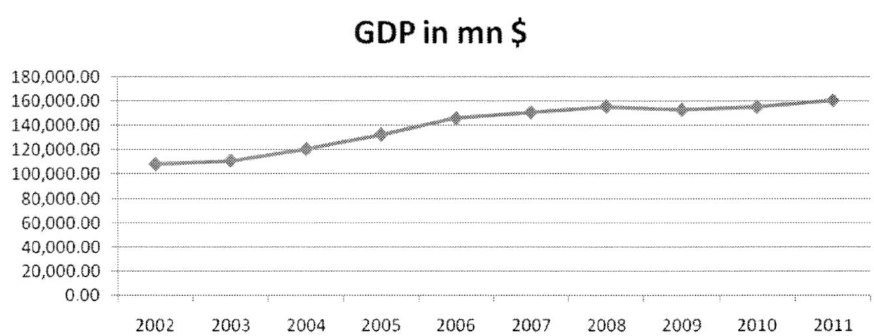

Fig. 3. GDP in mn $

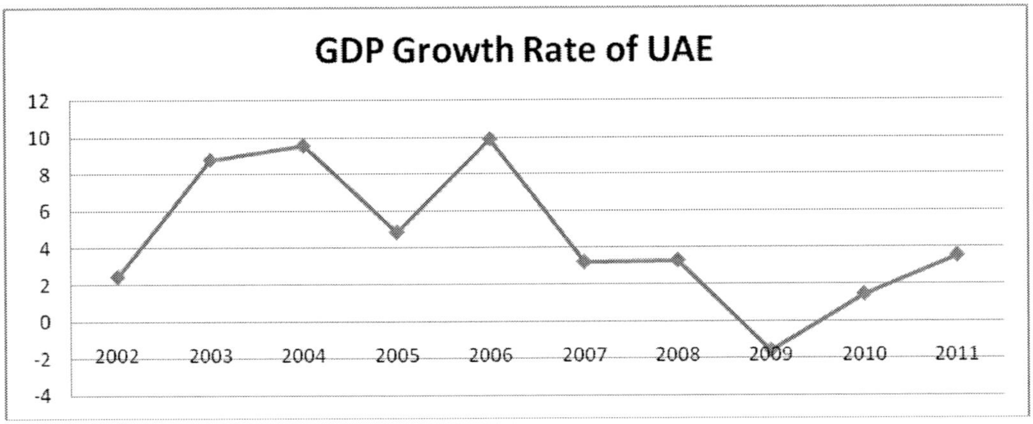

Fig. 4. GDP Growth Rate of UAE

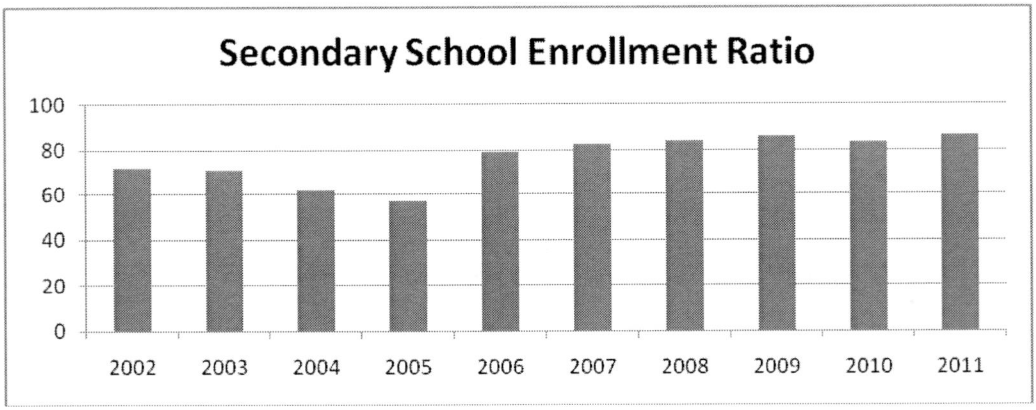

Fig. 5. Secondary School Enrolment Ratio

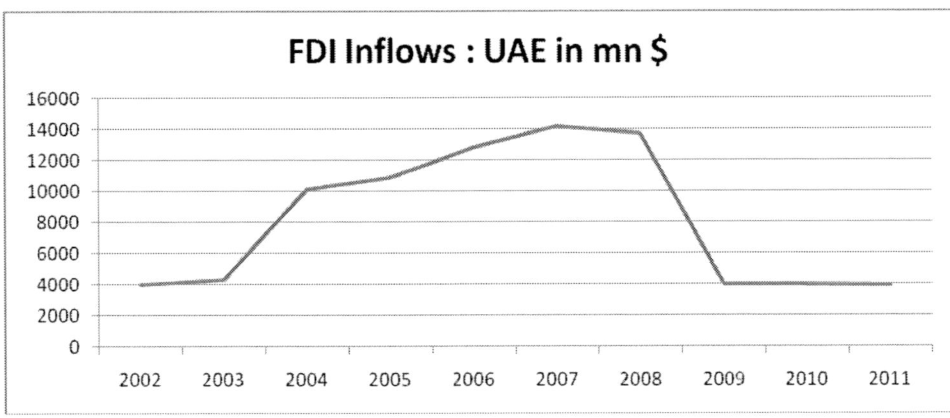

Fig. 6. FDI Inflows : UAE in mn $

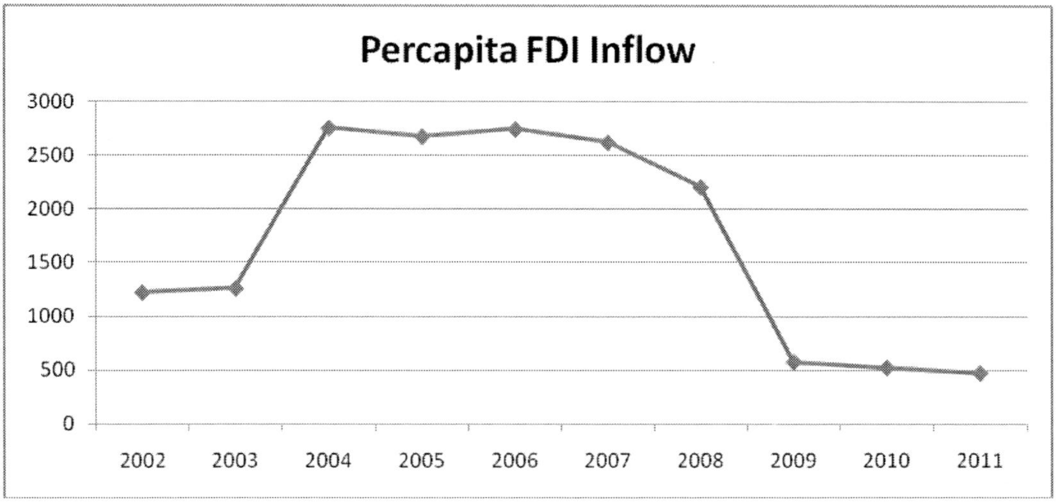

Fig. 7. Percapita FDI Inflow

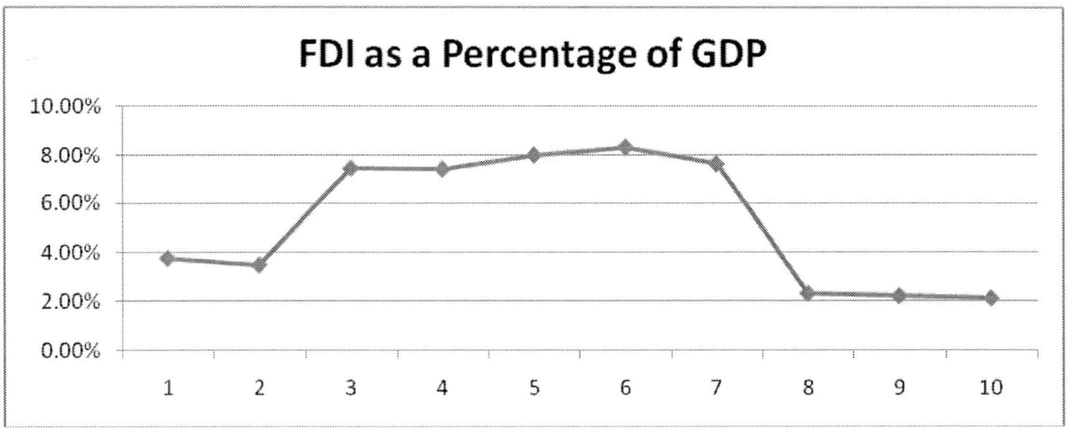

Fig. 8. FDI as a Percentage of GDP

Distributor Perspective on Implementation of SFA in FMCG Sector

Sandeep Puri, Bhavik Shah and Sahil Gupta

Institute of Management Technology, Ghaziabad

ABSTRACT

Perceived usefulness of sales force automation is the major central idea of research in most of research papers till date. However with the implementation of sales force automation with the intention to increase sales force productivity and lower inventory levels with profitable business, it is necessary to understand what is the impact of sales force automation at distributor point which includes both distributor sales representatives and other staff functions. Semi structured interviews were conducted with Owner, three Sales representatives and computer operator of a distributor of a FMCG company in Ghaziabad as a part of primary research.The main aim of the research paper is to evaluate the outcomes and effectiveness of sales force automation at distributor point which would give us insights on actual effectiveness of sales force automation at distributor level.

INTRODUCTION

Many studies suggest that Sales Force Automation (SFA) play a big role in simplifying business tasks and helps to improve the profitability. Research shows that SFA can help sales force to improve their productivity and it is done mainly to do things right (Efficiency) and to do right things (Effectiveness) (Clark et al, 2007). Another research proves that Sales Force Automation has an impact on Sales force motivation which translates in to better customer relationship management processes(Moutot and Bascoul, 2008). A study based on qualitative research tools identifies the benefits most valued by management in customer organizations – salespeople's professionalism, customer interaction frequency, salesperson responsiveness, and salesperson - customer relationship quality (Boujena et al,2009). Based on the research availableit can be said that SFA helps to increase in the sales force efficiency, increase in customer satisfaction, increase in sales and cost reduction.

Research papers are available which give us information about the process of sales force automation in multi-national companies (MNC's). However the Indian Fast Moving consumer goods (FMCG) companies are different from other MNC's. The distribution network in FMCG companies is multilayered and most of the distributors are independent distributors. For automation of sales force a high amount of coordination is required between the company and the distributor. To implement the sales force automation successfully, a company needs to convince the distributor about the benefits of SFA. Along with research showing increase in sales force productivity due to SFA and role of SFA in customer relationship management process, there was also a need to understand the impact of SFA at distributor level. It was felt necessary to know how sales force automation impact distributor and their sales representatives. A research by (Barker et al, 2009) answered the question of what might be the reasons for failures of sales force automation – Disruption of sales routine tasks, perceived loss of control by sales man, expectation gaps between management and salespeople, lack of commitment for implementation of system.In accordance of our research aim to find out the impact of SFA at the distributor point, we chose to understand the SFA at an Indian FMCG Company. Our research findings and suggested areas of improvement will help FMCG companies in achieving better coordination with its distributors. The company will be able to overcome the reservations distributors have about SFA.

SALES FORCE AUTOMATION IN FMCG SECTOR

Technology is the need of the business in the fast paced world nowadays. The technology is not just limited to the software companies and the head offices of the multi-national companies but it has also penetrated into the offices of channel partners.Sales force automation in FMCG companies is the classic case of technology penetration. The sales force automation ranges from using hand held devices for taking down orders in the market to complete automation of order processing and inventory management. P&G, HUL, Marico, Colgate Palmolive, Cadbury are some of the FMCG companies who have implemented sales force automation for increasing the effectiveness and efficiency of the supply chain and increasing the visibility of stock within the supply chain. This FMCG Companies have developed most comprehensive sales force automation software for the company owned and distributors' sales and services team to cut down on the non-productive time of both themselves and their distributors.The need felt by the FMCG companies few years back was to digitize and provide real time information about the product, schemes, offers, customer routes, prices, new product launch and receive information on orders and feedback from the field directly from the distributor sales representatives. Sales force automation was implemented because the sales team would be able to help increase the productivity and also coordinate with the distributors for order dispatch and indirectly help in increasing the supply chain surplus. Today, Area Sales Managers and Territory sales officers get access and real time overview of sales orders processed and a lead time to plan their sales pipeline, so they can forecast the demand with accuracy and increased confidence. Sales Force Automation helps companies to reduce costs i.e. by increasing the supply chain surplus and passing down benefits to the customers, helps to increases sales revenue i.e. by effectively meeting the unmet demand and reducing inventory carrying cost. Italso helps companies to get real time track of sales data and region wise statistics which helps sales managers to speed up back end processes fromthe instant feedback (from the sales representatives working in the field) which can be administered in central office. Thus sales force automation changed the way in which FMCG companies operated.

LITERATURE REVIEW

Sales Force Automation: Background

Companies implement sales force automation to improve the efficiency and effectiveness of supply chain and to improve the supply chain surplus. Sales force automation helps firms to convert the manual process to the electronic ones. For example, order book being replaced by electronic devices. Sales force automation can also be termed as a tool to create and disseminate new market information i.e. competition information and to make available information about the company's own products and services easily to sales representatives as they are available rather than mailing and printing the stuffs to them. Sales force automation help to reduce the time spent on support activities and thereby help in increasing the time spent on sales activities. Many companies have adopted sales force automation to decrease the supply chain mismatch. It helps companies to get real time and accurate visibility into its supply chain pipeline. So a collaborative effort could be made by all supply chain members to boost efficiency. Real time dashboards help company and its distributors to accurately forecast next day, month and year requirement by sub sequent supply chain member i.e. distributor and retailer respectively. Key features of sales force automation are – opportunity management, better customer relationship management, accurate sales forecasting and planning, proper quote and order management, appropriate incentive compensation depending on sales performance, effective and efficient coordination among supply chain members.

Ongoing Research

For the purpose of the study of sales force automation various research were studied to get insights on why companies go for sales force automation and what are the problems and implementation issues which come along with SFA. A longitudinal analysis for the factors leading to sales force automation gave the insights that salesperson attitudes have impact on intention to use new SFA systems prior to implementation (Jones et al, 2002).A research shows that use of knowledge management -based sales force automation has improved performance(Dong and Dennis, 2004)i.e. the more documents DSR's reads, the greater is his/her sales as a percent of quota. They also proved by the research that experience and expertise matters as not all sales representatives are benefitted equally from SFA system use. Research on reasons, barriers and support of SFA usage gives insights about how salespeople view the SFA in terms of efficiency gains and also in terms of fear of losing job (Buehreret al, 2005). Adding to the research on the efficiency gains, research suggest that efficiency gains are a primary motivation for investing in the Sales force automation and software ease of use and perceived usefulness would decide the success of implementation of SFA (Buttle et al, 2006). Other analysis suggests an increase in sales of about 2.5% due to use of sales force automation, which translates into hundreds of millions of dollars in revenue for the company. Sales Force Automation has the ability to help or hinder this relationship building process.Study shows that SFAcan help sales force to improve their productivityand it is done mainly to do things right (Efficiency) and to do right things (Effectiveness) (Clark et al, 2007).Automation in sales force work method is done finally for better customer relationship management. Research proves that Sales Force Automation has an impact on Sales force motivation which translates in to better customer relationship management processes(Moutot and Bascoul, 2008). Research on sales force automation tool shows that the use of tool depends on the perceived usefulness of tool both by sales people and management and if perceived usefulness of automation tool is more for salesperson, a sales person is more likely to take outcome based approached rather than activity based approach which help in increasing their efficiency (Mallin and DelVecchio, 2008).In the end, a study based on qualitative research tools identifies the benefits most valued by management in customer organizations. While interaction with the salespersons, customer perceive benefits in terms of four main dimensions – Salespeople's professionalism, customer interaction frequency, salesperson responsiveness, and salesperson –customer relationship quality (Boujena et al,2009).Based on the ongoing research, we followed following methodology to study complete sales force automation at an Indian company – Understanding the goals and objectives set by company for SFA, Implementation of SFA in a company, Identifying the outcomes due to implementation of sales force automation

Significance of the Topic

Successful implementation of SFA would require support of distributors and DSRs. The company would have to overcome the reservations distributors have regarding the automation of sales force. To maximize the returns from sales force automation the company should be aware of the impact SFA has at the distributor level. It must understand the improvements which are possible, which can further help DSR's. The present research available does not give an insight into the impact of SFA on channel partners. This research will provide information to companies which would help them in getting cooperation from distributors and maximize the returns on SFA.

RESEARCH METHODOLOGY

For the purpose of studying the sales force automation at a FMCG company, both primary and secondary research was conducted. For the purpose of research feasibility we conducted primary research by visiting distributor of a FMCG company in Ghaziabad. Primary research involved interviews with owner, three distributor sales representatives and computer operator of distributor. Semi structured interviews were conducted with above mentioned people. The main aim was to understand the pros and cons of sales force automation and how it impacted the sales process in the company. To understand the idea behind Sales force automation, three visits were made – One to the distributor to initiate the research, second one with the Distributor sales representative to the GhantaGhar market at few retailers/wholesalers in the market – third one again at the distributor to know exactly how PDA device work with MIDAS. The interviews also helped us to understand the areas where sales force automation can be improved. Visiting several markets with the sales representative helped us to understand how personal digital assistant is used by the sales representative and also how the device helps the salesman to achieve targets.Secondary research involved review of research papers and public information available on internet, newspaper and magazines. Research journal like journal of personal selling and sales management were of immense help.

OBSERVATIONS

The main aim of the research is to study the overall process of incorporating Sales Force Automation in an Indian company.A literature review was done to find out the process that should be followed while understanding the sales force automation in the FMCG Company.

General Overview

The need and requirement for sales force automation in the companywas primarily based on multiple reasons identified by primary and secondary research.Each distributor has their own sales representatives who have their defined territory to deal with everyday. Each day a representative goes to a particular beat (market) to take orders from the retailer in that beat (market). For entire week, daily a sales representative covers a new beat and takes the order from the retailers and wholesalers in that beat. On the very next day the orders requirements of the retailers and wholesalers in the beat are fulfilled. Thus the retailers and wholesalers received the orders on the very next day. Billing of the orders delivered is done in the next week when the DSR's revisits the same beat. Thus each beat is covered four times a month. Initially the routine processes i.e. order booking, collection and sales followed by Distributor Sales Representatives (DSR's) in the company were all captured and manually stored in order books.Sales representatives begin the day by delivering the previous day's orders and then go to the next beat to take the new ones. At the end of the day, the orders are entered in the order book manually by an operator. Each DSR's would update the daily orders received at the end of the day with operator sitting at the desk at distributor's factory. Manual order processing was having significant impact on efficiency of all supply chain members.

The three steps which were identified during literature review were studied thoroughly by primary and secondary research which gave detailed insights on the SFA in FMCG Company.

Step 1: Understanding the Need for Sales Force Automation:

Firstly, Company's Distributor Sales Representatives (DSRs), when out on the field, did not have access to information pertaining to stock levels at the distributor point and buying patterns of each outlet. Thus while taking up the order from wholesaler or retailer they were unaware of the stock available with distributor. Secondly, due to manual entering of details of the order by operator in MIDAS software, the process was time consuming and was prone to errors. Prior to the implementation of Sales force automation, each of DSR's need to sit with the operator to manually type their orders received from the beat (Market) on MIDAS software. Hence, only after a DSR is completely done with manual upload of orders received on that day does the other DSR get the chance to sit with operator to proceed with same work again. Thus the work was time consuming for both the operator and for DSR's and hence company was at loss as DSR's time was not utilized in the best possible manner. Thirdly, Each DSR's were unaware of their own previous P3M (Performance of past three months - Average sales for three months). To see their own past performance they needed to check on MIDA software about their performance for each SKU's in last three months which was practically difficult and not efficient method. DSR's had to keep checking MIDAS software to know what target they achieved and what target was left for the month. Thus the process was lacking in efficiency which was affecting the sales representative's performance which would be negatively affecting company's set targets in the highly competitive market. Fourth reason was based on the fact that the stock in hand information was not available easily with each DSR's when they took the order from retailer/wholesaler and hence the information pertaining to same was again needed to be fetched from MIDAS to further book orders from carrying and forwarding agents to replenish their own stock. The idea was cumbersome and was not effective and efficient enough to maintain appropriate inventory levels. Lastly, when DSR's went to each retailer/ wholesaler to take an order, they were unaware of the retailer/wholesaler capacity of purchase as previous month order data was not available. Hence while taking up a new order DSR's were missing out an opportunity to push more products to retailer/wholesaler based on past months data. This could be a probable loss to company and distributor for potential business from retailer/wholesaler. Due to all the above reasons in addition to diversified portfolio and entry of the FMCG companies in new categories over the time, the complexity and error probability in the system increased. With the exponential increase in the number of brands and the width and range of stock keeping units, company's realized the need to give distributor sales representatives focused information on demand so that he could execute sales plan and accomplish targets effectively with increase supply chain efficiency and co-ordination and get desired profits.

Step 2: Implementation of Sales Force Automation:

Based on the problem faced, company realized that the need of the hour was a Decision Support Tool which assist sales representatives during their visit to the beat (Market) and improve their overall efficiency with supply chain surplus. On primary research, it was found that the sales force automation took place in Ghaziabad roughly 6 months ago i.e. in May or June 2012. A Personal Digital Assistant (PDA) device – based Sales Force Automation Solution was developed using Microsoft .Net Compact Framework with SQL CE as the backend. PDA device was a Samsung galaxy ace smart phone with software installed in it. Costly PDA device with good touch and feel gave motivation for the sales reps during the times of change. Two day training was given together to all sales representatives from all distributors across Delhi/NCR on how to operate PDA device and how its usage would prove useful to DSR during their interaction with retailer/wholesaler. On primary research it was found that operating a PDA device was easy and no technical expertise is required for the same. The PDA application provided focused information about each outlet. It helps the DSR to drive channel-specific plans and make him productive right from the day one.

Step 3: Outcomes and Evaluation of Sales Force Automation

(a) Advantages of Sales Force Automation for FMCG Company:

(1) Ensuring more number of visits per salesman - The PDA device given to the salesman has a GPS system installed in it. The company at any point of time can find out the location of salesman. In order to ensure that salesman goes to the market daily, the salesman is required to punch the bill using PDA for at least 24 days a month. This ensures that of the 26 working days the salesman visits the market at least 24 days.

(2) Daily update of information at company's central server- After coming back from the market, the salesman enters the information in the MIDAS software which is then transferred to the central server. This helps the company to know which of the products are in demand and which all products are not selling.

(3) Daily Sales figure for TSO- With the implementation of Sales Force Automation, TSO also has access to daily sales figures. If weekly sales figure indicate that the sales are low, TSO can take immediate action on which products to be pushed and what primary and secondary schemes needs to be made for increasing the sales.

(4) Saving stationary costs- Before the PDA devices were given, the company had to provide order books to every distributor salesman. With the help of sales force automation the company is able to save these costs.

(5) Better demand forecasting - Everyday salesman covers one beat (market). In a particular beat there are many retailers/wholesalers. The sales representatives visit each retailer one after another. As a result the company is able to track the demand of every shop. This helps the company in better demand forecasting.

(6) Achieving higher sales -With the help of SFA the company is able to set target for every market shop wise. For every shop there are there are three fields in the PDA device. The first is P3M- Performance of last three months. It stands for the average sales made to the shop in the last three months. The second field is monthly target. The third is the MTD. It means the monthly sales made to the shop by the salesman. So every time the salesman visits a shop, he is aware of the percentage of target achieved. If the percentage is low, then the salesman can push the products in that particular shop.

(b) Advantage for Distributor and Sales Representatives:

(1) Helps the salesman return home at time and ensures complete coverage of market- If a distributor has four salesmen, then all of them return around 5.30 to 6.00. After returning the salesman sits with the computer operator and updates the orders in the server of distributor. If another salesman returned at that time then he would be required to wait till the first salesman transfers his to the computer. This could at times even cause a waiting time of thirty minutes. If the third salesman also came back at the same time then he might be required to wait for around 45 minutes. As a result the salesman reached his home late. In order to return early some salesman would not cover the entire market. After company implemented SFA and gave PDA to salesman, the salesman comes back from the market he first returns the money received to operator followed by entering data in PDA device and finally simply gives the update from PDA device to the MIDAS software and computer operator works on it and now sales reps are free to go. This helps in reducing the administrative tasks, helps salesman return home on time and also ensures that salesman would cover the entire market.

(2) Reduces Administrative overhead of salesman - Before the PDA device was given to the salesman, he was required to manually enter the routine information such as order booking, collections and sales in an order book. He would then manually enter the details into the distributor software at the end of the day. After distribution of PDA device, the salesman simply uploads the information to the Midas software. This helps in reducing the administrative overhead.

(3) Access to Daily Inventory Levels- While taking orders from the retailer the salesman can check the number of units left in inventory. This helps him deal with the demand in a much better way.

(4) Knowledge about each Individual shop –As sales reps now have the knowledge on what is the ordering capacity of each retailer/wholesaler; he now can push appropriate products to meet the targets more effectively.

(5) Increase in sales: Based on the primary research at the distributor point, it was found that the sales were increased up to 20% due to sales force automation. Main reason for this is that sales reps can now push effectively the products with no offers/schemes available. Without PDA sales representatives were able to remember the brands having offers/schemes available when they went to the market to take orders from retailer but not the brands without schemes. Thus they were able to push products with offers/ schemes more effectively. With the help of PDA device they can now know the inventory levels of the brands without schemes available with them and can now push them too effectively. This led to increase in sales.

(c) Disadvantages Pertaining to Sales Force Automation:

Sales Representatives are not using PDA device effectively. They take the orders on paper instead of PDA device when they visit the retailer due to two reasons: Convenience and fear. Convenience is one of the reasons as it's not feasible to enter orders directly into PDA device while taking orders from retailer/wholesalers. Fear is due to the fact that, in most of the cases the sales reps fear of losing the data of orders if upload from PDA to MIDAS software fails or if Internet or server is down at distributor point which happened in the case of sales representative who participated in the research. Thus sales representative is sometime reluctant to carry the PDA device to market as they find no use of it. Hence, this would not allow company to track the position of sales reps in the market. Another disadvantage of sales force automation is that despite being technologically advanced and efficient method for increasing supply chain efficiency, it does not help all sales reps to update the MIDAS in real time and know the availability of stock while taking up the orders in the market. This problem is critical due to the fact that all sales reps go to their respective market at same time and hence real time knowledge of inventory available at distributor point is not available. On interaction with distributor staffs, it was found that it was very difficult to put a system in place where each time sales reps give update to MIDAS from market and other sales reps are given the update on new available inventory in real time. But due to regular replenishment of stock at distributor point, this problem is not of much concern. Distributor follows the code of conduct of maintaining seven days of inventory and gets their inventory replenished within three days of order placed and due to these reasons the problem mentioned above is reduced to great extent.

MANAGERIAL IMPLICATIONS

(1) Use of PDA for qualitative research- During our visit to Ghantaghar beat in Ghaziabad, DSR found that PARAS(refined oil manufacturer) had occupied majority of the shelf space in many shops. It had tied up with shopkeepers for bulk space. Interviews with other DSR's revealed the similar strategy adopted by PARAS in other areas. The DSRs visit the market daily. They gain information about changing consumer trends, market strategies of the competitor and other important information. The PDA device should have fields where DSRs should be able to enter consumer insights and competitor strategies. This will help the company in market research as well. The managers should use PDA for Market Research.

(2) Guidelines should be issued to distributor- Distributors allow salesmen to take the PDA device to their home. DSR's children also use these devices for playing games. This might lead to breaking of PDA device and might also reduce the lifespan of the device. Managers should tell the distributors to ensure that PDA devices are kept at the distributor's place during night.

(3) Dual recording of data- Even after getting the PDA, salesmen use the copy to record the orders at retailer point. They come to the distributor and then enter the order data

in PDA. This leads to wastage of time. Let us understand why the DSR records the data twice. Then the data is uploaded to Midas software. After uploading the data, the data gets deleted from PDA device. If salesman had directly entered the data in the PDA, and after uploading the data some error occurs at the server, salesman would be required to upload the data again. But the problem is that, the salesmen won't have the data. He would have to go back to retailer and ask for the order. This actually happened with the DSR who would record the data directly in the PDA. The managers should ensure that data is deleted from PDA and Midas only after getting confirmation from server. This would help in saving more time and can be done during the next software update.

RESEARCH LIMITATIONS AND FUTURE RESEARCH

(1) As a part of primary research only qualitative research was conducted. As no qualitative data was collected, we cannot validate the results and recommendations by calculating p-value or other quantitative analysis.

(2) The salesmen interviewed during the primary research were distributor salesmen. Company salesmen were not interviewed during the research. To maximize gains from SFA, companies should also conduct a study on the impact of SFA on company salesmen. Our research does not cover this area.

(3) In the future quantitative research could be carried to test the validity of our research. Another important topic for future research can be to carry out similar research on company salesman.

REFERENCES

[1] Eli Jones, Suresh Sundaram, and Wynne Chin (2002), "Factors leading to sales force automation use: A longitudinal analysis",*Journal of Personal Selling and Sales Management*, Vol. 22, No. 3 (Summer, 2002), pp. 145-156.

[2] Dong-Gil Ko and Alan R. Dennis (2004), "Sales Force Automation and Sales Performance: Do Experience and Expertise Matter",*Journal of Personal Selling and Sales Management*, Vol. 24, No. 4.

[3] Stephan F. Gohmann, Robert M. Barker, David J. Faulds, Jian Guan (2005), "Salesforce automation, perceived information accuracy and user satisfaction",*Journal of Business & Industrial Marketing*, Volume: 20 Issue: 1.

[4] Paul Clark, Richard A. Rocco, and Alan J. Bush (2007), "Sales Force Automation Systems and Sales Force Productivity: Critical Issues and Research Agenda",*Journal of Relationship Marketing*, Volume 6, Issue 2.

[5] Jean-Michel Moutot and GanaëlBascoul (2008), "Effect of sales force automation use on sales force activities and customer relationship management process",*Journal of Personal Selling and Sales Management*, Volume 28, No 2.

[6] Michael L. Mallin,Susan K. DelVecchio (2008), "Salesforce automation tool selectivity:

[7] An agency theory perspective",*Journal of Business & Industrial Marketing*, Volume: 23, Issue: 7

[8] Othman Boujena, Wesley J. Johnston, and Dwight R. Merunka (2009), "The benefits of Sales Force Automation: A Customer Perspective",*Journal of Personal Selling and Sales Management*, Volume 29, No. 2, pp. 137-150

[9] Buehrer, R.E., Senecal, S. and Pullins, E.B. (2005), "Sales force technology usage – reasons,barriers, and support: an exploratory investigation",*Industrial Marketing Management*, Vol. 34, No. 4, pp. 389–398.

[10] Barker, R.M, Gohmann, S.F, Guan, J. and Faulds, D.J. (2009), "Why is my sales force automation system failing?", *Business Horizons*, Vol. 52, No. 3, pp.233–241

[11] Buttle, F., Ang, L. and Iriana, R. (2006), "Sales force automation: review, critique, research agenda", *International Journal of Management Reviews*, Vol. 8, No. 4, pp. 213–31.

Driving Sustainable Growth to Indian Pharmaceutical Industry through Field Force Excellence: A Study to Bring in Excellence to Pharmaceutical Sales Process

Rangin Lahiri, Ayon Hazra and Partha Chatterjee

Cognizant Business Consulting , Kolkata

ABSTRACT

Though the Indian Pharmaceutical Industry (Ranks the 3rd largest pharmaceutical market by volume and 10th by value with close to 2% of global sales) has been growing at thrice the speed of Indian economy, it has always been plagued with age old sales tactics, below par customer relationship management and lower field force maturity when compared to developing markets & their strategies of immersive physician engagement. To make matters more complex, the Indian Pharma market is characterized by high levels of branded generics, large number of players, minimal market exclusivity, and poised for a hyper competitive environment owing to expiry of patents of around $60 billion in 2012. Though the export market for generics would fuel growth till 2015, experts foresee imminent hurdles at sustaining its growth momentum given increasing regulations for prescription drug marketing, higher direct to consumer advertising and greater physician knowledge & collaboration due to social media and internet.

In this backdrop, optimizing current sales and marketing functions and building long term physician relationship through an effective but efficient field force process would be crucial to drive sustainable growth. A pan India survey of both Physicians and Medical representatives revealed lack of domain knowledge, professional salesmanship of field personnel and inability to respond to actual physician need. This paper features detailed analysis and recommendations on various areas like visit and call management, scientific selling and web based interaction with physicians which can bring field force excellence.

INTRODUCTION

Valued at around $13bn market contributing close to 2% of global pharmaceutical sales, India ranks the world's 3th largest pharmaceutical market by volume and the 10th by value (Chemical Business, June 2012, p. 59). McKinsey (Kumra et. al., Mckinsey, c. 2010) projects India's pharmaceutical sector to be the 10th largest market by 2015. The sector is fragmented with 2,872 genuine drug manufacturing units, of which 300 can be considered large scale producers. The top 10 companies account for 38% of the market as compared to 80% in the United States. The Indian Pharma market has been logging impressive growth rates between 14-17% owing to expiry of patents of around $13 billion worth blockbuster drugs in 2007 and another $60 billion in 2012 (Available from http://pharmabiz.com/NewsDetails.aspx?aid=71420&sid=1 , September 2012). This will create a bountiful export market for Indian generic companies fueling growth till 2015. Beyond 2015, they will need to look at sustaining its growth momentum when there will be no major drugs going off patent. Besides, with the government poised to set price control to more than 350 branded generics, a steep decline in the margins is imminent especially for multinational companies. The profitability in this market is driven primarily through brand loyalty and first-mover advantage. The company that brings a new molecule to market enjoys a brief period of pricing power before other entrants stoke competition. As a result, large companies often launch 30 to 40 new brands a year.

We believe Field Force Effectiveness would provide the impetus to sustainable growth in such a market scenario. Customer centricity is very typical of mature markets and companies need to be closer to their internal customer, the employees to become a customer focused organization. Similarly as the pharma market continues to mature, the growth rate would be driven by combining sales force effectiveness with marketing excellence, or customer excellence (Khater, March 2012, Available from http://www.youtube.com/watch?v=6P-x5lz8fBA&feature=player_embedded). Weidentified this need of Pharmaceutical Companies to understand the gaps in their current sales process and ways to minimize these gaps. For analyzing this we surveyed physicians to know their expectation from Pharma companies and also interviewed Medical Representatives to understand what companies are doing currently.

RESEARCH SIGNIFICANCE AND METHODOLOGY

After a brief period of sluggishness, the growth momentum in the domestic formulations market appears to be back on track. But with the ever increasing pressure to ensure maximum ROI, field force effectiveness would become a high priority area. The primary objective of this framework is to assess the maturity of pharma sales process on key parameters. Based on our CRM consulting experience in pharma industry, we have identified six key dimensions to evaluate Pharma sales process and suggest improvements that are to be undertaken. The following six dimensions that lay the foundation for **Field Force Excellence** evaluationFramework are:

- From manual call planning to integrated and systematic call planning cycle
- From offline and improper tracking of call notes and call objectives to real-time call detail capture
- From sales rep based call detailing to rep assisted/interactive based e-detailing

- From isolated sales call to marketing-focus call execution process
- From physician focus to key account focus
- From focus on sales channel to emphasis on other channels

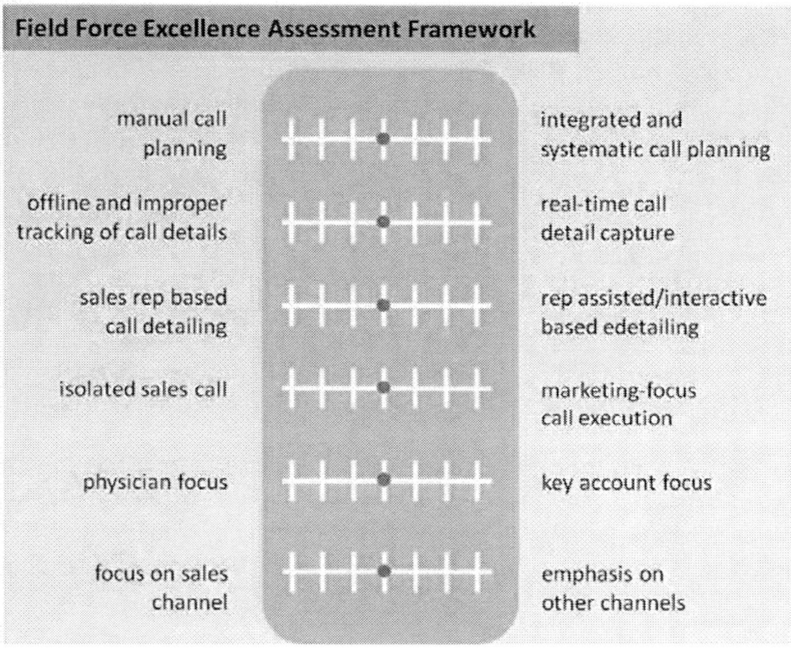

Fig. 1. Field Force Excellence Framework- Six Dimensions

Once all the initiatives and thus the dimensions are mapped to define the present state, a thorough gap analysis is done to identify improvement areas and the degree of improvement required. In order to reach to the final state on each dimension, the company needs to take focused actions after appropriate assessment of initiatives on three parameters- preparedness level, criticality of the function and business priority. The next and final step is to formulate a step-by-step roadmap to gradually build capabilities towards achieving sales force excellence. Throughout the evaluation and improvement process, organizations need to take conscious decisions in defining the short term initiatives and preparing long-term strategy for achieving sales force excellence.

LITERATURE REVIEW

Barclays Capital Equity Research in its report (n.d.) – India Healthcare and Pharmaceuticals (cited in Chemical Business, June 2012, p. 70-71) forecasts Indian pharma market to grow at 15% CAGR from FY12 to FY14. In recent times, the pharma industry has shown high interest in emerging economies like India due to its sustained economic growth, healthcare reforms and patent related legislation (Kumra et. al., Mckinsey, c. 2010). Historically, the impressive growth rates could be attributed to expiry of patents of around $13 billion worth blockbuster drugs in 2007 and another $60 billion in 2012 (Available from http://pharmabiz.com/NewsDetails.aspx?aid=71420&sid=1, September 2012). But beyond 2015, the companies need to focus on improving field force effectiveness built on new product launches and favorable pricing environment (Chemical Business, June 2012, p. 70-71).Apart from extensive internal research, we conducted a pan-India survey (Field Force Effectiveness Survey) wherein medical reps of top 50 pharma companies were covered and the experience of medical reps in the industry varied from 1year to 10 years. The coverage of respondents in our survey is illustrated in the table below:

Number of Medical Reps interviewed	150
Number of Doctors interviewed	75
Number of Pharma Companies covered	50

SURVEY ANALYSIS

In the first half of 2012, we conducted a pan-India survey on sales process followed by Indian pharma companies wherein we interviewed the Physicians and Medical representatives to understand the dynamics of the relationship between them and how betterment of this relationship can create differentiation in this highly competitive market. We have analyzed their feedbacks and suggestions for improvement and identified list of top initiatives that the Indian pharma companies need to take to be competitive with the top pharmaceutical companies of the world.

Observation1. The doctor today has more numbers of MRs waiting outside his clinic than patients. We analyzed why the number is increasing and how much time MRs spend waiting outside a doctor's clinic.

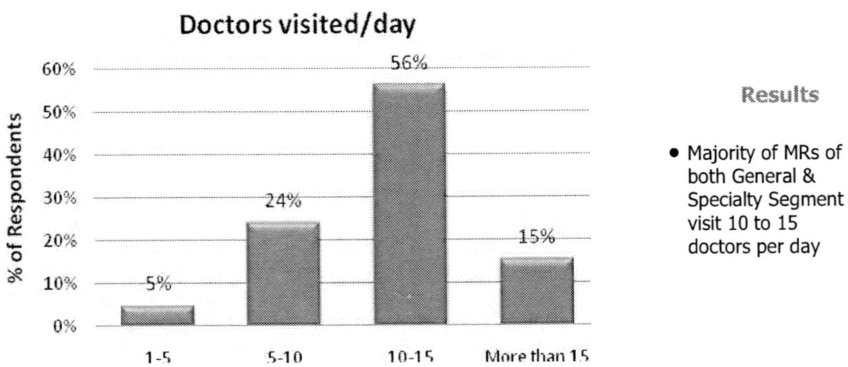

Fig 3:

Source Q: How many doctors do you visit per day?
Respondents: Medical Representative [N=150]

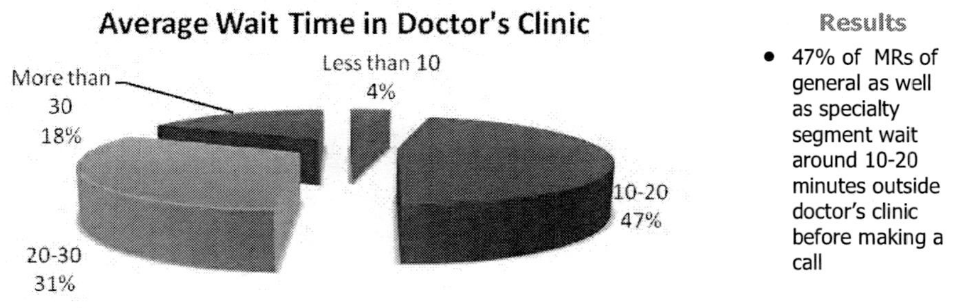

Fig 4.

Source Q: What is the average waiting time in physician's clinic /waiting room?
Respondents: Medical Representative [N=150]

Analysis

a. Effective Route Planning

One of the most critical components of doctor visit is effective route planning so that delay in meeting with a doctor is minimized and productive time spent with the doctor gets increased. Medical rep need to understand the geographic spread of his doctors as well as the potential category (high, medium, low etc) of doctors before preparing a route plan. An effective route plan entails for prior appointment with the doctors' office (in line with their preferred time to visit) as well as good coverage of various potential category of doctors to meet the call targets.

Observation 2. The effective detailing to physician is the key success factor of a brand communication. It is thus important to understand how many product an MR details per visit and how much time does he get to detail these products

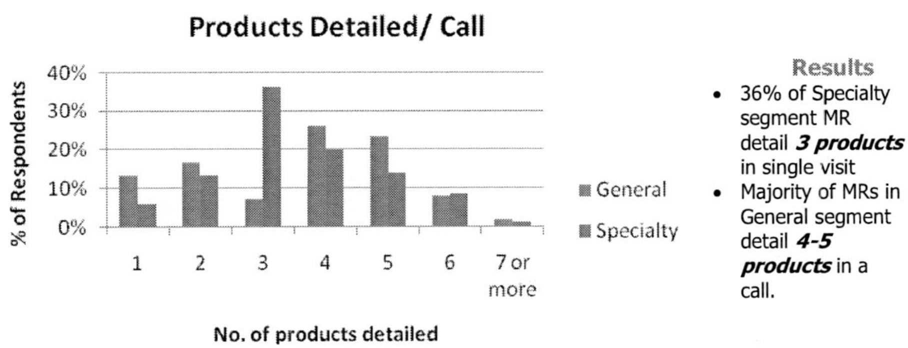

Fig 5.

Source **Q:** How many products do you detail in a single visit? (Average)
Respondents: Medical Representative [N=150]

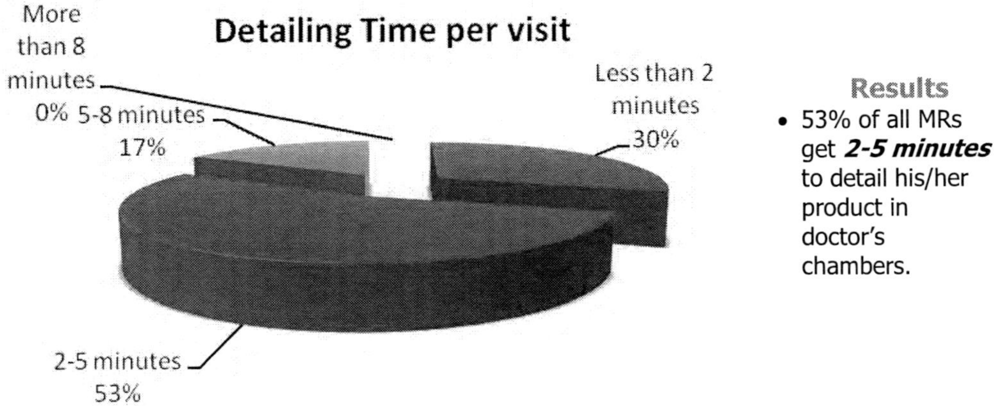

Fig 6:

Source Q: How much time do you spend, on an average, in detailing your product?
Respondents: Medical Representative [N=150]

Analysis

a. Electronic Detailing Technique

The survey findings point out that on an average a medical rep's portfolio consists of 21 products of which he/she can effectively detail out only 4 products in a call. This amounts to less than 20% product coverage in a call which significantly reduces the chance of recall in doctor's mind unless the product is outstanding in the market.

In order to increase the effectiveness of detailing a product, reps must take advantage of technology driven aids and techniques that are proven to be more effective and drives better value in terms of brand retention and brand recall in mind of doctors.Through interactive sessions that demands additional involvement of doctor and continuous learning opportunity, rep generates interest in the mind of doctors thereby increases the chance of prescription by doctors.

b. Product Categorization

One important aspect that came out of the survey is that most of the medical reps did not have clear cut product classification in their portfolio. Hence, it became extremely difficult for them to focus on specific set of products during a call detail session. This led to uniform weights get assigned to all the products in their portfolio. Medical reps based on their judgment detail out specific product(s) in a call to the doctors.

Product classification is one of the most important criteria marketing team would need in order to create differentiated product messaging for greater penetration. The most common classification used in developed countries is- Emphasis products and Non-emphasis products. Emphasis products are to be detailed on frequent basis within a month while non-emphasis products can be detailed based on the market demand conditions.

The study indicates that medical reps get less than a minute to detail a product in the call, hence it is paramount to classify rep's product portfolio associated with targeted messaging for maximum impact.

Observation3. Physicians interact with MR on a regular basis and hence it is important to understand what qualities he prefers in an MR. We also analyzed the improvement areas where companies should focus, as per MR that will improve his relationship with the Physicians.

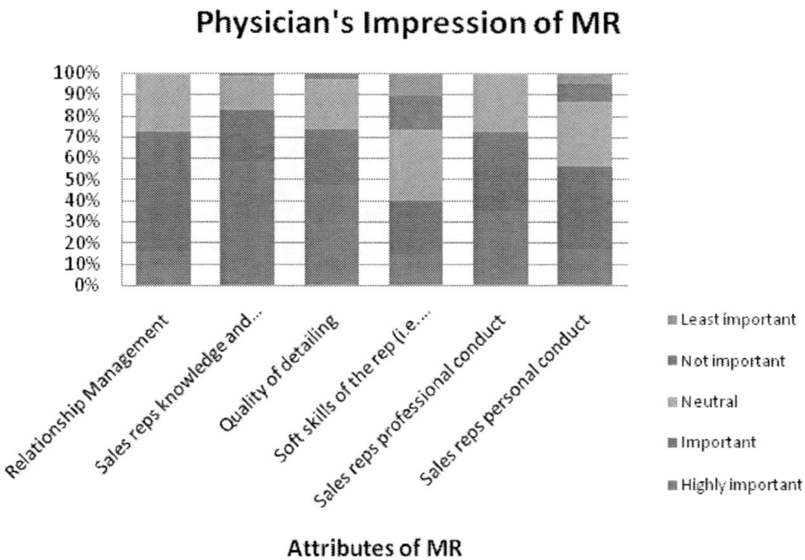

Results

- 60% of physician consider ***Medical Representative's knowledge*** about the therapy & drug that he is detailing as the most important attribute of MR.
- ***MR's professional conduct and his relationship management skills*** stand out overall as next most important attributes.

Fig 7.

Source Q: Please rate the following attributes of MRs based on their importance to you.

Respondents: Physicians [N=75]

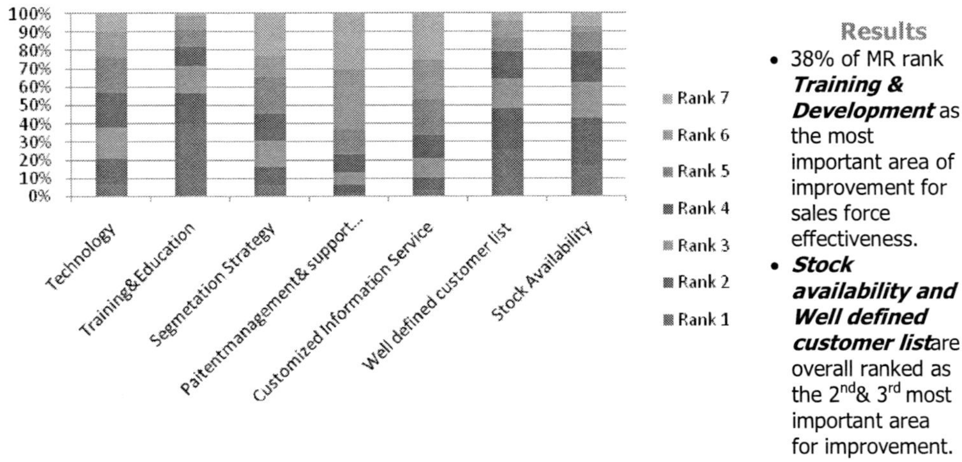

Fig 8.

Source Q: Following are the typical improvement areas Pharma companies are focusing on to achieve their sales force effectiveness. Please rank them in order of importance for your company. (1 is highest and 7 is lowest)

Respondents: Medical Representative [N=150]

ANALYSIS

a. Emphasis on Medical Training & Education

A Medical Representatives is the face of a company in front of customer. His interaction with physicians will make or break a company's image. It's thus very important to understand the key attribute that physicians look for in MR and we found that majority of physician prefer MRs having in-depth product knowledge. Companies need to have an ongoing training &development schedule for the field force to improve customer interaction and increase overall call effectiveness.

b. Integrated Customer Database

Majority of medical reps in our survey agreed that their marketing and customer service departments do not have proper visibility to customer information as well as customer interactions. This leads to ineffective segmentation and futile campaigns with marketing department doesn't have better understanding of customer preferences and customer feedbacks. The customer service department also resolves each case in isolation as they do not have the full history of customer interactions. In the survey with Pharma companies, when asked to detail out their focus areas they have identified the need of an integrated customer database as one of the top3 planned initiatives. This shows that although companies have planned for customer data management, no concentrated effort has been made to make it happen. Hence, we feel that there is an immediate need for pharma companies to invest in building strong customer database that will help the entire organization to better understand their customers.

c. Create a Professional Field Force

The professional conduct of Medical Representative is the first impression created even before the detailing starts. The well groomed and professionally smart MR creates a very impressive picture in front of the physician. Companies need to focus on the overall development of their field force and conduct training & workshops periodically to achieve the same.

Observation 4. The key to effective positioning of any drug is to know the parameters physicians consider for prescribing a drug. We analysed these parameters and also found out the preference of physicians for different marketing aids.

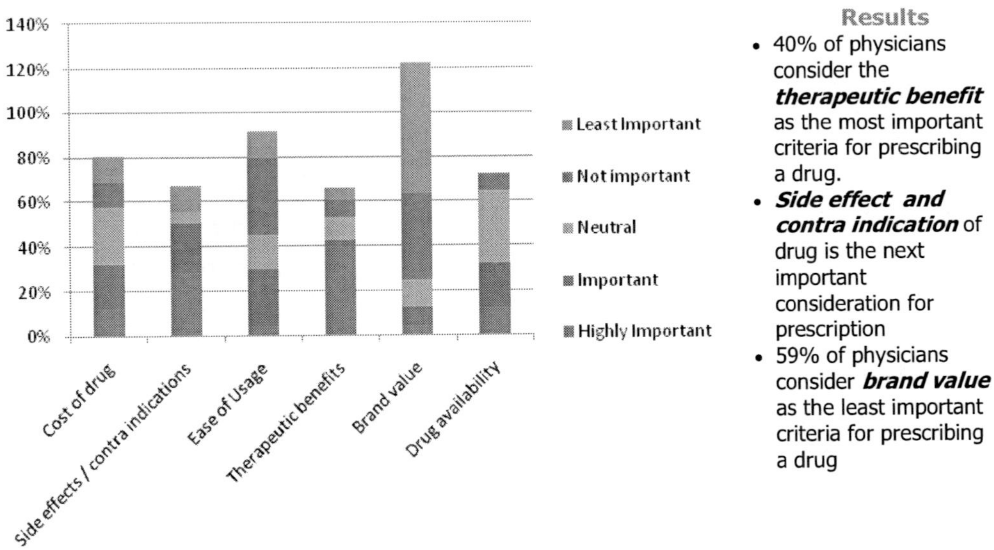

Fig 9:

Source Q: Following are some parameters typically considered while prescribing drugs. Please rate the parameters in order of their importance to you.
(1 Highly important, 5 Least important)

Respondents: Physicians [N=75]

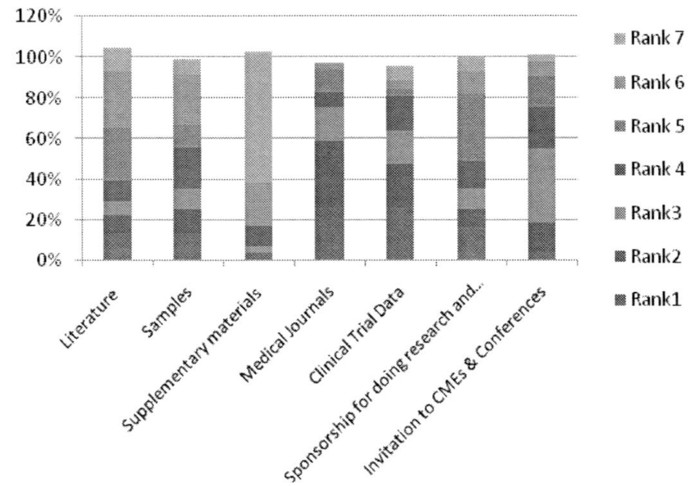

Fig 10:

Source Q: Please rank the following marketing aids in order of their importance to you? (1 is highest & 7 is lowest)

Respondents: Physicians [N=75]

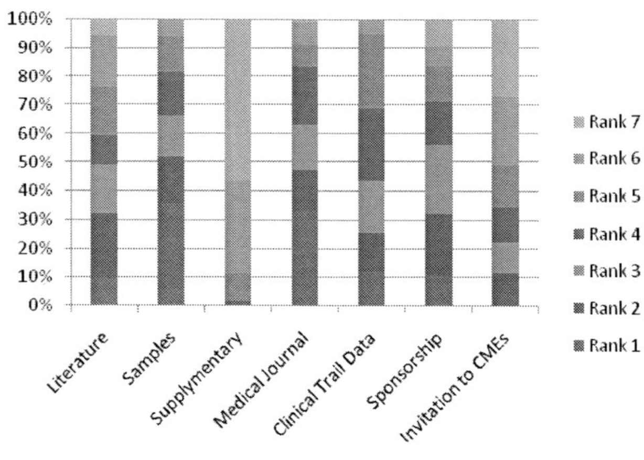

Results

- 33% of MR feel that both ***Samples*** and ***Medical Journals*** are most important inputs to physicians for generating Sales.
- Leave behind ***Literature and Sponsorship for Research*** are the next important input (22%)considered by MR for generating prescriptions.
- 55% of MR feel that the ***Supplementary Materials*** like pen, calendars etc have least impact on prescription generation.

Fig. 11:

Source Q: Please rank the following materials used as inputs to physicians for generating Sales? (1 is highest & 7 is lowest)

Respondents: Medical Representative [N=150]

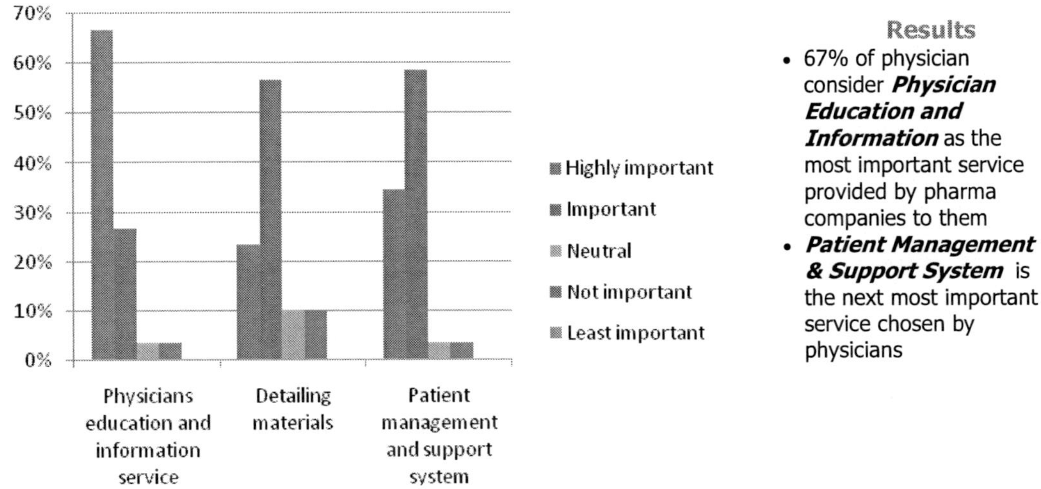

Fig 12:

Source Q: Please rate the following services of Pharma Companies in terms of their importance to you.

Respondents: Medical Representative [N=150]

ANALYSIS

a. Emphasis on Scientific Based Selling

The Physicians are more inclined towards getting the scientific information of a drug from the Pharma companies. They have preference for the marketing inputs like Medical journal & Clinical trial data which reinforces this fact. Companies should focus on providing scientific based selling and put emphasis on providing knowledge based seminars & convention to achieve better relationship with Physicians. Although Continuing medical education (CME) is not part of academic requirements but majority of physicians consider this as the most valuable source of receiving

b. Emphasis on Physician Education

Based on our study, if pharma companies stress upon proper medical education, providing the latest medical journals to doctors, it will have farfetched effect on bolstering relationship with doctors. Companies can use the web portal to provide rich information to the doctors on current trends and developments in a particular therapeutic area. They can invite experts from specific fields on to the website to share their opinions and blogs which doctors can reference to, if required. The companies can even provide a discussion forum to the doctors wherein they can share ideas, opinions and discuss about any problem they are facing in their specialty. We have researched top 30 pharma company websites and found that none of the websites provide this information. Therefore, there is an expectation gap between doctors and the pharma companies that needs to be bridged at the earliest.

c. *Effective Sample Management*

Samples assist in therapy initiation especially for drugs in chronic segment. It also assists MR to start a conversation with physician after providing samples. Effective sample management is one of the areas where companies should look at for improving sales process.

Observation 5. In current scenario there is an easy access to information. Physicians can get drug related information from many other sources other than MR. We analysed physician's preference for these channels of information.

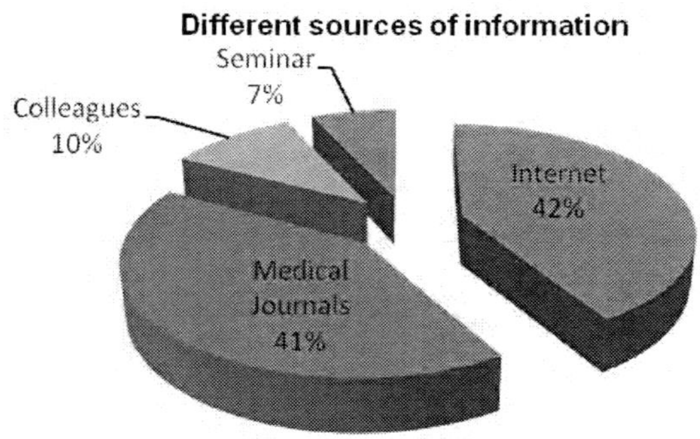

Results

- **90% of physician** get drug related information from sources other than MR.
- ***Internet search and Medical Journals*** are the most common source that physicians refer for getting information on drugs.

Key Insights

Companies need to make their presence felt in these sources which physicians constantly refer for drug related information.

Fig 13:

Source Q: Do you receive drug-related information from sources other than MRs? If yes, please specify the source.

Respondents: Physicians [N=75]

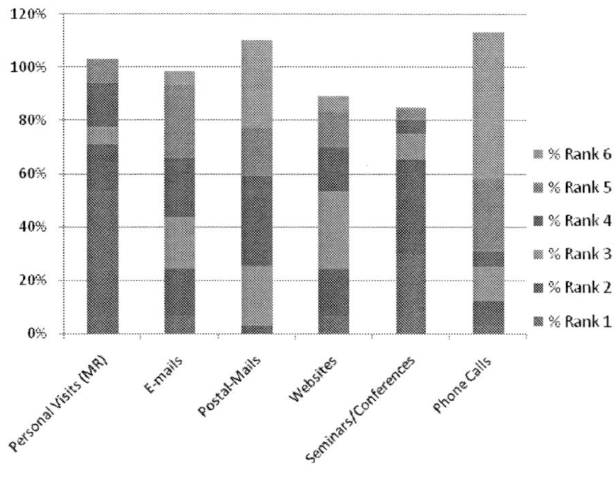

Results

- 54% of physicians find ***Personal visits of MR***as the most important channel for getting drug related
- ***Seminars & Conferences*** are the next most important channel of information. Information provided via phone is the least preferred channel by 56% of physicians
- Websites are also preferred channel of information with 35% of physicians giving it top 3 ranks.

Key Insights

The traditional method of MR visiting the physician is still the most preferred method of communication amongst doctors. Companies should focus more on improving Sales Force Effectiveness and benefit most from effective & efficient field force team.

Fig 14:

Source Q: Please rank the following channels of receiving information in order of preference. (1 is highest & 7 is lowest)

Respondents: Physicians [N=75]

ANALYSIS

a. Increase Web Based Interactions

The survey indicated Web as the potent channel second to Medical Rep in driving sales. As per the internal research on websites of top 30 pharma companies in India we found that the companies are not providing many initiatives to drive customers to their websites for placing orders or for resolving any service requests. However, from the survey it was clearly came out that physicians are interested in networking, open discussion forums and in web-based seminars on recent medical trends and developments. The importance of web as a channel has been established long back and Indian pharma companies should start investing in structured fashion to realize the true benefits of web-based customer interactions.

Observation 6. Medical Representative's view of his role in sales process defines how he is perceived by his customers. We analysed the total number of customers an MR has in his defined territory and how does he perceive his role in the entire sales process

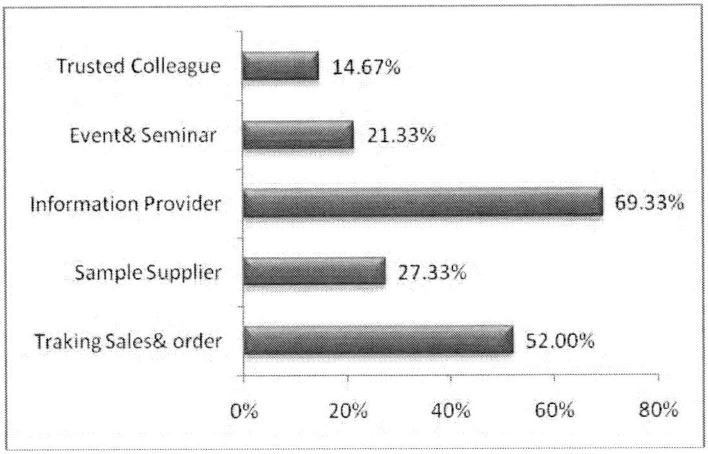

Results

- 70% of MR have feel that their main role in sales process is of ***Information Provider.***
- ***Tracking sales & order*** is their main role as mentioned by 52% of MRs.
- Very few MRs surveyed see themselves as ***Trusted colleague***

Fig 15:

Source Q: What do you think of your role in the Sales process? (You can mark more than one)

Respondents: Medical Representative [N=150]

Analysis

a. Medical Representatives should Build stronger Relationship with Physicians

Although majority of Medical Representatives feel that their primary role is to provide drug related information to doctors but it also comes out clearly in our survey that most of them do not consider themselves as trusted colleague. Most of Pharmaceutical companies today spend lot of time & money on building strong relationship with their customers. Thus it is very important for MRs to become a trusted partner for any drug related issue. Companies clearly needs to understand this and should assist MRs in building stronger relationship with their customers.

Observation 7. Indirect Sales is one of the major element of overall sales that pharmaceutical companiesfind difficult to compute and arrive at actual figure. We analysed the current traits and assessed the top methodologies used

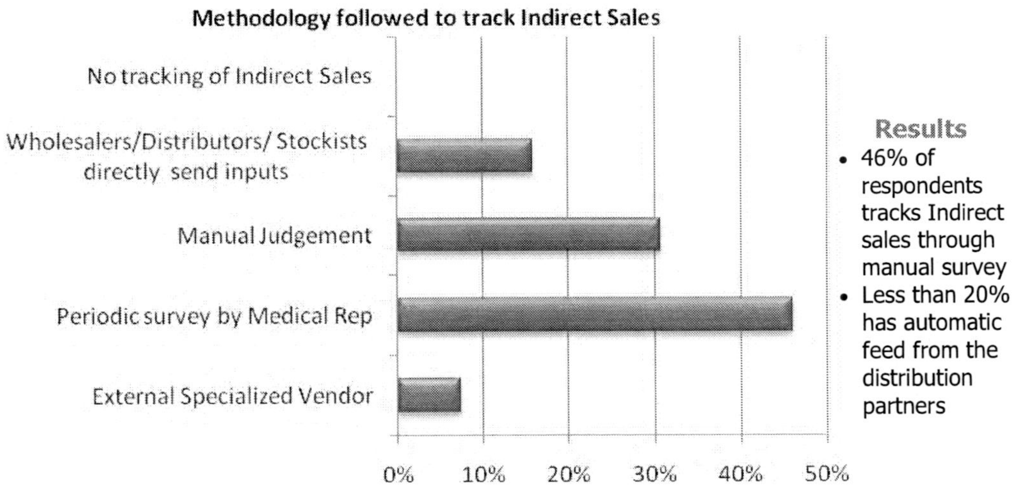

Fig 16:

Source Q: What is the methodology followed to track Indirect Sales? (You can mark more than one)

Respondents: Medical Representative [N=150]

Analysis

a. Companies Need to Maintain Reliable source to Gather Drug Distribution Data

From the feedback, we conclude that although every company has some way to track the indirect sales, most of them do not have an effective system and rely primarily on the data collected by medical reps on periodic visits and on their own judgment.

Therefore an external authentic database for maintaining this information is mandatory so that pharma companies can effectively optimize their distribution network and identify the growth contributors. In the developed countries, specialized vendors like IMS, CEGEDIM tracks the Drug Distribution Data (DDD) and provides their analysis to top pharma manufacturing companies. Cognizant would encourage Indian pharma companies to follow the same suite and identify specialized vendors focused on Indian pharmaceutical industry for such reports.

CONCLUSION

Competitive pressures in the domestic market are likely to sustain as MNCs become aggressive and domestic companies leverage on their expanded field force(Ghosh et. al., ICRA March 2012). However, its effectiveness and excellence would provide sustenance to this growth story. Through the physician's survey conducted pan India, the following key observations made were as follows:

- Physicians are more inclined towards scientific based selling and prefer medical journals and clinical trial data as input from Pharmaceutical companies. Physician's have strong inclination for services involving physician's education and participate actively in seminars and conferences.
- The in-depth knowledge of Medical Representative and good professional conduct are the main attributes physicians prefer in Sales Representative.
- Physicians show keenness in web based seminars and networking. Internet is becoming one of the most preferred channels for any drug related information apart from receiving it through the traditional medium, Medical Representative.

The Medical Representatives (Field Force) responses provided valuable inputs which could be summarized as follows:

- A Medical Representative (MR) gets less than 5 minutes in-clinic time to detail almost 4-5 products to a physician in a single visit. Most of them find this time inadequate and say that it affects their sales process.
- The customer databases maintained by most of the companies are inadequate according to most of MRs.
- According to majority of MRs training and development is the most important area where companies should focus on in order to improve their sales process.
- Most of the MRs has more than 150 customers in their territory and because of lack of planning they spend close to 4 hours daily waiting outside the doctor's clinic.

Based on the above insights, the study revealed that the Pharmaceutical companies should look at following areas of improvement in order to minimize the gaps and achieve excellence in their sales process:

1. Improve route planning activities to attain effective call planning and minimize the wait time outside doctor's chamber,
2. Invest in e-detailing to achieve more interactive sessions with physicians and increase the in-clinic interaction time
3. Keep appropriate portion for promotional budget for Physician's Education and Information service and focus more on such activities for the physicians.

4. Have an Integrated Customer Database which will help the field force to know better about their customers and effectively influence sales.
5. Stress more on scientific based selling and provide more scientific inputs to physicians.
6. Employ sample management system to achieve optimum benefits from sampling.
7. Increase web based interaction with physician.

Achieving the right pharmaceutical sales force structure and size are more important than ever in this highly competitive and dynamic environment. Christopher Wooden (June 2011), vice president for the Cegedim Strategic Data (CSD) Global Promotion Audit observes: "Effective sales force strategy and sizing are essential to achieving brand penetration and competitive share of voice. In mature markets, we see the challenge of 'right sizing' and it requires on demand data driven assessment to help optimize constrained resources." As the Indian Pharma sector continues to mature, we foresee future scope of research determining the Field Force Effectiveness metrics (Bates, June 2011) for emerging economies and the optimal mix of sales, medical education, advertising, PR, eActivitives for growth in market share.

ACKNOWLEDGEMENTS

This research paper is made possible through the help and support of many including the Physicians and Medical Representatives we had interviewed. We wish to thank Mr. Alok Saxena (Senior Manager, Cognizant Business Consulting) and Ms. Meenakshi Dandekar (Senior Business Analyst, Cognizant CSP Practice) for their contribution on the research methodology and as advisors in data analytics. Finally we sincerely thank our family and friends who had been a source of encouragement and support through various phases of this research.

REFERENCE LIST/BIBLIOGRAPHY

[1] Pharmaceutical Sales Force Effectiveness Metrics: Are You Measuring the Wrong Things? - 3rd Edition (Bates, June 2011)

[2] Favorable outlook forecast for the Indian Pharma Industry (Chemical Business, June 2012, p. 59)

[3] Indian Pharma market to grow at 15% CAGR by FY14 (Chemical Business, June 2012, p. 70-71)

[4] Indian Pharmaceutical Sector (Ghosh et. al., ICRA, March 2012) Available in http://www.icra.in/Files/ticker/Indian%20Pharmaceutical%20Sector.pdf

[5] Indian Pharma 2015 – Unlocking the potential of the Indian Pharmaceuticals Market (Kumra et. al., Mckinsey, c. 2010)

[6] Clear differences between emerging and more mature markets in pharma sales force levels (Wooden, June 2011) - Available in http://www.thepharmaletter.com/file/105065/clear-differences-between-emerging-and-more-mature-markets-in-pharma-sales-force-levels.html

Effective CRM: Assessing the Value Delivered Through Promotions

Priya Poddar

Institute of Management Technology, Ghaziabad

ABSTRACT

"There are 2 ways you can attract more business to your hotel, inn or guest accommodation. The first is to slash your prices so you are cheaper than the competition. But even if this does not bankrupt you, it still doesn't guarantee new business or business from the type of guests you want.

The second is to offer something so irresistible, so compelling, so different that not only your existing customers come clambering for it, but it also creates such a buzz that they tell all their friends too. And, of course, it's something that ***increases hotel revenues and your bottom line*** *too."*

The objective of this research paper is to find better techniques to measure the incremental sales generated by various promotions being run by an organization. A detailed study on each of the methodologies was done and suggestions on existing ones were also made.

INTRODUCTION

Promotions are all about **adding value.** And anything that adds value will **attract attention and stimulate sales** providing people know about it, so give people an incentive to try you out or make a return visit and set you apart from the competition. The aim of any promotion is to make something so irresistible to your customers they would be mad not to take up your offer. At the same time it is very important to find out that the promotions a company is running is actually adding value to them or not .i.e. whether they are generating incremental sales and profit or not . [Patrick Rooney, 2009,'Evaluating the impact of promotions', DMA Journal]

The methods of calculating incremental value through promotions being practiced as of now can broadly be classified into two categories:

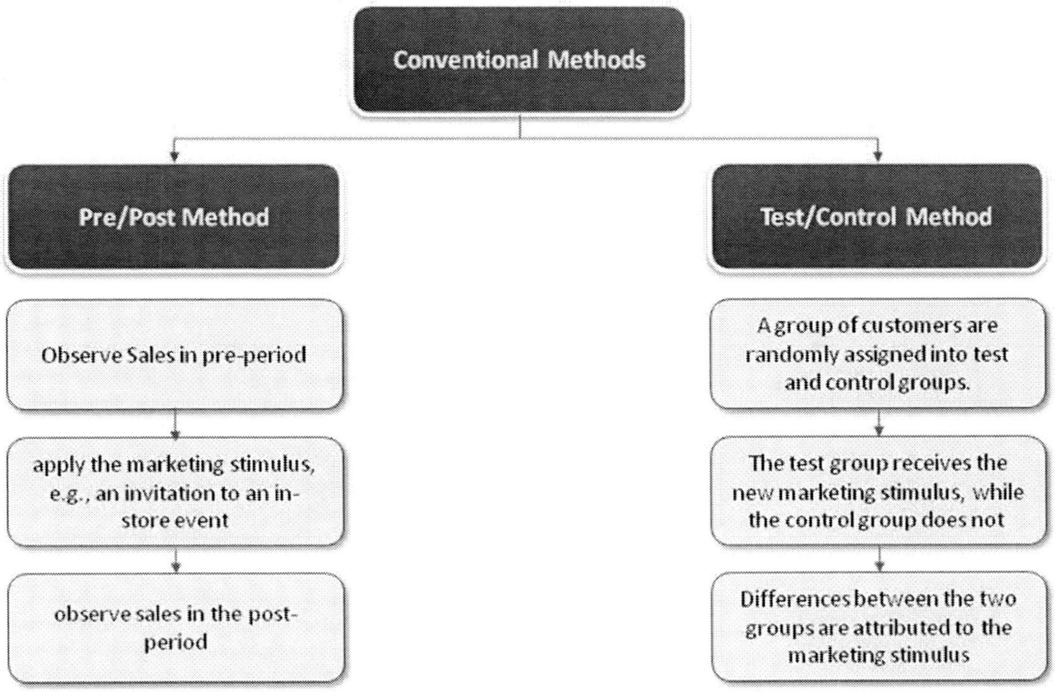

Need for New Methods

While the methods are extensively followed, there is a need for better methods due to the following reasons:

- **Effects of external environment:** Outside stimuli may effect outcome. For instance, there might be an increase in sales due to seasonal factors, but we might attribute it to promotional campaign.
- **Problems with matched control groups:** Random assignment of test and control groups may create errors. Issues like self-selection bias can cause incorrect approximation of actual incremental sales.
- **Need for better interpretation:** Statistical inferences which could predict how incremental sales would look like in the future and could benefit the respective organization.

A lot of research has already been done on the said issues. Some insights from the same are stated in table below:

S.No.	*Title*	*Key Insights*
1.	Evaluating the impact of promotions, Patrick Rooney, DMA Journal, 2009	• A combination of Pre/Post and Test/Control Design Method could be utilized • Incremental Sales = Observed Sales - Expected Sales • Expected Post-Test Group Sales = Pre-Period Test Sales * (Post-Control Sales / Pre-Control Sales)
2.	Propensity beginners' guide, Lorraine Dearden ,2011	It aims at forming matched control groups. The matching techniques that could be utilized are: • Nearest neighbor matching • Kernel based matching
3.	Direct Marketing for multichannel retailers, Behram J. Hansotia, 2002	Incremental metrics to measure the effectiveness of direct communications : • cost per incremental sale • incremental sales per dollar of direct marketing investment • incremental return on investment(ROI) • Incremental net present value (NPV), etc. Analysis and modeling techniques for multichannel promotions would require tree, or recursive partitioning-based approaches, like CHAID and CART, etc.
4.	Measuring marketing payback, ISBA, IPA, 2008	To measure incremental sales following could be adopted: • Econometric Modeling • Test and Control method • Trend Analysis Tips for measuring sales effect: • Monitoring sales growth is not enough • Look out for carry over effects • Think about revenue as well as volume • Keep the big picture in mind • Direct response data does not give you all the answers
5.	Payback and Return on marketing investment, Government Communication Network (UK) ,2011	Take the change in outcomes measured or forecast following the campaign. Exclude other factors by multiplying by the proportion of this effect that was attributable to the campaign. Then: • Add: the impact of relevant halo effects • Subtract: negative impacts and displacement • Multiply: the remaining impact by its financial value or proxy, to get Payback, then multiply by retention over time to get future Payback estimates Net Payback = Payback (NPV) – campaign cost (NPV) Then, ROMI = Net Payback (NPV) / campaign cost (NPV) ROMI can also be expressed as a percentage: ROMI (%) = (Net Payback (NPV) / campaign cost (NPV)) x 100%

Suggested Methodologies

Technique	*Methodology*	*Advantage*
Forecasting	Econometric Modeling (Linear Regression, ARIMA, etc.)	Statistical inferences could predict how incremental sales would look like in the future and could benefit the respective organization.
	Excel Based Methods (Monte Carlo Simulation, Sensitivity Analysis)	
	Trend Analysis	
Improving Test and Control Method	Combining Pre/Post and Test/Control Method	Most accurate and comprehensive measurement of incremental sales
	Forming Matched Control Groups	Reduces chances of Self- Selection Bias

FORECASTING

Forecasting situation vary widely in their time horizons, factors determining actual outcome, type of data, etc. Data can be intrinsic to company which can be controlled or can be uncontrolled extrinsic variables. It can be time series or can be causal variables. Patterns can be long business cycles or can show short seasonal influence. Forecast values can be obtained from qualitative as well as quantitative analysis but every model has its pros and cons. Hence it becomes very difficult to identify a model which is best suited for the forecast.

[ISBA, IPA, 2008, Measuring marketing payback]

Once data have been captured for the time series to be forecasted, the analyst's next step is to select a model for forecasting. Various statistical and graphic techniques may be useful to the analyst in the selection process. The best place to start with any time series forecasting analysis is to graph sequence plots of the time series to be forecasted. A sequence plot is a graph of the data series values, usually on the vertical axis, against time usually on the horizontal axis. The purpose of the sequence plot is to give the analyst a visual impression of the nature of the time series. This visual impression should suggest to the analyst whether there are certain behavioral "components" present within the time series.

The presence/absence of such components can help the analyst in selecting the model with the potential to produce the best forecasts.

After selecting a model, the next step is its specication. The process of specifying a forecasting model involves selecting the variables to be included, selecting the form of the equation of relationship, and estimating the values of the parameters in that equation.

After the model is specied, its performance characteristics should be veried or validated by comparison of its forecasts with historical data for the process it was designed to forecast. Error measures such as MAPE may be used for validating the model. Selection of an error measure has an important effect on the conclusions about which of a set of forecasting methods is most accurate.

FORECASTING MODELS

The following forecasting models were tested on specific datasets and following results were found:

S.No.	*Model*	*Applicability*
1	Regression	Low
2	Regression (With Seasonality)	Medium
3	Holt Winter	Medium
4	Simple Seasonal Exponential Smoothing	Medium
5	Holt Winter Multiplicative	High

Improving Test and Control Methodology

This can be done by two ways:

- Using a combination of test/control and pre/post design
- Forming matched control groups

Test/Control and Pre/Post Design Combination

This design combines the advantages of the two previous designs for evaluating the impact of promotions over a given time period.

In addition to making groups of customers comparable across both observed and unobserved covariates, it explicitly adjusts for changes between the pre- and post- periods that we would expect to see in the absence of the promotion.

Its relative disadvantages include: more time to set up; requiring two different groups; requiring random assignment procedures; and the fact that the concept of "expected sales," which is integral to the design, as explained in detail below, can be harder to present and explain.

[Patrick Rooney, 2009,'Evaluating the impact of promotions' , DMA Journal]

There are several measures of incremental sales using this design, one of which is described below:

The main highlights of this method would be:

- This design combines the advantages of both the designs for evaluating the impact of promotions over a given time period.
- In addition to making groups of customers comparable across both observed and unobserved covariates, it explicitly adjusts for changes between the pre- and post- periods that we would expect to see in the absence of the promotion.
- Incremental Sales = Observed Sales - Expected Sales
- Expected Post-Test Group Sales = Pre-Period Test Sales * (Post-Control Sales / Pre-Control Sales)
- When the Post-control group has higher sales than the Pre-control, the Pre-test group's sales will be multiplied by a number greater than 1; when the post-period sales are lower than the pre-period control group, the Pre-period Test group sales will be multiplied by a number less than 1, adjusting the "expected" sales downward.

Comparison of this technique with others is as follows:

Design	*Advantages*	*Disadvantages*
Pre / Post	Inexpensive (one group)	Takes time
	Easy to set up	Outside stimuli may affect outcome
	Easy to explain	
Test/Control	Easy to read	More expensive (two groups required) Random assignment (or more complex matching procedures) required
	Outside stimuli don't affect outcome	
	Quick	Random assignment (or more complex matching procedures) required
	Statistical inference easy	
Pre/Post and Test/Control	Most accurate and comprehensive measurement of incremental sales	Expensive
		Harder to explain
		Statistical inference harder (resampling may be required)

Hence, utilizing this method is a better option than utilizing the two methods individually.

Forming Matched Control Groups

This particular matching algorithm is most useful when there are at least twice as many untreated customers as there are treated customers. This makes it more likely that a set of untreated customers can be found that match as closely as possible the treated customers on a set of variables related to the outcome. The motivation for matching the two groups is that if they have similar pre-period purchase behavior and other characteristics (such as demographics and attitudes),then any differences we see during or after the promotion can be more plausibly attributed to the promotion, and not to pre-existing differences between the groups on the covariates. (One exception that remains a threat to this plausible inference is self-selection biases when customers "self-select" into receiving the treatment).[Lorraine Dearden ,2011, Propensity beginners' guide]

Some pointers to forming matched control groups would be:

- Often there cannot be random assignment for ethical or practical business reasons
- Used when there are at least twice as many untreated customers as there are treated customers
- **Greedy matching algorithm:** finds matched pairs of test and control customers that differ maximally by an amount specified by the user for each individual covariate
- **Optimal matching algorithm:** considers all potential controls to a given treated customer and selects the one that not only satisfies the maximum difference specified by the user, but also the pair that minimizes the differences over all matching variables.

Propensity Score

In the design of experiments, a propensity score is the probability of a unit (e.g., person, classroom, school) being assigned to a particular condition in a study given a set of known covariates. Propensity scores are used to reduce selection bias by equating groups based on these covariates.

In the analysis of treatment effects, suppose that we have a binary treatment *T*, an outcome *Y*, and background variables *X*. The propensity score is defined as the conditional probability of treatment given background variables:

$$p(x) \stackrel{\text{def}}{=} \Pr(T = 1 | X = x).$$

Propensity Score Matching

In the *statistical* analysis of *observational data*, propensity score matching (PSM) is a methodology attempting to provide *unbiased* estimation of treatment-effects. The possibility of "bias" arises here because the effectiveness of a treatment may depend on characteristics that are associated with whether or not a participant in an observational study chooses, or is chosen, to receive a given treatment.General procedure for propensity score matching is as follows:

1. Run logistic regression:
   - Dependent variable: $Y = 1$, if participate; $Y = 0$, otherwise.
   - Choose appropriate conditioning (instrumental) variables.
   - Obtain propensity score: predicted probability (p) or log[p/(1 " p)].
2. Match each participant to one or more nonparticipants on propensity score:
   - Nearest neighbor matching
   - Caliper matching
   - Mahalanobis metric matching in conjunction with PSM
   - Stratification matching
   - Difference-in-differences matching (kernel and local linear weights)
3. Multivariate analysis based on new sample
   - Use analyses appropriate for non-independent matched samples

Requirements for a good PSM are:

- Identify treatment and comparison groups with substantial overlap
- Use a composite variable—e.g., a propensity score—which reduces group differences across the covariates.

The two matching techniques with propensity score that can be employed are:

Nearest Neighbor Matching

- Each person in the treatment group choose individual(s) with the closest propensity score to them
- Can do this with (most common) or without replacement
- Not very efficient as discarding a lot of information from the control group

Kernel Based Matching

- Each person in the treatment group is matched to a weighted sum of individuals who have similar propensity scores with greatest weight being given to people with closer scores
- Some kernel based matching use all people in non-treated group whereas others only use people within a certain probability user-specified bandwidth

Advantages

- simplicity of method and presentation of results
- freedom from assumptions and constraints

Limitations

- it only adjusts for observed covariates
- self selection bias in this case could be a cause of concern

Future Research

- regression discontinuity design
- intervention analysis using time series modeling

RESULTS AND CONCLUSION

The two methods which could be employed to determine incremental sales can be forecasting techniques and also improvisation of current methodology.

Forecasting will give us baseline values for the coming months. Any deviation from the same would be attributed to promotions.

Various forecasting techniques through excel modeling were tried on the given dataset. Based on the MAPE, the applicability was found out. Also, factors such as trend and seasonality were kept into account while calculating forecast values.

For the second method, a combination of already existing techniques would enhance the accuracy of the calculation. Also, forming matched control groups rather than random selection of test and control groups would make chances of self selection bias lesser.

Hence, adopting the above said techniques would improve accuracy in predicting or estimation incremental sales. At the same time it will help the concerned organizations in better decision making.

RECOMMENDATIONS

- While following the conventional methods to generate incremental sales, it is important to look for other methods which would reduce chances of error and give a better measure of profitability of a promotion.
- Also, if the test and control groups being formed follow a certain method, their would be lesser chances of self selection bias. Hence, more incremental sales could be generated.
- A few other things to be kept in mind while calculating incremental sales would be:
- Incremental sales could be generated even after the promotion has been removed
- There could be post promotional dips as well
- Marketing one product may boost sales of other products in the portfolio: 'Halo effect'
- It may also lead to reduction in sales of other products: 'Cannibalization'

REFERENCES

[1] Patrick Rooney, 2009,'Evaluating the impact of promotions' , DMA Journal

[2] Lorraine Dearden ,2011, Propensity beginners' guide

[3] Behram J. Hansotia, 2002,Direct Marketing for multichannel retailers

[4] ISBA, IPA, 2008,Measuring marketing payback

[5] Government Communication Network (UK) ,2011,Payback and Return on marketing investment

[6] Kusum Ailawadi, 2006, Retail Promotion Profitability, Tuck Dartmouth Journal

[7] http://www.stochasticsolutions.com/pdf/CrossSell.pdf

Effect of Country of Origin on Brand Equity of Cars in India: A Study

Rohit Iyer, Chandana Mandal, Mohit Jain and AmbikaPaliwal

Institute of Management Technology, Ghaziabad

ABSTRACT

Marketers and consumer behaviour researchers generally accept that a product's or brand's country-of-origin is an important influencing factor in consumer decision-making. Most of the previous studies suggest that country-of- origin information which is indicated by the "Made in ..." label which serves several purposes in consumer decision-making. It acts as a salient attribute in consumer product evaluation. That is, the image that consumers have about a certain country will influence their perceptions of products from that country. Since consumers' perception of a particular country-of-origin influences their evaluation of products from that country, this will influence their preference, purchase intention and choice of a particular brand and hence has implications on the brand's equity. In this study the effects of brand's country-of-origin image on the formation of brand equity in two clusters i.e India. Here a high involvement category of Cars has been selected.

INTRODUCTION

In the arena of global marketing, building strong brands has become a top priority for marketers. Beyond, the marketing mix variables (advertising, distribution, price and product quality), the consumer's perception is influenced by the equity of a brand. Lost in the innumerable brands flow, consumer needs to reach him/herself to a strong brand, like an anchor, in which he can trust. Moreover, in numerous cases, in the process of buying, consumers are not only concern about the quality and price of a product but also other factors such as the brand's country-of-origin. Indeed many consumers use country-of-origin (COO) stereotypes to evaluate products for example, "German cars are excellent", "French wine is the best quality", "Japanese electronics are reliable", "Chinese clothes are bad quality" etc. These mental images enable the consumer to judge on the "superiority" or "inferiority" of a product, depending on their perception of the country. Sometimes also, the sale of a specific brands product could be simply forbidden in some country just because of the country-of-origin, like Coca-Cola in Cuba, Myanmar and North Korea. The dimensions of customer-based brand equity have been clearly proposed by Aaker (1991) and Keller (1993); they are brand loyalty, brand awareness, brand Distinctiveness and perceived quality

RESEARCH OBJECTIVES

The research questions studied are as follows:

1. To examine the effects of COO on brand equity in India.
2. To explore the moderators between COO and brand equity in India.

THEORETICAL FRAMEWORK

The proposed theoretical framework is as under:

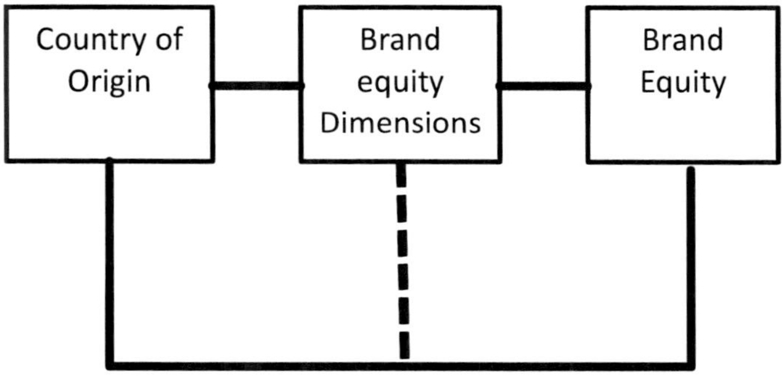

Country of origin. Innovativeness, Technology, Designing, creative, high Quality, prestige, advanced

Brand equity dimensions-Dynamism (Brand Distinctiveness), Hi tech (Brand Distinctiveness, innovative (Brand Distinctiveness)), sophistication (Brand Distinctiveness), distinctiveness (Brand Distinctiveness), Prestige (Brand Distinctiveness), excellence (Brand Distinctiveness),Buy(Brand Loyalty), premium (Brand Loyalty), think (Brand Loyalty), favorite (Brand Loyalty), Symbol(Brand Awareness), Imagine (Brand Awareness), Recall (Brand Awareness)

Brand equity: Prefer _ features, Choice, Prefer as good, Prefer same price, Prefer as good, Smart buy

RESEARCH HYPOTHESIS

Based on the results of the factor analyses the hypotheses were stated as follows:

H1. (a) Brand distinctiveness (b) Brand loyalty (c) Brand awareness/associations will have a positive relationship with brand equity.

H2. Brand's country-of-origin image will have a positive relationship with (a) brand distinctiveness (b) brand loyalty, and (c) brand awareness/associations.

H3. Brand country-of-origin image will have a positive relationship with brand equity through the mediating effects of (a) brand distinctiveness (b) brand loyalty,and (c) brand awareness/ associations

METHODOLOGY

To achieve the objectives of survey, a structured questionnaire was designed to collect primary data from respondents. The questionnaire consists of a five-point Likert scale ranging from "Strongly Disagree" to "Strongly Agree" option. This questionnaire consisted of 28 statements all of which were used by previous researchers NorjayaMohdYasin, Mohd Nasser Noor, Osman Mohamad, (2007). To choose the sample for this study, random sampling technique was used. Since the respondents were majorly Management students (which ensured they had sufficient awareness about foreign car brands and their country of origin) from various parts of India.

The survey was done administered from Ghaziabad on an national scale. The respondents so chosen from the cross-section of majority of management students were well-exposed to terms like brand equity, brand awareness, brand strength, country of origin, quality, research and development etc. As a measure of abundant precaution, we explained the necessary terms provided in the questionnaire to make it easy for them to respond correctly.

PROFILE OF RESPONDENTS

The total respondents for this study are 155 – 71 Indians .The study sample comprises respondents who vary on such characteristics as gender, age, marital status and living area. Such a difference is a natural reflection of the true consumer population for the India.

Hypothesis Testing (Indian Markets)

The regression analysis was employed to test the relationships posited in the model. Based on the conceptual model, the brand equity dimensions, which are treated as intervening variables in the model, are posited to influence brand equity.

Regression Brand Equity Dimensions Relationship with Brand Equity

The dependent variable brand equity was regressed on all these variables – brand distinctiveness, brand loyalty and brand awareness/associations. The results are shown below

Table 1 Regression: Brand Equity dimensions relationship with Brand equity

Model Summary

Model	R	R Square	Adjusted R Square	Std. Error of the Estimate
1	.651[a]	.423	.397	.4795532

a. Predictors: (Constant), Brand_Distinctiveness, Brand_Awareness, Brand_loyalty

b. Dependent Variable: Brand_equity

ANOVA[b]

Model		*Sum of Squares*	*df*	*Mean Square*	*F*	*Sig.*
1	Regression	11.305	3	3.768	16.386	.000[a]
	Residual	15.408	67	.230		
	Total	26.713	70			

a. Predictors: (Constant), Brand_Distinctiveness, Brand_Awareness, Brand_loyalty

b. Dependent Variable: Brand_equity

Coefficients[a]

Model		*Unstandardized Coefficients*		*Standardized Coefficients*		
		B	*Std. Error*	*Beta*	*t*	*Sig.*
1	(Constant)	.740	.649		1.140	.258
	Brand_Awareness	.215	.132	.179	2.029	.045
	Brand_loyalty	.338	.075	.457	4.516	.000
	Brand_Distinctiveness	.236	.114	.215	2.078	.042

a. Dependent Variable: Brand_equity

The model is significant at p=0.05 indicating 95 percent confidence in explaining the dependent variable. All the three variables – brand distinctiveness, brand loyalty and brand awareness/associations are found to have a significant and positive influence on brand equity at a significant level. The R square of 0.413 indicates that 41.3 percent of the variance in brand equity was explained by the variations in brand distinctiveness, brand loyalty and brand awareness/ associations. The standardized beta weights are in the hypothesized direction. These findings substantively support H1(a), H1(b) and H1(c). Looking at the beta coefficients of the dimensions of brand equity on brand equity, brand loyalty has the highest contribution towards brand equity, followed by brand distinctiveness and brand awareness.

Regression: Country of Origin image Relationship with BrandEquity dimensions

In testing the relationship between country-of-origin image and each of the dimensions of brand equity, results of the regression is shown below.

Model Summary

Model	*R*	*R Square*	*Adjusted R Square*	*Std. Error of the Estimate*
1	.408a	.167	.155	.5165932

a. Predictors: (Constant), COO_Image

b. Dependent Variable: Brand Distinctiveness

Coefficients

Model		*Unstandardized Coefficients*		*Standardized Coefficients*		
		B	*Std. Error*	*Beta*	*T*	*Sig.*
1	(Constant)	2.584	.471		5.485	.000
	COO_Image	.404	.109	.408	3.717	.000

a. Dependent Variable: Brand Distinctiveness

Regression: Country of Origin image V/s Brand Loyalty

Model summary

Model	*R*	*R Square*	*Adjusted R Square*	*Std. Error of the Estimate*
1	.304a	.093	.079	.8013617

a. Predictors: (Constant), COO Image

b. Dependent Variable: Brand loyalty

Coefficients

Model		Unstandardized Coefficients		Standardized Coefficients		
		B	*Std. Error*	*Beta*	*t*	*Sig.*
1	(Constant)	1.599	.731		2.189	.032
	COO Image	.448	.169	.304	2.653	.010

a. Dependent Variable: Brand loyalty

Regression: Country of Origin image V/s Brand Awareness

Model Summary

Model	*R*	*R Square*	*Adjusted R Square*	*Std. Error of the Estimate*
1	.234a	.055	.041	.4512924

a. Predictors: (Constant), COO Image

b. Dependent Variable: Brand Awareness

Coefficients

Model		Unstandardized Coefficients		Standardized Coefficients		
		B	*Std. Error*	*Beta*	*t*	*Sig.*
1	(Constant)	3.871	.412		9.407	.000
	COO Image	.190	.095	.234	1.995	.050

a. Dependent Variable: Brand Awareness

The significant F value for the three regressions is ,<=0.05, which indicates that the three regression models have 95 percent confidence in the ability to explain the dependent variables. From the above tables it is evident country-of-origin image, has a positive and significant influence on brand distinctiveness, brand loyalty and brand awareness at a significance level of p , 0:05. Therefore, H2(a), H2(b), and H2(c) are supported. Based on the R2 values, country-of origin image contributed 16.7 percent of the total variance in brand distinctiveness, 9.3 percent in brand loyalty, and 5.5 percent in brand awareness/associations.

Regression: Country of Origin image Vs Brand Equity

As significance value is greater than 0.05, no significant relationship exists between country of origin image and brand equity for cars segments in the Indian Market.

Table 2 Regression: Country of Origin image Vs Brand Equity

Model Summary

Model	*R*	*R Square*	*Adjusted R Square*	*Std. Error of the Estimate*
1	.160[a]	.026	.011	.5642826

a. Predictors: (Constant), Brand equity

b. Dependent Variable: COO Image

Coefficients

Model		*Unstandardized Coefficients*		*Standardized Coefficients*		
		B	Std. Error	Beta	T	Sig.
1	(Constant)	3.694	.450		8.206	.000
	Brand_equity	.147	.109	.160	1.345	.183

a. Dependent Variable: COO Image

In testing the mediating effects of the dimensions of brand equity in the country-of-origin image image – brand equity linkage, Baron and Kenny (1986) is consulted. They suggest that three requirements must be fulfilled:

1. Significant relationship between the independent and mediating variable;
2. Significant relationship between the independent and dependent variable; and
3. Significant relationship between the independent and dependent variable in the presence of the mediator.

To demonstrate mediation, Baron and Kenny (1986) further suggest that the effect of the independent variable on the dependent variable is reduced or even disappears in the case of full mediation.The first requirement is fulfilled by the results shown in the above parts. To fulfill the second requirement of the test of mediation, the relationship between country-of-origin image and brand equity is analyzed and the regression result proves to be insignificant and thus the second requirement is not fulfilled. So the mediating effects can no further be studied in this case.

CONCLUSION

Based on the results of the analysis of the data collected in Indian Market, It isobservedthat the country of origin does not significantly affect Brand equity in Indian market in the car segment contrary to the results found in few countries. Further exploratory research can be done to understand the reasons behind this behavior of Indian consumers. Nevertheless, this Behavior among Indian Consumers can be explained using the following arguments:

1. Indian Consumers make buy decisions based on the product performance and features for high involvement categories like cars and not based on its country's image
2. The contribution of country of origin towards brand equity of cars in the mind of Indian consumer is low.
3. Indians see cars as a status symbol. As a result, the ones who can afford it tend to buy the costliest one irrespective of its country of origin Image.

This result can be used by Indian car manufacturers to build brand equity by improving the car features and making it globally competent.

REFERENCES

[1] Norjaya MohdYasin, Mohd Nasser Noor, Osman Mohamad, (2007),"Does image of country-of-origin matter to brand equity?", Journal of Product & Brand Management, Vol. 16 Iss: 1 pp. 38 – 48

[2] Ravi Pappu, Pascale G. Quester, Ray W. Cooksey, (2006),"Consumer-based brand equity and country-of-origin relationships: Some empirical evidence", European Journal of Marketing, Vol. 40 Iss: 5 pp. 696 – 717

[3] Shamindra NathSanyal, Saroj Kumar Datta, (2011),"The effect of country of origin on brand equity: an empirical study on generic drugs", Journal of Product & Brand Management, Vol. 20 Iss: 2 pp. 130 – 140

[4] Aaker, David A. (1991), *Managing Brand Equity*, Free Press, N.Y.

[5] Aaker, David A. and Keller, Kevin L. (1990), "Consumer Response to Brand Extension," Journal of Marketing, 54 (January): 27-41.

[6] Alba, J.W. and Hutchinson, J.W. (1987), "Dimensions of Consumer Expertise," *Journal of Consumer Research*, March, 13(4):411-455.

[7] Barwise, Patrick (1993), "Brand Equity: Snark or Boojum?", International Journal of Research in Marketing, 10(1): 93-104.

[8] Biel, Alexander L. (1997), "Discovering Brand Magic: The Hardness of the Softer Side of Branding,"International Journal of Advertising, 16, 199-210.

[9] Biel, Alexander L.(1993), *Converting Image into Equity: Brand Equity & Advertising: Advertising's Role in Building Strong Brands*, Lawrence

[10] Erlbaum Associates, Inc., New Jersey.

[11] Chao, Paul(1993), "Partitioning Country of Origin Effects: Consumer Evaluations of A Hybrid Product," Journal of International Business Studies, 24(2): 291-306.

[12] Cobb-Walgren, Cathy J., Ruble, Cynthia A. &Donthu, Naveen (1995), "Brand Equity, Brand Preference, and Purchase Intent,"Journal of Advertising, 24(3): 25-40, Fall.

[13] Erickson, G.M., Johansson, J.K. and Chao, P. (1984), "Image Variables in Multi-Attribute Product Evaluations: Country-of-Origin Effects," *Journal of Consumer Research*, September, 11(2): 694-699.

[14] Gardner, Burleigh B., & Sidney J. Levy (1955), "The Product and the Brand,"Harvard Business Review, 33 (March/April), 33-39.

[15] Huang, Chun-Ying (2001), *The World of Marketing*, CommonWealth Publishing, Taipei.

[16] Insch, Gary S. and McBride, J. Brad. (1998), "Decomposing the Country-of-Origin Construct: An Empirical Test of Country-of-Design, Country-of-Parts and

[17] Country-of-Assembly," *Journal of International Consumer Marketing*, 10(4): 69-91.

[18] Kamakura, Wagner A. & Russell, Gary J. (1993), "Measuring Brand Value with Scanner Data,"International Journal of Research in Marketing, 10(1): 9-22, March.

[19] Keller, Kevin Lane (1993), "Conceptualizing, Measuring, and Managing Customer-Based Brand Equity,"Journal of Marketing, 57(January), 1-22.

[20] Keller, Kevin L. (1998), *Strategic Brand Management*, Prentice-Hall, New Jersey.

[21] Lassar, Walfried; Mittal, Banwari& Sharma, Arun (1995), "Measuring Customer-Based Brand Equity,"Journal of Consumer Marketing, 12(4): 11-19.

[22] Loomis, Anne M. (1998), "The Hidden Power of Global Branding,"Pharmaceutical Executive, 18(5): May 82-93.

[23] Morton, John (1994), "Predicting Brand Preference,"Marketing Management, 2(4): 32-44.

[24] Nagashima, Akira (1970), "A Comparison of Japanese and U.S. Attitudes Toward Foreign Products," Journal of Marketing, 34 (January): 68-74.

[25] Ofir, Chezy and Lehman, D. R. (1986), " Measurement Images of Foreign Products," Columbia Journal of World Business, 21(2): 105-108.

[26] Ogilvy, David (1963), *Confessions of an Advertising Man*, New York

[27] Park, C.W. and Lessig, V.P. (1981), "Familiarity and Its Impact on Consumer Biases and Hueristics," *Journal of Consumer Research*, September, 8(2): 223-230.

[28] Ries, Al (1999), *Focus: The Future of Your Company Depends on It*, HarperCollins, N.Y.

[29] Schoell, William F., &Guiltinan, Joseph P. (1990), *Marketing*, 4th edition, M.A.

[30] Zeithmal, Valarie A. (1988), "Consumer Perceptions of Price, Quality, and Value: A Means-End Model and Synthesis of Evidence," *Journal of Marketing*, 52(July): 2-22.

Examining Perceived Risks and Website Attributes Preferred by the Indian Online Users

Priya Mary Mathew and Sita Mishra[1]

Business and Technology Department, Pearl Academy, New Delhi
[1]Institute of Management Technology, Ghaziabad

ABSTRACT

With the Internet numbers crossing the figure of 100 million in 2011, India is witnessing a more mature growth among the users. The large internet user market despite a low penetration level also suggests that the online market of India has business potential. This research study examines the behaviour of online consumer in India in terms of internet usage, perceived risks, and website attributes influencing online users. A structured questionnaire was administered to 600 online consumers using field and online survey mediums. Findings show that the average time of internet usage of Indian online users is 2.6 hours daily. Results show that Indian online users had high level of perceived risks, highest fear being related to the delivery of products purchased online. Information quality, product range and after online sales service are most preferred website attributes which influence Indian online users.

INTRODUCTION

The internet has reached small metros and towns of India. Youth of India continues to form the major segment of the total online users (Internet and Mobile Association of India Report, IAMAI 2010 report). While the point of access in predominantly cyber café in India, the emergence of smart phones and 3G has resulted in use of mobile phones, I-pads and kiosks as emerging points of internet access.

The world has over 2000 million internet users with the internet penetration of 30 percent while India has 100 million internet users with just about 8 percent penetration level (Asia Internet usage and population, 2011). Despite low penetration level the e-retail market in India was worth INR 2000 CR in 2011 and is estimated to be worth INR 7000 CR by 2015 (Online retail industry by 2015). Though the internet penetration has shown tremendous growth in India (35% CAGR), capitalizing the market potential depends largely on how Indian online consumers actually use internet (internet usage or e-usage).

Despite high awareness of internet and high e-usage in India, the translation of e-users to into e-customers is low because of high perceived risks. To understand this, the study attempted to investigate the online consumer behavior of active Indian online users in terms of daily internet usage in hours, perceived risks of respondents, preferred website attributes that could influence e-users to become e-buyers.

LITERATURE REVIEW

Internet Usage

Studies on the influencers of internet usage have shown that perceived usefulness and ease of use encourages online users to use internet for longer duration (Davis, 1989). Loshe et al. (2000) showed that the longer the internet usage , the greater is the intent to do online purchase in future and the greater the chance of making a purchase online. This research studied the daily internet usage in hours to understand its influence on perceived risks of online users and preferred website attributes.

Perceived Risks

Perceived risk has been defined as feelings of uncertainty and possible adverse consequences about some future event (Cox and Rich, 1964; Bauer, 1960; Cunningham, 1967). Various types of risk identified were relative to physical, time, safety, financial, and performance dimensions (Cunningham, 1967; Dowling, 1986; Weber and Hsee, 1998, Lim,2003 ; Forsythe and Shi,2003). It was in 1999 that Mitchell suggested that perceived risk was powerful at explaining consumers' behaviour because consumers were more often motivated to avoid mistakes than to maximize utility in purchasing. The perceived risks of the Indian online consumers were studied by Sahneyet .al. (2008) and their study has established that reliability, security and trust were the most important factors that affect Indian online shopping behaviour.

Website Attributes

Online marketers and retailers should identify elements enhancing trust among potential customers. For entrepreneurs that depend totally on pure website-based businesses, designing their website is a central issue. Some of the elements identified as website attributes are: third-party approvals and endorsements; the site's usability and inter activity; the credibility of the online vendor; and the content elements including the aesthetic aspects of the online presentation and the marketing mix (Loebbecke, 2003; Chen and Chang, 2003; Demangeot and Broderick, 2007).

Research Gap

Unlike offline retail stores, the inability to interact with a salesperson and the merchandise, and the reliance on electronic payment methods increase perceived risks with regard to online shopping (Shim et al, 2001). The primary concerns for online users regarding online shopping have been privacy and protection of one's personal information, in the last two decades (Kolsaker et.al, 2004). Consumers look for cues from the online environment to make sure that they will not experience a loss when making a purchase online (Chang and Chen, 2008). A website is perhaps the only way an online store communicates with its customers (Chen et al, 2002).This present study tried to understand which website attributes help in reducing online shopping uncertainty.

RESEARCH METHODOLOGY

Objectives of the Study

The purpose of the study was to examine the online consumer behaviour of active Indian online users in terms of

- internet usage
- perceived risks
- website attributes
- relationship between website attributes and internet usage

Instrument

Based on extensive literature review, perceived risks of online consumers was in this study investigated based on following factors : Credit card information (Pennanen,K. et al, 2007); Privacy of Personal Information (Gefen, 2000; Walczuch and Lundgren, 2004); Trustworthiness of online retailer (Chaudhuri and Holbrook, 2001, Ruyter et al. 2001); Timely delivery of online purchases (Li and Zhang 2002); Delivered products must match those described on the website (Chang and Chen 2008); Products purchased online must be delivered undamaged (Li and Zhang 2002); Product returns must be easy for online purchases (Hahn and Kim 2009) and Contacting customer service must be easy for online purchases (Chang and Chen 2008). Eight website attributes, which are relevant to online retailers to entice online users, were included and the respondents were asked to rank each attribute (1 being the highest rank and 8 being the lowest).A structured questionnaire was used for the survey which had Cronbach's Alpha, á > 0.75.

Procedure

The respondents were selected using quota sampling technique. Based on IAMAI report (2010) first level of categorisation was based on Indian states that showed considerable penetration of Internet(Delhi, Mumbai, Chennai, Kolkatta, Gurgaon, Faridabad, Jaipur, Chandigarh, Hyderabad and Cochin). The second level of stratification was based on age groups. The quota decided was that one third of sample will be selected from each of these age groups :18 to 21 ; 21 to 30 and 31 above. Out of 600 filled questionnaires, 484 were found usable for data analysis.

Data Analysis Methods

Descriptive analysis was conducted on the data and non parametric methods were used. Regression analysis technique was used to explore and determine the relationships between the various decision variables. SPSS software was used to carry out the analysis.

Table 1. Demographic Profiling of the Sample Characteristics Summary (n=484)

Characteristic	*%*	*Characteristic*	*%*
Gender		*Annual Household Income*	
Male	45	Less than 5 lakhs	33
Female	55	5 to 12 lakhs	38
Age (years)		12 to 20 lakhs	17
18 to 21	37.6	More than 20 lakhs	12
22 to 25	28.7	*Internet Usage (hours per day)*	
26 to 29	14.3	Less than 2 hours per day	30.2
30 to 39	15.5	2 to 4 hours per day	47
40 to 49	3.3	5 to 7 hours per day	13.3
50 to 60	0.6	8 to 12 hours per day	8.1
Profession		More than 12 hours per day	1.4
Student	53.2	*Prior online purchase experience*	
Part time employment	7.2	Yes	61.3
Employed/Businessmen	33.5	No	38.7
Home maker	5.2		
Retired	0.9		

FINDINGS AND ANALYSIS

Internet Usage

The analysis of internet usage reflected that less than a half of the respondents (47%) access internet for 2 to 4 hours per day, while a third (30%)use internet for less than 2 hours per day and about one fifths (22%) are use internet for more than 5 hours per day. Thus the average time of internet usage of Indian online users are 2.6 hours daily.

Table 2. Internet Usage of Indian Online Users

Variables	*Findings*	*Percentage*	*Significance Tests Results*
Daily Internet Usage	Less than 2 hours per day	30.2	*T = 21.9*
	2 to 4 hours per day	47.0	*d.f. = 483*
	5 to 7 hours per day	13.3	$p < 0.05$
	8 to 12 hours per day	8.1	
	More than 12 hours per day	1.4	

Perceived Risks

The results (see Table 3) displayed that all the eight measures of perceived risk scored mean value higher than 6. This indicated that the respondents had high level of perceived risks in all the eight parameters. The respondents have expressed highest risk factors related to the delivery of products purchased online. More than three-fourths of the sample have given highest importance to the statement that "products purchased online must be delivered undamaged" (79 percent) and "delivered products must match those described on the website" (77 percent).

Table 3. Perceived Risks of Indian Online Users (ranked)

Perceived Risks (n=367)	*Mean*	*Percentage (in Likert Scale)*						
	(7 = Most Important, 1=Least important)	*Very important (Scale 7 to 5)*			*Neutral (Scale 4)*	*Least Important (Scale 1 to 3)*		
Products purchased online must be delivered undamaged	6.70	78.7	14.8	4.9	1.1	0.3	0.3	0
Delivered products must match those described on the Website	6.67	76.8	16.1	4.6	1.9	0.5	0	0
Credit card information used for online purchases must be secure.	6.58	78.2	10.6	5.4	4.1	0.5	0.8	0.3
Online purchases must be delivered in a timely manner	6.51	67.3	21.0	8.2	3.0	0.5	0	0
Online retailers must be trustworthy	6.49	70.8	15.5	7.9	3.8	1.4	0.5	0
Personal information provided for online purchases must be confidential	6.38	68.1	15.0	8.7	5.2	1.6	0.5	0.8
Contacting customer service must be easy for online purchases	6.11	51.0	25.3	11.4	8.4	3.3	0.5	0
Product returns must be easy for online purchases	6.08	51.2	22.1	13.4	11.4	1.1	0.5	0.3

Website Attributes

Indian online users were asked to rank eight website attributes with respect to any online buying website. The results(see Table 4) showed that attributes preferred in decreasing order were: Information quality, Product range, After online sales service, Visual design, Web atmosphere, Recommendation by relatives, Recommendation by other buyers and lastly, Fun ($p<0.000$).

Table 4. Most Preferred Website Attributes
(rank order, where 1 = highest rank, 8= least rank) (n=484)

Website Attribute	*Mean*	*Std. Deviation*	*t*	*Rank*
Information Quality	2.63	1.859	27.04**	1
Product Range	2.68	1.780	28.69**	2
After Online Sales Service	4.26	2.323	34.95**	3
Visual Design	4.29	2.279	35.91**	4
Website Atmosphere	4.33	2.144	38.53**	5
Recommendation by Relatives	4.48	2.139	39.94**	6
Recommendation by Buyers	4.87	2.087	44.53**	7
Fun	5.50	2.306	45.47**	8

Information quality was the most highly ranked. Content is king for online marketing (Hahn and Kim, 2009). Content quality deals with attributes such as information usefulness, completeness and accuracy. Information quality also refers to specific content, such as finding specific details about product and services, customer support, privacy policies and other important information. The second most preferred website attribute was the product range. Online consumers review an online retail firm highly only if the website displays a variety of product range. Consumers undertake a great deal of information search before actual buying. So the range of products available for online shopping matters considerably to online consumers.

Visual design was the third most preferred website attribute. Visual design refers to the visual attractiveness of a website, such as colors, fonts and multimedia features. A well-designed website can enhance the probability of a favourable impression as the viewer responds to visual cues, and a viewer with a favourable impression of a website is more likely to become a customer.

Relationship Between Website Attributes and Internet Usage

Time spent on internet is called internet usage Internet usage has significant influence on the behaviour of the online consumer.

The results (see Table 5) revealed that internet usage influences the ranking of preferred website attributes. When the duration of internet usage increases, the online user prefers information quality, after sales service, recommendation from other buyers and product range. Such a user's preference for the following website attributes decreases: recommendation from relatives, visual design, fun and website atmosphere. When we compare the two 'types' of website attributes according to increasing and decreasing preferences, we find that online users, with increasing usage, tend to prefer attributes which enhance utilitarian value and are less enamoured of website attributes that enhance entertainment (hedonic value). This shift in preference of website attributes with internet usage suggests that the confidence of the online internet shopper increases with greater internet usage.

Table 5. Ranking of Website Attributes (1 = highest rank, 8= least rank) based on Internet usage (n = 600)

Internet Usage	*Visual Design*	*Info. Quality*	*Pdt. Range*	*Web Atm*	*After Online Sales Service*	*Recomm Buyers*	*Recomm Relatives*	*Fun*
Less than 2 hours	179.6	198.4	184.5	175.6	193.0	175.5	179.4	174.8
2 to 4 hours	181.5	174.8	187.7	181.4	184.0	193.9	189.9	183.1
5 to 8 hours	187.3	181.8	160.9	187.3	160.2	157.7	158.4	189.1
More than 8 hours	187.4	151.4	167.1	219.8	152.6	165.4	186.6	196.2
Preference of website attributes with increase in internet usage ➔	decreases	increases	increases	decreases	increases	increases	decreases	decreases

DISCUSSIONS AND CONCLUSIONS

The study established that the highest perceived risks regarding online shopping that Indian online users have are those related to security of credit card information, confidentiality of personal information and trust in e-retailers. India does not have an adequate legal framework to support online consumers, something that is important for reducing uncertainties and building trust and confidence in the electronic marketplace. There is a need for legal frameworks that provide for the legal recognition of electronic documents and signatures and penalize common crimes and offences committed in cyberspace.

Converting online visitors into buyers is one of the biggest problems that many online businesses face in daily basis. During online shopping, trust is a vital factor for consumers to make purchase decision since consumers often perceive risks involved in online transactions. This study established that consumers may feel uncertain about purchasing products online, if they need to give out their personal information such as credit card numbers. Moreover in a populous country like India where one has to stand in long queues and travel dusty roads, given a choice, online user will buy travel tickets and do small item purchases (CDs, books, gifts) through the internet.Unlike in offline retail stores, the inability to interact with a salesperson and the merchandise, as well as the reliance on electronic payment methods, increases the perceived risk of online shopping. Hence, website attributes are highly important to induce online users to become buyers. The study found that website attributes preferred by Indian online users changed with internet usage and past online buying experience. Highly preferred attribute was recommendation by relatives and other buyers: India has a collective culture. Here the influence (referrals and recommendations) of friends, family, and media recommendations on shopping is very high. Recommendations of a retailer's online operations have dominant effect on online trust.

There have been certain limitations of scope in this study. However, these could be addressed in future research. Studies have established that psychological perception also influences online shopping trust, risk and benefit. A consumer's trust in a company can play an important role in reducing any uncertainty about online shopping. Future study can be done to understand how to enhance perceived benefit and trust in an online user.

REFERENCES

[1] Asia Internet usage and population, 2011accessed from http://www.internetworldstats.com/stats3.htm

[2] Bauer,R.A.(1960), "Consumer behaviour risk taking", in Zhao,A.L., Ward,S.H.P. and Goode, M.M.H.(2008), "Perceived Risk and Chinese consumers' internet banking services adoption", *International Journal of Bank Marketing*, Vol.26 No.7 pp.505-525

[3] Chang, H.H. and Chen, S.W. (2008), "The impact of online store environment cues on purchase intention: Trust and perceived risk as a mediator," *Online Information Review*,Vol.32 No, 6, pp. 818-841.

[4] Chaudhuri, A. and Holbrook, M. (2001), "The chain of effects from brand trust and brand affect to brand performance: the role of brand loyalty", *Journal of Marketing*, Vol. 65, pp. 81-93.

[5] Chen,S. and Chang, T. (2003), "A descriptive model of online shopping process: some empirical results" , *InternationalJournal of Service Industry Management*, Vol. 14No. 5, pp. 556-569.

[6] Chen, L.-D., Gillenson, M. L. and Sherrell, D. L.(2002), "Enticing Online Consumers: An Extended Technology Acceptance Perspective," *Information & Management* ,Vol. 39 No. 8, pp.705-719.

[7] Choi, J. and Lee, K.H. (2003), "risk Perception and e-shopping: a cross cultural study", *Journal of Fashion Marketing and Management*, Vol.7 No.1 , pp.49-64

[8] Cox,D.F. and Rich, S.U. (1964) in Korgaonkar, P. K. and Karson, E.J.(2007), "The Influence of Perceived Product risk on Consumers' e-tailer shopping preference," *Journal of Business Psychology*, Vol. 22, pp. 55-64.

[9] Cunningham, L.F., Gerlach, J.H., Harper, M.D. and Young, C.E. (1967), "Perceived risk and the consumer buying process: internet airline reservations", *InternationalJournal of Service Industry Management*, Vol. 16 No. 4, pp. 357-72.

[10] Davis, F.D. (1989), "Perceived usefulness, perceived ease of use, and user acceptance of information technology", *MIS Quarterly*, Vol. 13 No. 3, pp. 318-40.

[11] Demangeot, C. and Broderick ,A.J. (2007), "Conceptualising consumer behaviour in online shopping environments", *International Journal of Retail and Distribution Management*, Vol.35 No.11, pp.878-894.

[12] Dowling, G.R. and Staelin, R. (1986),"A model of perceived risk and intended risk-handling activity", *Journal ofConsumer Research* Vol. 21, pp. 119-135.

[13] Forsythe,S.M. and Shi, B. (2003), "Consumer patronage and risk perceptions in internet shopping", *Journal of Business Research*, Vol. 56 No. 11, pp.867-875

[14] Gefen,D. Rose, G.M., Warkentin,M and Pavlou,P.A (2005) "Cultural Diversity and Trust in IT Adoption: A Comparison of Potential e-Vote"" *Journal of Global Information Management*, Vol 13 No. 1

[15] Hahn,K.H and Kim, J (2009), The effect of offline brand trust and perceived internet confidence on online shopping intention in the integrated multi-channel context, *International Journal of Retail and Distribution Management* ,Vol. 37 No.2, pp.126-141

[16] IAMAI Reports (2005 to 2011), *Internet in India*, Internet and Mobile Association of India

[17] Kolsaker, A., Lee-Kelley, L. and Choy, P. C.(2004), "The Reluctant Hong Kong Consumer: Purchasing Travel Online," *International Journal of Consumer Studie,* Vol. 28, No. 3, pp. 295-304.

[18] Li, N. and Zhang, P. (2002), "Consumer online shopping attitudes and behavior: an assessment of research", Proceedings of 8th Americas Conference on Information System, 2002, pp. 508-17.

[19] Lim, N. (2003), "Consumers' perceived risks: sources versus consequences" , *Electronic commerce Research and Applications*, Vol.2 no. 3, pp. 216-28

[20] Loebbecke,C.(2003), "E-business trust concepts based on seals and insurance solutions", *Information Systems and E-business Management*, Vol.1 No.1, pp. 55-72.

[21] Lohse, G.L., Bellman, S. and Johnson, E.J. (2000), "Consumer buying behavior on the internet: findings from panel data", *Journal of Interactive Marketing*, Vol. 14 No. 1, pp. 15-29.

[22] Mitchell, V. (1999), "Consumer perceived risk: conceptualizations and models", *European Journal of Marketing*, Vol.33, pp.163-195.

[23] Online retail industry by 2015: Assocham http://www.livemint.com/2011/07/03111627/Online-retail-industry-to-reach.html Retrieved on 12 June 2011

[24] Pennanen, K., Tiainen, T. and Luomala, H.T. (2007), "A Qualitative exploration of a consumer's value based e-trust building process",*Qualitative Market Research: an International Journal,* Vol. 10, No. 1, pp. 28-47.

[25] Ruyter, K., Wetzels, M. and Kleijnen, M.(2001), "Customer Adoption of E-Service: An Experimental Study," *International Journal of Service Industry Management* Vol. 12, No. 2, pp.184-208.

[26] Shim,S., Eastlick,M.A., Lotz,S.L. and Warrington, P.(2001), "An Online Purchase Intention Model: The Role Of Intention To Search" , *Journal of Retailing*, Vol. 77 No.3, pp.397-416

[27] Ueltschy L.C., Krampf, R.F. and Yannopaulos,P. (2004), "A cross national study of perceived consumer risk towards online (internet) purchasing", *Multinational Business Review*, Vol.12 No.2, pp. 59-82

Experiential Marketing: With Examples of Starbucks and Disneyland

Sheeny Yadav

Institute of Management Technology, Ghaziabad

ABSTRACT

The paper discusses the commoditization of goods, services and now experiences to enhance the value delivered to the customer. This need has been created due to ease of imitation, and the only mode of differentiation left for the products was to provide better services. And as we all know, "Necessity is the mother of all inventions", all this led to the birth of Experiential Marketing *to entertain, stimulate and emotionally affect consumers. Experiences are further development of services and require customer as a co-producer – a co-creation of experience spaces between the firm and the customer. The management of today's firms is required to pull an experience by understanding customer needs to create appropriate value proposition through flexibility, innovation and learning. The experience sectors are primarily classified as*primary *and* secondary *sectors. The role innovation and internationalization play in these sectors is discussed through examples of two firms - Starbucks and Disneyland, who have utilized experiential marketing to reach the epitomes of providing memorable experiences.*

INTRODUCTION

It took a while for practitioners to realize the importance of bringing marketing into the boardroom. Before that, all the decisions were finance based. So what changed? The fact that marketers understood they had to present marketing in numbers too, so that the board could understand what difference the new marketing plan would create.

But marketing hadn't developed completely yet. It took an era to see a change between commoditization of goods to services. This need arose because goods could easily be imitated and the only mode of differentiation left was to provide better services. However, as per current scenario when everybody is providing first class services, a need has developed to go a step further. And hence has come up the need for experience marketing which focuses on selling an entire experience to the customer. However, while creating goods and providing services is in the control of the firm, what experience a customer goes through is not so much in their hands. Every customer will encounter a different experience over the same delivery. Commodities are fungible, goods tangible, services intangible and experiences memorable (*Pine and Gilmore).*

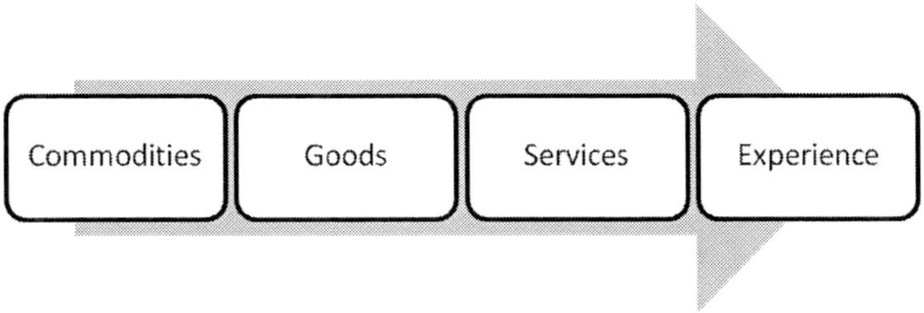

CREATING AN EXPERIENCE

Experiences are being valued above the rest as they are *unique, memorable and engaging* for every person in a different manner, while services are becoming commodities as they are homogeneous by day and are now chosen more on the basis of price and availability, than due to their uniqueness. As per Pine and Gilmore, only by creating unique and memorable experiences can service organizations achieve a lasting competitive advantage. Experiences draw on customer perspectives like psychology and sociology to explore symbolical, emotional and transformational significance for the individual and on managerial perspectives which focus on how organizations deliver experiences as value added offer.

Experience was earlier understood as a part of services, but a line is now slowly appearing between the two. Services aim to solve people's problems while experiences offer a mental journey. Experience is further development of service and requires customer as a co-producer. The customer and the company create between them '*experience spaces*', interaction in which helps come up with new ideas of how to offer new experiences as co-creators. Experience spaces allow dialogue, transparency and access to information due to which the customers can develop experiences to suit their own needs.Customers make different inferences of the experience based on their level of knowledge of the context, past experiences and social knowledge. This mental journey turns into a memory which they repetitively relive in their minds as the original experience. Experienced customers like sharing their experiences with novice users guiding them through the process, thus sharing value amongst them.

Holbrook and Hirschman examined the whole consumption process from pre-purchase to disposal and discovered that emotion is a crucial aspect of consumption. Consumers just don't respond to the experience but interact with it.The experience could be something like tourism for which you need to go the place, or it could be a movie on a DVD that could come right at your home on ordering.

Experience involves:

- Shift of emphasis from rational to emotional aspect of consumer decision making
- Transition from satisfying needs to fulfilling aspirations, desires and dreams
- Role of customer as an active participant rather than a passive consumer

- Substantial amounts of interaction with many parties in network and brand community

The job of the management is to create events that engage the consumer in a personal way, i.e., to regard work as theatre and every business a stage. According to *Pine and Gilmore*, 'An experience occurs when a company intentionally uses services as the stage, and goods as props, to engage individual customers in a way that creates a memorable event.'

What is required from the management is to pull an experience to:

- Chart and script each stage of customer encounter
- Understand the importance of staff customer interaction
- Teach staff to put a part of their own personalities into the roles
- Set the servicescape's environment and ambience in sync with the theme
- View service delivery as an integrated production

Customers needs have to be understood to create appropriate value proposition and requires flexibility, innovation and learning.

New techniques such as experience mapping, online brand based communities and theatrical scripting have come up to study experiences. Delivering the experience depends on the frontline staff, managers as well as the marketers. People remember not just the peaks of the excitement but the entire thing.

Three consumption motives are (*Hirschman and Holbrook*):

- ***Cognition seeking***: experience sought to stimulate thought processes
- ***Sensation seeking***: Experience sought to stimulate the senses
- ***Novelty seeking experiences***: desire to seek out novel stimuli.

Types of Experiences are

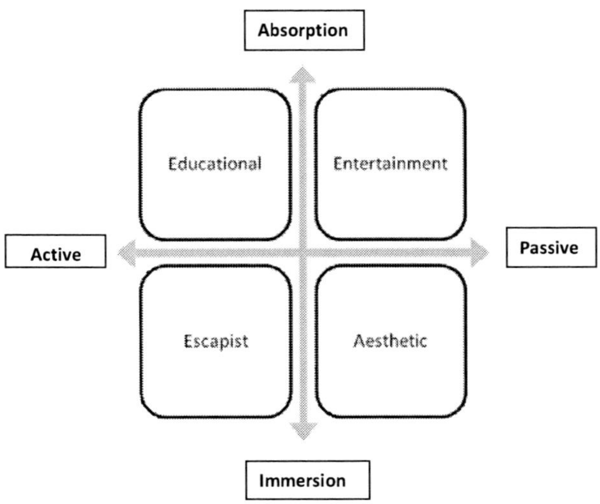

Role of Innovation in Experience Firms

Experience firms are identified on the basis of market demand, innovation effort and technology and require transformational leaders. Innovative experience firms have been observed to have more positive turnover than average firms.

The innovations required in this field don't ask for huge investments and hence economic risks connected with them are relatively low. Experience firms are generally very innovative and are driven by knowledge from customers and employees.Ideas for new innovations tend to emerge from interdependent relationship between the company, customers and the market factors. Experience firms are more innovative if there markets are international rather than national or local.

The Real Picture

The rise and continued interest in experience marketing is because it is the answer to the current problems being faced by the practitioners like difficulty of differentiating goods and services in the marketplace, recognition of the importance of customer experiences in the development of customer advocacy and a drive to achieve competitive advantage while simultaneously achieving a reduction in costs of production. When you provide customers with so much, they start expecting more. Thus, as services became inadequate, experience marketing got popular with a need to entertain, stimulate and emotionally affect consumers. Value is not added to goods or created by services but is embedded in the actual personalized experiences created through active participation.

The experience in all, can entertain, teach new skills, generate nostalgia with reminiscence and engage in fantasy of what the experience could have been. The customer goes through a pre-experience where he imagines, plans and budgets. He then lives through the experience seeking value and then in the post experience fantasizes, evangelizes, and learns from the nostalgia of the experience.

However, a major prerequisite for this experience creation is customer participation. But this in turn requires sharing of sensitive information by the people to engage in joint problem solving which they might not be comfortable with. Therefore, successful marketers need to provide proof of their trustworthiness, honesty and reliability and give their commitment for the entire consumption process, particularly at the post-experience age.

CLASSIFICATION OF EXPERIENCE SECTORS

Primary – These firms main aim is to produce experiences, e.g. tourism.

Secondary– These firms produce goods and services and use experience function as a value add-on and a marketing tool, e.g. agricultural, manufacturing and service firms.

Various experience firms could be films, festivals, sports clubs, computer game companies, design and architectural firms. While the secondary experience sector is performing well, the future trends predict that primary experience sector will soon take over. Hence innovation will be more specialized, professional and R&D based in the future.

STARBUCKS: AN EXAMPLE

Starbucks started with 4 stores in Seattle to over 17000 stores in 50 countries in 2011. They are now the world's leading retailer and roaster of brand specialty coffee. They have always placed their primary focus on quality and have a wide product range and a great service. Howard Schultz is the chief global strategist and is the man that has embraced the concept of experience and launched it in the company.

Howard Schultz: "We aren't in the coffee business, serving people. We are in the people business, serving coffee."

What differentiates them is there ***main objective***: *to serve people, not coffee.* They put the customer at the centre and then all the decisions and actions are taken keeping the customer's needs in mind. They try to offer high level of value and satisfaction by not only focusing on the product range but on the services as well.

Starbucks is the leading example of experience marketing in the world right now. The Starbuck's brand has elements of uniqueness and differentiation that are essential to create positive associations in the minds of the consumers. In 2007, they were placed 16th amongst*100 best companies to work for in Fortune magazine's list* beating their competitors,*Dunkin Donuts* and *Tim Hortons.*

Internationalization

Starbucks has been able to manage its brand image across stores in different countries with different cultures, by developed a new strategy for each country, thus strengthening their image worldwide.

They started a partnership with United Airlines to offer Starbucks coffee onboard which was a very bold step. The partnership turned out to be a huge success as they reached out to 80 million people travelling in flights annually.

They created a new range of cold coffees called *Frapuccinos* in alliance with Pepsi which won a lot of customers. They also started bottling it and this turned out to be such a huge success that they could not even keep track of the sales.

They have innovated by moving beyond making coffee to creating an environment where people want to drink coffee. They have also widened their product range to suit tastes of different people around the world and give them ample choices like, Power frapuccino and chai tea latte. They have even launched Starbucks Hearmusic which is the music you hear in a Starbucks café and can be downloaded on iTunes.

They look for ways to increase efficiency and cut down lines at customer stores, cut down delivery and management costs and increase density of number of cafes per area.

They aim to be the "*third place*" after home and work where people would like to spend most of their time. The environment is comfortable, relaxing and familiar. They have managed to retain their customers as well as employees.

Services

- They have proper trainings for all their employees. After passing the first two levels namely *Core 1* and *Core 2*, when an employee passes to a third level he/she is made a supervisor.
- The employees are given *blind tests* to become familiar with each and every product, its ingredient and flavor. Employees who respect and promote this culture are acknowledged and rewarded well.
- Employees are taught *Star skills*- describing different coffees to all customers who are not familiar with them along with nutritional information in case of diets and allergies.
- Every Starbucks café awards "*coffee master for the year*" to the employee who is best informed, most qualified and a great motivator. He is given a special status in the store and tells customers about their new products.
- The *Starbucks experience* is a very personal one where employees are encouraged to become more familiar with their customers, sometimes even being on first name basis and knowing preferences of their faithful customers.

They never promise more than they can offer, and never offer only what they promised.

DISNEYLAND: AN EXAMPLE

Walt Disney created what is called virtual/enhanced reality, unleashing his forces of Imagineeringto create a mesmerizing world of entertainment and adventure – called Disneyland on July 18, 1955. It was first of its kind place and was more than what was expected to be just another amusement park. It was like walking into an animated movie by absorbing people into a cinematic experience.

He wanted to create a "*Disney Experience*" like never before with a team of creative geniuses he called *Imagineers*.

While developing the area, he decided to keep just one entrance so that when people entered they all faced the same illusion. The first thing they saw was the looming Sleeping Beauty castle which takes you right into the world of Disney. When they walked from one place to the next, it literally felt like moving from one scene of the movie to the next. Even the vehicles to take them from one place to the next were horse carriages and fire wagons to keep up the essential first impression.

He had *brainstorming sessions* to solve practical problems being faced while making the park and to come up with new ideas to shape and define the park. The collaborative thinking process brought ideas both good and bad like*Utopia* cars and *Tomorrowland.*

He made rides which were more than just that. Peter Pan, his favorite ride made you feel like you were actually flying over landscapes. Guests would pass through the scenes by being on the dark rides and physically experience the live action scenes of the story. He made people believe, fantasy had turned into reality.

They achieved an unprecedented breakthrough in entertainment through three dimensional storytelling, causing people to directly experience and interact with the virtual world as stories and adventures came alive. Disneyland was a larger than life environment which was created by transferring blueprints into actual park virtual experience of a future world yet unknown.

Walt Disney was open to the idea of innovation and ***plussing***. He believed that Disneyland would never be done. In his words: "*Its something that will never be finished, something I can keep developing, keep plussing and adding to. Its alive*".

Disneyland has till date kept changing and upgrading, keeping its original footprint of the wondrous magical kingdom.Each frame has been created to achieve as closely a real life experience as possible.

In order to further create new illusions and keep adding to the Disneyland experience he started *Disneyland University which*trained park personnel not just to do their jobs but to perform as though they were onstage. The employees were taught to be cheerful and happy to further create the image of an optimistic world. They followed a proper dress code in line with the theme and followed special protocols.

He also made Disney characters walk around, but without talking to welcome the guests. These characters were asked to mingle with people, and pose for pictures but remain quiet all the time. This further enhanced the show compelling adults and children alike, of the world they had stepped into.

Although Disneyland is one of the best examples of what creating experience for the people can be like, it has faced a lot of criticism too. Disneyland has been dismissed as superficial and product-centred rather than being customer-centred. While there are definitely two opinions about Disneyland, experience marketing is surely here to stay, grounded in social and environmental values of the company in order to create added emotional value for the customer.

REFERENCES

[1] AnuHelkkula, ,Carol Kelleher, Circularity of customer service experience and customer perceived value, Journal of Customer Behaviour

[2] A. Talpau D. Boscor, Customer oriented marketing – A strategy that guarantees success: Starbucks and McDonalds, Bulletin of the Transilvania University of Brasov • Vol. 4 (53) •No. 1 – 2011, Series V: Economic Sciences

[3] Lars Fuglsang, Jon Sundbo and FlemmingSørensen, Dynamics of experience service innovation: Innovation as guided activity – results from a Danish Survey, The Service Industries Journal, Vol. 31, No. 5, April 2011, 661–677

[4] Caroline Tynan, Sally McKechnie, Experience marketing: A review and reassessment, Journal of Marketing Management, 2009, Vol. 25, No. 5-6, pp. 501-517

[5] Michael Morgan, Jorgen Elbe and Javier de Esteban Curiel, Has the experience economy arrived? The views of destination managers in three visitor dependent areas, International Journal of Tourism Research 11, 201-216 (2009)

[6] Gary DehrerImagineers in search of the future,The Futurist, March-April 2011

[7] Jon Sundbo, Innovation in the experience economy: A taxonomy of innovation organizations., The Service Industries Journal, Vol. 29, No. 4, April 2009, 431-455

[8] Luiz Carlos Jacob Perera, Roberto Borges Kerr, Herbert Kimura, FabianoGuasti Lima Starbucks – adding value to brand equity through an innovative brand image, Journal of Academy of Business and Economics, Vol.9, No.4, 2009

Impact of Advertising on Consumption of Beverages Especially Soft Drinks

Kumar Saurav, Ashok Sharma[1] and Lokesh Arora[2]

Institute of Management Studies, Ghaziabad
[1]Rajasthan University, Jaipur
[2]Jaipur NationalUniversity, Jaipur

ABSTRACT

Advertisement plays the major role in informing about the products and services to the target market. It is the paid form of communication to influence the behavior of the people with effective and efficient manner.The goal of advertising is to capture the largest part of the business. Most of the company especially FMCG and beverages spend huge money on advertisement but result in every cases don't same. There is a cut throat competition in market. Company think advertisement is the only weapon through which customers can know about their products and services. This is the reason company spends maximum on advertisement but this is not the real situation in market. There are many companies who spend very less on advertisement but doing well in market. On the other hand companies like HUL spends maximum amount on advertisement in spite of that company could not get result as company should. The main problem for a company is to know is it worth to spend more money on advertisement. This research paper is written for the purpose of knowing the relationship between advertising and its impact on consumption of beverages especially soft drink. 100 people have been considered for research purpose. Out of these 100 respondents70 are male and 30 are female. This research is based on empirical evidence and primary data has been collected from Alwar, a district in Rajasthan. In order to prove null hypothesis Chi-square test has been taken into consideration. Sample units are individuals especially management and engineering graduates. Researcher has collected the view of all these persons to know the relationship between advertising and its impact on consumption of beverages especially soft drinks.

INTRODUCTION

The food processing industry in India has a total turnover of around USD 65 billion which includes value added products of around USD 20.6 billion. The beverage industry in India constitutes of around USD 230 million among the USD 65 billion food processing industry. The soft drink market such as carbonated beverages and juices constitutes around USD 1 billion producing 284 million crates per year. In the peak season, the consumption capacity reaches 25 million creates per month and during off season the same goes down to 15 million crates in a month. Pepsi and Coca cola are the two leading brands in the Indian market.Advertising is one of the important parts of promotional tools of Marketing Mix, a term given by Neil Borden in 1964 in an article "*The concept of Marketing Mix*". Advertisement plays the major role in informing about the products and services to the target market. It is the paid form of communication to influence the behavior of the people with effective and efficient manner. The goal of advertising is to capture the largest possible proportion of the business. Consumption may be defined as use of final goods by a consumer until disposal. Final goods are goods that are ultimately consumed rather than used in the production of another good. A far as beverages is concerned consumption pattern of Indian people are changing day by day. In spite of awareness by different groups that consuming cold drink is not good for health, people specially youngsters prefer cold drink to fruit juice. There are many youngsters and middle and old age group person give importance to fruit juice because of rising level of health consciousness. Soft drink is a typical consumer product purchased by individuals to quench thirst and secondly for refreshment. Searching for the point of Indian soft drinks we first document on Gold Spot, this was the first brand soft drink in India. It was introduced by PARLE during later part of 40's.Cola giant, Coca-Cola was the first foreign soft drink to be introduced in India in 1965.Fruit drinks are popularly used in most urban households. If we go in history then we see the use of fruit juices began with consumption of orange juice, as a source of vitamin C to prevent scurvy disease. However, today markets are flooded with a large variety of juices *e.g.*, mango, apple, guava, litchi, grape, pineapple, etc. The main reason for increased consumption of fruit juices is changing lifestyles and rising level of health consciousness among consumers and parents. They believe that these drinks provide superior nutrition because of their fortified status and high beverage cost. Child preference, easy availability, convenience, naturalness and marketing strategies have given fruit drink industry

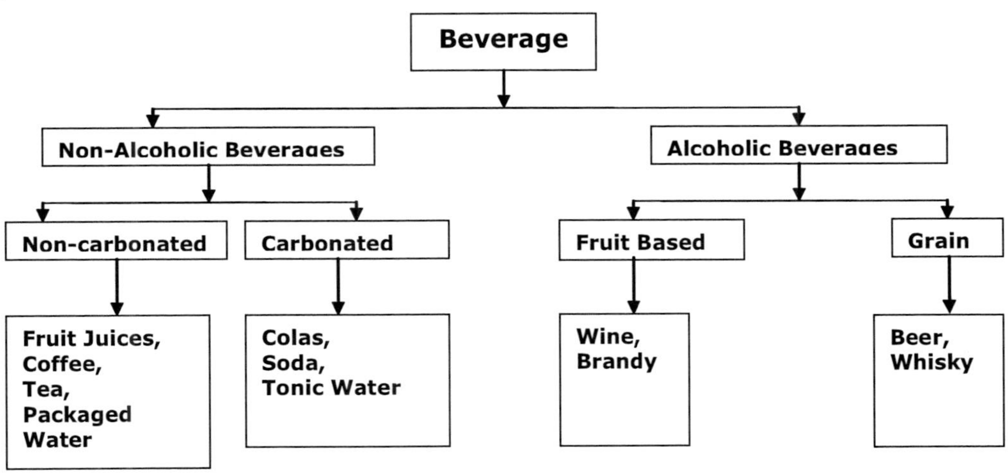

a booming growth. The exit of Coca-Cola from India in 1977 accelerated the growth of several Indian soft drinks. New soft drink in the form of Tetra pack entered the market among Frooti, Jump-In and Treetop were the prominent once.

SEGMENTATION OF SOFT DRINK PRODUCT

Segmentation on the basis of type of product

- Cola Product
- Non Cola Product

Cola products account for nearly 64% of the total soft drinks market which includes Pepsi, Coca- Cola, Thumps Up, Diet Coke and Diet Pepsi.

Non-cola segment which constitutes 36% can be divided into different categories based on the types of flavors available, namely Orange, Lime and Mango.

LITERATURE REVIEW

The impact of alcohol advertising and marketing on young people has received considerable attention. A substantial body of research has been devoted to the respective roles of family, peers, culture, social forces, media, and other significant factors in determining the decision by young people whether or not to drink. In fact, there is no compelling evidence of an unequivocal correlation between advertising and either drinking patterns among young people. Culture is one of the important reasons in consuming alcohol. It is likely that other forces, especially parental and peer influences, play a more significant role and that drinking patterns among young people are much more likely to be influenced by the prevailing culture around alcohol, than by advertising. The most powerful factors in shaping beliefs and attitudes about drinking are parental and peer influence. Alcohol advertising, on the other hand, plays only a small role.It is clear that drinking among young people is one of many risk-taking behaviors and part of a process of experimentation. For young people, as well as for adults, alcohol consumption is driven by long-term social trends. In the United States, for instance, the independent 1999 Report of the Federal Trade Commission (FTC) to the U.S. Congress found that alcohol consumption was lower than it had been in 1980. Among young people, alcohol consumption had also fallen during that period. The results from the study show that there is no clear relationship between alcohol advertising, its regulation, and either drinking patterns or problems among youth. Instead, the ESPAD Report points to the importance of culture in determining drinking patterns and problems in different societies.Denmark has a ban on all broadcast advertising except on low alcohol-content products, as well as various restrictions on print and outdoor advertising. At the same time, Denmark has one of the highest reported rates of intoxication among young people. Advertisement and consumption of alcohol is not related with each other among young people. This is culture which plays an important role while consuming alcohol. It is common belief that if a company invests heavily on advertising then market share of that particular company will increase. Advertising has a measurable effect on market share for particular brands and substitution between brands.Advertising does, however, have a measurable effect on market share for brands and a substitution effect between brands. This is not only about alcohol in fact other industries are also not restricted to advertisement. Consumer prefers only that product which suits them best. The lack of a demonstrable positive relationship between advertising and aggregate consumption is not unique to the alcohol market. In fact in other countries there is a reverse relationship between impact of advertising and consumption of alcohol. There was a sharp decline in the consumption of alcohol in spite of heavy advertisement. The experience of other industries with regard to their products is similar.In the Netherlands, Germany and the United Kingdom, alcohol consumption has declined despite increases in advertising expenditure. It is vital that companiesdifferentiate themselves from competitors by creating even more powerful, entertaining andinnovative advertisement messages, as well as sponsoring different events. However, as a consequence of long-term changes, such as the increase of a larger and morediverse range of media, as well as the arrival of new technologies, particularly the Internet,consumers have become better informed than ever, and as a result, some of the traditionaladvertising methods are no longer as effective as they used to be.Instead, firms have increasingly employed other marketing tools, such as corporatesponsorship of sports, arts and cultural events to name a few.

Advertising has a measurable effect on market share for particular brands and substitution between brands. Most of the children spend maximum time on watching television. Advertisers lured children by providing spicy food items during advisement. Children do not know the impact of that spicy food on health. They just try to have it whatever they have seen in advertisement. Children wish to buy those food items they watch on television advertisements. With the passage of time trends are getting change, many parts of the country have dozens of broadcast and cable channels and hundreds more may be on the way. Advertising's view of its audience is undergoing significant changes as well. While researchers and practitioners continue to argue the merits of globalized marketing in general and globalized advertising in particular, an intriguing phenomenon has emerged. Children are becoming more focus target market for many advertisers, and they are putting their extreme efforts to capture this valuable target market. Most of the advertisers are advertising those foods products which have above the standard level fats, more calories and salt such as confectionery, soft drinks, crisps and savory snacks, fast food and pre-sugared breakfast cereals are included in the daily lives of the children.This eating pattern is leading children towards heart disease, diabetes, hypertension and obesity in later stage of thelife.A major review of the field recently conducted by Hastings et al (2003) for the food standards agency has focused academic policy and public attention on the role that food promotion particularly television advertising plays in influencing children's food choices, defined in terms of food knowledge, preferences and behavior. Both research methods and findings addressed in this and other reviews are much contested (Paliwoda& Crawford, 2004 et.al) some reviews cover a wide terrain, examining the range of factors which may influence children's diet. Others are focusing on the direct effects of advertising on food choice. Lewis and Hill (1998) conducted a content analysis showing that food is the most advertised product category on children's television, and that confectionary, cereals and savory snacks are the most advertised.Hence, 60% of food adverts to children are for convenience foods, 6% for fast food outlets, and the remainder for cereals and confectionery.

OBJECTIVE OF THE STUDY

To find out the relationship between Advertising and its impact on consumption of beverages especially soft drinks.

SIGNIFICANCE OF THE STUDY

Beverages companies are spending lot of moneys on brand advertisement to attract customers but results are not same in every case. Study is to find out to what extent advertisement is effective for consumption of soft drink in beverage industry.

LIMITATION OF THE STUDY

- Due to lack of time, energy and money it was not possible to cover all areas of Alwar district so selected area have been taken into consideration.
- Respondents were reluctant to give answers especially female due to lack of time.
- Most of the respondents had problem in giving address and contact no.
- Working executives had no time in answering questionnaires.

HYPOTHESIS OF THE STUDY

H0: There is no significant difference between advertising and consumption of soft drinks.

H1: There is a significant difference between advertising and consumption of soft drinks.

RESEARCH METHODOLOGY

This study is based on empirical research. Researcher has collected primary data from Alwar a district of Rajasthan.

Area: Alwar, Rajasthan

Total sample size 100

Male	70
Female	30

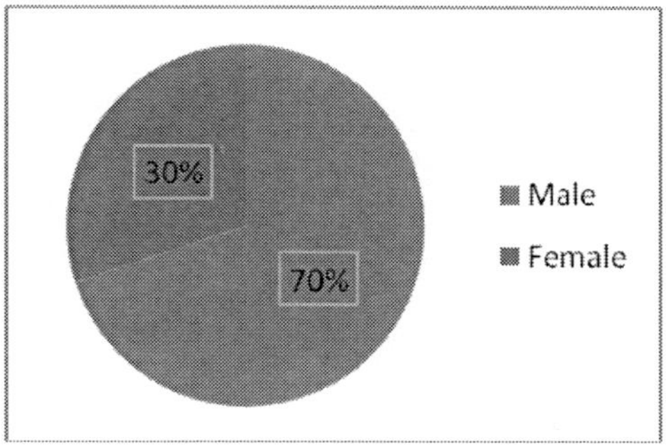

Graph 1: Total no of Male and Female out of 100 Respondents

Explanation of Graph 1

Total 100 respondents have been chosen for research purpose out of which 70% are male and 30% are female.

Sample Unit

Students of engineering and management colleges.

Testing

Chi-Square test has been considered to test null hypothesis.
Significance level: 5%
Degree of freedom: 1

Findings of the research work in the district of Alwar, Rajasthan

Total sample size:100

Pepsi: 37

Male: 32
Female: 5

Coke: 31

Male: 23
Female: 8

Others: 32

Male: 17

Female: 15

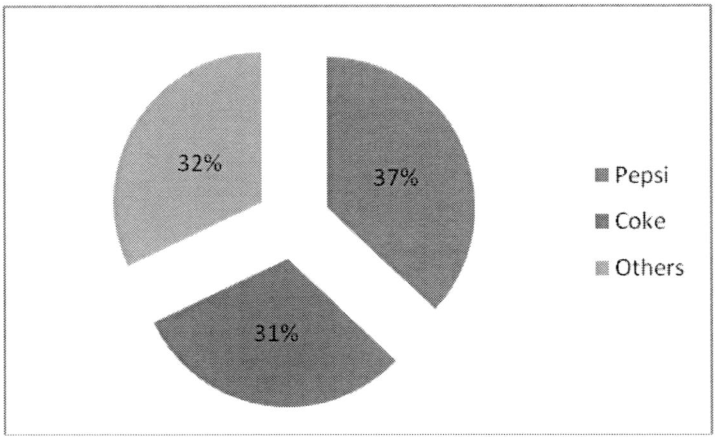

Graph 2: % of People Like Pepsi, Coke and Other Soft Drinks

Explanation of graph 2: Out of 100 respondents 37% like Pepsi, 31% like Coke and remaining 32% like others. Those respondents have included in others who does not know the varieties of Pepsi or Coke. They prefersoftdrinks other than Pepsi and Coke.

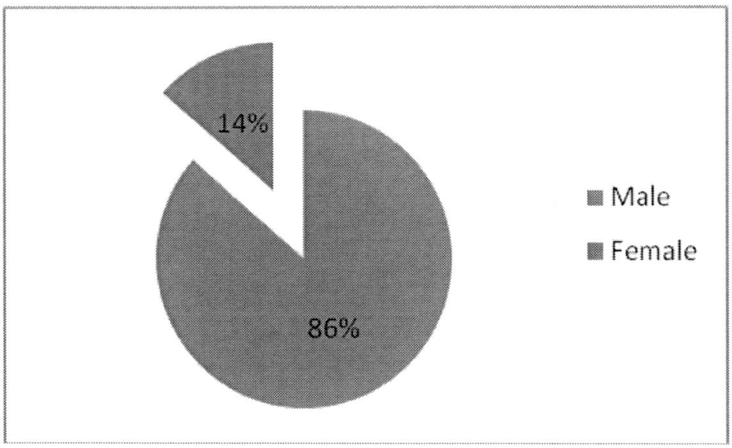

Graph 3: No. of People like Pepsi

Explanation of graph 3:

Out of 37 people like Pepsi, 86% are Male and 14% are Female.

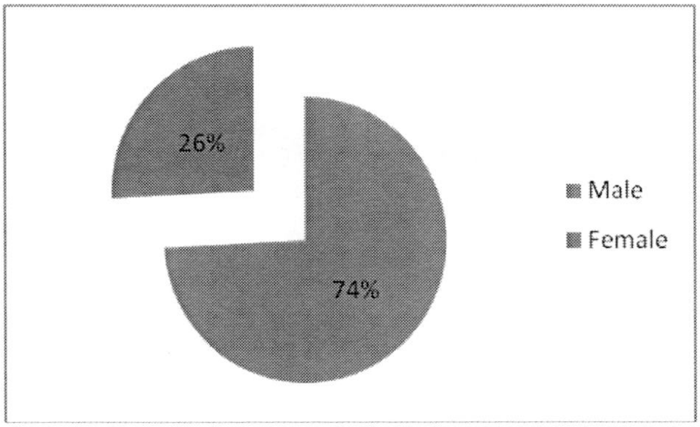

Graph 4: No. of People like Coke

Explanation of graph 4:

Out of 31 people like Coke, 74% are male and 26% are female.

Impact of Advertising on Consumption of Soft Drink

Advertisement effective: 68 (Male: 54 and Female: 14)

Advertisement not effective: 32 (Male: 29 and Female: 3)

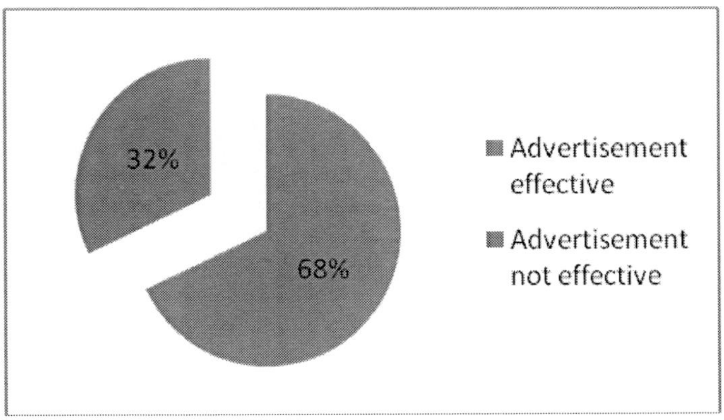

Graph 5: Advertisement Effectiveness on Consumption of Softdrink

Explanation of graph 5: Out of 100 respondents 68% said that advertisement is effective for consumption of soft drink and 32% said that advertisement is not affective for consumption of soft drink.

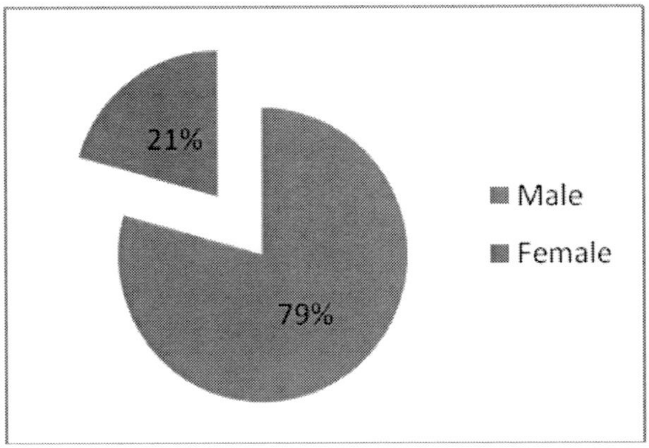

Graph 6: No of Respondents Like Advertisement

Explanation of graph 6: Out of 68 respondents who do like advertisement, 54 are male and 14 are female.

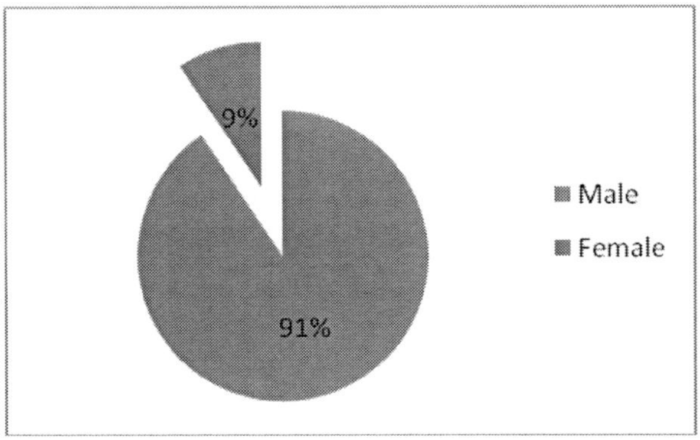

Graph 7: No of Respondents Does not Like Advertisement

Explanation of graph 7: Out of 32 respondents who does not likeadvertisement,29 are male and 3 are female.

Testing (Chi Square at 5 % significance level for 1 degree of freedom)

Data Type	*Male*	*Female*	*Total*
Advertising Effective	54	14	68
Advertising Not Effective	29	3	32
Total	83	17	100

The value of the test-statistic is

$$\chi^2 - \sum_{i=1}^{k}(O_i - E_i)^2/E_i$$

Where

x^2 = Pearson's cumulative test statistic, which asymptotically approaches a χ^2 distribution.

O_i = an observed frequency;

E_i = an expected (theoretical) frequency, asserted by the null hypothesis;

k = the number of cells in the table.

Observed Frequency (O)

Advertising effective for male	54
Advertising effective for female	14
Advertising not effective for male	29
Advertising not effective for female	03

Expected frequency (E)

Advertising effective for male	56
Advertising effective for female	12
Advertising not effective for male	27
Advertising not effective for female	05

Chi-Square Table

O	E	O- E	(O-E)2	(O-E)2/E
54	56	-2	4	4/56= 0.071
14	12	2	4	4/12= 0.333
29	27	2	4	4/27= 0.148
3	5	-2	4	4/5=0.8

- Calculated value of Chi Squarei.e.**(O-E)2/E = 1.352**

Degree of freedom = (c-1) × (r-1)

Where c is no of column and r is no of rows.

Here degree of freedom = (2-1) × (2-1) = 1

Table value of chi square for 1 degree of freedom at 5% significant level is **3.84.**

Testing of Null Hypothesis (Decision Making)

Since the calculated value of Chi square which is **1.352,**is less than the table value which is **3.84** at 5% significance level for 1 degree of freedom, so null hypothesis will be accepted. In this empirical study null hypothesis is "*There is no significant difference between advertising and consumption of cold drink*" So Null hypothesis is accepted.

CONCLUSION

It has been concluded from study on the basis of 100 samplesize that there is no significant impact of advertisement on consumption of soft drinks. If company doesnot give much importance to advertisement in spite of that customer would like to go for either Pepsi or coke. One and only thing is they should not compromise with quality of the product.

REFERENCES

[1] Agrawal and Kamakura (1995) July, "*The Economic worth of celebrity endorsers: An event study analysis*", Journal of Marketing, Vol 59, 56-62

[2] B. ZaferErdogan, Michael J. Baker and Stephen Tag (2001) June, "*Selecting Celebrity Endorsers: The Practitioner's Perspective*", Journal of Advertising Research, 39-48

[3] Erdogan (1999), "*Celebrity Endorsement: A Literature Review*", Journal of Marketing Research,15,291-314

[4] Goldsmith, Lafferty and Newell (2000), "The Impact of Corporate Credibility and Celebrity Credibility on Consumer Reaction to Advertisements and Brands", *Journal of Advertising*, Volume XXIX, number 3, 43-54

[5] McCracken, Grant (1989), "*Who is the Celebrity Endorser*?" Journal of Consumer Research, 16, (December), 310-321.

Impact of Consumer Behaviour on Social Media Marketing

Tanay Agarwal

Institute of Management Technology, Ghaziabad

ABSTRACT

Theadvent of user-generated content through a deluge of social media channelsfrom Web 2.0 era has had a colossal impact on the current commercialenvironment. Businesses and firms can no longer be satisfiedwith publishing content they desire potential customers to see. The social media landscape has instigated apower shift from the business towards the consumer. The qualitativeresearch in this study investigates the impact of consumer behaviour on these platforms. It further discusses how this has impacted traditional relationship marketing concepts, consumer expectations, conventional business-consumer relationship, relationship between user motivation and user responses towards social media, significance of positive online word of mouth and discusses about electronic word of mouth. This study explores the relationship between user motivations to use social media and user responses to social media marketing to examine the effectiveness of social media marketing.

INTRODUCTION: TARGETING THE RIGHT PEOPLE

In the bestselling marketing book, The Tipping Point, Gladwell (2000) suggests that big trends are startedby small groups of people that have the power to communicate with, inform and influence one another in society.Gladwell found that throughout history, the start and success of social, political and fashion trends can all be tracedback to specific types of people who can be categorized as connectors, mavens, or salespeople. The people that fallinto these special categories are capable of starting trends or ending them.

Connectors can help marketers communicate with the right people. Connectors are a special group ofpeople that have a gift of bringing people and ideas together and in a sense connecting people together. Any new media technology that has the ability to bring people together will have people whofunction as connectors.

Mavens are the ones thatessentially soak up information. They want to know the best deal and tell everyone about it. They arecredited with having the ability to start word-of-mouth trends with their charisma and social skills.

Sales people are individuals that have the ability to convince and sell people on new ideas. It is important to note that sales people are not hard core salesmen most people envision or even people that promote the selling conceptidentified by their ability to persuade others.

Both the mavens and sales people have the unique ability to be influencers in a consumer's decision-makingprocess. The word of mouth marketing campaigns that they can ignite can have huge ripple effects and create awave of interest and trends. In fact, "influential customers within branded customer communities can increase theeffectiveness of word-of-mouth marketing programs by as much as 50 percent" (Business Wire, 2009).

LITERATURE REVIEW

Social media, especially social networking sites (SNS), enable users to presentthemselves, establish and maintain social connections with others, and articulate their own social networks (Ellison,Steinfield, and Lampe 2007). Social media pertains to social networking amongusers, so marketing communication approaches in such user-canteredsocial networking contexts reflect the views of marketers (Mulhern 2009). The most prevailing communication approach focuses on the media features ofsocial networking, such that social connections transform intopersonal channels for brand communication (Russell 2009).

Recent studies show that experience with social networkingsites influences user responses to online shopping andadvertising (Cha 2009; Hoy and Milne 2009),and the intentions and social coherence of online community networks also shape perceptions of marketing communicationin SNS (Sohn 2009).

From a user perspective, social media use instead is driven by various gratifications, such as making new friends or locating old friends (Raacke and Bonds-Raacke 2008). Social capital and psychological well-being both drive social media use (Ellison, Steinfield, and Lampe 2007).

BEHAVIOURS IN SOCIAL MEDIA

The usage of social media in the past few years has amplified rapidly especially in the teenagers and middle aged users to communicate with each other and spend their leisure time. This existing trend and change makes people spend more time for simultaneous communication with their friends, establish friendships and spending a lot of time in the virtual world affecting consumer behaviours inexorably. Consumption related behaviours in social media can be primarily divided into two categories:

- *Before consumption* to decrease apparent risks and simplify purchasing
- *After consumption* to share satisfaction or dissatisfaction fromproducts with friends or firms.

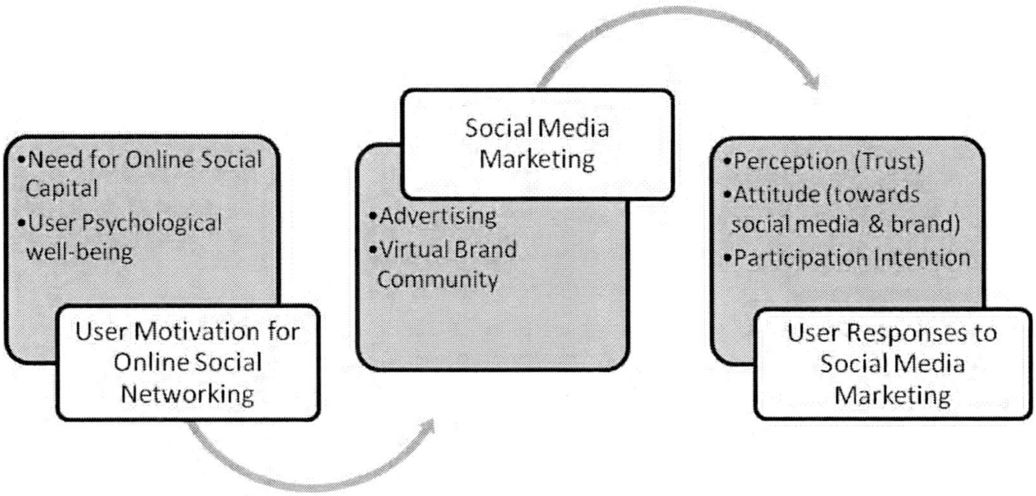

Fig. 1. Relationships between User Motivation and User Responses to Social Media Marketing

Moreover *online word of mouth* is a matter to be looked into since it is much more diverse from the traditional face-to-face word of mouth in terms of capacity to communicate with more people and likelihood of disseminating information to lots of people simultaneously.

Members of virtual communities can be believedto be a part of a promotion mix. Communications in these tools such as mailing platforms, blogs and virtual brand communities are importantmeeting locations which are created by customers that provide very useful feedbacks for firms. The monetary value of the word of mouth offered in these areas is paramount and it is seen that online word of mouth has more long term effects in comparison to the traditional word of mouth.

It is also worthwhile to mention that marketing managers should encourage online word of mouth. It isknown that most of the internet users of today's era meet at least on one social networking site and each of 50 social media sites have more than one million users in the US where they create personalized pages which consist of photos, music, books, popular links, area of intereststhereby constructing a social or professional network that covers friends and acquaintances. At this point, the probability of people stumbling upon ads has a huge prominence for firms. *Word of mouth marketing* is defined as activities of firms to encourage customer to customercommunication wilfully. Attainability and transparency of internet communication leadscompanies to follow and affect online word of mouth.

It is possible to classify the consumption related behaviours in social media asit can be concluded from the in depth interviews which were conducted on social media users:

- *Behaviours to influence other consumers*: Online opinion leadership, positive word of mouth (sharing positive experiences and advertisings, positive ideas, product rating, online linking etc.), negative word of mouth (sharing negative experiences and advertisings, negative ideas, complaints etc.)
- *Behaviours to be influenced by others for consumption*: Seeking information about products, following product review and ratings, learning new product, brand and promotions, being influenced by advertising and public relations activities.
- *Consumption related communication*: Making purchase decisions thorough social media (Social activities, entertainment, travel, etc.), communication with firm by social media, convey problems, dissatisfactions, satisfaction to firm etc.

These behaviours may take place before,after or during consumption and may be positive or negative. For understanding such situations in a better manner, word of mouth behaviour in social communication sites has tobe understood which is strongly related with repurchases and brand switching behaviours.

Persuasivenesslevel of social communication tools is closelyassociated with resemblance of interests of individuals and attitudes towardsforums. Therefore, this situation also affects the purchasing intentions of customers. High reliability,anonymity, low-cost and high interaction are stated as other characteristics of *Electronic Word of Mouth*.The suggestions which are generated in Electronic Word of Mouth are more reliable in terms of marketer generated information, since it's a customer to customer communication. Online networks consist of "nodes"(firm, country, person etc.) and "links" (friendship, kinship, interestetc.). Since word of mouth communication is animportant factor that affects consumer behaviours, this behaviour tendency has to be measured andmanaged. It has been observed in various studies conducted excessive satisfaction or dissatisfaction leads to more online word ofmouth behaviour.

Participants of social networks share personal preferences and experiences with each other.When network word of mouth is considered in terms of communication process, the sender contributesto theprocess enthusiastically and affects brand switching behaviours (especially with negative information), senderand receiver communicate in a free and opened virtual place, communication occurs efficiently andsimultaneously. At this point companies have to take attention true, reliable and customer driveninformation, create positive word of mouth, focus on the long term customer- firm relationships,encourage customers for these positive behaviours and emphasize on opinion leaders with a win-winstrategy. Moreover online word of mouth behaviour affects customer behaviours in shopping web sites.

Research indicates the direct and positive relationship between product ratings and sales. Moreoverpositive reviews are perceived as more qualified. But editor reviews affect negatively the web site meeting tendency accordingto same study. A study indicates that individuals have a tendency to make andread negative product evaluations which resulted to decrease brand value.

The online word of mouth communication is measured with two concepts

- online opinion leadership
- online opinion seeking level

Analysis and Discussion

From the data analysed it can be concluded thatthe relationship between the consumer and abusiness has changed significantly as a result ofsocial media. These platforms facilitate the formationof relationships in terms of customer acquisition,but they are more useful and regarded asmore appropriate for relationship maintenance asa customer retention platform thus impacting business-consumer expectations. The social media empoweredconsumer has emerged.

MOTIVATIONS

Users experience a sense of guilt for excessive useof these channels. Social media offers users theopportunity to interact with others, but it alsoallows the participants to observe individuals onthese platforms without revealing their presence.This anonymous observation has very negativeimplications for the respondents. These feelingsof guilt indicate to a perception of social media asan infatuationthat must be dealt with at the earliest. Participantswere found to be immenselydependent on social media asa means for both interacting with social connectionsand feeling involved and aware of what theirfriends are doing. In theculturewhere we live today, an individual's sense of belongingand thus a sense of one's self are inseparably linked tosocial media. This has created a type of virtualpeer pressure to consume social media as usersseek out activities and eventsthat are favourable to others.Users feel pressurised to interact with businesses bytheir online peers yielding to the functional aspect of motivation. The view of their online peers is very important to them. Marketers can increase brand value by activelyengaging the consumer in media experienceby providing them with an online space wherethey can generate their own material.

PERCEPTIONS

Social media is a realm where users are very awareof the fact that business and users within theircommunity can access their information and viewtheir actions. Thus, this hascreated a sense of paranoiaand many users are reluctant to accept businesses. It is in the interest of a business toemphasise on its social media platforms that itrespects the privacy of its users and does not distributethe personal information of its connections.In this way it increases the sense of trustbetween a user and the business and in turn thiscreates a long term relationship. In contrast, consumersdo see the personalisation of communications as favourable and are more open to marketingthat is relevant to their own personal interestsand needs.

CONSUMER CONTROL AND BRAND BONDING

The researchers found that consumers are morechallenging than ever before and have huge expectationsof their relationship with a business. Thereis an emerging egocentrism among social mediausers as a result of their empowerment and controlin the social media landscape. An inconsistency wasidentified between traditional relationship marketingand the relationships observed onlineas a result of consumer empowerment. This isbecause this relationship is now bi-directional andcontrolled by the consumer. The social consumerhas emerged: cynical, untrusting and highlydemanding. Relationship marketing strategies mustbe altered to accommodate this prevalent trend.With this in mind the researcher developed theconsumer contact cycle.

The Consumer Contact Cycle

The consumer contact cycle reflects the difficultya business can have in establishing a relationshipwith a consumer on a social media platform.Initially, a business requests the friendship of auser, or a user is suggested to befriend the businessby another contact. Though, the bond canbe severed by eroding consumer belief at eachwarning point. This cycle identifies the control ofthe consumer in the relationship formationprocess and it is not until all four stages are completethat brand bonding occurs and the consumeris considered to be in a relationship withthe business. Evidently it can be a complex task tosecure a relationship with a consumer on socialmedia, however, when brand bonding takes place the virtual value of the consumer can proveinvaluable to a business. This is because thebrand-consumer bond imitates a real life friendship.By virtue of being an arena originally establishedto enable friendship making among individuals,consumers associate accepting a businessas a contact with a real-life friendship. The bondis therefore strong; however, much like a humanrelationship trust is supreme and both partiesare expected to fulfil their side of the liaison.

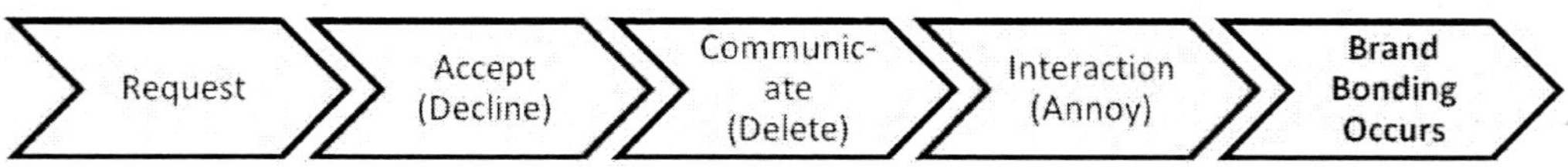

Fig. 2: Consumer Contact Cycle

Although the social media empowered consumercan be far more high maintenance than traditionalconsumers, they can also act as important sourcesof information. They can considerably influencetheir online communities in their buyinghabits and can eventuallybenefit a business in itsproduct and service strategies by assuming the roleof co-creators. This is the utmost level of value aconsumer can provide to a business, as once thesesteps have been accomplished a business can participatein *social CRM* and truly please its customers, thereby creatinglong term and co-operative relationships. Thisleadsus to the *virtual value ladder*of a social media consumer.

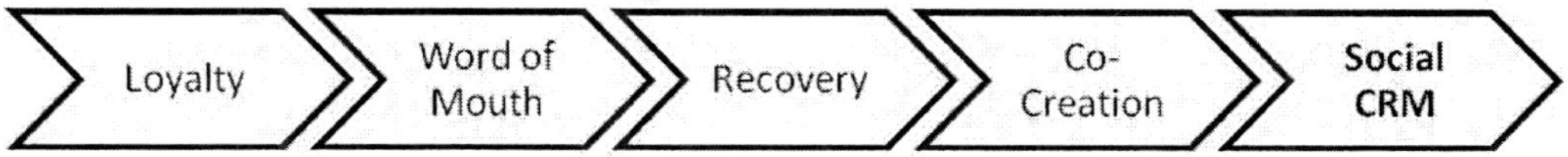

Fig. 3. Virtual Value Ladder

RELATIONSHIP RECOVERY AND WORD OF MOUSE

Consumers today are more critical anduntrusting of marketing communications than ever before in the history of social media. Social media allows a business to overcome these issues as unlike other mediums, often consumers are oblivious about the fact that they are being marketed toand conspicuousness alone can increase their brand awareness.Furthermore, businesses can target opinion leaders on these sites in order to stimulate an extensive audience.

CONCLUSION

There is adefinite perception among industry professionalsand consumers alike that there *is* a right and awrong way to carry out social media for business. In fact, it can be more detrimental to the reputation of a brand to ineffectively operate these platformsthan to refrain altogether.

The most noteworthyfactors for the consumer are *relevance*, *personalisation* and *the quantity of communications* they receive. From a professional point of view, social mediamust be regarded as a vital element to the marketing mix of a firm which should be managed by a social media educated manager on a constant basis. It is hereby recommended that it is essential to appoint a specific social media marketing manager within a business to control the running of the siteand preserve the *'face'* of the company. It is an avenue that allows the consumer to view a businessas a person, to form a real friendship, andthus it is of great value to a firm. Social mediais a medium that allows the consumer to see the human side of acorporation, which increases the possibility ofrecovery in a negative situation, providing a business with the opportunity to recuperate a consumers' trust.

Social Media has completely redefined the dynamics of the business to consumer relationship,transforming it from a one-dimensional occurrence to a bidirectional social bond.As a result of consumer empowerment, the power of word of mouth marketing and the emergence of social CRM, it hascertainly been found that traditional relationship marketing strategies require further updation.

REFERENCES

[1] Gladwell, M. (2000), "The tipping point: How little things can make a big difference", *New York: Little, Brown, and Company.*

[2] Research Reveals Word-of-Mouth Campaigns on Customer Networks Double Marketing Results, *Buiness Wire.* (27th October)

[3] Ellison, N. B., Steinfield, C. and Lampe C. (2007), "The Benefits of Facebook 'Friends': Social Capital and College Students' Use of Online Social Network Sites", *Journal of Computer-Mediated Communication*, Vol. 12, No.4.

[4] Mulhern, F. (2009), "Integrated Marketing Communications: From Media Channels to Digital Connectivity", *Journal of Marketing Communications*, Vol. 15,No. 2-3, pp. 85-101.

[5] Russell, M. G. (2009), "A Call for Creativity in New Metrics for Liquid Media",*Journal of Interactive Advertising*, Vol. 9 No. 2, pp. 3-24.

[6] Cha, J. (2009), "Shopping on Social Networking WebSites: Attitudes toward Real versus Virtual Items",*Journal of Interactive Advertising*, Vol. 10 No. 1, pp. 77-93.\

[7] Hoy, M. G. and Milne, G. (2010), "GenderDifferences in Privacy-Related Measures for Youn Adult Facebook Users",*Journal of Interactive Advertising*, Vol. 10 No. 2, pp. 28-45.

[8] Sohn, D. (2009), "Disentangling the Effects of Social Network Density on Electronic Word-of-Mouth (eWOM)Intention," *Journal of Computer-Mediated Communication*, Vol. 14 No. 2, pp. 362-367.

[9] Raacke, J. and Bonds-Raacke, J. (2008), "MySpace and Facebook: Applying the Uses and Gratifications Theory toExploring Friend-Networking Sites",*Cyber Psychologyand Behaviour*, Vol. 11 No. 2, pp. 169-74.

[10] Wright, E., Khanfar, N. M., Harrington, C. and Kizer, L. E. (2010), "The Lasting Effects of Social Media Trends on Advertising", *Journal of Business & Economics Research*, Vol. 8, No. 11, pp. 73-80.

[11] Chung C., and Austria, K., "Social Media Gratification and Attitude toward Social Media Marketing Messages: A Study of the Effect of Social Media Marketing Messages on Online Shopping Value", *Northeast Business & Economics Association*, pp. 581-586.

[12] Hutton, G. and Fosdick, M. (2011), "The Globalization of Social Media: Consumer Relationships with Brands Evolve in the Digital Space", *Journal of Advertising Research*, pp. 564-570.

[13] Chi,H. H. (2011), "Interactive Digital Advertising vs. Virtual Brand Community: Exploratory Study of User Motivation and Social Media Marketing Responses in Taiwan", *Journal of Interactive Advertising*, Vol. 12, No. 1 (Fall 2011), pp. 44-61.

[14] O'Brien, C. (2011), "The Emergence of the Social Media Empowered Consumer", *Irish Marketing Review*, Vol. 21, No. 1 & 2, pp. 32-40.

Impact of Sales Force Automation on Sales Force Productivity

AnkitaVarma, Esha Kumar and Daksha Shukla

Institute of Management Technology, Ghaziabad

ABSTRACT

Sales Force Automation (SFA)is a technology that complements the sales function. The technology enables organizations to manage sales pipelines, follow contacts and configure products. The discussion is initially focused on defining sales force automation, vendor segmentations and software details. The paper is an attempt to study the impact of SFA on sales force productivity. Current research in this domain stresses on efficiency issues within the firm, with key focus on technology implementation and reasons for high SFA failure rates. The authors review past literature and assess potential areas for future research.

INTRODUCTION

SFA systems are designed to provide technological support to the sales teams. Such applications came into being in the mid-eighties. Prior to SFA tools like sales forecasting and specialized tools for contract management were prevalent. These tools now form a part of a bundle of applications offered by vendors that are being used in business to business transactions. SFA is now looked at as a 'competitive imperative' (Morgan and Inks 2001) that offer 'competitive parity' (Engle and Bargnes 2000). Let us look at issues such as how SFA impacts the productivity.

DEFINITION OF SFA

Morgan and Inks in 2001 gave a definitions stating SFA systems make use of computer hardware and software to take data as input and provide automated collection, assimilation, analysis and distribution of information to improve the productivity. Another way to define SFA is as SFA applies technology to the selling function as stated by Pullig*et al.* in 2002.

As mentioned earlier SFA comes with a package of sales forecasting and contract management so in other words SFA complements the sales function by enhancing the performance of information flow among the sales team, consumer and organization (Speier and Venkatesh 2002). SFA systems include of centralized database systems which can be accessed via modem through remote computers making use of a specific SFA application so that a sales person can get instant update regarding various aspects of the job (Parthasarathy and Sohi 1997).

Therefore the definition of SFA can be stated as the application of information technology comprising both software and hardware to complement the sales function. SFA is a part of the company wide IT system connecting and integrating the sales activities with the other functions of the organization (J.Ranjan and S.Puri 2010)

SFA as a software records various stages of the sales process from automated collection, assimilation to analysis and distribution of information in order to enhance the efficiency and effectiveness of the sales force in a company. Some basic functionality offered by SFA are account management, incentive management, sales forecasting and workflow and process management. SFA application is most commonly available in two packages first as a part of CRM Suite and second as a part of Enterprise Suite or as SFA specialists a standalone SFA application. Some popular vendors of SFA specialists are Selectica, EzRoute, Salesnet etc., CRM Suites are offered by Siebel, Onyx and Enterprise Suite is offered by vendors like Oracle, SAP, Epicor.

NEED AND IMPACT OF SFA

A good sales force is the companies' lifeline. They form the top and the bottom line of a company and in today's dynamic environment the challenges faced by a sales force are very demanding. This is where SFA comes into play by managing the sales cycle from pre-sales to post – sales support needed by customers. By maintaining an automatized business data sheet SFA helps increase efficiency of the sales process. SFA reduces redundancy of data to prevent duplication of sales force effort and also preventing customer's negative reactions. By providing clear and detailed views of various aspects of sales such as list of potential customers or their contact details they make the overall decision making process easier from both ends – sales force and customer. The end result of a successful SFA implementation can dramatically shorten the overall sales cycle and increase revenues while increasing staff productivity and improving customer satisfaction levels(J.Ranjan and S.Puri 2010).

A detailed view of meetings, follow-ups, interaction with prospects, various stages of sales stages helping sales managers as well as sales representatives in doing their job more efficiently.

SFA implementations have both task and non-task outcomes as per Kraemer and Danziger (1990). The task outcomes like effects on productivity and the non-task outcomes can be accounted for in effects on job enhancement and social interactions. The research done on this topic is concerned mostly with task-related outcomes. Cronin and Davenport (1990) conducted one of the early studies to measure the benefits of SFA implementation in a single manufacturing company. Their findings indicated a number of hard and soft outcomes like improved knowledge management, better time management and, structural, cultural and motivational.

A few impacts that came across during the research were : on investigating a pharmaceutical company's operations in three countries, Engle and Barnes (2000) found a clear relationship between the adoption of SFA and the performance of salesperson. Ahearne and Schillewaert(2001) also found positive correlations between SFA implementation and sales representatives' market and technical knowledge, call productivity, adaptive selling, and targeting skills. Ahearne*et al.* (2004), in a later study consisting of 131 sales representatives from a mid-sized American pharmaceutical company, found a curvilinear relationship between SFA usage, as measured over a 3-month period, and salesperson performance, as measured by sales against quota.

WHY DO SFAs FAIL?

Prime reason for failure of SFA is the lack of general acceptance and usage among the sales people. Sales people need to be integrated with the SFA for better implementation and success of SFA. Another factor attributed to the failure of SFA is that technology cannot be implemented in each and every sales situation and it does not necessarily improve the performance. In fact it can be detrimental at times. Also SFA can be costly and take time for development. People expect it to be ready in a matter of days at a minimal cost, whereas they take 12-24 months for complete development. Also implementing the SFA today does not necessarily means instant results. It takes time for its acceptance and for it to provide results and can take few years. Lack of implementation can also be attributed to the fact that SFA needs to be focused on specific situations and on the best practices for the sales people. A lot of research is still required and for it many insights can be gained by focusing it on the firms and sales people where the implementation of SFA has been successful. To make SFA a success it is of utmost importance to make sure that future research delineates past failures. It should be more focused on the role of sales manager and sales personnel, and how technology can be beneficial to them both. Also sales manager have to play the role of educating and promoting successful usage of sales technology. Another point to make here is the organizational and environmental factors in the in the SFA adoption and usage.

Two different firms were investigated by Speier and Venkatesh (2002), where SFA technologies were withdrawn after implementation. A number of variables were examined such as age and sex, disposition towards technology, role perceptions and other organizational attributes such as management support and user involvement. There were many scales which were validated in other contexts but the salespeople turned against the system, demonstrating their dissatisfaction with increased absenteeism and voluntary turnover. Even the performance was not improved post SFA implementation. One of the most important reasons behind this was the misfit between the SFA tools and sales force in terms of technology. Following the performance of the company for another six months, they found out that post implementation, organizational job commitment, job satisfaction, salesperson organizational fit and salesperson-job fit had also decreased to a great extent.

WHY DO SFAs SUCCEED?

The major factor for the SFA to succeed is the people who are using it, the sales people. Much of the success of it depends on how salespeople use it and how they handle it the sales process. Success of SFA also depends on the two-stage implementation in which organization adopts it in the first phase followed by salespeople in the second phase. It should be a concentrated and rewarding effort so that everyone has a willingness to change. In these times of intense competition, SFA is a much needed tool. It enables businesses to effectively manage the entire sales cycle, from the lead generation to post-sales service and support to the customers. It enables sales management to capture and maintain up-to-date business data that will impact the entire sales process. Also a younger workforce helps in a smooth implementation of SFA (Speier and Venkatesh, 2002) as they are more technology oriented and have good understanding of it (Parthasarathy and Sohi, 1997).

Classification of Critical Success Factors (Puri, Singla, Malhotra and Wahie, 2011)

Category of Variable	*Item*
Organization/Cultural	Organizational encouragement and support; senior management facilitation and buy-in; entrepreneurial values; customer orientation; adaptive cultural norms.
Project-related	Deployment of a multidisciplinary implementation team; user group involvement; customer involvement; well-developed project plan; appropriate-to-task training.
Inter-personal	High levels of inter-personal trust; sensitive management of user expectations; information-sharing culture.
Intra-personal	Adaptability; perceived usefulness of the technology; perceived ease-of-use; strong belief that the technology will enable desired outcomes; skills in computer use.
Technical	Data availability; development costs; access to a competent IT/IS resource; degree of change required; technology fit to job role; fragmented and poor quality data.

SALES FORCE PRODUCTIVITY: QUESTIONS FOR RESEARCH

The adoption and implementation of technology among the sales force is still a very important area for research as it does focus on a critical aspect of productivity. 'User acceptance' is one of the key reasons cited for failure of SFA in management literature (Trailer and Dickie, 2006).

Success or failure of any technology depends on the willingness of people to adopt the technology. Companies continue to spend billions of dollars in Sales Force Automation applications every year. Unfortunately, most of the time the actual outcome of this implementation is rarely seen to be proportionate to the amount of investment made. One of the key reasons attributed to this in management literature is the failure of salespeople to perceive SFA as an empowering technology. Salespeople equate SFA with loss of autonomy, power and valuable data. Another cause of failure of SFA as a technology is the lack of willingness in salespeople to learn the technology.

EFFICIENCY ISSUES

A key efficiency issue is the SFA acceptance and usage among salespeople. Current selling environment calls for better understanding of why some sales force automation software implementationexperienced failure, demands of the current selling process and reasons for success in some cases.

Research focused on SFA failures is critical as it helps understand the antecedents of SFA failures. Complexity of sales environment calls for research with emphasis on sales manager/ salesperson interaction. Research which identifies environmental and organizational causes of SFA failure/success is critical. Research opportunities are also associated with how SFA can contribute in improvement of efficiency of each step of the selling process.

Another widely used application of SFA is contact management (Trailer andDickie, 2006). Using a metric based approach researchers can explore how SFA applications can play a pivotal role in improve the efficiency at each step of selling - prospecting, lead generation, and ultimately, qualifying potential customers.

Sales presentations are an important aspect of selling. Salespeople use a variety of devices to present during sales presentations. Technology enables salespeople to connect to central databases and repositories which contain fact sheets, customer testimonials, web pages, streaming media, etc., during sales presentations. Research is required to assess how this technology can be used for handling customer objections as well.

EFFECTIVENESS ISSUES

There is a significant opportunity to divert research efforts in understanding of the role of SFA on improving productivity from a relationship selling or an effectiveness perspective. Important SFA effectiveness issues in an organization include: a better understanding of SFA productivity from a relationship selling perspective, understanding the real versus the statistical customer, a better understanding of quality versus quantity of information, the importance of shared value between buyer and seller, and, determining ways to measure SFA effectiveness. (*Puri, Singla, Malhotra and Wahie, 2011*)

Literature review on the topic suggests that there is very little research effort that has been made on studying the effectiveness dimension of SFA. As a result areas such as relational SFA are not explored sufficiently. Future research on SFA needs to move beyond the traditional view of SFA as a transactional tool that is focused on sales efficiencies and throw light on the "relational" capability of SFA.

Information has never been as critical as it is today in the sales environment. Salespeople now need the right information at the right time, and must deliver it in the right manner to maintain and enhance customer relationships and productivity. In order to draw the entire potential of a SFA application in a relationship marketing context, the role of SFA in re-humanizing the customer to the organization is an important research topic. Baker and Leak (2006) recently reported that "mathematical modelling of humanity promises to be one of the great undertakings of the 21st century." The challenge lies in understanding how salespeople can derive benefit from the information available without minimum human judgement. Another future research topic with SFA is in understanding the relationship between the information and salesperson effectiveness. Sometimes SFA technologies can be an area of concern to the sales organization. One such case is information overload, which in turn may impact sales effectiveness. Almost all organizations are collecting data, but the productive use of the same is still a big challenge.(Jones *et al.* 2005).With the importance of data in a salespersons life, the potential of SFA to not only increase the amount of information available, but also the quality of information in a timely manner at the point of consumption to improve salesperson *knowledge* is of importance.

SFA literature indicates a gap in terms of studying the effect of SFA on customers. Organizations need to focus on customers along with technology innovations. In order to include customers into research studies, various metrics will need to be employed. Longitudinal studies that map changes in key metrics such as satisfaction, loyalty, repurchase intentions, trust, commitment, etc., should be used.

CONCLUSION

In the era of knowledgeable and demanding customers, sales force technology can help salespeople improve by many folds. From a research perspective it is critical to focus on both sides of the coin i.e. doing things right (efficiency) and doing the right things (effectiveness). The relational/shared value emerging from this technology should be explored from a relationship marketing context. With the pace at which the selling environment is changing future SFA research on effectiveness is critical.

REFERENCES

[1] Ahearne, M. and Schillewaert, N. (2001), The acceptance of information technology in the sales force, eBusiness Research Center, Working paper 10–2000, Penn State University.

[2] Ahearne, M., Srinivasan, N. and Weinstein, L. (2004), Effect of technology on sales performance: progressing from technology acceptance to technology usage and consequence,*Journal of Personal Selling and Sales Management*, 24(4), 297–310.

[3] Baker, S., & Leak, B. (2006), Math will rock your world, *Business Week*, Jan 23, 54.

[4] Cronin, B. and Davenport, E. (1990), Laptops and the marketing information chain: the benefits of sales-force automation, *International Journal of Information Management*, 10, 278–287.

[5] Erffmeyer, R. C. and Johnson, D. A. (2001), An exploratory study of sales force automation practices: expectations and realities, *Journal of Personal Selling and Sales Management*, 21(2), 167–175.

[6] Gohmann, S. F., Guan, J., Barker, R. M. and Faulds, D. J. (2005), Perceptions of sales force automation: differences between sales force and management, *Industrial Marketing Management*, 34(4), 337–343.

[7] Engle, R. L. and Barnes, M. L. (2000), Sales force automation usage, effectiveness, and cost–benefit in Germany, England and the United States, *Journal of Business and Industrial Marketing*, 15(4), 216– 242.

[8] Jones, E., Brown, S. P., Zoltners, A. A., &Weitz, B. A. (2005), The changing environment of selling and sales management, *Journal of Personal Selling and Sales Management,*2, (Spring), 105-111.

[9] Keillor, B.D., Bashaw, R.E. and Pettijohn, C.E. (1997), Sales-force automation issues prior to implementation: the relationship between attitudes towards technology, experience and productivity, *Journal of Business and Industrial Marketing*, 12(3/4), 209–219.

[10] Kraemer, K. L. and Danziger, J. N. (1990), The impacts of computer technology on the worklife of information workers, *Social Science Computer Review*, 8(Winter), 592–613.

[11] Morgan, A. and Inks, S. A. (2001), Technology and the sales force, *Industrial Marketing Management*, 30(5), 463–472.

[12] Parthasarathy, M. and Sohi, R. (1997), Sales-force automation and the adoption of technology innovations by sales people: theory and implications, *Journal of Business and Industrial Marketing*, 12(3/4), 196–208.

[13] Pullig, C., Maxham III, J.G. and Hair, J.F. Jr (2002), Sales-force automation systems: an exploratory examination of organizational factors associated with effective implementation and sales-force productivity, *Journal of Business Research*, 55, 401–415.

[14] Puri, S. and Ranjan, J.(2011) 'Value drivers for technology enabled sales force automation', *Int. J.Electronic Customer Relationship Management*, Vol. 5, Nos. 3/4, pp.259–271.

[15] Ranjan, J. and Puri, S.(2011) 'Sales force automation: research agenda', *Int. J. Value ChainManagement*, Vol. 5, No. 2, pp.141–150.

[16] Speier, C. and Venkatesh, V. (2002), The hidden minefields in the adoption of sales force automation technologies, *Journal of Marketing*, 66(3), 98–111.

[17] Taylor, T.C. (1993) 'Getting in step with the computer age', *Sales and Marketing Management,*March, Vol. 145, No. 3, pp.52–59.

[18] Trailer, B. andDickie, J. (2006), Understanding what your sales manager is up against, *Harvard Business Review,* (July/August), 48-55.

[19] Widmier, S., Jackson, D. and McCabe, D. (2002) 'Infusing technology into personal selling',*Journal of Personal Selling & Sales Management*, Vol. 22, No. 3, pp.189–198.

Influence of Children in Purchase Decision Making in a Family - A Study of Ghaziabad City

Eshwarya Pathak, Dhiraj Jain, Ved Shah and Dheeraj Goyal

Institute of Management Technology, Ghaziabad

ABSTRACT

Family as a consuming and decision-making unit is a central phenomenon in marketing and consumer behavior. Children are the most important elements in the family.In past, the purchase decision making in the family was confined to parents, children's were just the passive observers. But now with the changing scenario, children are given opportunities for decision-making and also influence the purchasing decisions of the parents.

The aim of this paper is to evaluate the extent of influence exerted by children on a family purchase decision-making. In this paper, child influence is studied from various perspectives. The degree of children's influence depends mostly on the type of product and stage of decision-making process. For some products, they are active initiators, information seekers, and buyers; whereas for other product categories, they influence purchases made by the parents.

To achieve the objective, primary research was conducted constituting 121 respondents of Ghaziabad city. The data was collected with the help of structured questionnaire containing questions about demographic profile and factors influencing purchase decision of children. Respondents include parents with children aged 3-15 years.The data was analyzed with the help of Microsoft Excel and appropriate hypothesis testing tools like Chi Square, ANNOVA and factor analysis will be applied. The study helped us to know the factors which influenced a child's decision making in a family and the extent to which they influence purchasing decisions.

INTRODUCTION

Family as a consuming and decision making unit is a central phenomenon in marketing and consumer behavior. Therefore,the domain has attracted the interest of marketers and marketing academics over the years. The family is a complex unit comprised of individuals with varied cognitive, emotional, and behavioral characteristics and abilities that can greatly affect family decision making across an individual's life-span. "Decision-making" describes the process by which families make choices, judgments, and ultimately come to conclusions that guide behaviors. The family has been identified as the most important decision making and consumption unit. Family decision-making implies that more than one member's input and agreement is involved. Children play very important role in family buying decision making for their own products as well as products used or consumed by other family members. Children today have a more important place in the society than their parents ever had. They not only are consumers but have a considerable influence may be direct or indirect influence in the family purchase decisions. It is seen that children not only influence family purchase decision but they also insist their parents to purchase the products they desire. Children's influence differs depending on the product category and decision-making stage. The purpose of this paper is to examine parents perception of their children's (3-20year's old) participation in and general influence on the family decision making process when purchasing in 09 different product categories.The degree of influence depends on various factors like age, gender family type etc. Also, the roles played by children with respect to various categories of products as initiator, influencer or final purchaser also is studied in this paper. The research conducted is descriptive and statistical tool like chi-square is used to analyze the factors influencing child for decision making.

LITERATURE REVIEW

Consumer behaviour" (Commuri and Gentry, 2000, pp. 1). There are many joint decisions, made by the consumers with the family members, which in turn has an effect on other family members. Family as a consuming and decision making unit is a central phenomenon in marketing (Foxall, 1977). Thus, Kotler (1972) identifies six roles that may be performed by various family members. A family member may play the role of initiator (recognize the problem or find the need for the item), influencer (he may persuades others in a purchase situation), information gatherer (he or more individuals may look for information related to the 12 possible purchase) or a decision maker (having the upper hand to make buying decision) – mostly joint decision are made. A marketer should carefully study the roles and be able to differentiate every family member's role (Kotler, 1972).

Boys were seen to be more influential for products like video games and CD's were as girls influence was seen to be high in household items like cloths, bakery items and writing [5, 6, 9]. Gender differences were also studied by Cowan &Avants[10], Maccoby[11] which indicated that boys and girls do not vary in their number of influence efforts, but do vary in their influence style.

Kapoor (2001) Investigated influence of children in family purchase decisions for consumer durables The consumer behavior of the children targeting on the adolescents is greatly influenced by peers (Campbell, 1969). Peer influence is maximum during early adolescence (age 14 years) and then it gradually decreases through middle and late adolescence (Brown, Clasen, &Eicher, 1986; Steinberg & Silverberg, 1986, as cited by Mangleburg). Reisman and Roseborough

(1955, as cited by Moschis and Churchill, 1978) speculated that children gain knowledge of expressive elements (styles and moods) of consumption from the peers.

The influence of television advertising on younger children takes place at various levels including the advertiser's "immediate product-persuasion effects" (Kaur, and of commercials over time (Kaur, and Singh, 2006). When a child's age increases their attitudes towards ads changes from positive to negative, where they become skeptical of advertising (John, 1999).

RESEARCH OBJECTIVES

- To study child's role in purchase decision making with respect to different product categories.
- To ascertain difference in degree of influence while buying different products.
- To study the impact of gender of children in family purchase decision making.
- To analyze the difference in amount of influence the child has in purchase decision making belonging to different family types.
- To ascertain the significance of child's age on his/her influence in purchase decision making
- To study the impact of family income on child's influence in purchase decision making with respect to different products.

RESEARCH METHODOLOGY

Research design	Descriptive nature
Sampling unit	Parents
Sampling size	121
Sampling method	Convenience sampling
Nature of data	Primary
Method of data collection	Schedule
Type of Schedule	Structured Schedule Containing questions having Likert type scale & ranking method.
Type of questions	Close ended questions
Statistical tools used	Chi-square test

DATA ANALYSIS

1. Daily time spend with the family

Time	*Frequency*
Less than 1 hour	3
1-3 hours	30
3-5 hours	42
More than 5 hours	46

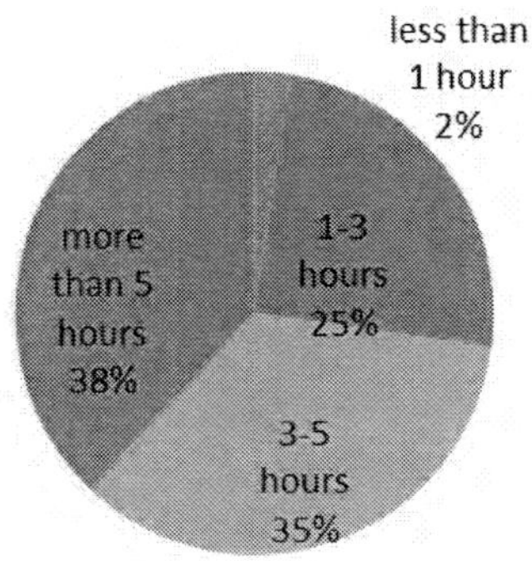

Fig. 1. Daily Time Spend with Family

From the results revealed in the figure1 it is clear that most the parents spend more than 5 hours with their children.

2. Opinion of children is considered while making purchase decisions

Response	*Frequency*
Yes	79
No	42

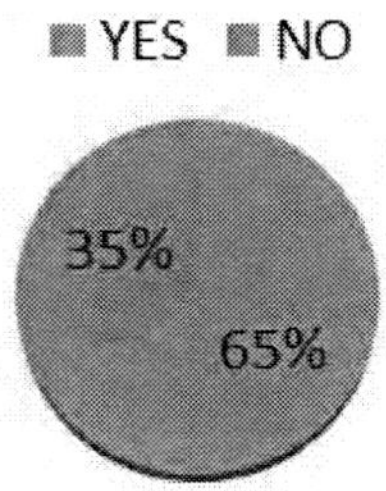

Fig. 2. Opinion of Children Taken while Making Purchase Decisions

Figure 2 shows that 65% of parents consider their child opinion while making purchase decisions.

3. Sources of information through which child gets aware of products and services

Sources	*Frequency*
Television	100
Friends& relatives	36
Internet	22
Others	04

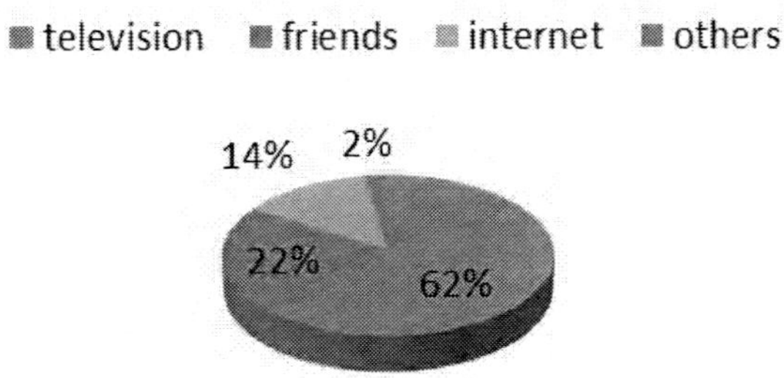

Fig. 3. Sources of Information of Children

From the results revealed in the figure3, it shows that most of children gets information through television and peer groups

4. Do parents get benefited from Child's advice

Response	*Frequency*
Yes	97
No	24

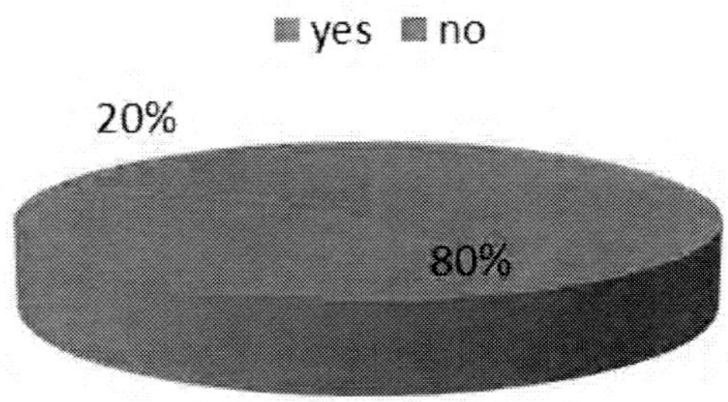

Fig. 4. Frequency of Child Advice Getting Benefited

From the figure 4, 80% of the parents are benefitted

Hypothesis Testing

H_o = Child's role in purchase decision making is indifferent with respect to different product categories.

H_a = Child's role in purchase decision making is different with respect to different product categories.

Table 1: Child's Role in Purchase Decision Making

Product Categories	*Roles*			
	Initiator	*Influencer*	*Final Purchaser*	*Total*
Packaged food items	39	41	41	121
Beverages	37	51	33	121
Cereals	40	59	22	121
Mobile phones	42	57	22	121
Television	35	64	22	121
Computer & laptops	45	56	20	121
Games	29	27	65	121
Restaurants	37	58	26	121
Holiday trips	50	53	18	121
Total	354	466	269	1089

$\chi^2_{calculated} = 87.47877$ $\chi^2_{tabulated(at\ 5\%\ degree\ of\ significant)} = 26.3$

From the table 1 it is revealed that child's role in purchase decision making is different with respect to different product categories. Child plays different roles as initiator, influencer or final purchaser for variety of products as per their use and need.

H_{01} = Child's influence on purchase decision is neutral with respect to product categories

H_a = Child's influence on purchase decision is different with respect to product categories

Table 2: Child's Influence on Purchase Decision

Product categories	*Ratings*					
	1	2	3	4	5	Total
Packaged food items	30	37	23	7	24	121
Beverages	19	45	29	15	13	121
Cereals	22	39	33	14	12	120
Mobile phones	12	33	30	21	24	120
Television	13	38	28	23	19	121
Computer & laptops	20	42	15	25	19	121
Games	24	48	13	13	24	119
Restaurants	20	40	27	26	8	121
Holiday trips	17	52	20	15	17	121
Total	176	374	218	158	159	1085

$\chi^2_{calculated} = 53.581$ $\chi^2_{tabulated(at\ 5\%\ degree\ of\ significant)} = 49.8$

The analysis provides enough evidence to reject the Null Hypothesis. In other words, child's influence on purchase decision is significant with respect to product categories. Children have different degrees of influence on different products depending on their need, wants and preferences.

H_{o2} = there is no impact of children from nuclear families on purchase decisions of different product categories.

Ha = there is an impact of children from nuclear families on purchase decisions of different product categories.

Table 3: Impact of Children from Nuclear Families on Purchase Decisions

Product categories	1	2	3	4	5	Total
Packaged food items	21	26	12	4	12	75
Beverages	12	27	20	9	7	75
Cereals	16	21	21	8	8	74
Mobile phones	10	25	14	12	13	74
Television	9	24	19	11	12	75
Computer & laptops	15	29	11	12	8	75
Games	16	32	6	8	11	73
Restaurants	14	26	18	10	7	75
Holiday trips	11	27	16	8	13	75
Total	124	237	137	82	91	671

$\chi^2_{calculated}$ = 29.25919 $\chi^2_{tabulated(at\ 5\%\ degree\ of\ significant)}$ =49.8

The analysis provides enough evidence not to reject the Null Hypothesis. In other words, there is no impact of children from nuclear families on purchase decisions of different product categories.

H_{o3} = there is no impact of children from joint families on purchase decisions of different product categories.

Ha = there is an impact of children from joint families on purchase decisions of different product categories.

Table 4: Impact of Children from Joint Families on Purchase Decisions

Product categories	*1*	*2*	*3*	*4*	*5*	*Total*
Packaged food items	9	11	11	3	12	46
Beverages	7	18	9	6	6	46
Cereals	6	18	12	6	4	46
Mobile phones	2	8	16	9	11	46
Television	4	14	9	12	7	46
Computer & laptops	5	13	4	13	11	46
Games	7	16	7	4	12	46
Restaurants	6	14	9	16	1	46
Holiday trips	6	25	4	7	4	46
Total	52	137	81	76	68	414

$\chi^2_{calculated}$ =49.06614 $\chi^2_{tabulated(at\ 5\%\ degree\ of\ significant)}$ =49.8

The analysis provides enough evidence not to reject the Null Hypothesis. In other words, Children of joint families do not have strong influence on purchase of various products especially games, computer & laptops, mobile phones, television etc.

H_{o4} = children having monthly family income less than 20000 do not have much influence on purchase decision with respect to product categories

Ha = children having monthly family income less than 20000 have much influence on purchase decision with respect to product categories.

Table 5: Influence of Children Having Monthly Family Income Less Than 20000

Product	1	2	3	4	5	Total
Packaged food items	9	13	9	0	7	38
Beverages	3	14	14	4	3	38
Cereals	2	13	11	7	5	38
Mobile phones	7	8	6	7	10	38
Television	5	10	8	7	8	38
Computer & laptops	9	13	4	2	10	38
Games	8	15	5	5	5	38
Restaurants	5	12	8	9	4	38
Holiday trips	3	18	6	3	8	38
Total	51	116	71	44	60	252

$\chi^2_{calculated}$ =38.9516 $\chi^2_{tabulated(at\ 5\%\ degree\ of\ significant)}$ =49.8

The analysis provides enough evidence not to reject the Null Hypothesis. In other words, families having monthly income less than 20000 do not have much influence on purchase of various products especially games, computer & laptops, mobile phones, television etc.

H_{o5} = there is no significant impact of family monthly income (20000-35000) on child's influence on purchase of various product categories.

Ha = there is significant impact of family monthly income (20000-35000) on child's influence on purchase of various product categories

Table 6: Influence of Children Having Monthly Family Income Between Rs 20000-50000

Product categories	1	2	3	4	5	Total
Packaged food items	3	3	6	2	2	16
Beverages	1	9	1	4	1	16
Cereals	3	2	9	1	1	16
Mobile phones	0	2	9	1	4	16
Television	3	5	2	3	3	16
Computer & laptops	2	7	3	2	2	16
Games	2	8	3	1	2	16
Restaurants	1	4	4	5	2	16
Holiday trips	1	11	1	1	2	16
Total	16	51	38	20	19	144

$\chi^2_{calculated}$ = 48.86755 $\chi^2_{tabulated(at\ 5\%\ degree\ of\ significant)}$ =49.8

The analysis provides that null hypothesis is accepted. In other words, families having monthly income from 20000-35000 do not have much influence on purchase of various products especially games, computer & laptops, mobile phones, television etc.

H_{06} = there is no significant impact of family monthly income (35000-50000) on child's influence on purchase of various product categories.

Ha = there is significant impact of family monthly income (35000-50000) on child's influence on purchase of various product categories

$\chi^2_{calculated}$ =27.5259 $\chi^2_{tabulated(at\ 5\%\ degree\ of\ significant)}$ =49.8

The analysis provides that null hypothesis is accepted. In other words, families having monthly income from 35000-50000 do not have much influence on purchase of various products especially games, computer & laptops, mobile phones, television etc.

H_{07} = there is no significant impact of family monthly income (>50000) on child's influence on purchase of various product categories.

Ha = there is significant impact of family monthly income (>50000) on child's influence on purchase of various product categories.

$\chi^2_{calculated}$ = 46.46695 $\chi^2_{tabulated(at\ 5\%\ degree\ of\ significant)}$ =49.8

The analysis provides that null hypothesis is accepted. In other words, families having monthly income above 50000 do not have much influence on purchase of various products especially games, computer & laptops, mobile phones, television etc.

H_{08} = there is no impact of gender of first child on high preference for different products

Ha = there is no impact of gender of first child on high preference for different products.

Table 7: Impact of Gender of First Child on High Preference for Different Products

Product categories	1	2	3	4	5	Total
Packaged food items	18	22	14	2	11	67
Beverages	12	22	20	7	6	67
Cereals	13	20	18	11	4	66
Mobile phones	7	23	14	12	10	66
Television	9	22	16	11	9	67
Computer & laptops	10	28	7	16	6	67
Games	10	30	10	2	13	65
Restaurants	11	23	21	9	3	67
Holiday trips	10	26	13	10	8	67
Total	100	216	133	80	70	599

$\chi^2_{calculated}$ =40.42528 $\chi^2_{tabulated(at\ 5\%\ degree\ of\ significant)}$ =49.8

the analysis provides that null hypothesis is accepted, i.e, there is no impact of gender of first child on high preference for different products

H_{09} = there is no impact of gender of child on high preference for different product categories

Ha = there is an impact of gender of child on high preference for different product categories.

Table 8. Impact of Gender of Child on High Preference for Different Product Categories

Product categories	*Girls*	*Boys*	*Total*
Packaged food items	36	54	90
Beverages	39	54	93
Cereals	43	51	94
Mobile phones	31	44	75
Television	32	47	79
Computer & laptops	32	45	77
Games	34	50	84
Restaurants	32	55	87
Holiday trips	40	49	89
Total	319	449	768

$\chi^2_{\text{calculated}}$ =2.089 $\chi^2_{\text{tabulated(at 5\% degree of significant)}}$ =15.507

the analysis provides that null hypothesis is accepted.,the result of table revealed that there is no impact of gender of child on high preference for different product categories.

H_{o10} = there is no impact of age of first child on high preference for different products

Ha = there is no impact of age of first child on high preference for different product

Table 9. Impact of Age of First Child on High Preference for Different Products

Product categories	*Age 1*	*Age 2*	*Age 3*	*Total*
Packaged food items	19.33594	27.89063	42.77344	90
Beverages	19.98047	28.82031	44.19922	93
Cereals	20.19531	29.13021	44.67448	94
Mobile phones	16.11328	23.24219	35.64453	75
Television	16.97266	24.48177	37.54557	79
Computer & laptops	16.54297	23.86198	36.59505	77
Games	18.04688	26.03125	39.92188	84
Restaurants	18.69141	26.96094	41.34766	87
Holiday trips	19.12109	27.58073	42.29818	89
Total	165	238	365	768

$\chi^2_{\text{calculated}}$ =4.051786 $\chi^2_{\text{tabulated(at 5\% degree of significant)}}$ =26.296

the null hypothesis is accepted, i.e, there is no impact of age of first child on high preference for different products.

CONCLUSION

The study showed that the children roles is different with respect to various product categories. It is evaluated that children plays different roles as initiator, influencer or final purchaser in accordance with their needs, wants and use.The degree of influence of children is not neutral for all the product categories. It is different for different products. There is no impact of gender of children on the family purchase decision making specially for high preference products. There is no impact of children of joint or nuclear families in decision making. There is no impact of family income on child's influence in purchase decision with 6.respect to various product categories. The major source of information through which the child gets aware of the various products is television and second most important is internet. Thus, most of the parents are benefitted by their child's advice and child plays an important role in family purchase decision. Thus it is very important for marketers to know the needs and wants of children as they highly influence purchase decisions in a family

REFERENCES

[1] Kapoor, S. (2001). Family Influence On Purchase Decisions- A Study with Reference to Consumer Durables, Unpublished Doctoral Dissertation, University of Delhi, Delhi.

[2] Gunter, B., &Furnham, A. "Children as consumers: A psychological analysis of the young people's market. London" Routledge, 1998

[3] McNeal, J. U. "Children are as a market of influences" Kids as customers-A hand book of marketing to children pp. 63-87, New York: Lexington Books. The free press, 1992

[4] John, D.R and Sujan, M (1990) „Age differences in Product categorization, Journal of Consumer Research, Vol. 16 (1990), pp.452-460.

[5] Jenkins R.L. (1979) „The influence of children in family decision-making: parents Perceptions, Advances in Consumer Research, Vol.6, pp. 413-418

[6] Young, B. M. "Television advertising and children", Oxford: Clarendon Press, 1990

[7] European Commission, European Commission White Paper: A New Impetus for European Youth (Brussels, 21 November 2001) (COM[2001]681 final)

[8] Paxton, J.G. and D.R. John. 1997. "The Emergence of Adaptive Decision-Making in Children." Journal of Consumer Research, 24 (June), 43-56

[9] oschis, G. P., & Moore, R. L. "Family communication and consumer socialization", Advances in Consumer Research, vol. 6, pp. 359-363, 1979.

[10] Moschis, George P. and Ray L. Moore. 1979. "Decision-Making Among the Young: A Socialization Perspective." Journal of Consumer Research.16 (September), 101- 111.

[11] Mangleburg, T.F., D. Grewal, and T. Bristol. 1999. "Family Type, Family Authority Relations and Adolescents' Purchase Influence." Advances in Consumer Research, 26, 379-384

[12] Advertising and Interpersonal Influences on Teenagers Participation in Family Consumption Decisions: Advances in Consumer Research, vol. 13, pp. 181-186.

[13] Isler, L., E.T Popper & S. Ward (1987). Children's purchase request and parental responses from a diary study, Journal of Advertisement Research, 27 (October/November)

Internet Marketing - Door to Success the Road Ahead for India

Sandeep Puri and Vidit Narang

Institute of Management Technology, Ghaziabad

ABSTRACT

Internet is becoming one of the fastest growing platforms that is playing a significant role in the lives of human beings. Marketing over Internet is gaining strength day by day. This paper attempts to begin a discussion on how the Internet evolved at a charged pace from network of computers to the world's truly international market; the consumers in internet market place; how a company add value to its operations by using the Internet; and more specifically, how India can use the Internet as the gateway to globalization and up to what extent this process has already started.

INTRODUCTION

Internet marketing is referred to as the marketing of products or services over the Internet. It is considered to be broad in scope as it not only refers to marketing on the Internet, but also comprises different marketing activities done with the support of e-mail and wireless media. Digital customer data and electronic customer relationship management systems are also often grouped together under internet marketing (Sinisalo et al.2007). In today's era of globalization not only the nations in the world and their communities have come closer to one another but most of the sectors have undergone significant changes. Needless to mention that the marketing sector has undergone significant changes and further is experiencing continuous changes. With the significant use of Internet it becomes important to study its impact on marketing field. It is true that the prime factor for the growth of Internet Marketing is the worldwide increase in the use of internet. Thus the new concept of Internet Marketing has emerged and is found to be dynamic in nature.

Internet is an increasingly expanding medium of interaction which has virtually eliminated geographical boundaries and overcoming previously existing obstacles of global business. It is considered to be an accidental mega-market born out of technology. Internet, the single most sophisticated online service, is simple and immediate to use; however, these attributes may not enjoy a perceived status of usability for those new and somewhat hesitant of advances in computer technology. Internet today offers India best opportunity to expand its market on more global scale. This network of computers represents perpetually open market without geographical barriers to prevent any business from reaching customers all over the world via a virtual market where trade, transactions, cash and commodities flow in form of electronic consumption.

With significant growth of internet usage, internet marketing is found to expand its horizons. Few companies which have revolutionized the way with regards to the use of internet in the field of marketing are Google.com, Yahoo.com, Amazon.com, Alibaba.com and Youtube.com. New online shopping model was brought up by giants like flipkart and ebay. The similar model is replicated in India by Jabong.com, homeshop18.com etc.

Internet marketing ties together the creative and technical aspects of the Internet, including design, development, advertising and sales (Charlesworth, 2009). Marketers are using iInternet marketing through different stages of the customer engagement cycle through search engine marketing(SEM), search engine optimization (SEO) and banner ads on specific websites. Internet marketing has brought various strategies such as affiliate marketing which consists of pay per view, pay per call and pay per click advertising. In addition to this e-mail marketing, viral marketing, blog or article based marketing, interactive advertising are also popular. New marketing techniques being invented all the time. It is important to know how the trend would be in future. Companies are inventing new techniques to find better ways to generate revenue and establish their brand on the internet.

Now days it is found that, the numbers of Indians are using Internet for search of information and other solutions online and also for their purchasing or selling of products through internet. Thus internet marketing focuses on 3 perspectives i.e. Consumer, Company and 3rd Party Agency. Consumer awareness plays important role in their interests to pursue internet marketing. Hence it would be useful both for companies and 3rd party agencies to understand the mind-set of the consumers as consumers would be the ones who would eventually drive internet marketing in a big way.

It is found that China is the leader among the Asian countries with 513 Million Internet users with respect to India, which has 121 Million internet users and was ranked at 2nd position. Use of internet by various nations is shown in Figure. 1

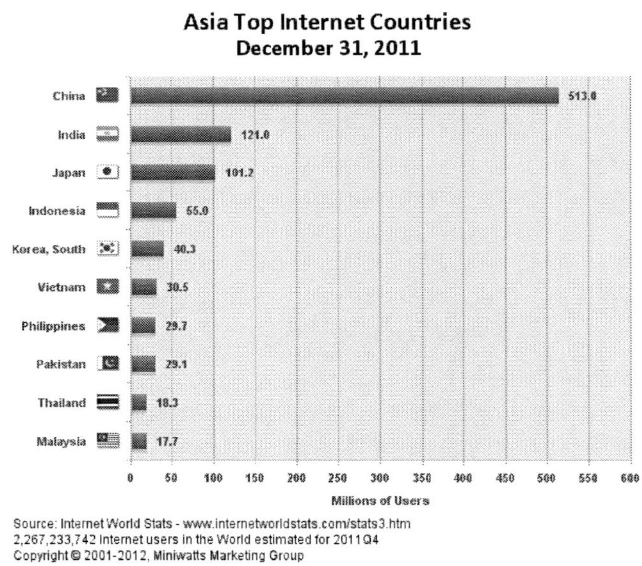

Fig. 1 Indicates the use of Internet by Various Nations.

Table 1: Use of internet in Asia, and Facebook Statistics

Asia Internet Use, Population Data And Facebook Statistics						
ASIA	Population (2011 Est.)	Internet Users, (Year 2000)	Internet Users 31-Dec-2011	Penetration (% Population)	Users % Asia	Facebook 31-Mar-2012
Afganistan	29,835,392	1,000	**1,256,470**	4.2 %	0.1 %	257,440
Armenia	2,967,975	30,000	**1,396,550**	47.1 %	0.1 %	282,700
Azerbaijan	8,372,373	12,000	**3,689,000**	44.1 %	0.4 %	782,000
Bangladesh	158,570,535	100,000	**5,501,609**	3.5 %	0.5 %	2,520,680
Bhutan	708,427	500	**98,728**	13.9 %	0.0 %	65,660
Brunei Darussalem	401,890	30,000	**318,900**	79.4 %	0.0 %	234,060
Cambodia	14,701,717	6,000	**491,480**	3.1 %	0.0 %	449,160
China *	1,336,718,015	22,500,000	**513,100,000**	38.4 %	50.5 %	447,460
Georgia	4,585,874	20,000	**1,300,000**	28.3 %	0.1 %	907,620
Hong Kong *	7,122,508	2,283,000	**4,894,913**	68.7 %	0.5 %	3,752,160
India	1,189,172,906	5,000,000	**121,000,000**	10.2 %	11.9 %	45,048,100
Indonesia	245,613,043	2,000,000	**55,000,000**	22.4 %	5.4 %	43,523,740
Japan	126,475,664	47,080,000	**101,228,736**	80.0 %	10.0 %	7,684,120
Kazakhstan	15,522,373	70,000	**5,448,965**	35.1 %	0.5 %	452,200
Korea, North	24,457,492	--	**--**	--	--	n/a
Korea, South	48,754,657	19,040,000	**40,329,660**	82.7 %	4.0 %	6,376,160
Kyrgystan	5,587,443	51,600	**2,194,400**	39.3 %	0.2 %	75,380
Laos	6,477,211	6,000	**527,400**	8.1 %	0.1 %	156,160
Macao *	573,003	60,000	**308,797**	53.9 %	0.0 %	204,920
Malaysia	28,728,607	3,700,000	**17,723,000**	61.7 %	1.7 %	12,365,780
Maldives	394,999	6,000	**114,100**	28.9 %	0.0 %	120,020
Mongolia	3,133,318	30,000	**355,524**	11.3 %	0.0 %	458,700
Myanmar	53,999,804	1,000	**110,000**	0.2 %	0.0 %	n/a
Nepal	29,391,883	50,000	**2,031,245**	6.9 %	0.2 %	1,396,800
Pakistan	187,342,721	133,900	**29,128,970**	15.5 %	2.9 %	6,412,960
Philippines	101,833,938	2,000,000	**29,700,000**	29.2 %	2.9 %	27,724,040
Singapore	4,740,737	1,200,000	**3,658,400**	77.2 %	0.4 %	2,602,880
Sri Lanka	21,283,913	121,500	**2,503,194**	11.8 %	0.2 %	1,235,080
Taiwan	23,071,779	6,260,000	**16,147,000**	70.0 %	1.6 %	11,877,620
Tajikistan	7,627,200	2,000	**794,483**	10.4 %	0.1 %	34,640
Thailand	66,720,153	2,300,000	**18,310,000**	27.4 %	1.8 %	14,235,700
Timor-Leste	1,177,834	0	**2,361**	0.2 %	0.0 %	n/a
Turkmenistan	4,997,503	2,000	**110,924**	2.2 %	0.0 %	5,860
Uzbekistan	28,128,600	7,500	**7,550,000**	26.8 %	0.7 %	128,780
Vietnam	90,549,390	200,000	**30,516,587**	33.7 %	3.0 %	3,173,480
TOTAL ASIA	**3,879,740,877**	**114,304,000**	**1,016,799,076**	**26.2 %**	**100.0 %**	**195,034,380**

LITERATURE REVIEW

The information superhighway is shaped by advances in digital telephone networks, personal computers, interactive cable television and, finally, the Internet. Internet has great potential for marketing and also great potential for abuse (McGeehan, 1996). Internet or World Wide Web has opened new avenues that are yet to be explored. Where else can you put your store in a mall where millions of customers can come and browse (Kanter, 2001). A research has been done in this field taking in account various important aspects like consumer privacy, consumer inclination and consumer personalization in field of Internet Marketing. Most of the literatures related to Internet Marketing which were referred had focus on three important perspectives, Consumer, Company and 3rd Party Agency. Most of the research undertaken so far intends to study the phenomena related to the growth and the trends in Internet Marketing. Nature of business on the internet

Internet began to grow dramatically in 1994 with the advent of a new, more user friendly application "World Wide Web" which provides companies to access to millions of new customers at a fraction of cost of print or television advertising, and in many cases, distribution. Web uses a technology called hypertext which allows users to leap from one computer data base to another by just clicking on highlighted images or text. It employs easy-to-use browsers to capture the public's imagination with a promise of navigable world of seemingly infinite amount of information. World Wide Web's popularity, has caused the entertainment media and the communication industries to re-evaluate their business models. The use of Internet to carry real time data, such as voice and video, in addition to traditional forms of data, which lent themselves more readily to packet switching technology.

Although the commercial market of Internet might be small today, it is likely to grow in the future. Millions of people all over the world can view the contents of worldwide Internet. It has become affordable and easy to access and most potential customers like to see companies represent themselves on online space. Customers can search products of company and can ask questions directly without having inconvenience of leaving home. However, a business's traditional strategies are not likely to be appropriate, and thus directly transferable, to electronic commerce. As businesses scramble to jump on the train before it leaves the station, they may ignore new rules that apply and hence make costly mistakes. Successful Internet marketers will need to recognize internet's peculiarities and embrace them with strategies custom-made for this new medium. The nature of Internet commerce is likely to take shape around several key factors, including:

- Consumer market is different.
- Internet users want control.
- Communication is direct.
- Authenticity is a must.

- Competition is open.
- Security is a big concern.

IMPACT OF INTERNET ON MARKETING

With substantial and rapidly growing Internet audience, wide variety of businesses has adopted the Internet as the means to conduct their marketing communications functions economically and more efficiently. Thousands of companies that provide goods and services to consumer market have invested in creation of company Web sites. The primary purpose of these Web sites is to raise awareness of the company and its offerings to those accessing the sites. As per today's standards, a company without a Web presence is considered to be living in the past. While most companies felt compelled to establish their Internet presence, they have not felt equally compelled to create a Web site with all substantive features and capabilities.

Taking into consideration different parameters that influence policy of companies which pursue internet marketing, it is important to know simultaneously about such aspects which influence consumers to actually use the internet either for shopping purposes or for some other particular service. The literature review has helped in in identifying following parameters which are of interest for consumers pursuing internet marketing:

- Consumer privacy
- Consumers decision making process in buying a product or using a service
- Consumers interaction and role of personalization in internet marketing
- How consumers evaluate companies in the field of internet
- Factors preventing consumers from indulging in internet marketing
- Effects of consumer gender differences on internet purchases

With the use of Internet there can be continuous customer support. Services can be made available through e-mail systems on internet. This saves time and money. In addition, feedback from marketplace can be collected on an on-going basis, and in many cases, in the form of "real-time" data. New products and services can be tested through interactive questionnaires on Internet. This feedback forms the basis of market identification and segmentation that enables marketers to better position their products.

CORPORATE RESPONSE TOWARDS INTERNET MARKETING

Companies have to take into consideration many parameters during their presence in the field of internet marketing. Some companies may be new entrants in internet marketing. Companies in internet marketing are driven by various factors. Basically companies should understand which marketing channel will be best for of their products or services. Companies also need to keep in mind what product information is to be disclosed and how to provide security for disclosed information so as to prevent hackers and malicious people from getting access to it. Company should be in a position to build confidence in buyers so that they can make purchases without the fear of credit card frauds. In addition to this, companies also need to understand about the sector which has an impact on the minds of people for example web mavens. The following parameters would be of the interest for companies using internet marketing:

- Drivers for internet marketing
- Marketing channel preference
- Importance of web mavens
- How to be successful in internet marketing
- Use of internet marketing in service provision
- Catering to consumer interest
- Focus on gender

INTERNET MARKETING- THE ROAD AHEAD

What does future hold for online/internet marketing? The acceleration of innovation in online technologies and the ways we can discover, consume and engage with information can be a challenge to keep up with. But as digital marketers that are more object opportunists, seeing future trends is exactly what they need to do in order to anticipate our place in digital universe.

It's not about where you can sell stuff to people right now, next month, next year, 5, 10 or more. That's why we think the concept of discover, consume and engage is important, because it transcends ideas like "social network" or "search engine" and focuses on consumers and technologies. Will we be using a search engine like Google in 5 years? Will we be using desktop computers in 5 years? What will future social networks look like? Answers to these questions are answers to future of marketing and customer engagement.

The future is bright for marketers who use Internet networking services. The evolution of virtual experience and promise of cyberspace have recently begun to open doors to information which was previously inaccessible. Everyone from public universities to big business is racing to cash on what promises to be future of information and communications. A totally paperless, highly dynamic environment has been created in which ideas and images are exchanged free from the burdens of the physical world. In this virtual space, there are no rules, no government regulation. Internet represents most massive amount of knowledge ever assembled on a common grid. It is for this reason that an Internet connection is fast becoming best way to reach the masses and provide input into a large percentage of the earth's composite knowledge. The implication of digital tomorrow on the way man conducts his day-to-day affairs is astounding.

How will the business traditions of the past fit into the binary stream of the future? The world of mass marketing is evolving at an alarming rate, and the vehicle which will bring business of future to the doorsteps of every human being lies in Internet.

GLOBAL INTERNET TRENDS AND INDIA'S STANDING

ComScore highlighted that worldwide online audience has jumped 7%, with Asia-Pacific markets adding more than 40 million users. India has been identified as the fastest growing online market during the same period, **with a 41% rise**. This is much higher than China (5%), Brazil(6%) and Russia (20%). With most online categories in Indian exhibiting an average reach below the global figures, the potential seems to be high.

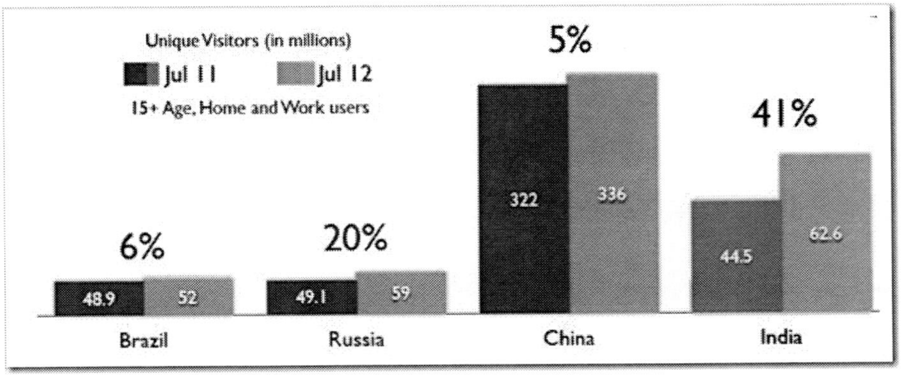

Fig. 2

http://trak.in/tags/business/2012/08/27/comprehensive-indian-internet-usage-statistics-report/

India's internet penetration is estimated at 10%, with 124.7 million users going online during July 2012.

India's Audience is Getting Younger

ComScore found 75% of the internet audience in India to be aged 35 years and below, promising to make it the **youngest online population in the coming years.**

Females formed 39.3% of the total audience, and the sharpest growth was observed among male and female segments in the age-group 15 to 24.

High Growth Areas

ComScore's findings show that travel, search, social networking and news arenas to be growing sharply in India's online world, crossing worldwide averages.

Table 2: These are the 'Super Seven' Categories Pointed out by the Data

Categories	*Year on Year Growth%*	*July 2012 Reach %*
Games	60	41
News	54	80.3
Search	43	91.5
Retail	43	59.9
Health	43	21.1
Social Networking	43	95.5
Travel	41	44

Source: http://trak.in/tags/business/2012/08/27/comprehensive-indian-internet-usage-statistics-report.

There's high potential for retail, games and health, since they fall below worldwide trends

The Online Retail Boom

As many as 3 in 5 internet users in India visit retail sites, which have registered a growth of 43% over the last year. The statistics indicate close contest between Snapdeal and Flipkart in horizontal retail, Jabong and Myntra in the lifestyle category, all of them fuelled by aggressive marketing and growing demand.

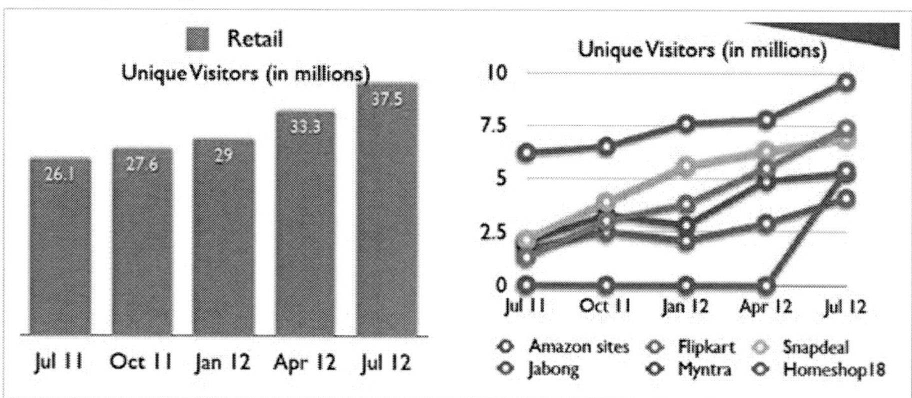

Fig. 3

Source: http://trak.in/tags/business/2012/08/27/comprehensive-indian-internet-usage-statistics-report/

Month of July saw a total of 37.5 million unique visitors from India coming to retail sites, with the apparel sub-category being the fastest growing sub-category at a year-on-year growth of 362%. Consumer goods, sports equipment and home furnishing have shown signs of growth as well. Vertical retail segments are expected to grow the fastest in the coming months.

Growth in the Travel Segment

India's online reach in the travel segment has crossed the worldwide averages, according to the ComScore statistics. Indian Railways tops the charts with a 19.2% reach in July 2012, followed by MakeMyTrip at 11.6% and Yatra Online at 8.3%

With a rise in people using private buses, **redbus.in shows a reach of 2% during July.**

E-Commerce Transactions in India

Direct debit or Net banking is the most popular payment method as per figures from the second quarter of 2012, with a 58% share. Visa and MasterCard follow at 21% and 12% respectively.

IRCTC averages at $17 (INR 935) per transaction, while Flipkart indicates $35 (INR 1925) per transaction.

Mixed Growth Witnessed in Other Categories

Business and finance has grown at 35%, with SBI being the most popular bank. ICICI Bank follows at the second position and HDFC at the third.

Real estate has grown 38%, **career services** have grown 30% and the **automotive category** has shown a growth of 18%.

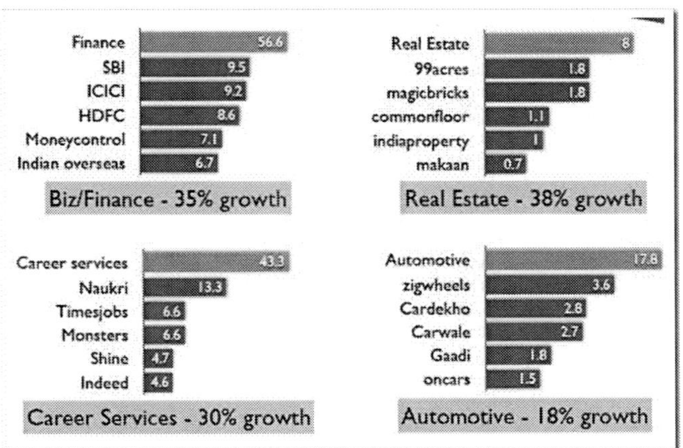

Fig. 1.4. title

Source: http://trak.in/tags/business/2012/08/27/comprehensive-indian-internet-usage-statistics-report/

Future Trends Concluded from Data

The statistics presented by ComScore suggest that smart phones and tablets are going to drive usage further through Wi-Fi access.

Going by predictions based on past trends, **entertainment will dominate the content growth** across both mobile devices and PC's, and categories like travel, news and career services are expected to continue showing decent growth.

There's a projected increase in cash-on-delivery payments, particularly in the retail category. With India's internet population expected to get even younger in the coming years, there's likely to be a boost in online advertising targeting the youth.

REFERENCES

[1] Alicia Aldridge, Karen Forcht, Joan Pierson, (1997),"Get linked or get lost: marketing strategy for the Internet", Internet Research, Vol.7 , No.: 3 pp. 161 – 169

[2] Charlesworth, Alan (2009). *Internet marketing: a practical approach.* Butterworth-Heinemann. p. 49.

[3] Comprehensive Indian Internet Usage statistics report by trak.in

[4] Craig S. Breitenbach, Doris C. Van Doren, (1998),"Value-added marketing in the digital domain: enhancing the utility of the Internet", Journal of Consumer Marketing, Vol. 15 , No.: 6 pp. 558 – 575

[5] Fred Palumbo, Paul Herbig, (1998),"International marketing tool: the Internet", Industrial Management & Data Systems, Vol. 98, No. 6 pp. 253 – 261

[6] Jaakko Sinisalo et al. (2007). "Mobile customer relationship management: underlying issues and challenges". *Business Process Management Journal* **13** (6): 772.

[7] Kanter R M (2001) "Evolve! Succeeding in the Digital Culture of Tomorrow",_Harvard Business School Press

[8] Lisa Harris, Geraldine Cohen, (2003),"Marketing in the Internet age: what can we learn from the past?" Management Decision, Vol. 41, , No.: 9 pp. 944 – 956

[9] McGeehan, P. (1996) "Cyber-Swindles Taking Root." USA Today, 31 January: 1A.

[10] Paul Herbig, Brian Hale, (1997),"Internet: the marketing challenge of the twentieth century", Internet Research, Vol. 7 , No.: 2 pp. 95 – 100

[11] Pallab Paul, (1996),"Marketing on the Internet", Journal of Consumer Marketing, Vol. 13, No.: 4 pp. 27 – 39

[12] Reports on internet statistics Asia region by internetworldstats.com

[13] Reports by internetsociety.org

[14] Reports by IAMAI

[15] Riyad Eid, Myfanwy Trueman, (2002),"The Internet: new international marketing , No.ues", Management Research News, Vol. 25 , No.: 12 pp. 54 – 67

[16] Shwu-Ing Wu, (2002),"Internet marketing involvement and consumer behavior", Asia Pacific Journal of Marketing and Logistics, Vol. 14 , No.: 4 pp. 36 – 53

[17) Stefan Lagrosen, (2005),"Effects of the internet on the marketing communication of service companies", Journal of Services Marketing, Vol. 19 , No.: 2 pp. 63 – 69

[18] T.C. Melewar, Nichola Smith, (2003),"The Internet revolution: some global marketing implications", Marketing Intelligence & Planning, Vol. 21 , No.: 6 pp. 363 – 369

[19] Thomas L. Ainscough, (1996),"The Internet for the rest of us: marketing on the World Wide Web", Journal of Consumer Marketing, Vol. 13 , No.: 2 pp. 36 – 47

Investigating the CRM Activities of SMEs in Jalandhar City of Punjab

Jaspreet Kaur Rai and Gagandeep Singh Kang[1]

Management Studies, Apeejay Institute of Management Technical Campus, Jalandhar-Punjab
[1]Department, Lovely Professional University, Phagwara, Punjab

ABSTRACT

It is observed that in this competitive and globalize environment no organization could grow or sustain until & unless it does not follow CRM Practices. This research conducted to identify the status of CRM in SMEs of Jalandhar and after thorough analysis some suggestions were given which could be effectively utilized by SMEs in the planning and implementation of CRM practices. The study conducted on six different sectors like Surgical, Rubber, Engineering, Sports, Hand tool and Electrical. This study is descriptive and analytical in nature. In Research methodology both qualitative and qualitative aspect of research has been used. Convenient and Stratified Sampling techniques were used while sample size was of 36 units.

This study helps in determine the advantage of CRM tools to Small & Medium Enterprises and to conclude what problems they face while implementing these tools. SMEs of Jalandhar are using traditional CRM practices like emails, telephones, fax, websites, salespersons, call centers and many more. Majority of SMEs in Jalandhar were partially computerized, so the installation of modern CRM software's is difficult task for them. However, Sick units in Jalandhar are facing trouble from competition and they have financial problems due to which they can't hire experts and CRM systems.

Small & Medium Firms require specific business strategies and procedures when exploring new technologies in order to co-exist with the dominating giants of the industry. SMEs need to determine what internal processes can be improved upon or replaced in order to better serve customers. For shaping future of Small & Medium Enterprises in Punjab, it's essential to implement CRM practices in a better way. E-CRM tools can also be implemented to reach the untapped customers and to get success in business.

INTRODUCTION

About Customer Relationship Management

Customer Relationship Management (CRM) understands customer needs and leveraging that knowledge to improve a company's long term profitability (Stringfellow et al). According to

Goff et al (1998), "CRM is a data-driven approach that enables companies to assess each customer's current needs and potential profitability and tailor sales offers and service. It often involves using multiple channels like the internet, direct mail, telesales and held sales to improve effectiveness and efficiency. A company can make contact with prospective customers through relatively low-cost direct mail or telesales". Strauss and Seidel (2004) claim that some see CRM only as a process driven by information technology, designed to optimize customer contact and experience. Barnes (2001) suggests that CRM is a data and product-driven process. He also suggests that companies sell more products through the data-mining capabilities of CRM.

ROLE OF SMALL MEDIUM ENTERPRISES

Research reveals that Small Medium Enterprises (SMEs) contributed more to Indian growth as compare to large scale industries. SMEs can be defined as enterprise set at small scale and on medium scale. At present, a small scale industrial unit is an undertaking in which investment in plant and machinery does not exceed Rs.1 crore, except in respect of certain specified items under hosiery, hand tools, drugs and pharmaceuticals, stationery items and sports goods, where this investment limit has been enhanced to Rs. 5 crore . The internal group set up by the Reserve Bank of India has recently recommended that the units with investment in plant and machinery in excess of SMEs limit and up to Rs. 10 crore may be treated as medium enterprises. *According to SME Chamber of India* "Small and Medium Enterprises (SMEs) play a vital role for the growth of Indian economy by contributing 45% of industrial output, 40% of exports, employing 60 million people, create 1.3 million jobs every year and produce more than 8000 quality products for the Indian and International Markets. SMEs Contribution towards GDP in 2009 was 17% which is expected to increase to 22% by 2012. There are 26.1 million SMEs Units in India and 12 million persons are expected to join the workforce in the next 3 years. SMEs are the fountain head of several innovations in manufacturing and service sectors, the major link in the supply chain to corporate and the PSUs. By promoting SMEs, the rural areas of India will be developed. SMEs are now exposed to greater opportunities than ever for expansion and diversification across the sectors. Indian market is growing rapidly and Indian entrepreneurs are making remarkable progress in various Industries like Manufacturing, Precision Engineering Design, Food Processing, Pharmaceutical, Textile & Garments, Retail, IT and Agro and Service sector.

CRM IN SMEs

CRM is about managing the relationships a business have with its customers. It has to do with managing the customers an enterprise has in order to give the customers satisfaction and increase profit. CRM helps in any industry to achieve the objectives properly for which the industry is actually set up. In case of SMEs also they want to beat their competitor and want to be in market for which they need to adopt CRM tools. Even many organization set up as small business enterprises are getting the advantage of CRM through maintaining their proper strategies to retain customer as government of India also helps the SMEs to get succeed and to be in competition. SMEs are the leaders in export marketing as many organizations set up trade fairs, exhibitions to promote SMEs skill in India as well as in foreign market. Small traditional enterprises, with poor support system and little exposure face difficulties in the new e-business environment. SMEs usually face difficulties while adopting IT applications or solutions based on IT. Limited human resources, especially those familiar with IT or corresponding backend processes, place these SMEs in an unfavorable position in an e-commerce environment, where the preferred physical channels of distribution and delivery still favors large enterprises. The Ministry of Small Scale Industries, Government of India has been promoting the use of IT in SMEs, as a part of the overall effort towards enhancing SME competitiveness, in the context of globalization. Most of the biggest companies are implementing CRM tools into their organizations, as they have realized about the importance of technology. To survive in the global market, focusing on the customer is becoming a key factor for companies big and small. It is known that it takes up to five times more money to acquire a new customer than to get an existing customer to make a new purchase. Therefore, customer retention is in particular important to SMEs because of their limited resources. A second aspect of CRM is that knowing the customer and his/her problems allow acquiring new customers more easily. It is important to note that establishing and managing a good customer relationship is a strategic endeavor. For this to happen business processes and company culture have to be redesigned to focus on the customer. The rapid development of Information Technology and the internet, however enable customer to have more choices than before regarding the purchase of products and services. Emerging electronic commerce has also been changed many aspects of existing business, business opportunities and process. SMEs need and should understand their customers better and focus their services towards their needs.SMEs export many products within nation and outside country as well so they require proper CRM systems which help these organizations to improve their market positions and increase customer loyalty. Good management is at the centre of every successful CRM. Customer care strategy and CRM software go hand in hand. In particular SMEs need CRM software that easily adapts to their customer care needs while still being low cost. In this paper it discuss about the benefits of modern technology for SMEs. Information Technology, particularly the Internet is making it easier for customers to find alternate providers for products and services. However when properly used, IT can help retain customers by building and managing the relationship.

REVIEW OF LITERATURE

According to Achuama & Usoro (2010) "Customer relationship management (CRM) with its current use of technology often termed electronic eCRM is widely recognized as inevitable in modern business. In this research, the results and their implications to developers, vendors and other interested parties are discussed. This research is based on the study of 240 small and medium scale enterprises in Nigeria selected randomly from the data base of Enterprises

Development Unit of Lagos Business School Nigeria. In order to have a successful CRM in an organization, it is important to consider these issues which have been brought together here as important ingredients for a successful CRM implementation for SMEs in developing countries. Any vendors, IT consultants or entrepreneurs trying to help SMEs in developing countries realize a successful CRM will have to consider those variables". *Sultan (2010)* concluded in his study that cloud computing is an emerging new computing paradigm for delivering computing services. The approach relies on a number of existing technologies e.g., the Internet, virtualization and grid computing. A case study of a cloud experience by a British SME is also presented in this study in order to further highlight the perceived values of cloud computing in terms of cost and efficiency for real small enterprise. *According to SMEs chamber of India (2010)* "the Small and Medium Enterprises (SMEs) play a vital role for the growth of Indian. SMEs are now exposed to greater opportunities than ever for expansion and diversification across the sectors. Indian market is growing rapidly and Indian entrepreneurs are making remarkable progress in various Industries like Manufacturing, Precision Engineering Design, Food Processing, Pharmaceutical, Textile & Garments, Retail, IT and ITES, Agro and Service sector". *According to Global SMEs Technological submits (2010)* "Global financial crisis and economic slowdown; many companies are affected in different degrees. But, with their inherent strength and resilience SMEs can weather adverse situations, as they are not dependent on public money. Many overseas companies are approaching Indian SME to outsource their manufacturing activities.SME Sector to identify and adopt latest the SME exhibitors will also get an opportunity to launch new products & services and exchange business information, identify potential buyers, sellers and investors. They can also obtain assistance to find out business partners for joint ventures, collaborations, technology transfer, contract manufacturing and other activities". *Hubert (2000)* stated in his study that Customer care strategy and CRM go hand in hand. In particular SMEs need CRM that easily adapts to their customer care needs while still being low cost. This paper discusses the benefits of CRM for SMEs and their special requirements i.e., CRM software. Business processes are not stable and need to be adapted when the business of the company changes. "The Governments can increase the affordability of ICT through grants, credits, leasing options and tax incentives. To encourage SMEs to use ICT equipment to increase productivity, the JapaneseGovernment allows corporations to deduct up to 6 percent of total lease payment onbrand-new machines from annual income tax payments. Ways that governments can help increase ICT adoption among SMEs include hosting training workshops that are flexible and tailored to specific industries, employee's position and role or software/hardware applications; providing subsidies for ICT training; and creating opportunities for firms to try the technologies hands on" *(by Kotelnikov , 2007).Buchanon Webster (2009)* studied that a pragmatic approach to CRM is much more appealing to the SME market and traditional approaches to CRM need to be redefined in order to get traction with SMEs. Step by step implementations are critical. Business objectives are often subject to change and large scale roll-outs do not suit the requirements of an SME. The backlash against CRM in the enterprise space has negatively impacted SMEs willingness to invest in the technology. There has been a lack of suitable products and a focus on back office products that directly impact the bottom line. *Kumar Manish (2009)* expressed in his study that CRM is one of the most exciting areas that organizations are looking at these days. He has mention three scenarios in his study which are clearly emerging in the Indian SME market from a CRM perspective. Firstly, the internal Call Center has to be CRMenabled to manage this steady flow of telephone calls, emails and other contact points from their prospects andcustomers. Invariably their telephony systems have also to be integrated with the CRM.Secondly, more and more organizations are seeking end to end solutions with best of breed offerings. Thirdly, hosted offerings are here to stay for SMEs looking for CRM application. The trend we see is of relatively smaller SMEs adopting this approach quickly as this minimizes investments in hardware, trained technical manpower and infrastructure. It also helps them get off the ground rapidly. *Stuti Kacker (2009*) expressed that today organizations are knowledge based and their success and survival depend on creativity, innovation, discovery and inventiveness. An effective reaction to these demands lead to innovative change in the organization, to ensure their existence. The rate of changes is accelerating rapidly, as new knowledge idea generation and global diffusion are increasing. Creativity and innovation have a bigger role in this change process for survival. SMEs have to learn and imbibe the process of innovation, in their day to day working, to remain competitive. Instead of looking for support from other agencies, they have to find their own ways of overcoming barriers. Despite all the barriers and gaps which I have stated before, Indian SMEs have continued on their path of progress.

RESEARCH PROBLEMS

- To study the CRM strategies adopted by SMEs situated at Jalandhar.
- To study the status of CRM in Small Medium Enterprises of Jalandhar.
- To highlight the problems in the way of CRM implementation by SMEs of Jalandhar.

RESEARCH METHODLOGY

Research Design:Descriptive Research and Analytical Research.

Data Collection:Primary and Secondary Data

Research Instruments: Structured Questionnaire- Both open and closed ended

Sample Size:Sample was consisted of 36 units. Sample size contained six different industries of Jalandhar which included Surgical, Rubber, Electrical, Hand tools, Engineering and Sports sector.

Sampling Technique: Convenient Sampling and Stratified Sampling techniques.

Data Analysis: When all of the information was compiled, the data was coded and entered in Statistical Package for Social Sciences (SPSS) 17.0. Frequencies, bar charts, mean, have been used to analyze the data. The results have been presented in the tabular and graphical forms at suitable places in the report.

DATA ANALYSIS AND INTERPRETATION

Table 1. Nature of Business Organization

		Frequency	*Percent*	*Valid Percent*	*Cumulative Percent*
Valid	Manual	7	19.4	19.4	19.4
	Semi automatic	23	63.9	63.9	83.3
	Automatic	6	16.7	16.7	100.0
	Total	36	100.0	100.0	

As reflected in table that 19.44% firms run their business operations manually. These enterprises are those which are still suffering from financial as well as technological problems. Tendency of mechanization also depends upon nature of product and competition prevailing in the market. It was observed that 63.89% small medium enterprises were semi automatic organization. It is observed that more is the level of automation, higher is inclination and success for CRM practices.

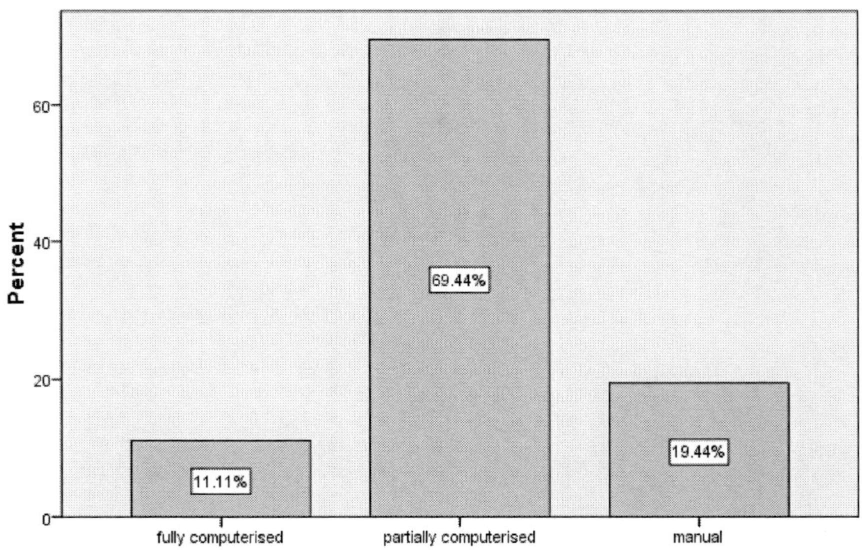

Graph 1: Status of IT and Computer in day to day operations in your company

SMEs scenario is changed now this development can be seen from the above figure of respondents who starts using computer applications to remain in competition. These companies realized the importance of Computer in their business, as seen that 69.44% respondents are partially computerized.

CRM Strategies Adopted by SMEs of Jalandhar

Most of the Small Medium Enterprises of Jalandhar adopt CRM Strategies for increasing sales, satisfying customers, increasing market share, increasing profits. These organizations are using many tools for achieving objectives for their CRM Strategy. Various tools used by SMEs of Jalandhar were e-mails & websites, trade sites, fax, sales persons, chat system, trade promotions, data records and much more.SMEs can achieve a competitive advantage by developing a more holistic view of interactions with customers who buy the products. In order to create a firm customer centric, company must need customer information. The successful firms deepen their relationship with their customer and able to convert them into loyal ones. Companies can only predict what their customers will do in the future if they keep a record of past behavior and know how to translate this information into knowledge about customers. Successful customer relationships draw on this knowledge and that is where the potential added value of customer relationship management lies. CRM strategies are often realized from the achievement of specific CRM objectives. To be successful, it's imperative that objectives are thorough, measurable and directly attributed to supporting the overall strategy. *During observation it is mostly observed that interviewing were clear that CRM is not only related to technology but it could be practiced manually also. If an organization has adequate resources and have long term plans they prefer CRM technologies. Such as internet, websites or software's otherwise they continue with traditional methods.*

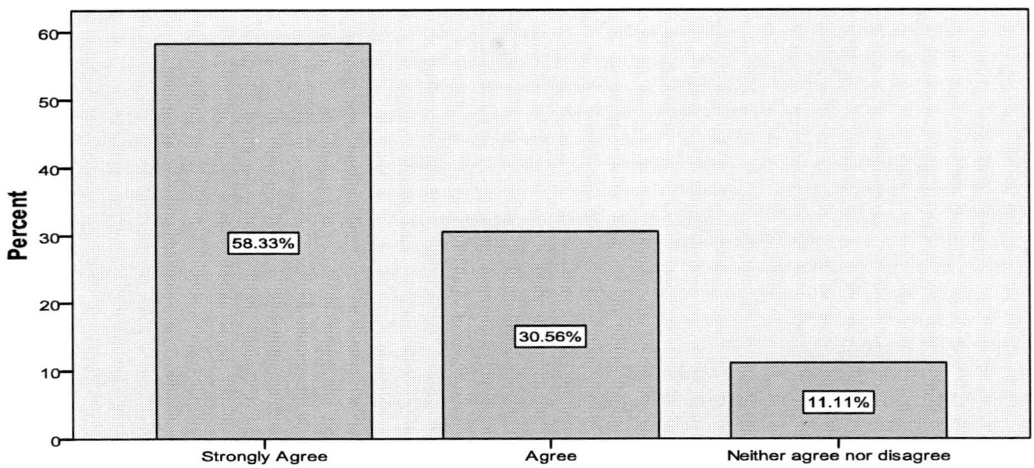

Graph: 2. CRM Helps in Winning Customer Loyalty

Table 2: Does your company believe that CRM helps in winning customer Loyalty

N	Valid	36
	Missing	0
	Mean	1.5278
	Minimum	1.00
	Maximum	3.00

The mean calculated fortable 2 is 1.5278which means that out of 36 respondents, maximum lies between 'strongly agree and agree'. It represents the responses of the respondents when it was asked from them that do they believed that CRM helps in winning customer loyalty. Maximum respondents were strongly agreed from the statement. As these organizations were successful in implementing CRM practices as compare to those who were just agree. 30.56% of respondents were agree from the statement because they believed that CRM helps in increasing business and to survive in a competition. These organizations believed that quality, better service and delivery on time are more important for them in order to win loyalty of customers. 11.11% don't want to rank any attribute so they just neither agree nor disagree. These organizations were those who were still struggling from problems during implementation of IT tools.

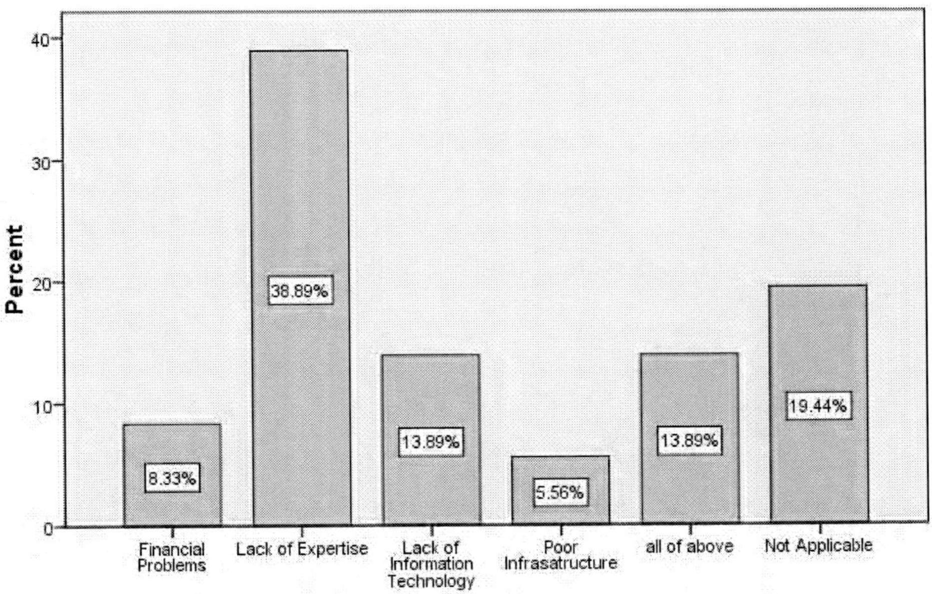

Graph 3: Kinds of Problems Faced by SMEs of Jalandhar in Using CRM Practices

Small Medium firms in Jalandhar still face many hurdles like financial problems, expertise, modern technology, poor infrastructure etc. 8.33% respondents faced financial problems while implemented CRM practices and 38.89% respondents faced lack of expertise problems which indicates that financial problem is not a much constraint for SMEs of Jalandhar. They were generated capital from number of schemes provided by government and from their business growth. They were doing good in their respected markets that's making their business profitable. 13.89% Small Medium firms have information technological problems. These firms basically are small firms which faced problems while installing IT tools for their business operationsproblems. However 19.44% respondent indicates the level of success of CRM implementation by them.

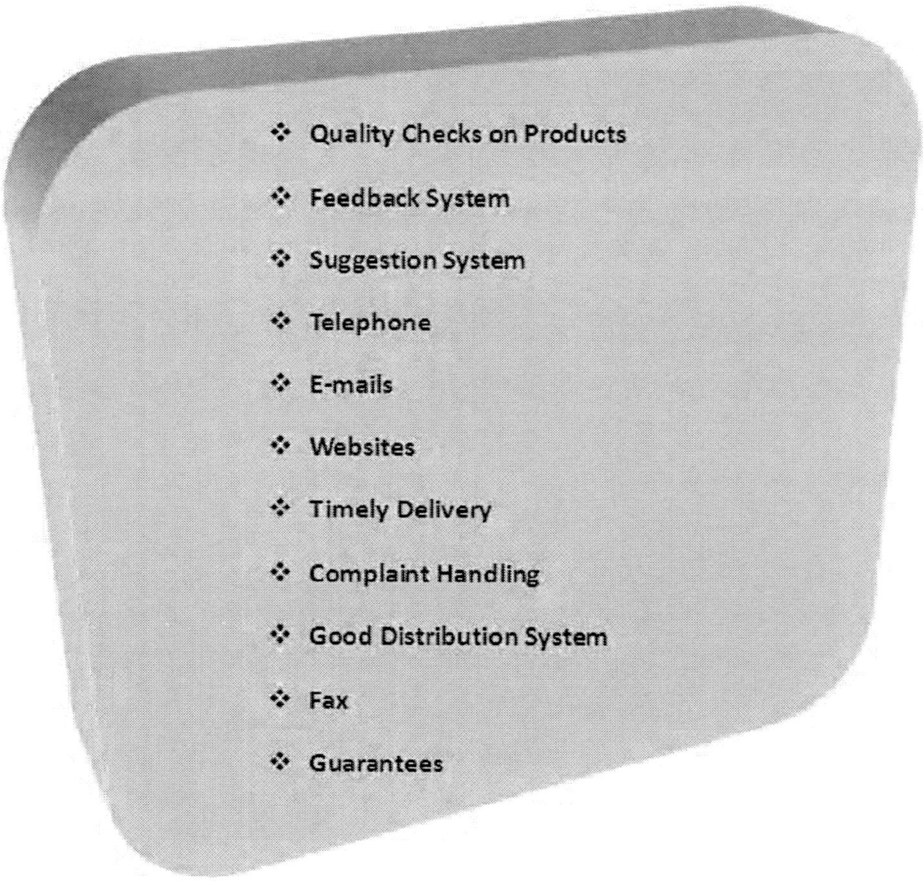

Fig. 1. Some Practices Implemented by SME of Jalandhar for Maintaing long Term Relations with their Customers

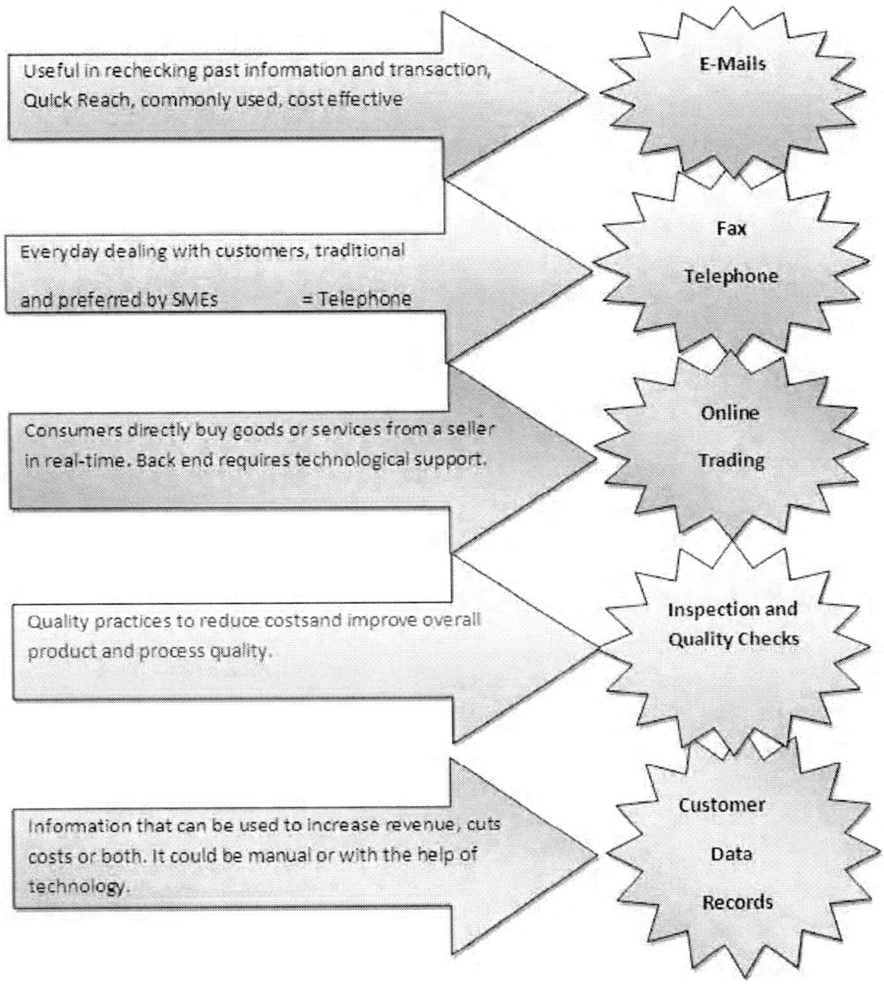

Fig. 2: Most commonly used tools of CRM by SMEs under the study

FINDINGS

As in changing scenario, SMEs also run their business with the help of IT and Computers. Maximum 69.44% SMEs under the study are partially computerized. In Jalandhar, Small Medium Firms are using IT tools for maintaining relations with their customers. Some SMEs even don't know about CRM strategy although they are implementing traditional CRM tools. It is found that many entrepreneurs are not professionally and technically qualified although they are running their business with their family grounds and experience but if short term programmes are plan and implement for them, it could lead to awareness about CRM and increase their business efficiency. IT Tools mainly used by SMEs of Jalandhar are emails, fax, telephone, websites, online chat, and delivery on time etc for delivering in better way to their customers. SMEs of Jalandhar believed on traditional way of CRM. They are using IT tools but still facing problems while using it. Customer Relationship Management helps small medium enterprises to satisfied customer needs and running as per the expectations of firms. Small Firms are not satisfied from government reforms. 58.3% SMEs of Jalandhar were strongly dissatisfied from government as they have not get any benefit from such a reforms. Sick units of Jalandhar are not able to get the benefits provided to them by government. Whereas medium firms are agree that government reforms help them but not always. Financial constraints are not major constraint in the implementation of CRM practices but it is mental blockage which makes reflected. If they recognized the importance of CRM for the growth and sustainability of their business then definitely they can arrange financial and other resources for them. It is observed that good number of SMEs in Jalandhar have adequate infrastructure and modern office.Good infrastructure helps to complete routine work in a better way at the same time whenever any customer approach physically it gives good impressions. SMEs of Jalandhar using CRM for focusing their existing customers and for increasing profits. They want to utilize their IT assets and try to improve their IT infrastructure so that they get more and more benefits from these tools. They could go for close customization as compare to big organization that usually practiced standardization to meet economies of scale and standard operations. This could project as competition advantage by SMEs during their CRM and marketing campaigns. Small Medium Enterprise is satisfied from their CRM practices used by them and very few were not satisfied from their CRM practices. All SMEs of Jalandhar under this study managing their clients in better way. They maintain their relations with customers by provided product delivery on time, having testing labs for checks on products before delivery, proper complaints handlings, replacing defected products. Companies in Jalandhar are using both traditional as well as modern tools of CRM properly. Traditional tools like feedback system, timely delivery, complaints handling, replacing materials etc and modern tools of IT like E-mails, Websites, Fax, Telephonic enquiries, Call centers etc. Customer Relationship Management Model adopted by Small Medium Enterprises of Jalandhar includes buyers (also fixed Buyers), government, partners, and exporters, Dealer's in other territories. Different people and different firms have their own views about CRM and many times it is slight different than the bookish meaning. Mostly firms mean with CRM that it is used to maintain good and long term relations with customers and satisfying them with good quality and timely delivery of products. Most of the SMEs of Jalandhar believed that CRM helps them in focusing on existing customers and increasing revenue opportunities. While others believed that CRM helps in increasing customer satisfaction. Rest mentioned some other benefits of CRM to their firms.

Mostly all the SMEs suggest some practices and tools to improve CRM role in Small Medium Firms which includes governments support, technological support by IT companies, many other schemes and programmes for SMEs development.

CONCLUSION

Customer Relationship Management is a complete approach through which SMEs can maximize their profits along with maintaining good relationship with their customers. The development of information and communication technology helps SMEs to collect data about their existing and potential customers and to inter collect detailed about individual customers. This study was conducted to determine the CRM practices adopted by SMEs of Jalandhar. SMEs of Jalandhar have implemented many tools to maintain relations with their customers. The most commonly used Customer Relationship Management tools by Small Medium Enterprises of Jalandhar are e-mails, websites, fax, online chat, trade sites, telephones, customer data mining, customer complaint handling department etc. SMEs of Jalandhar deal with their fixed buyers and with these fixed buyers; they were maintained a good relations from last many years. While more Small Medium firms get benefited from CRM tools, they were implementing IT tools for retaining old customers and serving the new ones. SME of Jalandhar was not implementing modern CRM tools. The basic problem SMEs faced was lack of expertise, modern technology and the head of the firms are not educated as per concern with IT knowledge, this is the reason that why they are not able to cope up changes. Their next generation will soon take responsibility to run the business, so new generation should be qualified and competitive enough to face tough competition. Many firms of Jalandhar under this study were those who run their business by their sons. Both father and son run the business collectively. Father knows the business from years to years on other hand son carry business with new ideas, innovations and creative thinking. For shaping future of Small Medium Enterprises in Punjab it's essential to implement CRM practices in a better way. E-CRM tools can be implemented to reach up to untapped customers and to get success in business. Leading software companies are providing low cost CRM software's for industries. Even many firms in Jalandhar are ready to implement more modern tools for maintaining relationship with their customers. In this research it is concluded that CRM Practices are becoming popular in SMEs and have a key role ahead.

REFERENCES

[1] Agarwal, A., Harding, D. & Schumacher, J. (2004). Organizing for CRM.*The McKinsey Quarterly 2004,* November 3,pp.81-91.

[2] Aghdasi, M. &Naude, P. (2008). Reasons for Success and Failure of CRM Projects from the prospectives of Advisors.*TarbiatModares University Faculty of Engineering Department of Industrial Engineering.*

[3] AS, M. &Arif, N. (2010). ERP – CRM Integration by Neural Networks.Proceedings of the International Joint Journal Conference on Engineering and Technology, pp.135-136

[4] Bhatia, G. (2007). Small and Medium Enterprises (SME) and Role of Competition Commission of India (CCI).*Competition Commission of India (CCI).*

[5] Bobbitt, L. M., &Dabholkar, P. A., (2001). Integrating attitudinal theories to understand and predict use of technology-based self-service - The Internet as an illustration, *International Journal of Service Industry Management*, 12, No. 5, pp. 423-450

[6] Carland, J. (2006). Academy of Information and Management Sciences Journal.Volume:9, No: 1.2006,ISSN 1524-7252.

[7] Chandra et al. (2009). A Report on CRM Strategies of Nokia.*CRM | PGDM 2008-10*

[8] Chesebrough. (2006). Knowledge Management A tool for SMEs to enhance competitiveness,CACCI Journal, Vol. 1, 2006.

[9] Cooper, D. R., and Schindler, P. S. (2006). *Business research methods, 9th Ed.*New Delhi:Tata McGraw-Hill., pp 1-35

[10] Coyles, S. &Gokey, T. (2002). Customer retention is not enough. *McKinsey Quarterly*, Vol. 11, No.2, pp. 75-81

[11] Das, K et al. (2009). Customer Relationship Management (CRM) Best Practices and Customer Loyalty Study of Indian Retail Banking Sector. *European Journal of Social Sciences*, Volume 11, Number 1 (2009), pp. 61-85

[12] Das, T. (2007). How CRM strategy does varies across Small and Large enterprises.Nottingham University Business School, 2007.

[13] Dholakia, R.R., & Kshetri, N. (2004). Factors Impacting the Adoption of the Internet among SMEs.*Small Business Economics* ,vol. 23 (4), pp. 311-322

[14] Dwyer, M., Gilmore, A. & Carson, D. (2009). *Innovative Marketing in SMEs'* European Journal of Marketing, Volume. 43, No. 1/2, pp. 46-61

[15] Gartner, J. (2002). CRM Trends for Small and Mid-size Businesses in North America. ©2002 Gartner, Inc. August 16, 2002.

[16] Gilmore, A., Carson, D. & Grant, K. (2001). SME Marketing in Practice: Marketing Intelligence & Planning, Volume.19 Issue 1, 2001, pp.6-11

[17] Globel SME Technology Summit. *(2010).* Small & Medium Business Development Chamber of India, Mumbai, November 2010.

[18] Goff, J. et al. (1998). A new way to reach small businesses.*The McKinsey quarterly* 1998, Number 3, pp. 172-176.

[19] Griffin, J. (2002). Growing by Knowing (Your Customer Base).*Source: http://www.crmguru.custhelp.com/app/answers.*

[20] Hildebrand, V. (2007). Drive Sustainable, Profitable Growth through CRM. *Wellesley Information Services (WIS),* Dec2007.

[21] India Global Summit on SMEs. (2004). Conference Proceedings, Emerging Challenges and Opportunities, pp. 23-24 Nov. 2004, New Delhi

[22] Internet & Mobile Association of India. (2010). Free for SMEs: Free and Low Cost ICT Solutions for SMEs. *IAMAI Knowledge Series 1*

[23] Islam. and Yang ,Yi. (2006). Service Satisfaction, Information Trust and e-CRM Performance in BSC model in the empirics of Financial Institutions.source: *http://www.sciencedirect.com*

[24] Kacker, S. (2009). Overcoming Barriers to Innovation for Indian SMEs.Joint Secretary, *Government of India, Ministry Small Scale Industries, New Delhi* – 110 011, India.

[25] Kale et al. (2010). Enterprise Resource Planning Implementation in Indian SMEs: Issues and Challenges.

[26] Kandie, W. & Chan, M. (2008). Towards Enhancing Collaboration in Small Enterprises.*Business Process Expert Community*, px.sap.com © 2008 SAP AG

[27] Koller & Schidler. (2009). *Business Research Methods*, 9th Ed.New Delhi: Pearson Publisher Ltd., pp 1-50

[28] Kotelnikov. (2007). Small and Medium Enterprises and ICT. Asia-Pacific Development Information Programme, source*: http://www.unapcict.org*

[29] Kotler, P. (2006) *Marketing Managemen*t. 12th Ed. New Delhi: Pearson Publishers Ltd., pp. 1-23

[30] Kotler, P., Keller, K. (2005). *Marketing Management.* New Jersey: Pearson Prentice Hall Ltd., pp. 1-40

[31] Kuada and Serles. (2006). Customer Relationship Marketing (CRM) Practices in Danish Small Businesses. *International Management Review, Vol. 2, No. 4, 2006.*

[32] Malhotra, K. (2009). *Marketing Management.* 5th Ed.New Delhi: Pearson Publication Ltd., pp 106-210

[33] Maria and Michelli. (2008). *SME's and Competitive Advantage.*Department of Economics, University of Padova, Via Del Santo, 33, 35123 Padova (Italy).

[34] Nargundkar, R. (2002). Marketing Resarch.7th Ed: Tata Macrgrew Hill., pp. 187-194

[35] Outlaw, J. (2002). CRM Trends for Small and Midsize Businesses in North America.2002 *.source:http://www. gartner.com.*

[36] Peck, K. (2010). Cheap Business Phone Service for Superb and Good Quality Performance.*source:http://www.articlealley.com/article.*

[37] Ramaswamy & Namakumari. (2007). Marketing Management. 3rdEd.New Delhi: Macmillan Publishers.,pp.151-161

[38] Rigby & Ledingham. (2004). CRM Done Right.*source:http://www.hbr.org*

[39] Rosenfield, R. (2002). Customer Relationship Management: A Brief History and Brief Mystery. Source: *http://www.jrosenfield.com/articles/CRM-History.htm*

[40] Sachdeva, J. (2009). Business Research Methodology.2009 Ed. New Delhi: Himalaya Publishers., pp.193-358

[41] Solano, P. &Canovas, G. (2008). Relationship lending and SME financing in the continental, pp. 465-482, European bank-based system.*Springer Science Business Media, LLC.* September 2008.

[42] Strickland, J. & Chandra, S. (2004). Technological Differences between CRM and E-CRM.*Issues in Information Systems,* Vol.5, No 2, pp. 408-413.

[43] Stringfellow, A. &Nie, W. (2005). CRM: Profiting From Understanding Customer Needs. source:http://www.hbr.org

[44] Tung, R. &Aycan, Z. (2008). Key success factors and indigenous management practices in SMEs in emerging economies.*Journal of World Business 43 (2008),* pp. 381–384

[45] Usoro. and Achuama. (2010). Dancing with the Stars: E-CRM and SMEs in Developing Countries. *Journal of Economic Development, Management, IT, Finance and Marketing,* Vol.2, pp.68-80, September 2010.Vol. 11, No.2, pp. 75-81.

[46] Zayman, Philip. (2003). Functional Requirement of CRM Solution for the South African SME's.M.Phil Thesis, Rand Afrikaans University.

Is Customer Satisfaction a Reflection of Employee Satisfaction in Context to Business Process Outsourcing?

Shreya Dhingra, Sarika Srivastava and H.N. Agarwal[1]

Jaipur National University, Jaipur
[1]*Saurashtra University, Gujarat*

ABSTRACT

Employee and customer satisfaction have been widely studied and are considered to be one of the most important outcomes of Business. To be successful, organizations must look into the needs and wants of their customers. It is a proven fact that organization with a quality foundation achieves high level of Customer Satisfaction, but some researches have shown that a specific key of achieving customer satisfaction is employee satisfaction. That is the reason why many researchers and academicians have continuously emphasized on the importance of customer satisfaction, loyalty and retention. Customer satisfaction is important because many researches have shown that it has a positive effect on an organization's profitability. There is also a positive connection between customer satisfaction, loyalty and retention. Therefore, customer satisfaction, loyalty and retention are all very important for an organization to be successful.

INTRODUCTION

There are many aspects of business upon which Human Resource managers need to focus, but the most important which is often considered is the customer. The importance of customers has been always highlighted by many researchers and academicians. Zairi (2000) said "Customers are the purpose of what we do and rather than them depending on us, we depend on them. That is the main reason why organizations today are focusing on customer satisfaction, loyalty and retention. A business cannot exist without a customer—article after article and book after book remind us of this truth. But at times this emphasis on the customer may us from the pivotal resource that makes it possible to satisfy the customer—the employee.

Kotler and Keller (2007) describe highly satisfied customers as behaving positively towards firms in the following ways. They stay loyal by buying more and are less sensitive to price. They speak positively about the firm in comparison to newer customers; they are also less expensive and easier to serve.

It is self evident that without employees the business's product or service simply could not exist. Just one person cannot drive a business by oneself; one cannot make an actual organization that produces goods and services. For this people are needed. No matter the size of the organization, the employees will ultimately be responsible for dealing with customers, either face to face, on the telephone, through correspondence, or on the company website. To the customer, your employees are the organization. Employee satisfaction is the key element in achieving customer satisfaction. Without employee satisfaction, customer satisfaction will never be achieved. It is the linkage between employee satisfaction and customer satisfaction that is critical. One major goal of this paper is to highlight the link for improving employee satisfaction as one way to effectively improve the customer satisfaction.

This paper is based on the findings of the research on relationship between employee satisfaction and customer satisfaction with a special reference to BPO industry in India.

LITERATURE REVIEW

Customer Satisfaction

Many research studies have narrated the importance of customer satisfaction. Kotler (2000) defined satisfaction as a person's feelings of pleasure or disappointment resulting from comparing a product's perceived performance (or outcome) in relation to his or her expectations". Hoyer and McInnis (2001) also explained that satisfaction can be associated with feelings of acceptance, happiness, relief, excitement and delight.

Reich held (2006) states that a dissatisfied customer can act as a detractor and can drive up service costs by reporting numerous problems. Unhappy customers can damage the firms' reputation, reducing its ability to attract the best people in the industry. In addition to it customers may demoralize frontline employees with the amount of demands and complaints that they are inclined to make. There are many factors which affect the customer satisfaction. Most important among them is the dissatisfaction of employees. According to Hokanson (1995), these employee satisfaction factors include friendly employees, courteous employees, knowledgeable employees, helpful employees, service quality, good value, billing clarity and quick service. Call centre manage flow of information and communication between Organization and the customer via telephone (Malhotra & Mukerjee, 2004). Call centre also allow a company to build, maintain and manage customer relationship by solving problem and resolving complaints quickly.

Effect of Customer Satisfaction on Profitability, Customer Loyalty and Retention

Customer satisfactions have a positive effect on an organization's profitability. According to Hoyer and McInnis (2001), satisfied customers form the foundation of any successful business as customer satisfaction leads to repeat purchase, brand loyalty, and positive word of mouth.

As stated by Zairi (2000): "There are numerous studies that have looked at the impact of customer satisfaction on repeat purchase, loyalty and retention. Satisfied customers are most likely to share their experience with other people, similarly dissatisfied customers would share their negative experience. Aaker (1995) said that the strategic dimension for an organization includes becoming more competitive through customer satisfaction/brand loyalty, product/service quality, brand/firm associations, relative cost, new product activity, and manager/employee capability and performance (Figure 1).

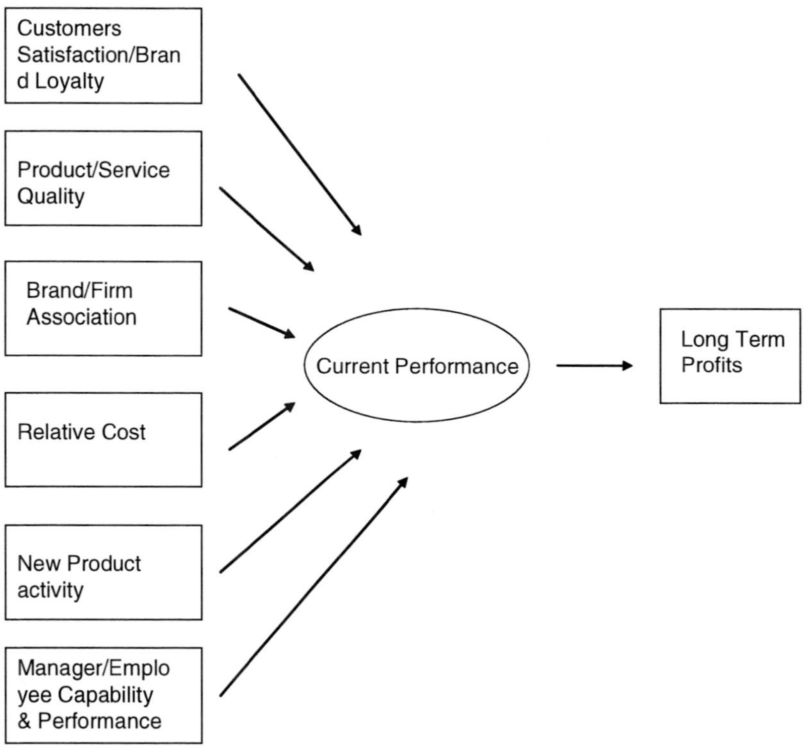

Fig. 1. Performance Measures Reflecting Long-Term Profitability

Source: The Importance of Customer Satisfaction Relation to Customer Loyalty and Retention; Aaker (1995)

Employees in the call centre need to answer call by customer 24 hour throughout 365 days per year. Therefore, employees who work in a call centre are under a certain amount of tension. The management realizes that is it vital to make sure their employees are satisfied in order for them to deliver good service to customer.

Relationship Between Customer and Employee Satisfaction

Call Center employees are the primary contact between the company and the customer and therefore are one of the important influencer of customer satisfaction. Many researches have shown that one key for achieving the customer satisfaction is employee satisfaction. Therefore it is said that in reference to call centre, employee's job satisfaction influences the quality of service which they provide. Thereby Berry (1997) explained that great efforts are required to improve employee's job satisfaction, which in turn creates the satisfied customer and a successful organization. Nilson, Johnson and Gustafson (2001) said that long established organizations with a quality foundation have better leverage for achieving high levels of customer satisfaction. There is also a "positive and significant relationship between customer satisfaction and employee satisfaction" these relationships are "positive, statistically and substantively significant". According to Brown and Lam, (2008). Employee satisfaction is significantly related to service quality and to customer satisfaction, which in return influences the profitability of the organization leading to a satisfaction-quality-profit cycle.

So satisfied employees are more productive, innovative and loyal, which in turn leads to customer retention. Of course, dissatisfied employees will likely lower customer satisfaction. Employee satisfaction therefore becomes a critical leading indicator. According to Koyes,(2006), what else can be interpreted from this other than that employee satisfaction plays a "strong, central role" in predicting profitability and organizational effectiveness. Kozzani and Oakley, (2005) explains the direct links between employee satisfaction and customer satisfaction, and between customer satisfaction and improved financial performance, it is important to understand the elements that drive employee satisfaction

Heskett et al. (1994) proposes a relationship between profitability, customer loyalty, and employee satisfaction. The service profit chain was developed by analyzing the profitability of the organization which centered the employees of the company and customers needs as the main focus area of the management. The motive of the service profit chain was to make the employees and customers paramount to organizational profitability and performance.

DISCUSSION AND IMPLICATIONS

The BPO industry is identified by various job-related characteristics that is regularly found in organization, some of which eventually become the reasons for employees' dissatisfaction from a typical BPO job – high stress levels, monotonous nature of the job, demand-supply disparity and lack of career growth potential on the professional front, loss of identity, mismatch with normal cycle, complete change of life style and lack of comfort on the personal front. All such reasons lead to mounting dissatisfaction in BPO employees. Increased dissatisfaction leads to reduced motivation, which in turn results in diluted efficiency because of which employees are not able to give their expected output which eventually results in their leaving the job.

Based on the past literature, it can be said that employees working in outsourcing environment confront a varied work environment, which is highly controlled; closely monitored and strictly measured against targets though employees are encouraged to take responsibility for both their team and their own performance. According to Berry (1997), employ the satisfied employee will lead to the creation of satisfied customer, resolve the actual problem in the management of call centre industry, create good environment for call centre employees.

Factors Affecting Employee Satisfaction: Challenges Facing the Job Satisfaction

Much of literature is available which states a BPO job is repetitive, less skilled, and less challenging and thus affects the attitude of the employees towards it, Taylor and Bain, (2006) mentioned some job related factors which affect the employee satisfaction. Thus, some of the major job-related factors in BPO employees identified are namely challenges in the job, supervision, working conditions, salary, accountability, authority, recognition, career progression, company policies and interpersonal relationships which effect the satisfaction of employees.

Supervision. It is always found that BPO employees at the Indian sites feel that close supervision and restricted freedom make the supervision ineffective on the part of their team leads and often causes discontent among the employees.

Working conditions. Working conditions is an important dimension of BPO job as it affects employee satisfaction, willingness to work and subsequently efficiency. Numerous studies have investigated effects of working conditions on strain; employee complaints job satisfaction and affective commitment over time, and, in turn, enhance intentions to quit a job.

Salary. According to Sharma and Jyoti (2006), Salary is a vital job-related characteristic, which affects employees' liking towards a job, their satisfaction level and even their commitment to the organization. Salary and promotions are related to company policies, which in turn affect employees' attitude towards work.

Accountability, authority, recognition. These job-related characteristics often affect job satisfaction and employee motivation at workplace. It gets converted into an ingredient of self-esteem and hence affects employee self-fulfillment.

Career progression. Career progression is another critical job-related characteristic which affects employees' satisfaction and their willingness to stay with the organization.

Company policies. Policies matter to organizations and employees alike; they will shape employees' perceptions of fairness and justice, and hence, their commitment to the organization.

Interpersonal relationships. Interpersonal relationship in an organization is quite a binding factor and affects employee satisfaction to a large extent. Lack of it in a workplace often leads to social stressors.

Factors Affecting Customer Satisfaction

It is always said that in a service Industry, there is always a direct link between job and employee satisfaction and on the other hand there also exist a relation between customer satisfaction and loyalty. In today's world, organization realize that is it important to keep their worker satisfied as human resource is the important assets for the organization to keep their business running. With satisfied workers, they will deliver the better quality service to the customer which indirectly will increase customer satisfaction

Fig. 2. Factors that Affect Customer Satisfaction

Source: The Importance of Customer Satisfaction Relation to Customer Loyalty and Retention; Hokanson (1995)

CONCLUSION

The purpose of this paper is to examine the relationship between employee satisfaction and and customer satisfaction in reference to BPO employees. Since satisfaction of internal customers, i.e. employees, is linked to satisfaction of external customers (Heskett et al., 2008), internal marketing aims at satisfying the needs and wants of "internal customers", so that they show the right attitude and dedication and remain committed to the organization, which is crucial for delivering good quality service and satisfying customers. It is crucial for Indian call centre organizations' to find out ways, as part of the "internal marketing strategy", to ensure that the frontline employees are motivated to be customer conscious, and remain committed to their organizations'.

REFERENCES

[1] Aaker, D. A., 1995, Strategic Market, New York, John Willey and Sons, Inc.

[2] Berry, L.M. (1997). Psychology at Work, San Francisco: McGraw-Hill Companies Inc.

[3] Bernhardt, K. L., Donthub, N. and Kennettc, P. A. (2000). A longitudinal analysis of satisfaction and profitability. Journal of Business Research, 47 (2), pp. 161-171.

[4] Brown, S. P., and Lam, S. K. (2008). A meta-analysis of relationships linking employee satisfaction to customer responses. Journal of Retailing, 84 (3), pp. 243-255.

[5] Grebner, S., Semmer, N.K., Faso, L.L., Gut, S., Kalin, W.and Elfering, A. (2003), "Work conditions, well-being, and job-related attitudes among call centre agents", European Journal of Work and Organizational Psychology, Vol. 12 No. 4, pp. 341-65.

[6] Hoyer, W. D. & MacInnis, D. J., (2001), Consumer Behavior. 2nd edition, Boston Houghton Mifflin Company.

[7] Heskett, J.L., Jones, T.O., Loveman, G.W., Sasser, W.E. Jr and Schlesinger, L.A. (2008), "Putting the service-profit chain to work", Harvard Business Review, July-August, pp. 118-29.

[8] Hoyer, W. D. & MacInnis, D. J., 2001, Consumer behavior. 2nd edition, Boston, Houghton Mifflin Company.

[9] Hokanson, S., January 2, (1995), The Deeper You Analyze, The More You Satisfy Customers, Marketing News, p. 16.

[10] Kozzani, C.A., and Oakley, J. L. (2005). "Linking organizational characteristics to employee attitudes and behavior: A look at the downstream effects on market response and financial performance". Forum for People Performance Management & Measurement, pp. 1-15.

[11] Koys, D. J. (2006). The effects of employee satisfaction, organizational citizenship behavior and turnover on organizational effectiveness: A unit level longitudinal study. Personal Psychology, 54 (1), pp. 101-114.

[12] Malhotra, N., & Mukherjee, A. (2004). The relative influence of organizational commitment and job satisfaction on service quality of customer -contact employees in banking call centers. Journal of Services Marketing, 18 (3), 162-174.

[13] Nilson, L., Johnson, M., and Gustafsson, A. (2001). The impact of quality practices on customer satisfaction and business results: Product versus service organizations. Journal of Quality Management, 6 (1), pp. 5-27.

[14] Reichheld, F. F., (1996), The Loyalty Effect: The Hidden Force Behind Loyalty, Boston, Harvard Business School.

[15] Sharma, R.D. and Jyoti, J. (2006), "Job satisfaction among school teachers", IIMB Management Review, Vol. 18 No. 4, pp. 349-63.

[16] Taylor, P. and Bain, P. (2004), "Call centre outsourcing to India: the revenge of history", Labour and Industry, Vol. 14 No. 3, pp. 15-38.

[17] Zairi, M., (2000), Managing Customer Dissatisfaction through Effective Complaint Management Systems, the TQM Magazine, 12 (5), pp. 331-335.

Is the Extension of Brand "Dairy Milk" Non-functioning Among Today's Indian Youth? A Research Study

Malay Bhattacharjee and Prithviraj Banerjee

Globsyn Business School,Block EP&GP,Sector 5, Salt Lake City, Kolkata

ABSTRACT

It has been observed over a long period of time that brand Cadburys' have been very successful in promoting its various products concerning different types of chocolates. But a closer look would also make one understand that "Cadburys" have created different 'sub-brands' in the likes of "Dairy Milk, Temptation, Bournville, Celebrations" etc. These sub-brands were "extended" along with the principle "brand - Cadburys".

Undoubtedly it has been a part of the company's strategy to extend the brand as well as the sub-brand side by side simultaneously. This study has been an endeavor to look closely and ascertain if the sub-brand "Dairy Milk" is really working as envisaged by the makers. Using a structured survey questionnaire, we find that even if Cadbury withdraws its sub-brand extension of 'dairy milk' other than the chocolate popular as "Cadbury Dairy Milk" chocolate it would hardly have any affect into it's market among the youth of this country.

INTRODUCTION

Cadbury is a British confectionery company owned by Mondelçz International Inc. and is the industry's second-largest globally after Mars, Incorporated. The company was known as Cadbury Schweppes plc from 1969–2008 until its demerger, in which its global confectionery business was separated from its US beverage unit (now called "Dr Pepper Snapple Group").

In 1905, Cadbury launched its Dairy Milk bar, with a higher proportion of milk than previous chocolate bars, and it became the company's best selling product by 1913. Fruit and Nut was introduced as part of the Dairy Milk line in 1928, soon followed by Whole Nut in 1933. By this point, Cadbury was the brand leader in the United Kingdom. These were accompanied by several other products: Flake (1920), Cream-filled eggs (1923), Crunchie (1929) (Crunchie was originally launched under the Fry's name but later adopted by Cadbury's) and Roses (1938).

Cadbury India Ltd. is a part of Mondelçz International. Cadbury India operates in five categories – Chocolate confectionery, Beverages, Biscuits, Gum and Candy. In the Chocolate Confectionery business, Cadbury has maintained its undisputed leadership over the years. Some of the key brands are Cadbury Dairy Milk, Bournvita, 5 Star, Perk, Bournville, Celebrations, Gems, Halls, Éclairs, Bubbaloo, Tang and Oreo.

In India, Cadbury began its operations in 1948 by importing chocolates. After over 60 years of existence, it today has six company-owned manufacturing facilities at Thane, Induri (Pune) and Malanpur (Gwalior), Bangalore and Baddi (Himachal Pradesh) Hyderabad and 4 sales offices (New Delhi, Mumbai, Kolkata and Chennai). The corporate office is in Mumbai.

Cadbury India enjoys a value market share of over 70 percent in the chocolate category and our brand Cadbury Dairy Milk (CDM) is considered the "gold standard" for chocolates in India. The pure taste of CDM defines the chocolate taste for the Indian consumer.

CADBURY DAIRY MILK

Cadbury Dairy Milk (CDM) entered the Indian market in 1948, and since then for consumers across India, the word Cadbury has become synonymous with chocolate. CDM remains at the top of the Indian chocolate market not only because of its most delicious, best tasting chocolate but also because of its memorable communication.

In the early days, the brand had a huge fan following among kids. In order to build stronger appeal among older age groups, the brand re-positioned itself through the classic 'Real Taste of Life' campaign in 1994. The campaign positioned Cadbury Dairy Milk as the chocolate that awakened the little child in every grown up and very soon, both teenagers and adults, were hooked on to this bar of pure magic.

With the launch of the Rs. 5 pack in 1998, CDM became more affordable and hence more accessible for the masses. The ensuing positioning of 'Khaane Waalonkokhaaneka Bahana Chhayie' made consumption into a joyful, social occasion.

In 2004, the 'KuchMeetha Ho Jaaye' campaign was launched, seeking to increase CDM consumption by making it synonymous with traditional sweets (Mithai). With Amitabh Bachchan as the face and voice of the brand, the campaign went on to become a huge success. People could relate to the commercials that were aired to promote Cadbury Dairy Milk. How many can forget the 'Pappu Pass Ho Gaya' commercial? The country cheered on as Pappu fell in love in the Pappu Love Test commercial. Then came'MissPalampur' and the country celebrated the beauty pageant with a difference. The'Kenya' commercial that was aired in 2008 celebrated the spirit of cricket and that of true sportsmanship. In 2009, we aired another commercial under the 'KuchMeetha Ho Jaaye' platform, called the 'Pay Day' commercial.

In the year 2010, the 'ShubhAarambh' campaign was launched, drawing lines from the traditional Indian custom of having something sweet before embarking on something new. With 'ShubhAarambh', Cadbury took the Dairy Milk journey a step further into the hearts of its million lovers.

With the current campaign 'Khaane Ke BaadMeethe Mein Kuch Meetha Ho Jaaye', the company aims to introduce the thought of having a CDM as a post dinner meetha (dessert).

LITERATURE REVIEW

Brand Extension is nothing new to any given industry all around the globe in the present scenario. But the meaningful purpose of any such brand extension also needs to be well justified from the point of view of the consumers. The company might go for a brand extension just because a given brand has been successful over a fairly long period of time. But it needs to be seen whether the consumers have also understood the meaningful purpose of the said brand extension in the same light as that of the brand makers. Academic studies (Aaker& Keller (1990), Farquhar, Herr & Fazio (1990), Park, Milberg & Lawson (1991), Roedder&Loken (1991)) have been trying to understand how consumers within the target market could get to understand and evaluate the mechanism of the said brand extension.

Most of the previous research has revolved around the issue of "fit". Most of these studies have taken up the issue of "fit" as a generalized concept applicable across industries and all types of product categories. "Fit" is that element which would translate the workable relationships between the consumer perceptions of the parent brand, its product categories, the extension, pre-determine the ease with which the parent brand can extend (Farquhar, Herr & Fazio (1990), Park, Milberg & Lawson (1991), Boush&Loken (1991)). Roedder John &Loken (1991) have gone one step further to determine the relationship between the parent brand and the said brand extension in terms of harmful or damaging or uncalled for "feedback" effects wherein not understanding or not keeping in toes of the brand extension or failing to notice a said brand extension has been a crucial subject matter.

Bridges (1991) has examined extensions in terms of product features and image associations and their role in preserving schema cohesion.Meyers-Levy &Tybout (1989) have examined the optimal degree of fit, or schema (in)congruity. These researches were mainly based on consumer responses (feedbacks) in U.S, wherein either they were consumers or they were students under the pretext of hypothetical extensions presented in an experimental setting.

Gil McWilliam of London Business School in his research titled "The Effect of Brand Typology on Brand Extension Fit: Commercial and Academic Research Findings" (1993) states that, practitioners do not operate from a single homogeneous view of branding, but rather utilize various branding typologies to help them understand brand extension evaluations.

The present work is motivated by the above McWilliam (1993), Bridges (1991), and Meyers-Levy &Tybout (1989) studies and tries to prove that every extension does not happen to be a fruitful extension. Also, that part of the extension which is not functioning as expected needs to be revisited and would call for necessary logical decisions to be taken, however bold.

Research Objective

The main objective of the research is to understand if the extension of the brand "Cadbury" along with the sub-brand "Dairy Milk" simultaneously is justified and happens to be working in the diffusion of various types of chocolates of various categories belonging to various price ranges, as well as serving various segments of the market.

Research Methodology

Data Collection: Primary data was collected through a structured questionnaire on a one-on-one structured in-depth interview based on the given questionnaire containing several multiple choice questions pertaining to the given issue. Some of the questions were of 'open end' nature which gave ample scope to the respondents to come through with their own understandings out of their perception which were then incorporated for analysis.

Sampling Technique: The sample used for the purpose of this research has been the product of two stage sampling. At first the 'stratified sampling' has been used to earmark and ensure that the sample likely to be collected should correspond to the age barrier of 18 – 23 years of both the sexes. Furthermore, it was also looked after that all the respondents are students of under graduate programs or post graduate programs. Once this was ensured then the second stage used for the physical data collection has been 'convenient sampling'.

Sample Size: The total sample size used for this research stands at 170 respondents who are either college students or university students. The break-up of sample stands as 100 young males and 70 young females of the city of Calcutta.

Research Design: The research primarily focuses on the subject of the purpose of the extension of the sub-brand "Dairy Milk" and its effects on the given target market. Because of the exploratory nature of the research, it was decided upon to conduct in-depth interviews with a structured questionnaire amongst the youth population of the city that are in all probabilities exposed to the said brand as also the brand extension. The nature of the data restricted us to perform the chi-square tests with the help of Excel, as well as constricted us to come about with data representations through pie-charts, bar diagrams, area diagrams.

Analysis & Findings

H_0 (1): All given choices are equally preferred by the customers while going for a Dairy Milk chocolate (bar) at the time of purchase.

H_1 (1): All choices given are not equally preferred by the customers while going for a Dairy

Milk chocolate (bar) at the time of purchase.

For testing the hypothesis above, we employ the chi-square goodness-of-fit test. The results are:

	Cadburys'	Dairy Milk	Cadburys' Dairy Milk	None
Observed	0	67	3	41

Chi-sq	111.667
d.f.	3
Critical value	3.841

Since the calculated value of chi-square (111.667) is greater than the critical value of chi-square for 3 d.f. (3.841) at the 5% level of significance, we reject the null that the choices are equally preferred.

We also test the following

H_0 (2): Gender and preference of the customers while going for a Dairy Milk chocolate (bar) are independent.

H_1 (2): Gender and preference of the customers while going for a Dairy Milk chocolate (bar) are not independent.

For testing the hypothesis above, we employ the chi-square test of independence of attributes. The results are:

	Cadburys'	*Dairy Milk*	*Cadburys' Dairy Milk*
Male	0	41	2
Female	0	26	1

Chi-sq	1.020
d.f.	3
Critical value	3.841

Since the calculated value of chi-square (1.020) is less than the critical value of chi-square for 3 d.f. (3.841) at the 5% level of significance, we fail to reject the null that gender of the participants and response to the following questions are independent.

The diagrammatic expression stands like this.

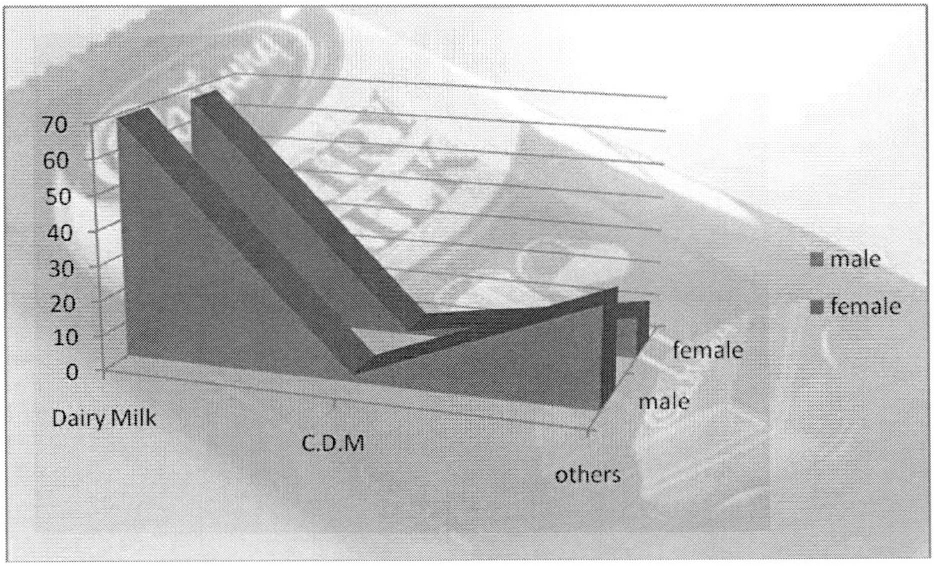

Interpretation

- It is observed from the following test that majority of the people from this age group take a "Cadburys' Dairy Milk Chocolate" bar accepting the fact that it is "Dairy Milk". In their selection, the word "Cadburys'" hardly has any role to play.
- It might even be that they have a fair level of knowledge and understanding about 'Dairy Milk' being a product of "Cadburys" which is why the very words "Dairy Milk" comes to them with sufficient reinforcement about it being a Cadburys' product.

H_0 (3): All given choices are equally preferred by the customers while going for a Dairy Milk Silk chocolate (bar) at the time of purchase.

H_1 (3): All given choices are not equally preferred by the customers while going for a Dairy Milk Silk chocolate (bar) at the time of purchase.

For testing the hypothesis above, we employ the chi-square goodness-of-fit test. The results are:

	Cadburys	Dairy Milk	Silk	Cadburys' Silk	Cadburys' Dairy Milk - Silk	none of these
Observed	0	0	33	2	2	0

Chi-sq	6509
d.f.	5
Critical value	11.07

Since the calculated value of chi-square (6509) is greater than the critical value of chi-square for 5 d.f. (11.07) at the 5% level of significance, we reject the null that the choices are equally preferred.

We also test the following

H_0 (4): Gender and preference of the customers while going for Silk are independent.

H_1 (4): Gender and preference of the customers while going for Silk are not independent.

For testing the hypothesis above, we employ the chi-square test of independence of attributes. The results are:

	Cadburys	*Dairy Milk*	*Silk*	*Cadburys' Silk*	*Cadburys' Dairy Milk - Silk*
Male	0	0	24	2	0
Female	0	0	9	0	1

Chi-sq	3.373
d.f.	5
Critical value	11.07

Since the calculated value of chi-square (3.373) is less than the critical value of chi-square for 5 d.f. (11.07) at the 5% level of significance, we fail to reject the null that gender of the participants and response to the following questions are independent.

The diagrammatic expression stands like this.

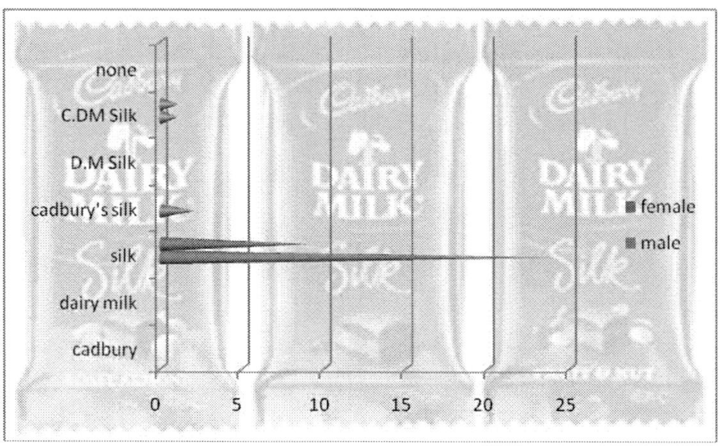

Interpretation

- This part of the study reveals the fact that "Cadburys' Dairy Milk Silk" is somewhat being accepted by the people in the name of "Silk" only.
- This also suggest that the customers as well as the end consumers know the fact that "Silk"

is a Cadburys' product, and that it is a milk chocolate.

- This might trigger in them the required "brand recall' without the aid of the words "Cadburys' Dairy Milk" while purchasing SILK.
- This might also be indicative of the fact that the word "Dairy Milk" is not at all required to identify "Silk".
- Dropping the words "Dairy Milk" would help Cadburys' increase their product range just as it has increased it through "Temptation, Bourneville, Celebration" etc.

H_0 (5): All given choices are equally preferred by the customers while going for a Cadburys' Dairy Milk Éclairs .

H_1 (5): All given choices are not equally preferred by the customers while going for a Cadburys' Dairy Milk Éclairs .For testing the hypothesis above, we employ the chi-square goodness-of-fit test. The results are:

	Cadburys'	*Dairy Milk*	*Éclairs*	*Cadburys' Dairy Milk*	*Cadburys' Dairy Milk Éclairs*	*None of these*
Observed	0	0	170	0	0	0

Chi-sq	173061
d.f.	5
Critical value	11.07

Interpretation Since the calculated value of chi-square (173061) is greater than the critical value of chi-square for 5 d.f. (11.07) at the 5% level of significance, we reject the null that the choices are equally preferred.

The diagrammatic representation is given below:

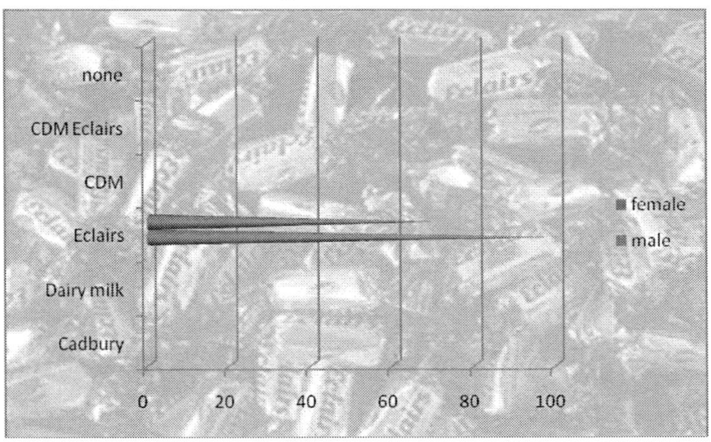

Interpretation

- The study reveals a very crucial element here. That, people buy "Cadburys' Dairy Milk Éclairs" just as Éclairs.
- It has been understood from the research that such is the power of the word called "Éclairs" that most of the respondents have been found to be not knowing the fact that the words "Dairy Milk" happens to be a part of Éclairs.
- Therefore, if brand "Cadburys" drops the word "Dairy Milk" from that of "Éclairs" it would hardly make any difference in the market as well as to the buyers.

H_0 (6): All given choices are equally preferred by the customers while going for a chocolate.

H_1 (6): All given choices are not equally preferred by the customers while going for achocolate.

For testing the hypothesis above, we employ the chi-square goodness-of-fit test

	Chocolate	*Candy*	*Cadburys'*	*Amul*	*Cadburys' Chocolate*	*Amul Chocolate*	*Nestle*	*Nestle Chocolate*	*Others.*
Observed	0	0	159	0	8	2	0	0	2

Chi-sq	227836
d.f.	8
Critical value	15.507

Interpretation Since the calculated value of chi-square (227836) is greater than the critical value of chi-square for 8 d.f. (15.507) at the 5% level of significance, we reject the null that the choices are equally preferred.

The diagrammatic expression stands like this.

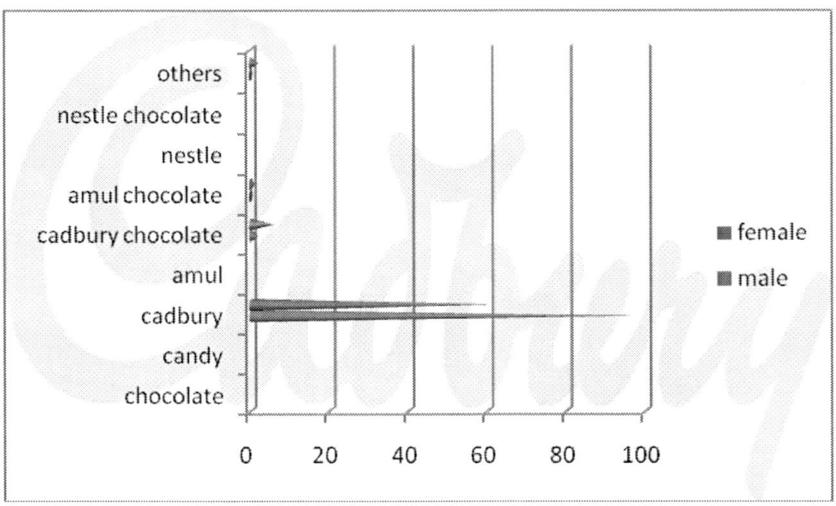

Interpretation

- This part clearly reflects the understanding that to this section of the customers and consumers Cadburys' is not a brand but a product which is essentially a chocolate.
- Therefore, those who do not prefer brand Cadburys' and hence are buying other competing brand's products for their own consumption or for others are also identifying them as "Cadburys" when communicating.
- This might be because of the fact that to them "Cadbury" is a product and not a brand. Had it been more of a brand then the brand preference could have been more as perceived and expected.

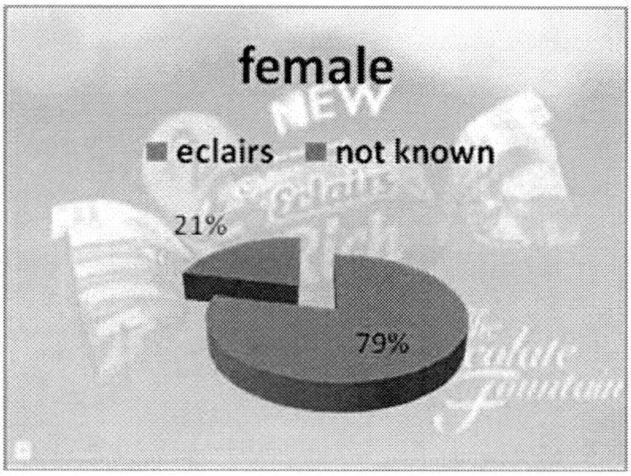

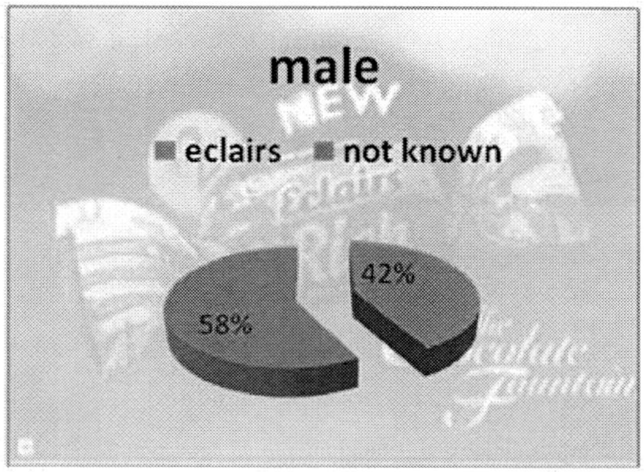

Interpretation

- Cadbury Éclairs Brownie has become quite familiar among both the genders without the aid of the 'dairy milk' within a very short period of time.
- This might also prove the fact that Cadburys' have understood or observedthe non functioning role of 'dairy milk' and so have consciously dropped the extension strategy of the sub brand 'dairy milk'.

CONCLUSION

Results from the analysis indicate the very fact that 'Cadbury' as a principle brand has a deep penetration into the minds of the people. Any extension done of the principle brand is quite justified as it is deep rooted in the minds of the youth of present India. It also indicates that to an average Indian the concept of a chocolate boils down to the fact that they identify it in the name of 'Cadbury'. This has enabled Cadbury to open up new dimensions in the field of chocolate bars. But at the same time it also reveals the fact that Cadburys' effort of identifying itself as 'Cadbury Dairy Milk' is not working as envisaged other than the chocolate ear marked as "Dairy Milk". If people take an 'éclairs' in the name of éclairs, a 'silk' bar in the name silk, a 'fruit and nut' bar in the name of 'Cadbury Fruit & Nut' then it is of no use extending the sub-brand "dairy milk". Therefore, it can even be arrived at that, if "Cadbury" takes off the sub-brand "Dairy Milk" from all other chocolates other than the particular chocolate popular as "Cadbury Dairy Milk" chocolate it would hardly make any difference to the end users and that its market domination would hardly be affected.

REFERENCING

[1] Aaker, David A., and Kevin L. Keller (1990), "Consumer Evaluations of Brand Extensions", Journal of Marketing, 54, January, 27-41.

[2] Bridges, Sheri (1991), "A Schema Unification Model of Brand Extensions", Paper given in Special Session at Association of Consumer Research Conference, Chicago.

[3] Boush, David M and Barbara Loken (1991), "A Process-Tracing Study of Brand Extension Evaluation", Journal of Marketing Research, Vol 28 February, 16-28.

[4] Ehrenberg A.S.C. (1974), Repetitive Advertising and the Consumer, Journal of Advertising Research, 14 (2), April, 25-33.

[5] Farquhar, Peter H. (1989), "Managing Brand Equity", Marketing Research, September, 24-33.

[6] Farquhar, Peter H., Paul M. Herr, and Russell H. Fazio (1990), "A Relational Model for Category Extensions of Brands", Association of Consumer Research, 17, 1-5.

[7] Kapferer, Jean-Noel (1991), Les Marques, Capital de L'Entreprise, Les +ditions D'Organisation, Paris.

[8] Lannon, Judy and Peter Cooper (1983), "Humanistic Advertising: A Holistic Cultural Perspective", International Journal of Advertising, 2, 195-213.

[9] Loken, Barbara and James Ward (1990), "Alternative Approaches to Understanding the Determinants of Typicality", Journal of Consumer Research, 17, (September), 111-126.

[10] McWilliam, Gil (1991), "Consumers' Involvement in Brands and Product Categories", Proceedings of EMAC 1991 Annual Conference, Dublin, 21-23 May, p 404-424.

[11] Meyers-Levy, Joan and Alice M Tybout (1989), "Schema Congruity as a Basis for Product Evaluation", Journal of Consumer Research, 16, 39-54.

[12] Park, C. Whan, Robert Lawson and Sandra Milberg (1989), "Memory Structure of Brand Names" Association of Consumer Research, 16, 726-731.

[13] Park, C. Whan, Sandra Milberg and Robert Lawson (1991), "Evaluation of Brand Extensions: The Role of Product Feature Similarity and Brand Concept Consistency", Journal of Consumer Research, 18, September, 185-193.

[14] Roedder John, Deborah and Barbara Loken (1991), "Diluting Brand Equity",Working Paper, University of Minnesota.

[15] [http://www.mondelezinternational.com/in/en/About/ourbusinessinIndia.aspx]

Key Sales Performance Indicators: A Literature Review

Sandeep Puri, Meenakshi Arya and Harsh Ajmera

Institute of Management Technology, Ghaziabad

ABSTRACT

It is imperative to have less key performance indicators for a sales organisation for easy assessment and tracking of performance. The indicators should be balanced mix of outcome based indicators and behaviour based indicators but the relative weightage will ultimately depend upon the goals important to a particular organisation, product and service offering and organisation work culture. This article is aimed at the compilation of the learning from the past research work done on key indicators of the sales organisation performance.

INTRODUCTION

Key sales performance indicators are the most important and efficient way to determine how well the individual sales people as well the entire organisation has performed over the given period of time. Although it is impossible to determine with precision the performance evaluation approaches used by sales organisations, several studies have produced sufficiently consistent and relevant information to warrant some general conclusions. This article reviews the previous research work done on the kinds of performance indicators used in various industries as well as the various drawbacks associated with them along with special scenarios.

NEED FOR PERFORMANCE INDICATORS

According to the research done by *Zallocco, Pullins* and *Mallin* in 2009, one of most significant concerns in sales management is the measurement of sales performance and the most obvious measure of sales performance is the resultant sales. Nevertheless, with the increasing significance of factors like customer satisfaction, long term relationship management and customer knowledge management, companies have starting looking beyond the short term interests like unit sales and immediate revenue while quantifying and assessing the sales force performance. Since more and more sales personnel deal with complex issues it becomes imperative for the organisations to come up with comprehensive performance metrics. In this regard, key sales performance indicators are the measures of strength and vigour of the sales and business development system of an organisation which lead to understanding of strengths and weaknesses of the sales force. During carrying out the past research review the key indicators used by most of the firms were analysed and then the most significant indicators in the various industries were selected. Also, most of the researchers emphasize that key indicators should be less in number for easy tracking and avoiding replication. The classification of the indicators is based on several parameters like chronology and skills to be measured.

KEY SALES PERFORMANCE INDICATORS - CLASSIFICATIONS

Outcome-based Indicators and Behaviour-based Indicators

It is potentially insightful to evaluate sales force performance both in what they do (e.g. sales skills) as well as the outcomes (e.g. sales results) that are attributed to them. This view suggests that sales force performance can be studied both as behaviour performance and as outcome performance (Anderson and Oliver, 1987; Behrman and Perrault, 1982; Challagalla and Shervani, 1996; Cravens *et al*., 1993; Oliver and Anderson, 1994).

Outcome based Indicators: These are those indicators which can be quantifiable and analysed numerically to arrive at the results. These can be explained on the basis of percentage increase or decrease and are attributable to salesperson performance. Outcome based indicators require less monitoring and objective methods of evaluation are employed to analyse them. Following are the most important outcome based indicators used:

Sales: The sales figures can be defined in terms of number of units sold or value in dollars. The further analysis of sales figures leads to various other indicators which are used to gauge the performance of sales organisation:

(a) Market Share: Market share is an indicator of market competitiveness with respect to sales of product and services of a particular firm. This metric, supplemented by changes in sales revenue, helps managers evaluate both primary and selective demand in their market. Generally, sales growth resulting from primary demand (total market growth) is less costly and more profitable than that achieved by capturing share from competitors because of less efforts being put in increasing sales. Market share is invariably measured in terms of unit market share and revenue market share.

(b) Sales Growth: Sales growth is defined as percentage change in sales over the last period. It is to be ensured that measurements are calculated on an appropriate time period, long enough to avoid being fixated on constantly fluctuating numbers, but short enough to uncover trends to get the big picture. Formula used is: (change in sales / sales in previous period) × 100

(c) Sales per Representative: This indicator applies to sales personnel who are little experienced and are in the field for quite some time, and is generally measured over the course of a month or quarter in order to provide an accurate measure of an individual representative's performance. This can be used to provide additional details such as type of customer (new/ repeat) or normalized to track performance against target quota for the period. Benefit of this measure is to into each individual's performance based on sales revenue generated. Formula used is: actual Sales / quota Amount = percentage on target

Profitability: According to a research paper published by Piercy *et al* (1998) even when the sales of a particular product line is doing good in terms sales volume it can be an unprofitable product for the company, which can be attributed to the distribution costs of that product. Certain firms lay emphasis on profitable territories, products and salespersons in order to decide future sales strategies. For Example, IBM's worldwide sales force of 30,000 had incentive pay based on profitability (60 per cent) and customer satisfaction (40 per cent). The main critique of this indicator was given in the research done by James Poon TengFatt in 2000 on "criteria used for evaluating salesperson" which is that the profitability is the ultimate objective of most for-profit firms and the evaluation of sales person performance on the basis of profit-based criteria can be unjust to sales persons as profitability is influenced by so many other factors which are much less controlled by sales persons.

With respect to Profitability, the emphasis on the specific measures may vary according to business type classification (Fatt*et al.*, 2000). The emphases in this evaluation criteria group are as follows:

1. Distribution firms: Cancelled orders, net orders per repeat order, selling expense versus budget, order/call ratio.

2. Manufacturing firms: Average cost per call, net orders per repeat order, selling expense versus budget, selling expense as a per cent of sales.

3. Service firms: Cancelled orders, selling expense versus budget, selling expense as a per cent of sales, order/call ratio.

Businesses mostly do not focus on maximizing sale profitability per unit of sales. This means that they strike a right balance between the profitability and the volume of sale. Beyond a certain point, per unit profitability leads to lesser number of units sold and hence appropriate product mix is one of the ways to nullify that. However, it has to be looked at carefully, because product mix decisions are not driven purely by the sales profitability. There are many other factors like product risk, sustainability of product etc.

While measuring the sales profitability, direct cost (cost of sales and sales expenses like sales compensation, sales offices) are included. However, there is always a question on whether the field operations (like processing of sales orders) or whether the indirect costs need to be allocated. Sales profitability can be measured with different level of expense allocations (starting from direct costs to allocating all indirect expenses).

New customers: According to a research conducted by Menguc and Barker (2005) mentions that addition of new customer base to the existing one requires social networking skills of the sales force to use establish relations. This indicator is strongly used as an acid test when the market conditions are poor so spontaneous addition of new accounts is not seen and hence sales force effectiveness plays an important role. This metric can also be analysed to arrive at the switch made by the customers of the competition and hence growth in new customer acquisition gives the boost to the sales force morale.

Customer Satisfaction/Repeat Purchase: Customer Repeat purchase or usage value is a good indicator of long term business sustainability of organization because it points to higher overall customer lifetime value and potential of retaining the customer. This KPI measures the fresh activity (purchases/usage) done with in a period of time. Customer repeat purchase value is the sum of the sales value of all purchases or usage done by a same customer within a given period of time. *For example: A corporate customer gives repeat order for desktop to a hardware vendor; A customer buying his second car from the same dealer or manufacturer, a customer doing high use of a credit card, Bank balance maintained by the customer, high mobile usage by the customer.* The criteria used for finding the performance of the company based on this indicator is the assumptions made about product pricing, usage and margins. Reference to industry experts and reports on customer segment or product based average usage is also made.

Behaviour Based Indicators: A contemporary approach based on certain theoretical and empirical studies suggests that insights into salesperson performance come from evaluating salesperson work behaviour, rather than just the outcome results attributed to them (Anderson and Oliver, 1987; Challagalla and Shervani, 1996; Cravens *et al.*, 1993). This aspect of performance is concerned with the various skills and activities that are important to fulfil the responsibilities of the sales job. Behaviour based indicators require constant monitoring and require subjective measures of evaluation. Certain indicators of behaviour performance indicators are:

1. *Selling skills*: By definition, selling skills comprise both declarative and procedural knowledge. Leigh and McGraw (1989, p. 17) define declarative knowledge as "the set of situational cues that enable a salesperson to recognize or classify a particular selling situation as an instance of a more general selling category". For example, attentively listening to their customers to better identify and understand their concerns and problems is one example of a salesperson using their declarative knowledge (Sharma *et al.*, 2000). Procedural knowledge can be defined as "a set of learned behavioural routines that fit various selling situations" (Leigh and McGraw, 1989, p. 17). For example, working out solutions to customers' questions and objectives is an example of the use of procedural knowledge. Research by Menguc and Barker (2005), classified selling skills as need assessment skills, understanding unique problems and concerns of the customers, using established contacts to develop new customers, sales presentation skills and problem solving skills. They also talked about agency theory (Eisenhardt, 1985, 1989) which emphasizes the alignment of goals and objectives between principals (sales manager) and agents(salesperson) wherein the sales manager (principal) may want the

salesperson (agent) to spend more time on selling skills, while the salesperson may wish to spend that extra time seeking out new accounts.

2.Collaborative Skills: According to the research done by Menguc and Barker (2005), these skills comprise of generating considerable sales volume from team sales, building strong work relationships with other people in the company, working closely with non-sales employees to close sales, discussing selling strategies with people from various departments. Collaborative skills are difficult for competitors to copy due to both path dependencies and co-specialization. In addition, collaborative skills are unprogrammable, non-routine, and voluntary in nature. Salespeople's inter and intra-unit collaborative skills allow them access to the social resources and information that are set in within their social networks. These skills contribute to their social capital pool and are acquired by systemic knowledge-based resources which are specific to a particular organisation.

3. Adaptive Skills: Adaptive skills are part of selling skills but several researchers pay additional emphasis on these skills because of their nature of acquiring them over the period of time by doing things. According to the research paper by Johlke (2006), they can be defined as altering of sales behaviours during a customer interaction or across customer interactions based on perceived information about the nature of a selling situation. It has been treated as a determinant of salesperson productivity as well as a measure of sales performance. For example, in their study, Pettijohn*et al.* (2000) found positive relationships between adaptive selling and performance ranking, sales volume, and closing ratio. Research paper by Menguc and Barker, (2005) stated that adaptive selling requires declarative selling skills.

According to a research article by Piercy *et al.* (1998), when senior sales managers were asked to rate the importance of a variety of behaviour-based and outcome-based performance indicators, they ranked almost all the behaviour-based factors higher than conventional outcome factors which shows that while sales managers continue to keep scores mainly using sales results, they do recognize the importance of the components of salesperson behaviour that lead to sales results.

LAGGING INDICATORS AND LEADING INDICATORS

According to a business development advisory firm "Beyond Referrals", some researchers have classified sales performance indicators on the basis of time of measurement that is chronological criterion which has been depicted as follows:

1. *Lagging Indicators*: Lagging indicators are the past measures that are helpful in knowing the past and determining if the success was achieved. Most of the financial indicators are lagging indicators because they validate how well the company has performed based upon past performance. These indicators are final result of certain activities or behaviour by the sales force or organisation as a whole and once they are measured there is little scope of changing them. Examples of lagging indicators are total sales revenue, profitability, market share, number of new clients obtained and customer satisfaction.

2. *Leading Indicators*: Leading indicators are task based metrics that are measured early, can be influenced to affect future outcomes and have predictive power of success. They are measured in present to check if goals will be met tomorrow. They are measured early and often enough to allow for changes that can impact the outcomes they predict. Most of the time, lagging indicator is an activity rather than an effect. In this case the indicators tell if any action has to be taken in order to achieve the goal. For example: number of closing opportunities at a particular point of time, one of the factor that pushes closing opportunities may be number of outbound calls to potential customers. Low KPI refers to a decrease in calls frequency due to external influences and to rectify the poor KPI value, the firm will choose to take steps to increase the activity of telephone introductions.

INTERNALLY ORIENTED INDICATORS AND EXTERNALLY ORIENTED INDICATORS

1. *Internally oriented indicators*: Research done by Zollacco*et al* (2009) identifies internally oriented indicators focussing on the working of the organization. An investment in skill development of the salesperson increases the likelihood that these skills will be used to achieve performance goals that are shared by the salesperson and sales organization. These include measurement of salesperson competencies, capabilities and skills such as *teamwork, product/ technical knowledge and communication.* These measures tend to be derived from the use of organization's internal resources used to develop the salesperson.

2. *Externally oriented indicators*: These indicators are market driven and marketplace will dictate the conditions of the sale (i.e. fair price, required service levels, acceptable quality). Market driven organisations outperform those that are not; therefore the market driven model is desirable, Zollacco*et al* (2009), found external measures to be positively related to salesperson's job satisfaction while selling skills were not so much linked to job satisfaction. Some of the external performance indicators are *market share, relative share, customer satisfaction, market coverage, product awareness, relative quality, relative price and customer preferences.*

SPECIAL SCENARIOS

1. B2B: Internally oriented indicators play an important role in these kinds of selling scenarios because of emphasis on relational selling rather than transactional selling. For major accounts management where building long term customer relationship is the key, performance measures that combine characteristics of externally oriented and effectiveness should be used. Here both the needs of the customer and the selling goals of the salesperson/organisation can be best satisfied. For mid-size customers, measures combining aspects of internally oriented with effectiveness can be utilised. For small customers internally oriented indicators with efficiency aspects of performance indicators can ensure that salespersons are providing adequate market coverage to a large base of small businesses (Zollacco*et al, 2009).*

2. *New Products*: In their research for new product selling in Netherlands, Hultink*et al.,* (2000) formulated the hypothesis that product newness to the firm is negatively related to selling performance. The selling process for "new to the firm" products may be of a trial-and-error nature. Because salespeople have to adapt their selling techniques and need to establish the best way to sell a new product, it has been argued that they are more likely to engage in dysfunctional behaviours. Thus the research stated that one of the important metric to judge the sales force performance in this case is the feedback from the sales manager based upon certain objectives set by the sales manager like good market share, generating sales and identifying major accounts, exhibiting that outcome based indicators played more significance than behavioural indicators. The research also indicated that positive feedback is informational as well as a motivational, and that negative feedback primarily serves an informational role in improving sales performance. Where sales managers provide effective feedback, salespeople feel less ambivalent about their role, and they will be better armed to experiment and take risks in selling, and refrain from dysfunctional behaviour.

3.Group Performance: According to a research conducted by Zollacco*et al.* in 2009 a pattern called organization theory (Ouchi, 1979) focused on the difficulty of obtaining cooperation among a group of individuals (e.g. a sales team) who share only partially congruent objectives. Typically, when this group yields a single output (e.g. sales) the performance of each individual team member may be unequal. In light of this, team mates will channelize their future efforts, and certainly the entire team will not perform to its potential. To deal with this problem of measuring and assessing group sales performance (Ouchi, 1979) suggests that one performance evaluation strategy can be grounded on the idea that market dynamics will drive the sales. It is suggested that this is a very efficient form of performance measure, in that when the required market conditions are met, goal incongruity (between buyer and seller) is reduced. Therefore, salesperson's performance may be impacted by external organizational factors such as gaining/ utilizing customer feedback, obtaining competitor knowledge, staying abreast of technological developments. All this suggests that organization theory paradigms can be used to provide a theoretical basis for sales managers' utilization of performance evaluation strategies based on selling goals, tasks, availability of performance measures, and marketplace conditions.

CONCLUSION

While there have been exhaustive efforts in an endeavour to identify effective and dependable indicators of sales force performance that would be useful to managers, the large number of studies conducted have made only a limited contribution to improving understanding of sales performance. However, it remains uncertain whether this deficit reflects attention to inappropriate performance indicators, choosing the wrong dimensions or features of performance, or merely the solicitation of poor measures.

Conventionally, sales management focusses on recruitment and selection of right candidates to sales jobs and use incentives to provide motivating stimulus with the ultimate goal of producing sales outcomes. This approach has suffered from the limitations that would be expected, given the incomplete understanding of the underlying drivers of sales force performance.

Also, one acute and persistent problem facing managers and researchers in the area of sales management control is simply the ambiguity of the results achieved when common conventions about the results of different types of control are tested empirically.

Although many researchers and authors have tried to decipher the overall indicators of sales force performance and have come up with a wide gamut of indicators but the relevant indicators can only be found after understanding the kind of product or service offering, the variables suitable for the firm and criteria for deciding the variables. They should be formulated such that they are helpful in connecting the firm's goals and strategies to its activities and outcomes, keeping the higher management informed of the health of organisation.

This note limits itself in that most of the research papers are based upon the studies conducted in US and UK and hence have constraints as far as application in other countries is concerned. The findings of this note can be best summarised by suggesting that managers should select indicators of performance to not only "do the right things" (outcome), but also to do those "right things the right way" (behaviour). For managers, this decision will be task-dependent. This literature review also raises additional research questions as to whether managers in practice are using the right performance indicators (i.e. outcomes-based versus behaviour based) in various sales situations. When developing key performance indicator framework for any firm, the manager should attempt to have few KPI's because of convenience and precise measurement of performance. Thus it is recommended to have not more than 4-5 indicators with a good mix of outcome based, behaviour based, lagging, leading, internally oriented and externally oriented indicators depending upon the parameters which the organisation wants to lay emphasis on.

REFERENCES

[1] Bruce D. Keillor, R. Stephen Parker, Charles E. Pettijohn, (2000),"Relationship-oriented characteristics and individual salesperson performance", Journal of Business & Industrial Marketing, Vol. 15 Issue: 1 pp. 7 – 22

[2] BulentMenguc, Tansu Barker, (2005),"Re-examining field sales unit performance: Insights from the resource-based view and dynamic capabilities perspective", European Journal of Marketing, Vol. 39 Issue: 7 pp. 885 – 909

[3] EminBabakus, David W. Cravens, Ken Grant, Thomas N. Ingram, Raymond W. LaForge, (1994),"Removing Sales force Performance Hurdles", Journal of Business & Industrial Marketing, Vol. 9 Issue: 3 pp. 19 – 29

[4] Erik Jan Hultink, KwakuAtuahene-Gima, Iris Lebbink, (2000),"Determinants of new product selling performance: an empirical examination in The Netherlands", European Journal of Innovation Management, Vol. 3 Issue: 1 pp. 27 – 36

[5] Inés Küster, Pedro Canales, (2008),"Some determinants of sales force effectiveness", Team Performance Management, Vol. 14 Issue: 7 pp. 296 – 326

[6] James Poon TengFatt, (2000),"Criteria used for evaluating sales persons", Management Research News, Vol. 23 Issue: 1 pp. 27 – 32

[7] Leyland F. Pitt, Pierre R. Berthon, Matthew J. Robson, (2000),"Communication apprehension and perceptions of salesperson performance: a multinational perspective", Journal of Managerial Psychology, Vol. 15 Issue: 1 pp. 68 – 82

[8] Mark C. Johlke, (2006),"Sales presentation skills and salesperson job performance", Journal of Business & Industrial Marketing, Vol. 21 Issue: 5 pp. 311 - 319

[9] Nigel F. Piercy, David W. Cravens, Neil A. Morgan, (1998),"Sales force performance and behaviour-based management processes in business-to-business sales organizations", European Journal of Marketing, Vol. 32 Issue: 1 pp. 79 – 100

[10] Ronald Zallocco, Ellen BolmanPullins, Michael L. Mallin, (2009),"A re-examination of B2B sales performance", Journal of Business & Industrial Marketing, Vol. 24 Issue: 8 pp. 598 – 610

[11] Websites: www.klipfolio.com; www.executionmih.com; www.beyondreferrals.com

Lead User Research for Smart Phone Apps

Dhiraj Sharma, Yogesh Upadhyay[1] and Shiv Kumar Singh[2]

Institute of Management Technology, Ghaziabad
[1]Institute of Management, Jiwaji University, Gwalior
[2]Institute of Commerce, Jiwaji University, Gwalior

ABSTRACT

Today Indian market is flooded by local and international brands of new and newer smart phones. Companies are trying to figure out how to win the smart phone war. On the other hand,due to ever increasing competition and decreasing voice revenues to rock bottom, Indian mobile service firms are also struggling for keeping average revenue per user from decline. At this instance, smart phone apps that are unique and preferred by the smart phone users seem to be the answer to the problem faced by both the kinds of players. Present study tries to find out possible answers to– what kind of apps can make Indian users pay for them; what kind of features are anticipated/ needed in the smart phone operating system for these apps; and other similar questions.

INTRODUCTION

Smart phones makers are flooding the markets with newer models. Companies are trying to figure out how to win this smart phone war. Apart from the hardware, screen size and mega pixels, it is increasingly clear that an important strength is an open platform on which apps can be developed by developers around the world, on shared revenue model. These apps greatly enhance usability of the mobile handset to its users.

There is a set of customers in high-tech market who absorb latest innovations both in smart phone market and in apps. These users suffer increasingly from the needs they discover and scout app stores to find apps to satisfy their needs. They are evolving smart phone functionalities by adding apps and forcing companies to evolve hardware and design of these smart phones. In India with the advent of 3G, surfing for apps and adding apps has become easier. Success of 3G depends on increase in data usage and smart phone apps are instrumental in driving up data usage, also due to frequent updates. Hence, betting on successful apps makes sense not only for developers and smart phone manufacturers but mobile service providers too. IT service providers also look at successful apps to deliver similar solutions to their clients. The benefits of these apps also extend to advertisers and marketers and thereby to larger business community.

Researchers through this research intend to discover answers to questions similar or related to the following –What kinds of apps are popular among Indian smart phone users?Apps are on revenue sharing model and these are only hope for Indian mobile service firms for revenues as competition has driven voice revenues to the bottom. What kind of apps can make Indian users pay for them?How apps are forcing smart phone makers to evolve hardware?What features are anticipated/ needed in smart phone hardware?What features are anticipated/ needed in smart phone operating systems?

RESEARCH OBJECTIVE

This research aims to find features, functionalities or attributes of trending apps. What makes popular apps; paid or free, popular? What more users of these apps are looking for? What makes users pay for apps? Study concludes the list of features or functionalities which users eagerly wait for, in future apps.

RESEARCH QUESTIONS

- What are major platforms on which apps are being developed and distributed? Here to ascertain the importance of a platform we take number of apps developed on it, as measure.
- What are all-time top apps paid and free on each of these platforms? Ranking of these apps is taken as given on online market place of these platforms. These ranking may be based on number of downloads or ratings given by users or it can be a function of both.
- What are trending (new and popular/highest rated) top apps paid and free on each of these platforms?
- What are functionalities, features or attributes of all these apps?
- What do users, who rate these apps as highest, like about them?
- What do users, who rate trending (new and popular/highest rated) apps as low, want more in them?

RESEARCH DESIGN

Lead users have been an elusive lot for product designers and marketers but in the age of internet they flock in user forums and on Facebook and/or likedin pages to seek help or knowledge on product use. Moreover, smart phones are introduced from one or the other player almost every month and all of them try to differentiate from the rest. Because there is greater chance of smart phone bought becoming obsolete in a year; buyers also try to make an informed decision by seeking advice from sophisticated users. These users are known to be aware of latest and best handsets. These users are usually young and technically well-versed.

Lead User Research

The term 'lead user' was coined by Prof. Eric Von Hippel et al. (1986). According to Eric Von Hippel, lead users are:

- Lead users face needs that will be general in a marketplace – but face them months or years before the bulk of that marketplace encounters them, and
- Lead users are positioned to benefit significantly by obtaining a solution to those needs.

Since lead users are familiar with conditions which lie in the future for most others, they can serve as a need-forecasting laboratory for marketing research. Moreover, since lead users often attempt to fill the need they experience, they can provide new product concept and design data as well.

Lead User Research is a multi stage approach aiming to generate innovative new product concepts and to enhance the effectiveness of cross-functional innovation teams.

The first two stages out of the four stages of the Lead User Research as proposed by Eric Von Hippel focus on identification of lead users. However, it has been observed that the lead user research is relatively hard for consumer markets as compared to industrial goods. Lead users for technology/ industrial goods are easier to find as industrial products are typically only applied to limited, industry-specific user group. Since only specific users will be involved, these users can be targeted and located relatively easily. And then, lead users can be filtered out from the specific user group by survey or questionnaire, etc. While, for consumption product industry with millions of consumers, it's almost impossible to filter lead users by ways such as survey.

Netnography: Identification of Lead Users

In our case however, Smartphone & apps being high technology products, netnography(Kozinets, 2010; Belz and Baumbach, 2010) was used to identify lead users for smart phone mobile apps. Netnograhy adapts ethnography research method in online world to observe and study emerging communities through their communication. Users of smart phone apps flock on online market places of respective smart phone platforms and operating systemsto rate the apps they use and provide feedback to developers. These feedbacks would prove very useful to the Mobile companies as they can often come up with new product concept or innovative add-ons in the same product.

As and when new apps come up for any platform, many users come and give their reviews and/or suggestions on the app. This data comes very useful for the companies as well as any other users sifting through the company/ platform website for same/ similar apps. Also data about these users can be collected by these websites to track the characteristics of these users and whether or not they can be classified as lead users based on their previous records and current usage patterns.In high technology areas like these, it is very easy to track lead users because of these platforms. Only ardent technology users would visit these sites and leave their feedback to report their requirements/ suggestions for improvements, primary characteristic of lead users.

Lead User Study Stage-1: Project Planning

The deliverable of this stage of our lead user research is a specific data collection plan focused on key questions (e.g. market trends) and key resources (appropriate experts and literature). We visited websites of various app platforms and Smartphone companies to find out the latest technology and the users interested in that technology. We found out the number of apps that were offered by the platforms (like Android for Google and appstore for iPhone) and the apps that were most popular. There were different categories of apps, relevant to different users. There were apps for books, music, media, fitness, business and what not. Some of these apps were available for free, while some had to be paid for.

This information led us to observe various patterns and raised many questions. The users for such phones were usually young and aware of latest technology. A lot of research went into purchase of any new Smartphone or any related technology. And this information was usually gathered from various user forums where people who have already used the technology (lead users) and faced some, if at all, problem using it. These kinds of forums become primary source of information, both for users as well as companies who keep looking for improvement to stay alive in the cut throat competition.Key questions on which data collection plan would be centered are detailed under heading of Research Objective above.Key resources in our data collection plan are forecasts by technology experts, popular technology blogs, industry reports, user forums and user reviews in applications stores.

Lead User Study Stage-2: Trend/Needs Identification

The new smart phone applications market is very dynamic and not a day goes by without a new entry to the market or an announcement from a major player that has a significant impact upon the mobile market.

After Apple launched its Apple App Store in 2008, the download of these applications went quite high in a very short time. Developers upon realizing this, started developing a lot of such applications. In 2009 the market boomed with tens of thousands of new apps, making it highly difficult for individual apps not to be lost in the long tail.

Trends and Predictions – Worldwide Smartphone Application Market

As smartphone applications market entered a new phase. The main developments can be summarized in terms of six major trends, according to research2guidance.com.

- **Increased market growth**: The market almost tripled in 2010 from what it was in 2009.
- **Deceleration of price decline:** During the first two years until the end of 2009 the average price of an application dropped from US$20 to almost US$4. At the same time

this trend is accompanied by major price movements within app stores which demonstrate price increases of as much as +30%, and similarly declines as steep as -30%. This indicates greater market transparency and simpler arbitrage processes.

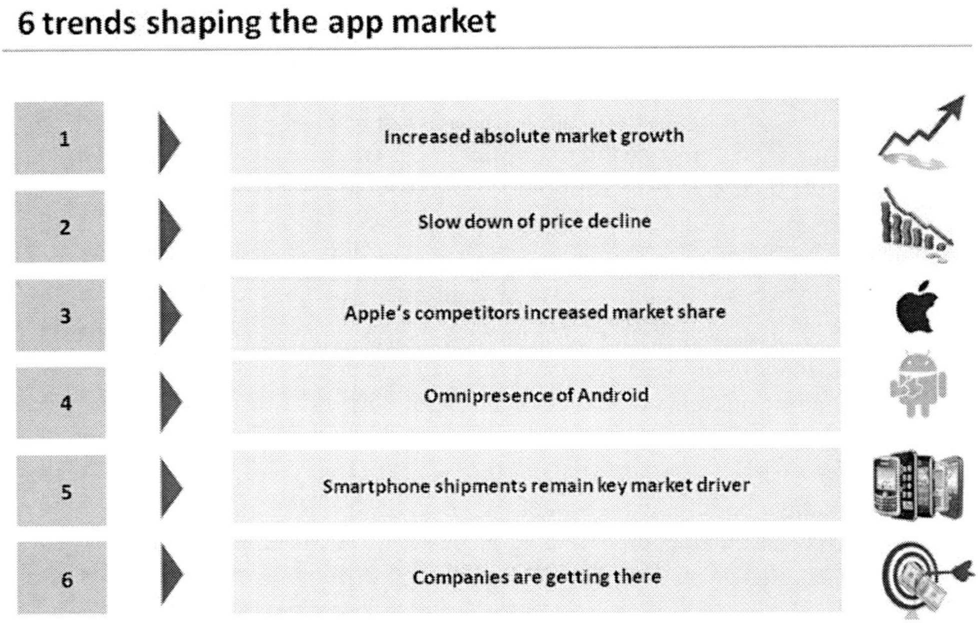

Source: research2guidance.com

- **Apple's competitors increased their market share:** Apple's competitors also started developing such applications and started having an impact on Apple's market share. In 2010 developers and smartphone users started to focus on platforms alternative to Apple, who lost almost 10% of market share in the first half of 2010.
- **Omnipresence of Android:** At the end of 2009 only six devices were useing the Andoid operating system. During the first six months of 2010, however, smartphone device manufacturers released a new Android device every 2-3 days. In 2010 the number of smartphone models using an Android system overtook the number with other OS platforms like Windows and Symbian for the first time since the launch of the Apple App Store in 2008.
- **Smartphone shipments remain the main market driver:** The shipment of smartphones has already reached almost 30% in some industrialized countries. Furthermore the number of smartphones shipped in the first HY 2010 was already 70% of that reached throughout 2009. All of these smartphones provide easy access to application stores, and this in turn drives application download numbers.

- **Companies are getting in on the act:** By the end of 2009 less than 10% of global companies had a presence in one or more app stores. But now, most of the companies have brought smartphones in the market. In addition to branding, companies are also increasingly using applications to link to their core products or to build transaction business.

Few other notice worthy trends are summarised in following picture-2 and picture-3 below:

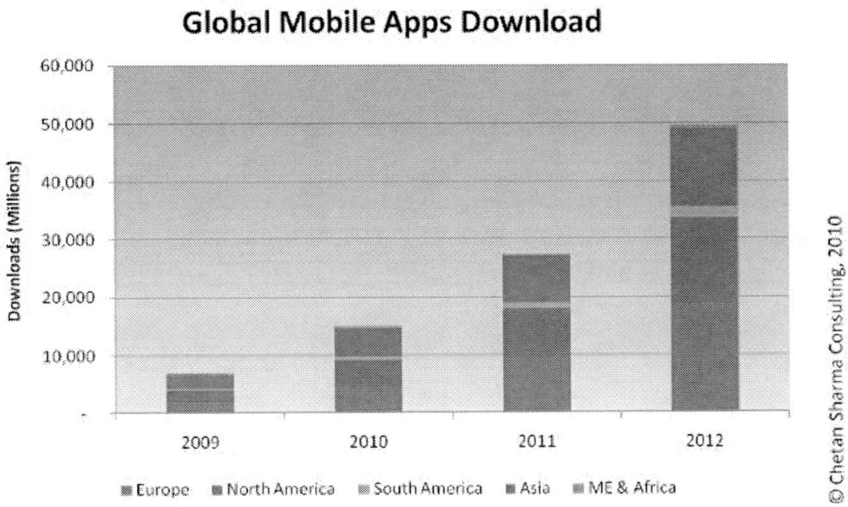

Source: comscoredatamine.com

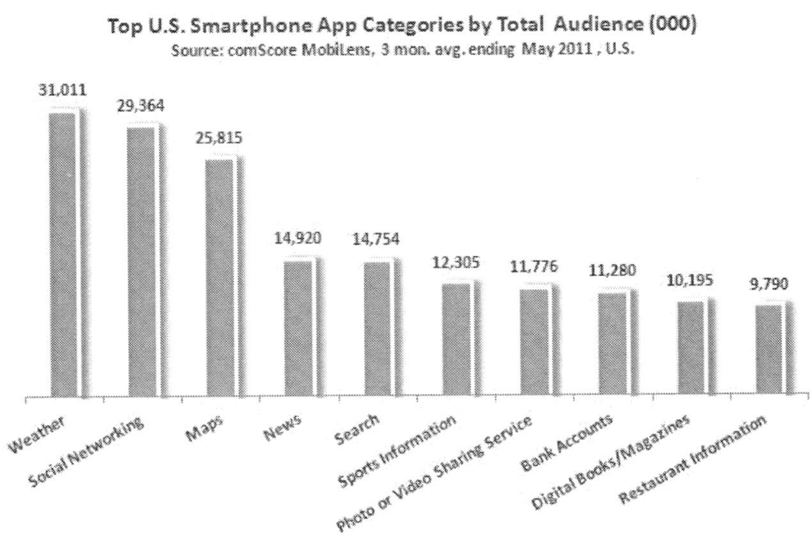

Source: comscoredatamine.com

A look at the top smartphone app categories reveals that Weather apps had the largest audience reaching 31 million smartphone owners, or 40.4% of the total U.S. smartphone audience. Social Networking apps closely followed with a smartphone audience of 29.4 million (38.2% reach).

Predictions for the Top Smartphone Apps in Near Future (Expert Views)

Mobithinking.com reported on Gartner's November 2009 prediction that the Top 10 consumer mobile applications for 2012 will be:

Money Transfer: According to Gartner, within their first year of operation most services offering person-to-person transfers, using Short Message Service (SMS), signed up several million users within their first year. This means consumers want and are using mobile(m) features that include m-banking, m-payments, and definitely m-commerce, they want to check bank balances, make payments, and buy stuff from mobile web stores or through mobile coupons.

According to Mobilthinking.com's report, "In 2009, eBay's mobile gross merchandise volume ("GMV") was over $600 million. eBay expects to generate $1.5 billion in GMV through mobile commerce in 2010," according to eBay (October, 2010).

Location based Services: Gartner predicts that from 2009 the LBS user base will grow globally from 96 million to more than 526 million in 2012.

*Mobile Search:*The information from Gartner suggests that, "The user experience of mobile search needs to improve to drive customer loyalty and drive sales and marketing opportunities." What this means for businesses is that they need to understand search engines, mobile web portals, and what works on Smartphones and other mobile devices.

Mobile Browsing: Gartner's report stated that, "60 percent of handsets shipped in 2009 can browse the mobile Web, rising to approximately 80 percent in 2013. Therefore, the mobile Web will be a key part of most corporate B2C mobile strategies."

Mobile Health Monitoring: Gartner stated in 2009 that using IT and mobile telecommunications for remote patient monitoring is limited to pilot projects at that time. This technology has taken major leaps in the last year and at a recent 2010 Las Vegas Technology show, health care apps for Smartphones were demoed that monitored heart rate, blood pressure, and more. There are now thousands of healthcare apps available for consumer self-monitoring and apps that will relay vital signs to doctors.

Mobile Payment: This includes all the types of goods and services customers and businesses might want to purchase over the mobile web. Mobile financial services will include online banking, online shopping, and online services like ticketing.

Near-Field-Communication Services: Gartner suggests that, "NFC allows contactless data transfer between devices and terminals typically to pay for transport or to cash in a mobile coupon."

Mobile Advertising: From US$530.2 million in 2008, Gartner projected mobile advertising spending to reach US$7.5 billion in 2012. One report by the MMA and Lightspeed Research done in October 2010 found that, "In UK, France and Germany, 45 percent of consumers (especially younger people) noticed mobile advertising and of these, 29 percent responded to it. Of those that responded to the ads, in Germany 49 percent, UK 47 percent and in France 22 percent went on to make a purchase."

Mobile Instant Messaging: Gartner believes that, "Users really desire Mobile IM, especially in developing markets. This presents an opportunity for mobile advertising and social networking."

Mobile Music: Music Apps are number ten on the list. Not just downloading entire songs, but also the ring tones and ring-back tones. This service has turned into a multibillion-dollar service all on its own.

All time top 10 free iphone apps: According to a list released by Apple, the all time top ten free iphone apps are as following:

1. Facebook : This free app can be used to manage the facebook account.
2. Pandora: This is a free music app. One needs to say what type of music he/she wants to listen to, and Pandora generates a free streaming radio station customized to your tastes.
3. Google Mobile App: This app gives one touch access to all google features. This can also be used to search the web using your voice.
4. Shazam: It is a music app. It can be used to find out the information about a song. One just needs to let the app hear to song to know about the artist and the album.
5. Flixter: This app can be used to watch movie trailers, read movie reviews and also know about the show timings of a movie.
6. The weather channel: This app is used to keep track of current and upcoming weather conditions.
7. Google Earth: It can be used to browse the satellite images of earth.
8. Bump: Bump exchanges your contact information with others using bluetooth.
9. Skype: Skype is an app for text based chat and also for affordable international calls.
10. Papertoss: It is one of the simplest and most popular games on appstore.

All time top 10 paid iphone apps

According to the list released by Apple, the top ten paid iphone apps are:

1. Doodle Jump: It is highly popular game on Appstore.
2. Tap Tap Revenge 3: This is a music based game.
3. Pocket God: This is a game where you control an island of primitive people.

4. Angry Bird: One of the most popular games of the recent times, it deals with flinging birds at pigs in an effort to win back stolen eggs.
5. Tap Tap Revenge 2.6 : It is a popular music based game.
6. Bejewelled 2: This is a gem matching game.
7. Traffic Rush: It is a very popular game with arcade style gaming.
8. Tap Tap Revenge Classic: This is a nice game for guitar lovers. One can strum along with his/her fingers with this game.
9. AppBox Pro: This app includes a level, a tip calculator and a date countdown.
10. Flight Control: This is a game dealing with safely landing of planes.

Top 10 Free Android Apps

According to a list by TechCrunch, the top 10 free Android apps are:

1. Kindle: It is a great app for reading ebooks in a pocket format.
2. Skyfire: It is fast web browsing and video streaming app.
3. Google Voice: This app can be used to route calls to various paths, and take advantage of tons of advanced features like voicemail transcription, free texting, cheap international calling.
4. EverNote: This is a centralized notebook and note creation system that synchs to the cloud.
5. Barcode scanner: This app is used to scan books, movies and music to get information and pricing.
6. Lookout: This is used to scan installed apps and downloadable files for virus.
7. Facebook: This is used to remain connected to the social networking site.
8. Layar Reality Browser: It overlays on the camera as it scans the real world and gets up to date information about it.
9. Mint: This app helps in aggregating all the finances.
10. Places Directory: It lets you know of restaurants, movie theatres etc. in an area.

Top 10 paid Android Apps

According to a list by TechCrunch, the top 10 paid Android apps are:

1. Root Explorer: It is a comprehensive file manager to access and manipulate all files on the device.
2. Advanced Task Manager: It keeps all system tasks and apps in line to increase the efficiencey and speed of the phone.
3. Beautiful Widgets: It is used to customize the device with lots of skind and widgets.

4. SetCPU for root users: It is used to overclock, underclock or tweak the device's performance.
5. MyBackUp Pro: It can be used to create a backup of the file on cloud.
6. CacheMate for Root Users: It is a cache clearing app.
7. Soundhound: It helps in finding about the music.
8. Drop Box: It is used for synching files between phone and computer.
9. LogMeln Ignition: It is used to acees a computer remotely using the phone.
10. DroidAnalytics: It is a google Analytics client.

Lead User Study Stage-3: Preliminary Concept Generation

The new products which are coming are enough to satiate the customer's needs and demands. They have defined new products of their own choices, stating their requirements.

Quick Office PRO- Create, Edit and Share Microsoft® Office files!:

Lets the user Create, Edit, Access & Share Microsoft Office files. It includes PowerPoint editing, footnote/endnote support, faster file loading, and more. It takes mobile productivity to the next level with this must-have, award-winning productivity suite for Android smartphones. You can work with Word documents, Excel spreadsheets, and PowerPoint presentations while conveniently accessing files remotely from your Google Docs, Dropbox, Box.net, Huddle, SugarSync, and MobileMe accounts. For viewing PDF files, advanced PDF viewer is included, as well.

Talking Tom Cat

Talking Tom repeats everything you say with a funny voice.People love it as it encourages a cheeky little laugh & smile. Good fun & loaded easily.

Calorie Counter PRO

MyNetDiary is the easiest to use and most comprehensive diet app available on the Android Market. With over 40 screens and a 416,000+ foods database, MyNetDiary's Calorie Counter PRO brings all of our top-ranked paid iPhone and iPad apps features.Provides Lots of features, big food database.

ESPN Radio

Listen to LIVE ESPN internet broadcasts & MORE on your Android-powered device.

ESPN Radio is now available for Android-powered phone!

Fantasy Football Monster

Lets you Manage your Yahoo, ESPN, and NFL.com fantasy football teams with one app!

Provides All leagues in 1 app and it gives more info than the app that goes with the league. But users also want tablet support or atleast landscaping support.

Camera Zoom FX:

Camera ZOOM FX combines powerful camera functions with stunning post processing - creating magic moments is fun and fast!!

Over 90 unique FX - combine these in a non-destructive way to create infinite processing options. Takes a MUCH better picture than the phone's original camera.

Block Breaker Unlimited

Grab power-ups, trigger switches and blast through gateways to reach new areas as you push your way towards the top.

Innovative new scrolling level design adds depth to all 100 of the game's stages

Lead User Study Stage-4: Final Concept Development

Netnography and depth interviews with lead users of the age group 22-48 years, revealed certain Points regarding apps as following:

- Apps generally used included entertainment, social networking, mails, infotainment, news, sports, business related and other general information.
- They were highly satisfied and did not demand for significant changes either in the quality of apps or their genre.
- i-phone users or other smartphone users did not complain regarding the crashing of apps.
- However, the points of dissatisfaction were there:
  - o The free apps were irritating with the ads of the sponsors in between them
  - o It needed a Wi-Fi connectivity all throughout to get the latest updates
  - o The problem of Wi-Fi could be overcome with the advent of 3G Technology
- App sometimes cut out every 5 min when listening to live radio consistently. So it needs to be made consistent
- The drop down lists and check boxes that work on the laptop do not work on smartphone.
- Few apps do not stretch to tablet size well, so you cannot read any text due to the wrong background (dark) being behind dark text.

CONCLUSION

As per the research work carried out, Indian customers still have a need gap which can be capitalized by the companies effectively and efficiently. They can design apps which are:

- More customer friendly
- Synchronizes with mail
- Gets updated continuously with news, mails, RSS feed
    - o Youtube needs internet that bothers the consumer
- Inbuilt internet connectivity
- Free Apps Without sponsors ads
- Features Synchronization of calendar
- Drop down support should be given for the word docs.
- Lists, bullets, paragraph formatting can also be included
- Ads which generally come along with the download can be removed.
- Takes long time to load so streaming issues should be rectified.
- Few specific demands
    - o Finance tutorials
    - o More News apps since Bloomberg is the favorite of the category surveyed

REFERENCES

[1] Alex Ahlund, Top 30 Android apps of all time, Oct. 2010. Available at: http://techcrunch.com/2010/10/30/top-30-android-apps/

[2] Anonymous, Top U.S. Smartphone App Categories, July 2010. Available at: http://www.comscoredatamine.com/2011/07/top-u-s-smartphone-app-categories/

[3] Anonymous, Mobile Web: latest facts and stats forecast a rosy outlook, Aug. 2009. Available at: http://www.mobithinking.com/latest-mobile-stats

[4] Chetan Sharma, Sizing up the global Mobile Apps Market, Chetan Sharma Consulting for Getjar, Mar. 2010. Available at: chetansharma.com/sizing_up_the_Global_Mobile_Apps_Market.pdf

[5] Dylan Love, All-Time Top 10 Free iPhone Apps, Jan. 2011. Available at: http://www.businessinsider.com/all-time-top-10-free-iphone-apps-2011-1

[6] Eric Von Hippel, Lead Users: A Source of Novel Product Concepts, Management Science, Vol. 32, No. 7, 1986.

[7] Frank-Martin Belz, and WenkeBaumback, Netnography as a Method of Lead User Identification, Creativity and Innovation, Vol. 19, No. 3, 2010.

[8] Glen L Urban, and Eric Von Hippel, Lead User Analysis for the Development of New Industrial Products, Management Science, Vol. 34, No. 5, 1988.

[9] Liviu LICA, Mobile and Social: Ten Best Practices for Designing Mobile Applications, InformaticaEconomica, Vol. 14, No. 3, 2010.

[10] RohinDharmakumar, Mobile Apps in India: Not an Apt Offering, Forbes India [Online], Dec. 2010. Available at: http://business.in.com/article/real-issue/mobile-aps-in-india-not-an-apt-offering/19692/1

[11] R. de Waele, Mobile Trends 2020, Mobile Trends for the Next 10: A Collaborative Outlook, mTrends Blog, Jan. 2010. Available at: www.m-trends.org/2010/01/mobile-trends-2020.html.

[12] Ralf-Gordon Jahns, Six Major Trends Shaping the SmartPhone App Ecosystem in 2010, Oct. 2010. Available at: http://www.research2guidance.com/6-major-trends-shaping-the-smartphone-app-ecosystem-in-2010/

Leveraging Big Data for Advantages in Retail Analytics

Jayanthi Ranjan, Ritwik Vijayan and Vaqar Merchant

IMT, Ghaziabad

ABSTRACT

'Big Data' is the buzzword today owing to the generation of large amounts of data attributed to the preponderance of internet and growing means of communication. Emergence of social media sites Facebook, Twitter etc. and networked sensors in cameras, mobile phones and other devices have added to the already mounting piles of data.

One of the industries for which analysing 'Big Data' is imperative to gain competitive advantage is retail industry. Analysing data is essential for retail companies to understand consumer's buying propensity, satisfaction, and consumer's intention to purchase.

Along with the significant advantages that Big Data can offer to traditional as well as online retail, it is still a new concept that not all businesses have adopted and understand which brings with it a lot of challenges with respect to acceptance as well as application which must be carefully weighed, understood and overcome.

INTRODUCTION

The world is seeing a torrential flow of data in every sphere of economy and business. Proliferation of internet, social networking sites e.g. Facebook, LinkedIn, Twitter etc. growth of mobile phones, smart phones and networked sensors have led to unimaginable explosion of data. It is estimated that enterprises globally stored more than 7 exabytes of new data on disk drives in 2010, while consumers stored more than 6 exabytes of new data on devices such as PCs and notebooks. One Exabyte of data is the equivalent of more than 4,000 times the information stored in the US Library of Congress. Every month people send 1 billion Tweets and post 30 billion messages on Facebook. More than 1 trillion mobile devices are in use today and mobile commerce is expected to reach $31 billion by 2016.

An MGI report on Big Data (2012) says that in the year 2007, a study sponsored by EMC was conducted by the research firm IDC on the amount of digital data that was being created and replicated each year. These studies showed that for the first time, the amount of data created in a year exceeded the world's data storage capacity. The total amount of data created and replicated in the year 2009 was 800 exabytes (10^{18}) and this volume is to grow 44 times by the year 2020. Simply put, the study revealed that a huge gap existed between the amount of data generated and the amount that could be stored and this gap is only set to increase with each passing year. Estimates show that the volume of data is expected to increase at the rate of 40% every year. If all this data was to be converted into DVD's there is enough data to create a staircase long enough to carefully walk us to the moon - and back – thrice.

A lot of this implosion of data can be attributed also to the kind of data that is generated today. Earlier, most data that was generated was simply in the form of text, so, if we were to convert all of William Shakespeare's works into text we would require all but 5 Megabytes (10^6) of storage space. In the 1980's global storage of data was 99% in the analog form and 1% in digital form, by the year 2007 these positions have been significantly reversed with 94% of data in digital form and only 6% in analog form. Today, however, data is created from many different sources and in many different forms such as text, audio, video. This data also has many more sources today, such as, sensor data, machine data, transactional data, and social network data. This deluge of data requires being carefully stored or indexed and this is referred to as Metadata (data about data).

WHAT IS BIG DATA?

"Big data" refers to datasets whose size is beyond the ability of typical database software tools to capture, store, manage, and analyze. This definition is intentionally subjective and incorporates a moving definition of how big a dataset needs to be in order to be considered big data—i.e., we don't define big data in terms of being larger than a certain number of terabytes (thousands of gigabytes). We assume that, as technology advances over time, the size of datasets that qualify as big data will also increase. Also note that the definition can vary by sector, depending on what kinds of software tools are commonly available and what sizes of datasets are common in a particular industry. With those caveats, big data in many sectors today will range from a few dozen terabytes to multiple petabytes.

An alternative definition of big data will be "Big Data can be defined as massive amounts of stored content (structured or unstructured) that can be easily analyzed in real time (a reasonableamount of time to get a useful answer)."(Arnold, 2012)

How 'Big' is 'Big Data'?

Big Data can essentially be classified based upon 3 of its characteristics (Manghani, 2012):

Volume: The reason why the definition of Big Data is vague is the fact that the classification may vary from industry to industry. While some industries may regard data above 3 Terabytes as Big Data, other may go so far to stretch it up to 5 Petabytes and above. It is also important to note that data is not classified as big simply based on the size of the data. Organizations store data in much sophisticated forms with the help of database management systems. Data which requires being stored in a large number of records, transactions, tables and files may also be classified as voluminous and hence Big Data.

Velocity: Data velocity essentially implies the frequency with which data is generated. Every minute on the internet sees 48 hours of content being uploaded on Youtube, over 2 million search queries on the popular search engine Google and Facebook users sharing more than 684,400+ pieces of content. This is simply a sample of the data being generated from Personal Computers and mobile devices, there is much the same data coming from sources such as sensors and robotics manufacturing, video cameras and other electronic gadgets. Data from these and other sources may not be sizeable but the pace at which it is being generated means it all adds up to become an important characteristic of Big Data.

Variety: This refers to the different sources from which all this data is generated. The internet and the options it provides in terms of sharing and putting up content in the form of video, audio, pictures, graphics on social media as well as other hosts is well known; data also has a very important role in all businesses today with data continuously being generated every minute and the careful storing, analysis and application of this data is what provides businesses with the much needed competitive edge. This variety includes Point-of-Sales data at retail outlets and shops, customer food preferences at hotels and restaurants, RFID (Radio Frequency Identification) data from supply chains, Business to Business processes data and many such sources; all contributing to the characteristic of data variety.

As mentioned above, businesses and organizations generate a tremendous amount of data, being able to sift through all this data, pick out the data which is relevant to their business and which is right and will be helpful in gaining a better understanding of their business is the challenge. These activities require qualified business data analysts, a commodity which is in short supply throughout the world.

CAUSES ATTRIBUTED TO GROWTH OF BIG DATA

Big Data market is slated to be $50 billion by 2017, with several companies either above or closing in on the $100-million sales threshold, according to Wikibon, a professional community dedicated to solving technology and business problems via an open source collaboration of free advisory knowledge. This global phenomenon of amplification in volume of data can be used for the benefit of enterprises around the world by improving their competitiveness. It is estimated that a retailer using Big Data has the potential to improve his operating margin by 60%. IBM, one of the leading players in this emerging space, estimates that 2.5 quintillion bytes of data are created every day from a variety of sources, including sensors, social media and billions of mobile devices around the world. IDC estimates the market for big data technology and services will grow at an annual rate of nearly 40 percent to reach $16.9 billion by 2015.

Big Data has now become ubiquitous in every sector of the economy and has become an essential asset for growth and competitive advantage. The value of big data lies in its ability to analyze data which previously could not be accessed due to its sheer size.

More reasons attributed to growth of big data are:

- Continuous increase of computing power.
- Decrease in cost of storing huge volumes of data due to emergence of cloud computing. It has become easier to store, access and analyze Big Data. Thus enabling organizations to take advantage of new knowledge streams. Cloud technology enables renting of memory space instead of buying dedicated high memory space.
- Development of open source data analysis tools like "Hadoop".

BIG DATA AND ANALYTICS

Big data and analytics are complementary. Analytics is the discovery and communication of meaningful patterns in data. One of the most common uses of analytics is to mine business data to describe, predict and improve business performance.

Specific areas of analytics include enterprise decision management, retail analytics, marketing and Web analytics, predictive science, credit risk analysis and fraud analytics. Retail, marketing and customer management have been key areas of focus for leading vendors.

Performing Big Data Analytics

Data may be structured into structured or transactional data and unstructured data which can be obtained from all over the internet in the social media, sensor information and websites. The integration of data from these two sources followed by the harnessing of this data with the help of sophisticated tools provides insights which could not have been thought of before. Finally, feeding these insights and data into a Business Intelligence environment allows for the visual representation and discovery of results which in turn provide business value.

Cassandra: an open source database management system which manages huge amount of data on a distributed system – multiple computers communicating and solving smaller aspects of a larger problem – was originally developed at Facebook. Advantages of the distributed system include lower cost, higher reliability & scalability.

Dynamo: proprietary distributed data storage system developed by Amazon.

Hadoop & MapReduce: an open source software framework for processing huge datasets on distributed systems was originally developed by Yahoo!

Mashup: an application that combines and data presentation or functionality from two or more sources to create new resources.

R.: an open source programming language and software environment for statistical computing and graphics. It has become a standard for developing statistical software development and data analysis.

Stream processing: technologies designed to process large real-time streams of event data. It is used in areas such as financial services trading, RFID event processing, fraud detection, process monitoring and location based services in telecommunication.

Visualization: refers to the techniques and technologies used for creating images, diagrams or animations to communicate, understand and improve the results of big data analyses.

Tag cloud: a type of visualization technique where words which appear more frequently are larger and words appearing less frequently are smaller.

Clustergram: another visualization technique used for cluster analysis where individual members of a dataset are assigned to clusters as the number of clusters increases.

History flow: a visualization technique that charts the evolution of a document as it is edited by multiple contributing authors.

Spatial information flow: a visualization technique that depicts the amount of internet protocol data showing spatial information flows. For example the amount of information flow between the NYSE in New York and cities around the world.

'BIG DATA' ADVANTAGE FOR ONLINE RETAIL

The retailing sector has been collecting data for a long time to identify, segment and retain customers and retailers are at the forefront of the big data revolution. Big Data will empower retailers to track the behavior of individual customers from internet click streams, update their preferences and model their likely behavior in real time. This will enable retailers to recognize when customers are nearing a purchase decision and nudge the transaction to completion by bundling preferred products, offered with reward program savings. This real-time targeting, which would also utilize data from the retailers' multitier membership rewards program will increase purchases of higher margin products by its most valuable customers.

Some online businesses, such as Amazon, are already leading the field in this area. The site uses collaborative filtering technology, which allows it to develop automatic recommendations for customers based on their purchase history data.

We have on number of occasions experienced Big Data at work. We buy a shirt online, put it in our virtual shopping cart, but then for some reason change our mind. Afterwards, every site we visit features an ad for that very shirt at that same online store. Online retailers can give us a virtual identification number and track us as we hop from site to site and direct purchase targeted ads for products they already know we are attracted to.

Big data offers retailers the benefit of analyzing large data sets compared to smaller ones. Thus big data can identify business trends, combat crime and recognize real time traffic conditions enabling retailers to sell more of its products. Big data is combined with sales data to help optimize store layout, product placement and consumer interest.

The retailer can combine information it has about past purchases with details about the customer collected through the customer's Facebook page and elsewhere to determine exactly what price to sell the item and if it is right to negotiate.

Segmentation is most effectivewhen big data is used. It allows more micro-segments to be created and more personalization using information such as click stream web data, which logs how people browse a particular site.

The next stage for many brands that have already achieved detailed segmentation is to add in new areas. Social media sites provide brands with data for sentiment analysis, which can be integrated with retail EPOS data from to better understand how the way people feel about the brand. When this is achieved, people who already like a brand can be targeted individually in-store or with relevant DM and email content, effectively linking the on- and offline environments where consumers interact with a brand.

'BIG DATA' ADVANTAGE FOR TRADITIONAL RETAILERS

In the era of Big Data, it's those physical stores that seemed destined to be left out in the cold. But the vast majority of purchases – somewhere around 90% — still occur in a traditional retail setting. And brick and mortar retailers are looking towards big data to help them stay relevant.

One aspect of big data is video analytics, where traditional retailers analyze security video. Video analytics can be used:

- To alert management when a VIP customer enters the store and serves a role in customer relationship management.
- Analytics can provide insight into customer shopping and traffic patterns, which can guide staffing decisions.
- It can provide an alert to management if check-out lines are long or wait times are excessive.
- It can estimate customers' relative age and gender, which can provide valuable demographic data related to customer patterns.
- Analysis of customer traffic patterns can guide design of marketing materials and their location in the store.
- Analysis of customer traffic patterns using video analytics and observing customer shopping habits can provide data on the effectiveness of an end cap display and/or guide optimum location of merchandise on a shelf.
- Analysis of the time customers linger in front of a display can gauge its effectiveness, and analysis of relative age and gender can measure a display's appeal to various demographics.
- Analyzing transactions, for example, by specifying 'no sales' or all transactions above a certain number, can help to pinpoint questionable sales, and associated video can

clarify what really happened and supply irrefutable evidence for investigation and possible prosecution.

Smartphones can bridge the gap between the online and offline worlds, because users always have their phones with them, even when they're not browsing the Internet. Retailers can learn about a customer through their online shopping behavior and then offer them short-term discounts through a cell-phone when the consumer is near that stores brick-and-mortar location.

One company that hopes to give traditional retailers the kind of analytic tools available to ecommerce firms is RetailNext. The firm has developed a computer program that uses a store's security cameras to give managers all kinds of information about how consumers interact with the store. Using this program, Retail Next can show exactly how many customers are in a given store at a time, which parts of the store they explore, which specific items customers spend a lot of time perusing — and which they do not. RetailNext can combine this information with other variables like staffing levels, weather, product assortment and placement to determine what does and doesn't boost sales. Luxury retailer Mont Blanc has used RetailNext's services to improve its staffing levels and its product arrangement within its stores, increasing same-store sales 20% in the process. Retailers like American Apparel and Family Dollar have also successfully utilized RetailNext's services to improve the layout of their stores and increase same-store sales.

BIG DATA APPLICATIONS FOR BRICK AND MORTAR STORES

Smart Shopping Cart: The smart shopping cart extends the trend in using sensors and RFID technology to provide new sources of customer interaction data. Much like what we're seeing across other industries (smart grids, the connected car, Positive Train Controls, intelligent appliances, Progressive Snapshot), the smart shopping cart will capture the in-store shopping behaviors and traffic patterns of customers. When coupled with the customer loyalty card information, this will enable brick-and-mortar retailers to compete on equal footing with the on-line retailers in their ability to capture key in-store information like time in store, store routing, and time spent at specific store destination areas.(Schmarzo,2012)

Personalized Shopper: Leveraging the smart shopping cart, or just a smart phone app, coupled with QR and RFID codes, retailers can create a shopping experience customized to the shoppers buying behaviors and shopping objectives.

- Construct the optimal shopping list (given that the customer has input their shopping and meal objectives)
- Optimize the shopper's route through that particular store's layout. Make customer-specific product and meal recommendations
- Provide real-time coupons based upon what's already in the shopping cart
- Optimize the shoppers budget (given the customer has input budget constraints)

Shopping Budget Optimization "Dashboard": Instead of focusing on just selling products, retailers have the opportunity to become the trusted shopping advisor. For example, instead of a sales receipt that really tells the customer nothing new, what if you leveraged the customer's historical purchase data to provide a "spending report" much like financial services companies provide to their customers.

Designing a new receipt: It could provide some of the following shopping optimization capabilities and act like a shoppers shopping budget dashboard:

- Provide benchmarks against like or similar shoppers' buying preferences across different product categories, stores and geographies
- Highlight individual purchase trends in the types of products and product categories, and the frequency of those purchases
- Provide Amazon-like product recommendations to make specific product or meal recommendations
- Provide insights and specific recommendations to help customers optimize their shopping budgets

CHALLENGES IN BIG DATA

In larger organizations today, business intelligence (BI) applications typically provide information that is at the core of their businesses. These apps address the organization's mostcritical aspects, but they only represent a small part of the data that can be analyzed. BI vendors admit that there is more data yet to analyze outside these software systems, which they are now working to integrate and leverage. In its recent 2012 report, "Big Data—Extracting Value From Your Digital Landfills," AIIM Market Intelligence Industry Watch puts it simply: Some organizations (26%) are still struggling to organize their content, and 30% of organizations admit to having poor reporting and BI capabilities.

There is a severe shortage of necessary talent possessing analytical capabilities to exploit Big Data advantage to its fullest. It is very difficult to develop this kind of talent as it requires years of training.

- Privacy is an important issue for consumers, for instance, data pertaining to health and financial records is considered very sensitive by consumers
- Clarity regarding intellectual property rights of data and ownership of data is still ambiguous
- Legal framework regarding responsibility for negative consequences of inaccurate data is still not in place
- Organization leadership may lack insights regarding value of Big Data and ways to utilize it for organizational benefit
- Organizations still dependent on legacy systems will find it difficult to access and process consumer data available via social media sites and networked sensors.

CONCLUSION

The implosion of data in walks of life and fields of business means that there is a lot of business & competitive intelligence that can be gained out of recording all this data. This in turn means that Big Data as a concept is here to stay and qualified professionals who are capable of sifting through the relevant data, choosing data which is right and relevant and who are capable of analysing this data will be in vogue. Its advantages as well as opportunities in the field of retails analytics have been extensively discussed upon and will continue to be an area of much interest to businesses as these will be the source of much of their competitive intelligence and will help them in maximising their returns through targeted marketing and interaction with consumers.

REFERENCES

[1] Zalud, Bill (2012) 'Video Analytics:Big Retail Deal with Big Data', *securitymagazine.com*

[2] Manghani, Amit (2012), 'Big Data explosion deriving insight',*Cloudbook Journal Vol 3 Issue 1*

[3] Arnold,Erik (2012) 'The Big Deal About Big Data', *Information Today*

[4] Taft, D., (2012) 'Big Data offers big opportunities for Retail, Financial and Web companies', *Eweek*, Available at: http://www.eweek.com/enterprise-apps/big-data-offers-big-opportunities-for-retail-financial-web-companies/

[5] Arthur, L., (2012) 'Big Data brings holiday vheer to retailers like Macy's', *Forbes* Available at: http://www.forbes.com/sites/lisaarthur/2012/11/07/big-data-brings-big-holiday-cheer-to-retailers-like-macys/

[6] Barth, P. & Bean, R., (2012) 'Who's really using Bog Data', *Harvard Business Review*, Available at: http://blogs.hbr.org/cs/2012/09/whos_really_using_big_data.html

[7] Matthews, C. (2012), 'Future of Retail: How companies can employ Big Data to create a better shopping experience' ,*TIME Business & Money*, Available at: http://business.time.com/2012/08/31/future-of-retail-how-companies-can-employ-big-data-to-create-a-better-shopping-experience/

[8] Al-Greene, B. (2012), 'Are retailers ready for Big Data', *Mashable Business*, Available at: http://mashable.com/2012/10/12/big-data-infographic/

[9] Schmarzo, Bill (2012), 'Big Data in traditional Retail', *InFocus*, Available at: http://infocus.emc.com/william_schmarzo/big-data-in-traditional-retail-part-ii/

[10] Manyika, J., Chul, M., Brown, B., Bughin, J., Dobbs, R., Rozburgh, C. & Byers, A., (2011) 'Big Data: The next frontier for innovation, competition & productivity', *McKinsey Global Institute*

[11] http://www.inc.com/ss/best-industries-2012/jj-mccorvey/big-data-5-companies-capitalizing-on-this-business-opportunity#4

[12] http://www.marketingweek.co.uk/big-data-embracing-the-elephant-in-the-room/3030939.article

[13] http://blogs.hbr.org/cs/2012/09/will_big_data_kill_all_but_the.html.

Marketing to Rural Consumers in M.P.

Anil Dhagat and Shubhangi Dhagat[1]

Department of MBA, Gyan Ganga Institute of Technology & Sciences, Jabalpur Madhya Pradesh

[1]Govt. M.K.B. Women's Autonomus College, Jabalpur, Madhya Pradesh

ABSTRACT

"Contemporary issues and strategies in marketing of goods and services to Rural consumers in Madhya Pradesh."

INTRODUCTION

Marketing process, as defined, relates to identifying, creating, and promoting needs of end consumers and ensuring that they are fulfilled by the producers at all level .Rural marketing is a mix of farm and non farm produce marketing activities .In the view of liberalization as emphasized in the new economic policy, there emerges a challenge for many unveiled sectors of economy to position themselves in a better defensive place to sustain in the changing economic environment. Agribusiness is one among which need to be made aggressive in performing businesses. The marketing in rural products, either rural to rural, or rural to urban, or urban to rural in developing countries like India, is being performed under unstructured conditions and does not assume any organized functioning pattern.

The status of rural marketing need to be understood in view of Geographic, social & cultural dynamics and also from the point of view of various economic and operational gaps therein. Thus appropriate planning for rural product marketing in terms of trade channels, infrastructure, technology, and behavioral dimensions need grater emphasis for achieving better economic efficiency. Marketing to poor, and rural consumers, is a big challenge for producers and manufacturers and importers in India, This is an issue carrying many fold challenges and opportunities for holding increasing market share to various industries and service sectors. On the other side the agenda of governance by the ruling parties also always talks about growth and development of rural and backward society, hence opportunities for marketing in rural areas and marketing of products and services to poor and rural consumers has become a matter of priority concern. Increasing literacy rate in rural India, increasing per capita income in rural India and increasing information technology, and media in rural India and also increasing infrastructure base due to better governance strategies followed by administration, rural demands have increased significantly, but in India there are vide gaps between markets available for marketing to poor, they are mainly geographical, social, economical and cultural and environmental as a whole. In the light of these differences in India there shall be a need of different strategies and studies to reach to rural and poor consumers. On the other side, if , marketing from rural to urban does not find significant support and does not get proper coordination to cope up with reciprocal exchanges, the issue of socio economic enlistment of rural and poor society will be un-reached.

Madhya Pradesh is a state of comparatively slow economic growth and has many fold socio economic entities of its population which is residing in 51806 villages, 244 Tahaseels, and 313Blocks. The demographic picture of M.P. according to primary data of 2011 censes shows significant opportunities and scopes for rural marketing and scopes for reaching to poor and rural consumers, but at the same time it has many fold issues of challenges and problems which need a proper management and efforts to be made to cultivate desired results of success in catering poor society and consumers by the global business society, who look forward to see M.P. as a destination for Marketing various products and services.

This research paper aims to discuss and analyze and review the present status of rural marketing and marketing to poor people in Madhya Pradesh as a whole. It also focuses on different issues which are directly or indirectly involved in rural marketing in the state and deals with challenges and difficulties in reaching poor consumers and problems of maintaining supply chain systems to ensure rural marketing. The paper describes socio economic, Cultural, and demographical challenges for rural marketing in M.P. and suggests road maps and paths to achieve success in marketing to consumers of rural and poor society in Madhya Pradesh.

Research Methodology

Paper provides an overall review of rural marketing positioning M.P. based on analysis and interpretation of secondary data basically and also deals with primary data on the issues where opinion and expressions of consumers and supply chain system and authorities involved in providing necessary infrastructure and environment for marketing in rural areas. Statistical tools such as averages, correlation and percentage are used in analyzing the facts and graphical presentations make study easy to understand.

Results and Discussions

The study reveals some Demographic , Geographic and Socio-Economic , factors that play very important role in buying behavior of rural and poor consumers of rural society, Cost effectiveness and assurance of availability of product or services are major issues which makes consumer to believe in brand , Social issues and cultural strengths of rural society in M.P. plays a vital role in their buying behavior, Media effects are progressively positive in buying behavior of poor and rural society , Packaging in mini pouches and personal selling skills are even more effective in changing brand by the poor and rural consumers , Increasing Literacy and increasing cross cultural movements have shown a remarkable change in buying behavior of rural society of M.P.

Geographically distances between villages, and their inter connectivity and also timely assured supplies, inventory management, and prizing are some established challenges in rural marketing in M.P. Socio economic changes and disguised unemployment , marginal farming and lack of irrigation facilities becomes reasons for deviating buying behavior because monsoon uncertainty and non connectivity during rains either stop or decrease demand and supply either side. Migration of effective population to- wards urban or semi urban areas affects demand cycle of products and services. With this all there are some challenges for marketing in rural areas of M.P. they are:

(i) How rural marketing can be low cost at the end in the hands of rural and poor consumer?

(ii) How a product mix / Service mix can be made to be marketed in rural segment in possible lower and competitive price?

(iii) How handling, storing, and transportation cost of the products can be minimized?

(iv) How rural publicity and rural promotion activities can be managed controlled, and be made effective in the light of diversified socioeconomic entity of rural and poor customers of rural M.P.?

(v) How distribution channels be created to ensure regular supply and availability of goods and services in remote areas of rural population to sustain brand loyalty in rural and poor consumers?

(vi) Which are the expected areas of good governance in rural M.P. to ensure a smooth support and strength to marketing to poor and rural consumers?

(vii) How cross linkage can be developed between Rural V/S Urban areas, and Urban V/S Rural areas of M.P. are some issues which may require discussion and further researches to suggest future action plans and strategies?.

Implications

The research work provides many fold basic information's related to rural marketing issues and problems and possibilities of ensuring growth in rural marketing in M.P. and also highlights major socio economic ,Cultural issues , and cross cultural and demographic characteristics which may an important information's to further researches , may be used by Rural strategic marketing in M.P., A extended study on rural consumer behavior can be useful to marketers interested in M.P.

The government and local self governments can read the issues from their socio economic development point of view, and can determine their priorities for future socio -economic enlistment of the poor and rural society of M.P.

CONCLUSION

Rural Marketing in India was never been an issue in Indian and in global society before 1975, but Rural population in India was always an issue of concern for the governments for rural and Poor's upliftment, and villages were always a priority for electrifications, Irrigation facilities, Road and Rail Connectivity, Literacy and Education, Economic Growth, Employment, and Cultural integration of rural society. But even after completion of Eleven Five years plans, the conditions of rural society and rural markets, and consumers economic status have not shown any countable growth which can ensure high turnover from rural markets of M.P. After 56 years of independence still per capita consumption of rural society in M.P. has not reached to the level of even a marginal living standard, which is expected by the marketing world. This might be a situation that can be seen from the point of view of future markets in the state. The growth of per capita income in rural areas is uncertain due to dependency on non irrigated marginal farming, slow growth of ssi,s and lack of employment opportunity in rural areas, and also poor infrastructure is a challenge and hurdle in consistency of rural demands as well assurance of supply of products and services in the rural areas of M.P. Problems are : How to reach them, how to educate them about products and services, how to ensure supply of affordable quantity and quality of products and services in time to their Endeavour. How existing and reached market can be extended by strategies which can incorporate socio economic and behavioral effects and strategies which can en-cash mood and emotional entity of poor and rural consumers of M.P. are important issues.

M.P. is a developing state surrounded by five states out of five three states are developed. Literacy and education in M.P. has shown a significant growth, Media has covered app.70% population, and reaching to villages has become easier comparatively due to the implementation of national connectivity schemes and schemes of village connectivity run by the central government and state government. The rural population is also brought under minimum number of day's employment schemes which is bringing demands for regular consumption in the rural areas. Micro financing have shown a significant growth in the rural society of Madhya Pradesh which can be treated as support to income increase of rural society of the state. Kissan Credit cards scheme has initiated a new dimension for agro products in the state of M.P. The rural social welfare schemes and the schemes of economic empowerment of women , free education to girl child, Mid day meals schemes have given encouraging support to general education level of rural society specially women segment of the rural society. Invitation to Foreign Direct Investment in the state has made government to ensure well connectivity, improved communication and infrastructural base are some optimistic seen for ensuring marketing to rural and poor people in the state of M.P.

REFERENCES

[1] Raj Gopal :'Rural Marketing –Development,Policy,planning,& practice' Rawat Publications New Delhi ISBN-81-7033-469-4 1998.

[2] Makarand Wath & Preeti Agarwal: Exploring Indian Rural Market- The way Ahead, International conference on technology and business management March 28-30 2011.

[3] H.M.Saxena : Indian Rural marketing Rawat Publications New Delhi 2008.

[4] Aualkh, Harbans Singh: Changing Food grain market structure in India, BR Publishing corp. New Delhi 1983 pp vi + 312.

[5] Jain Vijay K. : Marketing Management for Small Units, Management publishing company Dehradoon 1988 pp.x+ 182.

[6] Prasad R : Making Rural Markets an Effective Instrument for small Firms Development . Bihar Journal of Agriculture Marketing, 1993-1 (1) 14-26.

[7] Dr.Kavaldeep Dixit: Competitive And Innovative Marketing Strategies for Tapping Vast Rural Potential in India , International Journal of Multidisciplinary research Vol.1, Issue 7, November 2011,ISSN 2231 578.

[8] Strategic Marketing Forum Times of India Panel discussion Published in: Strategic Marketing volume I issue III: Challenges in Rural Marketing July August 2002 page 22-29.

[9] Deepti Shrivastava : Marketing to Rural India: A changing Paradigm, APJRBM Volume 1 Issue 3 (December , 2010) ISSN 2229-4104

Order of Entry: Impact of Firm Level Variables on Firms' Sales

Devika Vashisht

Marketing and Stategy Department, IBS Hyderabad

ABSTRACT

Literature on business performance and order of entry suggests that early entrants tend to have a higher market share across various types of goods and firms. The paper suggests that firms invest heavily in marketing strategies like packaging, advertising, distribution and promotions to prevent entry of other firms, in FMCG and Consumer durables industries. Firms are divided into early and late entrants by taking liberation effect as a criterion. Results show that the early entrants outperform late entrants and their firm level variables have high impact on firms' business performance.

INTRODUCTION

India has undergone a lot of changes in the last century and has improved a lot in terms of its business environment. The credit for such an improvement in India goes to the industrialization which has shaped its business environment. After the inception of Industrial delicensing in 1985 and the *1991 economic crisis*, the central government *launched economic liberalization*. India has turned towards a more *capitalist* system and has emerged as one of the fastest growing large economies of the world. Before 1991, most of the industrial industry was dominated by family owned businesses. During that time period the numbers of players in the market were very few. Post 1991 the economy had a new look with the onset of many small and medium sized enterprises that started to contribute significantly. With the reorganization of share holding patterns, the private capital outperformed the public capital. Family based conglomerates changed into corporations managed by proficient and competent managers. With such a transition in the economy, the demand for the human capital increased which led to the development of education and training system of the country. More and more technologically advanced segments started emerging. Such changes had great impact on market place too. Before liberalization the competition was low as the numbers of players in the market were very few. But after liberalization when the trade barriers were decreased, the number of players increased, many companies came into the picture. The companies which used to enjoy monopoly or stable market, no longer could do that. They had to do various changes in their marketing strategies and activities, shareholding patterns, HR policies, operations and investments in research and development in order to survive in the market and to continue their business. Hence, industry growth, competition, marketing intensity and available resources are the major factors which significantly affect the sales of an industry. Here the concept of "order of entry" of a firm is introduced which acts as decisive factor in deciding the sales of companies. The order of entry strategy refers to the firm's or brand's timing of entry and sequence into new markets (Schoenecker and Cooper, 1998). Hence, this study examines the impact of firm level variables on firm's sales taking the order of market entry phenomenon into consideration in the Indian context.

LITERATURE REVIEW

When entering a specific market or product category time is a crucial factor for a firm. Many researchers have contributed a lot on the effect of the order of market entry on business performance of firms. Bowman and Gatigon (1996) studied the impact of order of entry into a market on the effectiveness of a firm's marketing mix decisions. They portrayed how price effectiveness, market response to quality, advertising effectiveness and distribution effectiveness are affected by order of entry. They examined the effectiveness of marketing mix variables on market share in five product markets (two-durable, three-non-durables) and 55 brands. The findings showed that the responsiveness of marketing mix variables like price and promotions on market share reduced with order of entry. The main effects of order of entry on market share were insignificant. The results in similar direction were observed by Kalyanaram and Wittink (1994) in their study to investigate the effect of marketing variables, like price, distribution, promotion and advertising expenditure on a relative market share. Log-linear regression was used on the 220 weeks data collected for 19 brands in five packaged goods categories. While the results conform to earlier findings, heterogeneity in entry affects the market share across different categories. Lieberman and Montgomery (1988) investigated the advantages and disadvantages of early entrants. Numerous sources of advantages, such as formation of ideal self, availability of scarce resources, barriers to entry by investing in marketing strategies, like advertising, distribution and R&D, influencing buyer's choice and others have been suggested in favor of the early entrants (Kardes and Kalyanaraman, 1992). The firms entering market with a full-scale launch and the pioneering firms enjoy advantages in terms of competitive position that mediates the relationship of order and scale with profitability. Such advantages are controlled by the availability of marketing and R&D. David Stewart (1996) used the Canadian automobile market data to explain effect of promotional expenditure on sales. Market share, market growth and the interaction between the both were the explanatory variables. The study revealed that expenditure on promotional activity is clearly an important aspect in the total marketing costs incurred by many organizations. Gerard R. Butters (1977) used sales density model where the model demonstrates the effect of advertising expenses and distribution expenses on sales. Cheaper the advertisement lower is the sales prices distribution & greater is the total sales.

Nam John Woo (2001) used Korean manufacturing firms' data to study the impact of R&D on sales. They estimated the elasticity of R&D expenditure with respect to sales by taking the derivative of log (R&D) with respect to log (sales). They explained the behavioral difference between scientific and non scientific firms by dividing the firms in large, medium and small sized firms' categories. They found that mean of R&D to sales ratio is more for scientific than for non-scientific firm. William T. Robinson & Joengwan Chiang (2002) did a study on the product development strategies for established market pioneers, early followers & late entrants in the market. In the study it is discussed that at the time of entry, market pioneers are known for emphasizing major product development projects. Data from 2273 established manufacturing businesses revealed that market pioneers engaged them more in the product development activity which is a combination of product R&D expenses and new product sales. On the other hand, late entrants were less likely to engage in product development. Horsky Dan (1977) discussed the impact of the brand's advertising expenditure, both present and past, the brand's other marketing activities such as pricing, product quality, new variety introductions, distribution, and dealer activities and other industry factors such as the product's primary demand and competitors' activities on sales of any brand. Niel E. Backwith (1972) highlighted sales responses of five competing brands to advertising with parameters of simple market response for all brands estimated jointly. This study revealed the effect of decision variables, including total advertising expenditure for a firm's brands, allocation of advertising monies between brands, introduction of new brands, and discontinuance of promotion for existing brands on sales. Kuvykaite1, Dovaliene and Navickiene (2009) discussed the packaging role in marketing communications, especially in the point of which in turn influenced consumer's purchase decision there by affecting the sales of the product. They used Milk and washing-powder as the two different products from the group of convenience goods for their study. The study revealed the impact of package elements on consumers buying behavior, thus in turn its effect on sales of the companies.

SIGNIFICANCE OF THE PAPER

With the reorganization of economy business environment changed drastically and thus the market place. Companies underwent lots of changes in their marketing strategies, ownership patterns, human resource policies, operations and research and development investments, to survive in the market. Thus, firm level variables affect companies' sales (Kardes and Kalyanaraman, 1992), but do these variables have equal impact on sales of the companies established before liberalization and the companies incorporated after liberalization. This issue acts as a motivating factor to take this study for research in order to find out the effect of these firm-level variables on the sales of the companies across two industries before and after liberalization. The reason behind choosing FMCG and Consumer durables industries is that despite strong competition these industries have always exhibited remarkable growth. Thus, provides a lot of old and new players for the study.

Hypotheses: The existing literature has shown that the firm level variables such as advertising, promotion (marketing), packaging and distribution affect the sales of the firms. Also, order of entry literature has highlighted the importance of the time when a firm enters a market or a product category, as a deciding factor for firm's performance and sales. Hence based on the literature available the following hypotheses are framed.

Null Hypothesis

H_0: There is no significant difference between the impact of marketing variables such as advertising, promotion, packaging and distribution on the sales of companies established pre-liberalization when compared to companies incorporated post liberalization.

Alternative Hypotheses

H_1: The impact of packaging expense on sales of companies established pre liberalization will be more when compared to companies established post liberalization.

H_2: The impact of advertising expenses on sales of companies established pre liberalization will be more when compared to companies established post liberalization.

H_3: The impact of marketing expense (promotions) expense on sales of companies established pre liberalization will be more when compared to companies established post liberalization.

H4: The impact of distribution expense on sales of companies established pre liberalization will be more when compared to companies established post liberalization.

Impact of firm level variable on sales is more for companies established pre liberalization than that of companies established post liberalization is the expected outcome for every firm level variable taken in the study, which highlights the importance of order of entry phenomenon.

Proposed Model: To measure the impact of the firm-level variables on firm's sales, the following model has been proposed.

$$S = \alpha + \beta_1 (PACK) + \beta_2 (ADV) + \beta_3 (DIST) + \beta_4 (MKT) + \varepsilon$$

Where, α = Intercept, β_1= Coefficient of packaging expenses, β_2= Coefficient of advertisement expenses, β_3= Coefficient of distribution expenses, $\beta 4$= Coefficient of marketing expenses and ε = Error term

S = Companies' sales

ADV = Advertisement expenses

DIST = Distribution expenses

MKT = Marketing Expenses

PACK = Packaging expenses

Literature available highlights that the ADV (Advertisement expenses) and DIST (Distribution expenses) of brands affect sales (Horsky Dan, 1977). A Canadian automobile market study shows that MKT (Marketing Expenses) or promotional expenses form a major part of marketing mix that in turn impacts the firm's sales (David Stewart, 1996).

Literature available on packaging shows that it plays an important role in marketing communications. It influences consumer's purchase decision, thus affecting the companies' sales (Kuvykaite1, Dovaliene and Navickiene, 2009). Hence, early entrants tend to have a higher market share as suggested by the literature available on marketing variables affecting business performance and on order of entry. Also, these firms invest heavily in marketing strategies like packaging, advertising, distribution and promotions to prevent the entry of other firms. This study aims to generalize the findings in the Indian context for FMCG and Consumer durables industries.

RESEARCH METHODOLOGY

The data analysis was carried out using SPSS 16.0. Data on the variables mentioned above was collected for various firms industry-wise in Indian FMCG and Consumer durables industries from Prowess database. Prowess is a corporate database service provided by CMIE. It contains detailed information on over 10,000 firms starting from the year 1990. A company wise search was done and a set of 30 companies based on their sales, incorporated before liberalization (1991) and another set of 30 companies which had significant sales in 2009, established after 1991 were selected and used for the study. In every industry all those companies were discarded whose information was not available. Thus it resulted in a set of 21 companies established before liberalization and another set of 13 companies established after liberalization for FMCG industry. Also a set of 24 companies established before liberalization and another set of 15 companies established after liberalization for Consumer Durable industry. The analysis of these two industries is divided into two separate studies.

RESULTS AND ANALYSIS

The objective of the study is to examine the difference in the effect of marketing variables on sales of FMCG and Consumer durables companies established pre and post liberalization. For each industry a student *t*-test was used to test the differences in mean of all the variables between the two sets of companies (one established pre liberalization and the other established post liberalization) in each of these industries. Then regression analysis was done on the pooled data of pre and post companies together. Separate regression was carried out for companies established pre liberalization and companies established post liberalization with sales as dependent variable and advertising expenses, marketing expenses (promotion), packaging expenses and distribution expenses as the independent variables for each of these industries.

Study I. FMCG Industry

Exhibit 1: Descriptive Statistical Information of Various Measures of FMCG industry (in crores)

		N	*Mean*	*Std. Deviation*
Sales	1	21	1.0001E3	1360.67059
	2	13	2.7815E2	297.69920
Pack	1	21	81.2271	114.37520
	2	13	9.6631	13.17355
Adv	1	21	92.4948	197.76796
	2	13	.7015	1.28554
Mkt	1	21	11.7205	20.33388
	2	13	5.2777	5.05654
Dist	1	21	34.1824	52.18109
	2	13	8.3285	11.10153

1: Companies established pre liberalization

2: Companies established post liberalization

Exhibit 2: Regression Analysis of pooled data (FMCG Industry)

Model		*Unstandardized Coefficients*		*Standardized Coefficients*	*t*	*Sig.*	*Collinearity Statistics*	
		B	*Std. Error*	*Beta*			*Tolerance*	*VIF*
1	(Constant)	84.998	41.100		2.068	.048		
	Pack	2.919	.996	.248	2.931	.007	.114	8.786
	Adv	1.261	.454	.179	2.778	.009	.196	5.091
	Mkt	5.254	3.241	.076	1.621	.116	.368	2.721
	Dist	14.851	1.863	.566	7.973	.000	.162	6.183
R	R^2	Adjusted R^2	F - value	Sig. F Change				
.988	.976	.973	299.971	.000				

Exhibit 3a: Regression Analysis of pre-liberalized FMCG companies

Model		*Unstandardized Coefficients*		*Standardized Coefficients*	*t*	*Sig.*	*Collinearity Statistics*	
		B	*Std. Error*	*Beta*			*Tolerance*	*VIF*
1	(Constant)	74.001	61.406		1.205	.246		
	Pack	3.080	1.197	.259	2.572	.020	.120	8.310
	Adv	1.235	.538	.180	2.296	.035	.199	5.016
	Mkt	5.818	3.940	.087	1.477	.159	.352	2.844
	Dist	14.436	2.241	.554	6.442	.000	.165	6.059

Exhibit 3b: Regression Analysis of pre-liberalized FMCG companies

Model	*R*	*R Square*	*Adjusted R Square*	*Std. Error of the Estimate*	*Change Statistics*				
					R Square Change	*F Change*	*df1*	*df2*	*Sig. F Change*
1	.990[a]	.980	.976	212.45108	.980	201.096	4	16	.000

Exhibit 4a: Regression Analysis of post-liberalized FMCG companies

Model		*Unstandardized Coefficients*		*Standardized Coefficients*	*t*	*Sig.*	*Collinearity Statistics*	
		B	*Std. Error*	*Beta*			*Tolerance*	*VIF*
1	(Constant)	95.955	59.233		1.620	.144		
	Pack	9.199	6.840	.407	1.345	.216	.185	5.420
	Adv	-61.416	78.690	-.265	-.780	.458	.146	6.830
	Mkt	-11.963	8.722	-.203	-.372	.207	.770	1.298
	Dist	23.957	6.671	.893	3.591	.007	.273	3.660

Exhibit 4b: Regression Analysis of post-liberalized FMCG companies

Model	*R*	*R Square*	*Adjusted R Square*	*Std. Error of the Estimate*	*Change Statistics*				
					R Square Change	*F Change*	*df1*	*df2*	*Sig. F Change*
1	.930[a]	.865	.797	134.08593	.865	12.788	4	8	.001
a. Predictors: (Constant), Dist, Mkt, Pack, Adv									

Results

For each hypothesis mentioned above, we have compared the beta coefficients for the two sets of companies. The support or rejection of the hypothesis has also been discussed. In case of packaging expenses, it is significant (p<0.05) for pre-liberalized companies but not significant in case of post-liberalized companies (p > 0.05) although the standardized â coefficient for pre-liberalized companies is less (0.259) than that of post- liberalized companies (0.407). Therefore, H1 cannot be accepted. In case of advertising expenses, â is significant (p<0.035) for pre-liberalized companies but not significant in case of post-liberalized companies (p<0.458). Also the standardized â coefficient for pre-liberalized companies is more (0.180) than that of post- liberalized companies (-0.780). Therefore, H2 is supported. When marketing expense is considered, it is found out that it is not significant (p<0.159) for pre-liberalized companies and also not significant in case of post-liberalized companies (p<0.207). Therefore, H3 is not accepted since marketing expenses was not at all affecting sales for FMCG companies. Now, in the case of distribution expenses, it is found out that it is significant (p<0.000) for both pre-liberalized companies and post-liberalized companies (p<0.007). But, here the case is opposite. The standardized â coefficient for pre-liberalized companies is less (0.087) than that of post-liberalized companies (0.893). Therefore, H4 is not supported.

Discussion

Study of Indian FMCG industry shows insignificant mean differences between the companies established pre liberalization and those established post liberalization in their dependent and independent variables. The results from the separate regression equations indicate that although there is significant positive impact of packaging, advertising and distribution on sales for companies established pre-liberalization, we cannot compare these impacts with the post-liberalized companies as these companies do not show any significant impact of these independent variables on their sales. The only variable that has a significantly different impact on sales of pre and post liberalization companies is distribution. The observations suggest that since distribution expenses play a critical role in the FMCG industry for easy availability of the products at the doorsteps of the consumers, post liberalized companies spend significantly more on distribution to get significant impact on sales than spending on marketing and advertising. For the post-liberalized companies, the effect of distribution is much more that the pre-liberalized set of companies. This is because, newer players in the market seek to gain better exposure and penetration and as a result focus more on the distribution channels. They initially spend heavily and succeed in creating a strong distribution network. Once such a network is in place, the post-liberalized companies have to spend less on the distribution expenses to achieve similar or even more sales and revenue than the pre-liberalized companies. Also we observe that packaging and advertising have significant impact on sales of pre liberalized companies but no significant impact on sales of post liberalized companies. Since the early players are not new to the market thus customers have better brand awareness, thus their expenses lead to significant impact on sales but this is not the case with late entrants or new players. This specifies the significant role played by order of entry of in deciding the sales and business performance of the companies.

Study II. Consumer Durables Industry

Exhibit 5: Descriptive Statistical Information of Various Measures of Consumer Durable industry (in crores)

		N	*Mean*	*Std. Deviation*
Sales	1	24	255.0517	250.58112
	2	15	263.6587	275.39687
Pack	1	24	6.3463	9.53085
	2	15	4.3880	4.55267
Adv	1	24	4.1283	9.39286
	2	15	2.2567	5.46869
Mkt	1	24	6.9983	11.58757
	2	15	4.5187	8.61365
Dist	1	24	4.208	5.0527
	2	15	4.2067	4.99494

1. Companies established pre liberalization
2. Companies established post liberalization

Exhibit 6: Regression Analysis of pooled data (Consumer Durable Industry)

Model		*Unstandardized Coefficients*		*Standardized Coefficients*	*t*	*Sig.*	*Collinearity Statistics*	
		B	*Std. Error*	*Beta*			*Tolerance*	*VIF*
1	(Constant)	79.995	35.622		2.245	.031		
	P_P	1.450	5.851	.045	0.248	.806	.328	3.049
	Adv	1.829	4.634	0.058	.395	.696	.509	1.964
	Mkg	.267	3.248	0.011	.082	.935	.614	1.628
	Distribution	38.608	8.135	.746	4.746	.000	.437	2.286

R	R Square	Adjusted R Square	F - value	Sig. F Change
.795	.632	.589	14.612	.000

Exhibit 7a: Regression Analysis of pre-liberalized Consumer durable companies

Model		*Unstandardized Coefficients*		*Standardized Coefficients*	*t*	*Sig.*	*Collinearity Statistics*	
		B	*Std. Error*	*Beta*			*Tolerance*	*VIF*
1	(Constant)	91.155	44.725		2.038	.056		
	Pack	5.365	6.905	.204	.777	.447	.250	3.994
	Adv	-2.996	6.532	-.112	-.459	.652	.288	3.471
	Mkt	4.987	5.895	.231	.846	.408	.232	4.302
	Dist	25.502	14.605	.514	1.746	.097	.199	5.021

Exhibit 7b: Regression Analysis of pre-liberalized Consumer durable companies

Model	*R*	*R Square*	*Adjusted R Square*	*Std. Error of the Estimate*	*Change Statistics*				
					R Square Change	*F Change*	*df1*	*df2*	*Sig. F Change*
1	.820[a]	.672	.603	157.93320	.672	9.725	4	19	.000

a. Predictors: (Constant), Dist, Mkt, Adv, Pack

Exhibit 8a: Regression analysis of post-liberalized Consumer durable companies

Model	*Unstandardized Coefficients*		*Standardized Coefficients*	*t*	*Sig.*	*Collinearity Statistics*	
	B	*Std. Error*	*Beta*			*Tolerance*	*VIF*
1(Constant)	80.773	82.895		.974	.353		
Pack	-3.034	21.310	–.050	–.142	.890	.316	3.164
Adv	4.422	10.021	.088	.441	.668	.991	1.009
Mkt	-.251	6.342	–.008	–.040	.969	.997	1.003
Dist	44.537	19.424	.808	2.293	.045	.316	3.164

Exhibit 8b: Regression analysis of post-liberalized Consumer durable companies

Model	*R*	*R Square*	*Adjusted R Square*	*Std. Error of the Estimate*	*Change Statistics*				
					R Square Change	*F Change*	*df1*	*df2*	*Sig. F Change*
1	.780[a]	.608	.451	204.09439	.608	3.873	4	10	.038

Results

For hypothesis testing, a comparison of the beta coefficients for the two sets of companies has been done. In case of packaging expenses, the standardized â coefficient for pre-liberalized companies is more (0.204) than that of post- liberalized companies (-0.050).However â is insignificant ($p > 0.05$) for pre-liberalized companies but for post-liberalized companies ($p = 0.05$). Therefore, H1 cannot be accepted. Taking advertising expenses under consideration, the standardized â coefficient for pre-liberalized companies is less (-0.112) than that of post-liberalized companies (0.088).However it is not significant in both the cases i.e. pre-liberalized companies ($p > 0.05$) and for post-liberalized companies also ($p > 0.05$). The standardized â coefficient for pre-liberalized companies is less (-0.112) than that of post- liberalized companies. When marketing expense is considered, it is found out that the standardized â coefficient for pre-liberalized companies (0.231) is more than that of post- liberalized companies (-.008) but it is insignificant for ($p > 0.05$) for pre-liberalized companies and post-liberalized companies ($p > 0.05$). Therefore, H3 cannot be accepted. Whereas in the case of distribution expenses, the standardized â coefficient for pre-liberalized companies is less (0.514) than that of post-liberalized companies (0.808) and this difference is significant at $p < 0.05$ level. Hence H4 cannot be accepted as well.

Discussion

The results show that Indian Consumer Durable companies established in the pre-liberalization period is observed to spend more than that of the post-liberalized companies but this difference is not significant for sales, marketing expenses, advertising expenses and packaging hence cannot be interpreted. Only distribution expense is observed to have significantly greater mean for pre liberalized companies. With time, the demand for consumer durable has increased hence it becomes necessary for pre established industries to invest more on their distribution network so that their customers can have easy accessibility of their products and thus they can survive in the market. The pooled regression results reestablish the same result as; they have done huge investments in setting up their distribution network and have been able to create its higher impact on sales.

CONCLUSION

In this research, an attempt is made to inspect two research questions. Firstly to find out whether there is any significant difference in the sales figures and marketing variables of the year 2009 between the two sets of two different types of industries (one set comprised of the companies established in pre liberalization period and the other set is of those which incorporated in the post liberalization period). Secondly to find out how do the marketing variables affect the sales of these two sets of companies to witness the effect of order of entry. The results reveal that among all other firm level variables in Indian FMCG industry, only the packaging expense is the one which has a higher mean for pre liberalized companies than that of post liberalized companies. On the other hand in Indian Consumer Durable industry distribution expenses has a higher mean for pre established companies as these companies are using network expansion strategy to sustain the competition and hence in the market. The study also highlights the role of order of entry on the impact of marketing variables on sales of companies established pre liberalization and those established post liberalization. Significant differences between the two sets of companies of Indian FMCG industry in terms of packaging expense have shown the effect of order of entry phenomenon. Similarly significant differences are observed between the two sets of companies of Indian FMCG industry in distribution expenses, but it is inconsistent with the order of entry effect which leaves us with the scope of further research. Even their impact on companies' sales for pre liberalized companies is higher than that on post liberalized companies' sales. Hence, taking liberalization effect as the criteria of splitting the firms into early entrants and late entrants and order of entry on a cross-sectional data set of Indian companies, the results show that the pre-liberalized companies (early entrants) outperform post-liberalized companies (late entrants). Also, their firm level variables have high impact on firms' business performance. Thus, the study demonstrates that early entrants invest heavily in marketing strategies like packaging, advertising, distribution and promotions to prevent the entry of other firms.

LIMITATIONS AND MANAGERIAL IMPLICATIONS

The study has certain limitations. Only two industries are considered for the study but still there is a huge scope to explore the order of entry effect across various other industries where one can analyze whether this trend is chased in all other industries or not and by what extent. Thus more far-reaching study including all the sectors can be done. To better understand the order of entry's phenomenon, supplementary strategies and firm performance measures can be exercised. In the same way, complete analysis of each industry segment can be done with much more detailed data.

One comprehensible implication for managers is that, one should go for an early entrant strategy in the existing Indian economic set-up along with a complete knowledge of the competitive, political, economic, social and technological conditions of market.

REFERENCES

[1] Alpert F H, Kamins M A, Sakano T et al. (2001), "Retail Buyer Beliefs, Attitude and Behavior towards P and Me-too Follower Brands," *International Marketing Review*, 18 (2), 160-187.

[2] Assmus Gert, Farley John U, and Lehaaann Donald R. (1984), "How Advertising Affects Sales: Meta-Analysis of Econometric Results," *Journal of Marketing Research,* 21, 65-74.

[3] Bowman Douglas and Gatignon Hubert (1996), "Order of Entry as a Moderator of the Effect of the Marketing Mix on Market Share," *Marketing Science*, 15 (3), 222-242.

[4] Carpenter G S and Nakamoto K (1989), "Consumer Preference Formation and Pioneering Advantage," *Journal of Marketing Research*, 27, 285-298.

[5] Farris Paul, Olver James, Kluyver Cornelis de (1989), "The Relationship between Distribution and Market Share Author," *Marketing Science*, 8 (2), 107-128

[6] Gerard R. Butters (1977), "Equilibrium Distributions of Sales and Advertising Prices," *The Review of Economic Studies*, 44 (3), 465-491

[7] Horsky Dan (1977), "Market Share Response to Advertising: An Example of Theory Testing," *Journal of Marketing Research*, 14, 10-21.

[8] Kalyanaram G, William Robinson and Glenn Urban (1995), "Order of Market Entry: Established Empirical Generalizations, Emerging Empirical Generalizations and Future Research," *Marketing Science*, 14 (3), 212-221.

[9] Kardes F R and Kalyanaram G (1992), "Order-of-Entry Effects on Consumer Memory and Judgment: An Information Integration Perspective," *Journal of Marketing Research*, 29, 343-357.

[10] Kuvykaite Rita , Dovaliene Aistë , Navickiene Laura (2009), "Impact of Package Elements on Consumer's Purchase Decision," *Economics and Management*, 14, 72-78

[11] Lieberman Marvin B and Montgomery D B (1988), "First-Mover Advantages," *Strategic Management Journal*, 9, 41-58.

[12] Marnik G. Dekimpe and Dominique M. Hanssens (1995), "The Persistence of Marketing Effects on Sales," *Marketing Science*, 14, 11-21.

[13] Nam J Woo (2001), "Non Parametric Quantile Regression Analysis of R&D Sales Relationship of Korean firms," *Empirical Economics*, 26, 259-270

[14] Neil E. Beckwith (1972), "Multivariate Analysis of Sales Responses of Competing Brands to Advertising," *Journal of Marketing Research*, 9 (2) , 168-171

[15] Stewart David (1996), "Allocating the promotional budget: revisiting the advertising and promotion-to-sales ratio," *Marketing Intelligence & Planning*, 14 (4), 34-38.

[16] William T. Robinson and Jeongwen Chiang (2002), "Product Development Strategies for Established Market Pioneers, Early Followers, and Late Entrants," *Strategic Management Journal*, 23 (9), 855-866

[17] Zou Shaoming and Özsomer Aysegül (1999), "Global Product R&D and the Firm's Strategic Position," *Journal of International Marketing*, 7 (1), 57-76

Relationship Between Customer Satisfaction and Loyalty Among Passenger Car Users (An Empirical Study Conducted in Bangalore City Among Small Passenger Car Users)

R. Srivats and R.K.Gopal[1]

Amity Global Business School, Bangalore
[1]MBA Department,CMR Institute of Technology, Bangalore

ABSTRACT

Customer satisfaction is the extent to which a product's perceived performance matches buyer's expectations. If the product's performance falls short of expectations, the customer is dissatisfied. If it matches expectations, the customer is satisfied. If it exceeds expectations, the customer is highly satisfied or delighted. The marketing companies, who want to be successful in the long run go out of the way to keep their customers satisfied and delighted. They strive to match customer expectations with company performance. Some companies aim to delight customers by promising only what they can deliver, than delivering more than they promise.

This paper aims to emphasize the Relationship between satisfaction and loyalty of customers with specific reference to small passenger car brands like the Maruti, Hyundai and Chevrolet.

To succeed in the business and to compete effectively, the firms must build long lasting relations with customers and also aim to create superior customer value. Loyalty comes out of satisfaction and loyal customers are likely to patronize a company's products and services for a long time. Therefore to attract and retain customers, an organization should constantly seek ways to deliver superior customer value and satisfaction. Finally the paper concludes the relationship between Customer satisfaction and loyalty.

INTRODUCTION

Overview of Buyer Behaviour

In general, predicting individual human behaviour is a complex phenomenon as they often seem it difficult to study their own minds. It is seldom easy, and sometimes impossible, to generalize about human behaviour because, each individual is a unique characteristic of personality, perception, attitude, behaviour, and environment. Predicting such a varied behaviour of people is a difficult and complicated task, filled with uncertainties, surprises and governed by risks. Therefore marketers must effectively predict human behaviour, which enables them to yield vast fortunes by understanding their buying patterns and designing products to suit their needs and wants and thereby gain customer satisfaction, while inaccurate/wrong predictions can lead to loss of millions of rupees. Today, business world is highly competitive and centers on customers. A successful business always recognizes that, the "customer is the king. This becomes all the more important in knowing why and how people consume products. This helps marketers to understand how to improve/modify existing products, what types of products are needed in the market place, or how to attract consumers to buy their products.

INDIAN AUTOMOBILE INDUSTRY-AN OVERVIEW

India is emerging as one of the most attractive automobile markets destination in the globe and is poised to become key sourcing for the automotive vehicles & also auto components The Indian automotive sector has a presence across all vehicle segments. It has more than 80 percent market share and also has greater volumes in the automobile sector. The passenger car market also has 135% share. The passenger vehicle market consists of utility vehicles and passenger cars.

Initially, the industry had few players and was protected from the global competition till early 90s.After the government lifted the licensing, during the early 90's i.e. after 1991, 17 new ventures have come into the Indian market. At present there are 13 manufactures of passenger cars 5 manufacturer of multi utility vehicles (MUVs), 9 manufacturers of commercial vehicles 12 of two wheelers 4 of 3 wheelers, besides 5 manufacturers of engines. With the entry of global players, the Indian automobile sector has become highly competitive. The growth curve of Indian automobile industry has been on and upswing for the past few years. It is the fourth largest passenger car vehicle market India and is 25th fastest growing car market in the globe, with a growth of 20%. Continuing the upswing, the sector posted impressive growth of 9% says the economic survey 2009-10

REVIEW OF LITERATURE

Edward Conlon, Sarv Devaraj, Khalil F Matta (2001) in this paper, relationship between quality represented by consumer rating and quality related activities by the consumer, represented by maintenance activities in the automotive industry. Based on several converging theoretical perspectives, a model is presented and it is tested, relating vehicle initial quality ratings to consumers' routine maintenance.

Audhesh K Paswan, Nancy Spears and Gopala Ganesh (2007) the purpose of this study is to focus on the feeling associated with being rejected by the preferred service brand, and its effect on consumer assessment of the alternate brand. Data for this study were collected using self-administered questionnaire in the context of higher education services targeted at the international market. Findings revealed that consumers who do manage to get their preferred service brand tend to be more satisfied with the features of the product.

Bernt Krohn Solvang (2007) through this paper develops and tests model to explain the variation is repurchase behavior between customers shopping for grocery products and furniture. The analysis and results of the research is based on interview data collected from 400 adult consumers in four different stores in Kristiansand, Norway. While researching the question of what were the main differences in the factors influencing repurchase in grocery stores compared to the furniture stores..

Larry P Pleshko, Samar M. Bager (2008) this study investigates the relationships among customer satisfaction, customer loyalty and market share in a sample of students pertaining to their usage of health club. Data for the study was gathered from a buyer group in a large university town in Southeast USA. Sampling framework comprised of Relationship between customer satisfaction and loyalty under graduate business students.

John Andy Wood (2008) in this paper explains the influence of environmental factors on organizational buyers' satisfaction with service providers using survey data from a cross section of organizational types in a business research context. This research introduces and tests on explicit conceptual connection between perceptions of the environment and buyers' assessments of satisfaction through the evaluation ser of alternatives in a structural equation model. Further, the model tests the positive relationship between satisfaction and intention to continue in the exchange relationship.

NEED FOR THE STUDY

The above study will aim to explore the buying behavior of car purchasers in the Indian context. The Customer satisfaction in the context of purchase process, after sales service will be explored. An attempt is undertaken to understand consumers' expectations and customer satisfaction and its effect of loyalty towards the Next purchase.

Statement of Problem: The Problem under study is to find out the relationship between customer satisfaction and loyalty. The effect of loyalty in repeat purchase of the brand of car will also be studied.

Objectives of the Research Study: The objectives of the research study undertaken are as follows:

1. To study the relationship between gender and Loyalty with reference to the Brands of Car owned.
2. To explore the relationship between Dimensions of Customer Satisfaction.
3. To understand the relationship between loyalty and the brand of car owned by the user.

4. To find out the association between demographic variables and the Brand of cars owned by the users.

Scope of the Study: The study will be conducted among small car owners of Maruti, Hyundai and Chevrolet. These are the three prominent players in the small car segment. The brand owners **of Swift, Alto and Zen from the Maruti Udyog Limited** will be considered for the study. Owners of **Santro, Getz and i10 from the Hyundai** stable will be the respondents for the study. From **Chevrolet owners** of Spark, Aveo and Aveo U-VA will be third set of respondents considered.

Respondents: Car owners from each company adding up to a total of 450 respondents and 50 respondents from Tata Nano will be empherically tested for the study. Owners of more than two years and less than six years are considered for the study, as they are the potential customers who will plan to either go in for a new car in the same segment .Small cars owners who will plan to upgrade from a small car to a medium size/luxury car will also be considered for the study. Samples will be restricted to Bangalore.

HYPOTHESIS

The hypothesis indicates the degree of association between variables. There were 3 major hypothesis formulated for the purpose of study which was as follows:

Hypothesis 1: There is significant difference between gender and loyalty with respect to the brand of cars owned.

Hypothesis 2: There is significant positive correlation between Dimensions of customer satisfaction.

Hypothesis 3: There is a significant difference between loyalty and the brand of car owned by the users.

Hypothesis 4: There is significant association between age, Income and the Brand of cars owned.

Methodology: Questionnaire was constructed addressing to the objectives of the study. Reliability was checked for the instrument.

- **Research Design**: An exploratory study followed with Descriptive study.
- **Sampling Method**: Convenience sampling method was used.
- The **sample size** was 500.

ANALYSIS

A Study was undertaken for 500 customers (Users) of Small Car. The actual sample for the final study will be 500 Small Passenger Car Users. As a thumb rule 10% of the Sample i.e. 50

was selected for Pilot Study. The Questionnaire was administered to 500 selected samples. Detailed Statistical Analysis was carried out using SPSS Software. Some of the Results of Study are discussed in Further Section of this paper.

Reliability Analysis Results

Table 1. Indicating Reliability Values

Cronbach's Alpha	*Internal Consistency*
a> .9	Excellent
.9> a > .8	Good
.8> a > .7	Acceptable
.7> a > .6	Questionable
.6> a > .5	Poor
.5> a	Unacceptable

The Results of reliability test are as shown in Table 2 Cronbach alpha is the coefficient of reliability of test score for a sample of respondents. Cronbach alpha will generally increase as the inter-correlations among the test items increase and is thus known as consistency estimate of reliability of test scores. In general a value of 0.7 is acceptable. According to above Table cronbach value of 0.7 is acceptable. The scores, which are within the limits of the acceptable range, are used for further statistical applications. From Table 2 it can be seen that the alpha value for the first variable viz. Purchase Process to the fifth variable perceived value before purchase is within the acceptable range, i.e. the alpha values were good.

Inference

The range of alpha values for all the variables is between 0.7 and 0.9. Thus the instrument was highly reliable.

Table 2. Indicating Cronbach Alpha Values for Variables

Variables in Q9-13	*Mean*	*Std. Deviation*	*Variance*	*Skewness*		*Kurtosis*	
	Statistic	*Statistic*	*Statistic*	*Statistic*	*Std. Error*	*Statistic*	*Std. Error*
Purchase process	28.36	3.885	15.092	-.586	.337	-.019	.662
After sales service	22.58	3.928	15.432	-.309	.337	-.491	.662
Vehicle performance and perceived value	39.16	5.449	29.688	.103	.337	-.802	.662
Loyalty	38.24	4.805	23.084	-.270	.337	-.568	.662
Perceived Value Before Purchase	35.76	9.352	87.451	-.789	.337	-.276	.662

Table 3. Indicating Combined Means, SD, Variance, Skewness and Kurtosis

Variables in Q9-13	*Mean*	*Std. Deviation*	*Variance*	*Skewness*		*Kurtosis*	
	Statistic	*Statistic*	*Statistic*	*Statistic*	*Std. Error*	*Statistic*	*Std. Error*
Purchase process	28.36	3.885	15.092	-.586	.337	-.019	.662
After sales service	22.58	3.928	15.432	-.309	.337	-.491	.662
Vehicle performance and perceived value	39.16	5.449	29.688	.103	.337	-.802	.662
Loyalty	38.24	4.805	23.084	-.270	.337	-.568	.662
Perceived Value Before Purchase	35.76	9.352	87.451	-.789	.337	-.276	.662

The Table 3 indicates the analysis of descriptive statistics for the variables that are reliable. The variables from Question 9-13 Includes the purchase process (Includes 7 sub variables), after sales service (Includes 6 sub variables), vehicle performance and perceived value (Include 10 sub variables), loyalty (Includes 10 sub variables), perceived value before purchase (Includes 8 sub variables).

From the above Table 3 it is evident that combined means of the variables except purchase process and after sales service is between 35 and 39. This indicates that the majority of customers are quite happy with these factors i.e. vehicle performance, loyalty, and perceived value before purchase with respect to the Brands Maruti, Hyundai and Chevrolet.

Skewness measures to what extent a distribution of values deviates from symmetry around the mean. A value of Zero (0) represents a symmetric or evenly balanced.

Distribution. A positive skewness indicates a greater number of smaller values and a negative value of skewness indicates a greater no of larger values and a value between ±1 .0 is considered excellent for most psychometric purposes. From the above Table 3 it is seen that except variable 11, all the other variables have negative skewness value. It indicates that the variables have greater number of larger values.

Kurtosis is a measure of the peakedness or flatness of a distribution. A kurtosis value near zero indicates shape close to normal. A positive value of the Kurtosis indicates a distribution more peaked than normal. A negative value of Kurtosis indicates a shape flatter than normal. A kurtosis value of ±1 is considered excellent for most psychometric purposes. Finally from the above Table 3, it is indicative that all the variables have a value of Kurtosis, which is negative and one of the values are towards zero. The negative value indicates that the curve is more peak. The first variable i.e. Purchase process has a value which is closer to zero

T-TEST RESULTS

Hypothesis 1: There is significant difference between gender and loyalty with respect to the brand of cars owned.

For the hypothesis I, Independent Sample T Test*, was used to test the above hypothesis, which was related to **objective 1**, the results of which are discussed in the following sections. The Independent Sample T Test output Table is indicated in **Appendix Table AB 1-AB 9**

Table 4. Indicating Independent Sample T Test Table for H_1 for Brand Maruti

Dimensions of CS	*Gender*	*N*	*Mean*	*Std. Deviation*	*T value*	*P Value*
Loyalty	Male	127	33.97	3.899	1.830	0.069
	Female	23	35.52	2.695		

Results: Since the P value is marginally greater than 0.05 in case of brand Maruti, the hypothesis is accepted at 5 percent level of significance. Hence it is concluded that there is significant difference between gender and loyalty, with reference to the Brand Maruti.

Discussions: It is seen that the P value is greater, hence it is inferred that there is difference between loyalty and brand maruti, with respect to both male and female customers. . It is also further observed that female customers are more loyal as compared to male customers with respect to the brand Maruti

Table 5. Indicating Independent Sample T Test Table for H_1 (b) for Brand Hyundai

Dimensions of CS	*Gender*	*N*	*Mean*	*Std. Deviation*	*T value*	*P Value*
Loyalty	Male	104	32.26	3.491	1.008	0.315
	Female	46	31.57	3.769		

Results: The P value is greater than 0.05 in case of the brand Hyundai; the hypothesis is rejected at 5% significance level. Hence it is concluded that there is no significant difference between gender and loyalty for the brand Hyundai.

Discussions: In case of the brand Hyundai, the P Value is significantly greater, hence it is inferred that loyalty does not differ from male and female customers. They exhibit equal importance to the loyalty. Further it is observed that Male customers exhibit marginally more loyalty as compared to female customers towards the brand Hyundai.

Table 6. Indicating Independent Sample T Test Table for H_1 (c) for Brand Chevrolet

Dimensions of CS	*Gender*	*N*	*Mean*	*Std. Deviation*	*T Value*	*P Value*
Loyalty	Male	134	33.08	4.913	1.057	0.292
	Female	16	34.44	4.211		

Results: The P value is greater than 0.05 in case of the brand Chevrolet; the hypothesis is rejected at 5% significance level. Hence it is concluded that there is no significant difference between gender and loyalty for the brand Chevrolet.

Discussions: In case of the brand Chevrolet, the P Value is significantly greater than 0.05. Hence it is inferred that gender and loyalty do not differ significantly with respect to the brand Chevrolet. Further it is observed that female customers exhibit marginally more loyalty as compared to male customers towards the brand Chevrolet.

Table 7. Indicating Independent Sample T Test Table for H_1 (d) for Brand Tata Nano

Dimensions of CS	*Gender*	*N*	*Mean*	*Std. Deviation*	*T Value*	*P Value*
Loyalty	Male	44	31.93	2.999	0.782	0.438
	Female	6	30.83	4.750	.	

Results: the P value is greater than 0.05 in case of the brand Tata Nano, in case of both male and female customers; the hypothesis is rejected at 5% significance level. Hence it is concluded that there is no significant difference between gender with respect loyalty in the case of the Brand Tata Nano.

Discussions: In case of Tata Nano, the P value is significantly greater; hence it is observed that gender and loyalty have no significant difference with respect to the brand Tata Nano. Further it is observed that Male customers exhibit significantly greater loyalty than that of female customers; hence they are more loyal towards the brand Tata Nano as compared female customers.

Hypothesis 2: There is significant Positive association between Dimensions of customer Satisfaction

For Testing the above Hypothesis, Correlation Analysis was used. The results of Correlation are given below.

Table 8. Indicating Correlation Coefficient Between Dimensions

Dimensions of Customer Satisfaction	*Purchase Process*	*After Sales Service*	*Vehicle Performance and Perceived Value*	*Perceived Value before Purchase*	*Loyalty*
Purchase process	1	.569(**)	.498(**)	.443(**)	.181(**)
After sales service	-	1	.572(**)	.489(**)	.220(**)
Vehicle performance and perceived value	-	-	1	.498(**)	.235(**)
Perceived Value before Purchase	-	-	- -	1	.248(**)
Loyalty	-	-	-	-	1

* Correlation is significant at the 0.05 level (2-tailed)

** Correlation is significant at the 0.01 level (2-tailed)

Results: The correlation coefficient between purchase process and after sales service is 0.569 which indicates nearly 57% positive relationship between purchase process and after sales service and is significance at 1% level. The correlation coefficient between purchase process and vehicle performance is 0.498, which indicates nearly 50% of positive relationship between purchase process and vehicle performance and perceived value and is significant at 1% level.

The correlation coefficient between purchase process and perceived value before purchase is 0.443, which indicates nearly 43% positive relationship between purchase process and perceived value before purchase and is significant at 1% level. The correlation coefficient between purchase process and loyalty is 0.181, which indicates nearly 18% of positive relationship between purchase process and loyalty and is significant at 1% level.

Similarly, the correlation coefficient between after sales service and vehicle performance is 0.572, which indicates nearly 57% positive relationship between the 2 dimensions and is significant at 1% level. The correlation coefficient between after sales service and perceived value before purchase is 0.489, which indicates nearly 49% positive relationship between the two dimensions and is significant at 1% level. The correlation coefficient between after sales service and loyalty is 0.220 which indicates nearly 22% positive relationship between after sales service and loyalty and is significant at 1% level. Similarly the correlation coefficient vehicle performance and perceived value before purchase is 0.498 which indicates nearly 50% of positive relationship between vehicle performance and perceived value and is significant at 1% level. The correlation coefficient between vehicle performance and loyalty is 0.235 which indicates 24% positive relationship between vehicle performance and loyalty and is significant at 1% level. Lastly the correlation coefficient between perceived value before purchase and loyalty is 0.248 which indicates nearly 25% of positive relationship between perceived value before purchase and loyalty and is significant at 1% level. Since the P value is less than 0.01, the null hypothesis is rejected at 1 percent significance level. Hence it is concluded that there is relationship between the dimensions of customer satisfaction.

Discussions: The upper portion of each cell identifies the corresponding correlations between the dimensions of customer satisfaction accurate to three decimals. The middle portion indicates the significance of each corresponding correlations. The lower portion records the number of subjects involved in each correlation. The notes below the table identify the meaning of the asterisks and indicate whether the significance levels are one tailed or two tailed. The diagonal of 1.000s shows that a variable is perfectly correlated with itself. It is seen from the table that all the dimensions of customer satisfaction are perfectly correlated with itself. It is also noticed that there is strong positive relationship between loyalty and perceived value before purchase which has ($r = .248$, $p < .001$). Similarly it is also noticed that all the dimensions of customer satisfaction have strong positive correlation p values. The correlation Table is Indicated in Table 8.

Hypothesis 3: There is significant difference between loyalty and Brand of Car owned by the user.

For testing the Hypothesis one way ANOVA was used. The results and the mean plots are indicated below.

Table 9: ANOVA Output for Hypothesis III for Loyalty and Brand of car owned by the user.

Loyalty	*Sum of Squares*	*df*	*Mean Square*	*F*	*P value*
Between Groups	434.152	3	144.717		
Within Groups	8385.560	496	16.906	8.560	0.000

Table 10. ANOVA Output for Hypothesis III for Loyalty and Brand of car owned by the user

Dimensions of Customer Satisfaction	*Brands of Car*	*Mean*	*Std. Deviation*	*F value*	*P value*
Loyalty	Maruti	34.21[b]	3.774	8.560	0.000
	Hyundai	32.05[a]	3.890		
	Chevrolet	33.23[b]	4.848		
	Tata Nano	31.80[a]	3.213		

Mean Plot Chart 4.1 Indicating Brand of Car Vs Loyalty

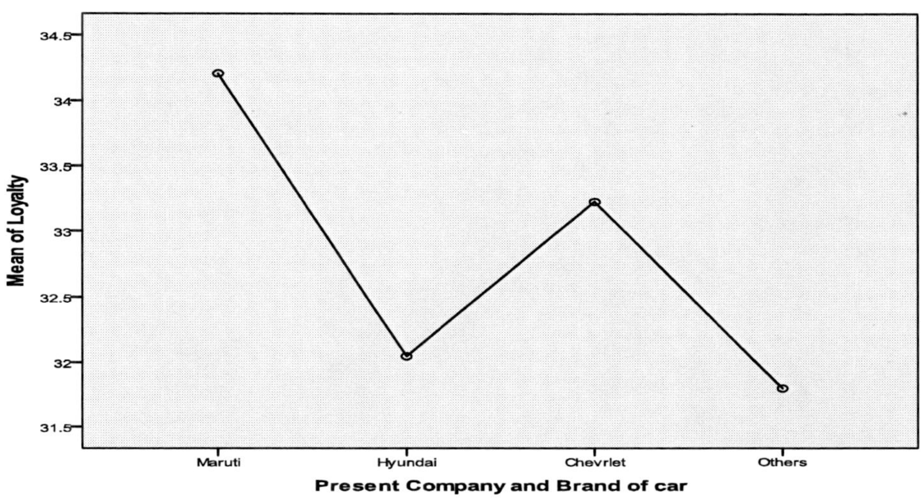

Results: Since the P value is less than 0.01, the hypothesis is accepted at 1 percent significance level. Hence it is concluded that there is significant difference between loyalty and Brand of car owned by the user.

Discussions

It is indicated from the Mean Plot 4.1 that, the Mean values are greater for Maruti, followed by Hyundai, Chevrolet, and the least Mean Value corresponds to the brand Tata Nano. Hence it is signified that the respondents depict greater loyalty towards the Brand Maruti, followed by Chevrolet, Hyundai and Tata Nano. Further it is seen that the brand Maruti has more loyalty in the minds of the users since the customers are satisfied with overall performance of the car and it is also a Trusted Brand. The four dimensions of customer satisfaction also contribute to loyalty towards a particular brand.

Hypothesis 4: There is significant association between demographic variables such as age, income and Brand of cars owned.

For testing this hypothesis, Chi Square was used; its results and Clustered Bar Charts are indicated below.

Clustered Bar Chart 4.2 Indicating Association between Age and Income

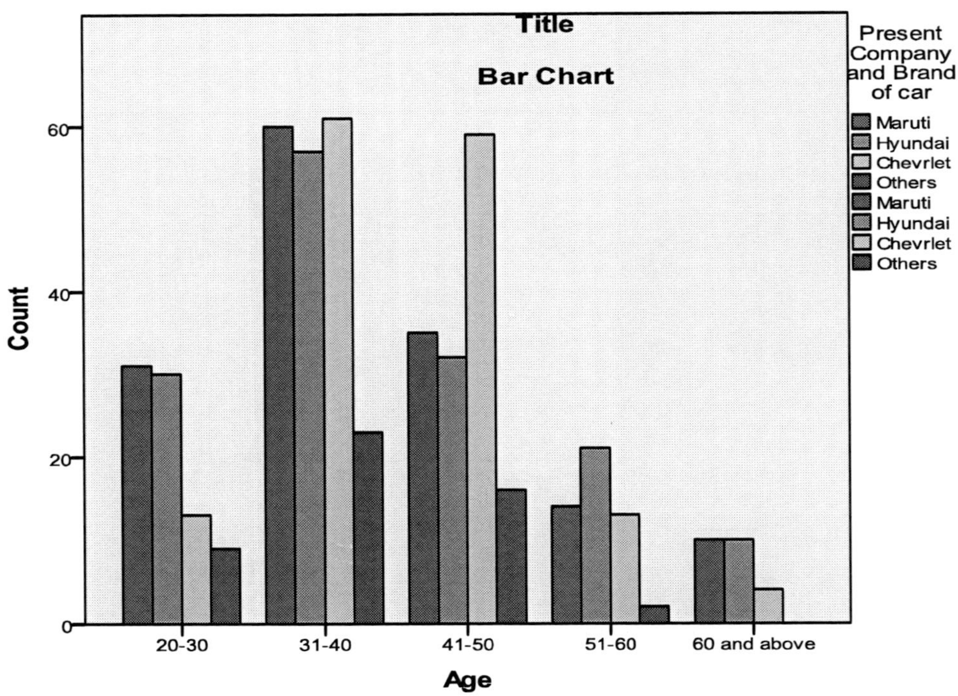

Table 11. Indicating Chi-Square output for age group Vs Brand of Cars for Hypothesis IV

Age Group of Respondents	*Present Company and Brand of Car*			*Others*	*Total*	*Chi-Square Value*	*P Value*
	Maruti	*Hyundai*	*Chevrolet*				
20-30	31	30	13	9	83	29.962	** 0.003
	(24.9)	(24.9)	(24.9)	(8.3)			
	[37.3]	[36.1]	[5.7]	[10.8]			
31-40	60	57	61	23	201		
	(60.3)	(60.3)	(60.3)	(20.1)			
	[29.9]	[28.4]	[30.3]	[11.4]			
41-50	35	32	59	16	142		
	(42.6)	(42.6)	(42.6)	(14.2)			
	[24.6]	[22.5]	[41.5]	[11.3]			
51-60	14	21	13	2	50		
	(15.0)	(15.0)	(15.0)	(5.0)			
	[28.0	[42.0]	[26.0]	[4.0]			
60 and above	10	10	4	0	24		
	(7.2)	(7.2)	(7.2)	(2.4)			
	[41.7	[41.7]	[16.7]	[0]			
Total	150	150	150	50	500		

Note: ( ) indicates Row Total, [ ] Indicates Column Total,
** Indicates Significant at 1 percent level

Results and Discussions: Since the P Value is less than 0.01, for the variable Age, the hypothesis is accepted at 1 percent significance level. Hence it is concluded that there is significant association between Brands of car with respect to age of the users.

Discussions: It is indicated from the **clustered bar diagram and Table 11** that, in the age group of 20-30, Maruti was preferred by maximum number of users, followed by Hyundai, Chevrolet and Tata Nano. In the age group 31-40 and 41-50, Chevrolet was preferred the most followed by Maruti, Hyundai and Tata Nano. In the age group 51-60, Hyundai, Maruti were the most preferred brands, followed by Chevrolet and Tata Nano. Similarly in the senior citizen age group Maruti, Hyundai had equal preferences, while Chevrolet had third preference with Tata Nano having no preferences in the Senior Citizen i.e. above the age group of 60.

Interpretation: The Leading brands like Maruti, Hyundai and Chevrolet was preferred by all age groups, while Tata Nano was preferred by all age groups except senior citizens.

Table 12. Indicating Chi-Square output for Income Vs Brand of Cars for Hypothesis IV

Family Monthly Income	*Present Company and Brand of car*				*Total*	*Chi-Square Value*	*P Value*
	Maruti	*Hyundai*	*Chevrolet*	*Others*			
25000-45000	32	18	11	4	65		
	(19.5)	(19.5)	(19.5)	(6.5)			
	[49.2]	[27.7]	[16.9]	[6.2]			
45001-65000	48	29	31	20	128		
	(38.4)	(38.4)	(38.4)	(12.8)			
	[37.5]	[22.7]	[24.2]	[15.6]			
65001-85000	25	28	86	22	161		**
	(48.3)	(48.3)	(48.3)	(16.1)		119..120	0 .000
	[15.5]	[17.4]	[53.4]	[13.7]			
85001-105000	15	28	14	2	59		
	(17.7)	(17.7)	(17.7)	(5.9)			
	[25.4]	[47.5]	[23.7]	[3.4]			
105000 and above	30	47	8	2	87		
	(26.1)	(26.1)	(26.1)	(8.7)			
	[34.5]	[54.0]	[9.2]	[2.3]			
Total	150	150	150	50	500		

Note: ( ) indicates Row Total, [ ] Indicates Column Total,

** Indicates Significant at 1 percent level

Since the P Value is less than 0.01, for the variable Income the hypothesis is accepted at 1 percent significance level. Hence it is concluded that there is significant Difference between Brand of car with respect to Income, of the users.

Discussions: It is depicted from the Table and clustered bar diagram that in the Income category of 25,000-45,000, the most preferred brands were Maruti, Hyundai, Chevrolet and Tata Nano. In the Income category of Rs. 45,000-65,000, Maruti was preferred by majority of respondents, followed by Hyundai and Tata Nano. In the category of Rs.65, 000-85,000, Chevrolet was preferred by majority of respondents, followed by Hyundai, Maruti, and Tata Nano. Similarly in the higher Income category between Rs.85, 000-1, 05,000 and above Rs.1, 05,000, the most preferred brands were Maruti, Chevrolet and Tata Nano.

Clustered Bar Chart 4.3 Indicating Brand Vs Income

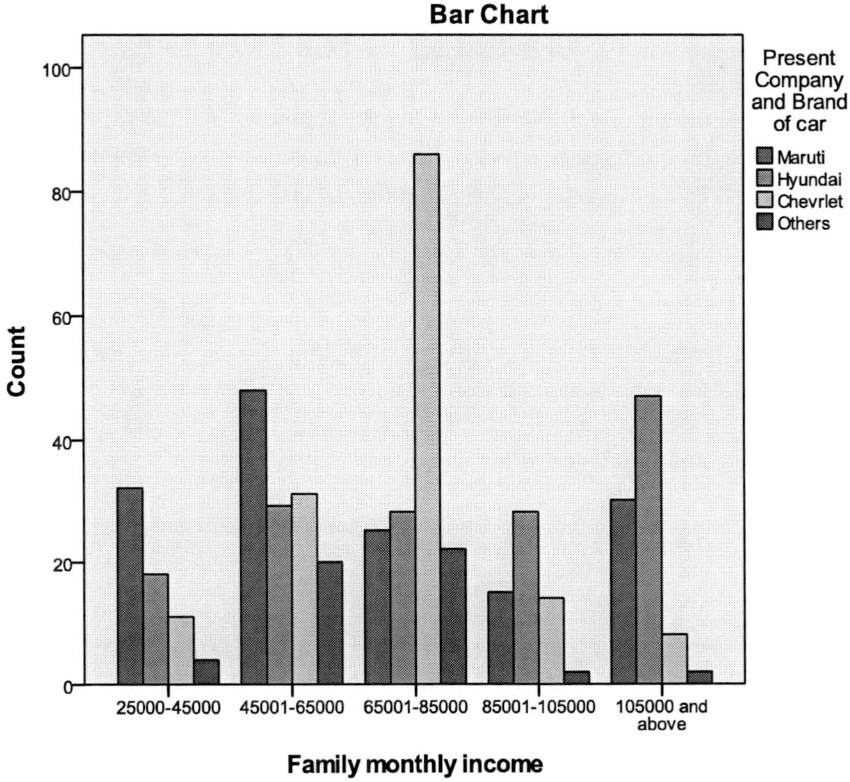

FINDINGS: The following are some of the key findings of the study

- It was seen that there was a positive relationship between gender and loyalty.
- It was inferred that females depict greater loyalty as compared to male customer for the Brand Maruti.
- Male customers exhibit more loyalty as compared to female customers towards the brand Hyundai.
- It was also inferred that Female customers are more loyal as compared to male customers towards the Brand Chevrolet.
- In case of Tata Nano, the Male Customers were more loyal as compared to female customers.
- Loyalty is one of the variable influencing purchase dimensions.
- Customers are more loyal towards the brand maruti, followed by Hyundai, which were having greater market share in the passenger car market.
- There is positive association between the Dimensions of customer satisfaction such as Loyalty and other Dimensions such as Purchase Process, after sales service, Vehicle performance and perceived value and perceived value before purchase.

- It was found that the in the age group of 20-30, the most preferred brands was Maruti. Similarly in the age group of 31-40 and 41-50, Chevrolet and Maruti were the most preferred brands. In the age group of 51-60, Hyundai and Maruti were the most preferred brands, followed by Chevrolet and Tata Nano. Lastly in the senior citizen age group of above 60, Maruti and Hyundai had equal preferences, while Chevrolet had the third preference. The Brand Tata Nano did not have any preference among the Senor Citizen age group.
- Finally it is observed that income is one of the important parameter that customers consider for the purchase of passenger car.

CONCLUSIONS

The study is indicative that there is a positive relationship between Gender and Loyalty with reference to Brand of cars owned. The Dimensions of customer satisfaction namely loyalty and other dimensions of customer satisfaction such as purchase process, after sales service, vehicle performance and perceived value and perceived have positive correlation or positive association. Futher the customers depict greater loyalty towards the brand maruti. Finally there is significant association between age group and Brand of cars owned by the user.

REFERENCES

[1] Audhesh K Paswan, Nancy Spears and Gopala Ganesh (2007). The Effect of Obtaining Ones Preferred Service Brand on Consumer Satisfaction and Brand Loyalty. Journal of Services Marketing. 21/2 pp 75-87.

[2] Bernt Krohn Solvang (2007). Satisfaction, Loyalty, and Repurchase: A study of Norwegian Customers of Furniture and Grocery Stores. Journal of Customer Satisfaction, Dissatisfaction and Complaining Behavior 20 pp 110-122.

[3] Edward Conlon, Sarv Devaraj, Khalil F Matta (2001). The Relationship between Initial Quality Perceptions and Maintenance Behavior: The Case of the Automotive Industry Management Science 47 (9) pp 1191-1202.

[4] John Andy Wood (2008). The Effect of Buyers' Perception of Environmental Uncertainty on Satisfaction and Loyalty. Journal of Marketing Theory and Practice 16 (4) pp 309-320.

[5] Larry P Pleshko, Samar M. Bager (2008). A Preliminary Study of the Relationships among Consumer Satisfaction, Loyalty and Market Share in Health club Consumers: Allied Academies International Conference-Proceedings of the Academy of Marketing Studies, 13 (1).

[6] George D Mallery P (2003). SPSS for Windows Step-by-Step: A simple guide and Reference 11.0 update (4th Ed.). Boston Allyn and Bacon.

[7] Rajendra Nargundkar, Marketing Research 2nd Edition, Text and Cases, TMH

[8] CRISIL Research cars and utility vehicles- Annual Review

Strategies for FMCG Marketers to Use Internet as an Effective Medium for Sales and Communication

Sandeep Puri and Prity Jha

Institute of Management Technology, Ghaziabad

ABSTRACT

Internet marketing is an accountable and measurable medium to attain both selling and branding objective. Internet is serving as an effective medium for Sales and Communication. Major ways of online promotion are Website, Social Networking, Search Based Advertising (keyword search, pay per click, impression based), Email Marketing, Online Public Relations (blogs, discussion forums etc.), and Media Sharing Sites. Some other emerging ways include Pod-casts, Social Bookmarking and Micro Blogging etc.This study examined the current practices of FMCG firms in using Internet for marketing to the digital generation and emerging trends in the world of Internet-based selling and advertising. The Study also examined in-depth, use of 'social media' as a tool by marketers to engage with consumers and develop lasting relationships.

INTRODUCTION

The world of digital media is evolving at a phenomenal pace. It is not only transforming how we obtain information, but how we interact, communicate and share as well. It is also changing the way consumers chose or buy products or services(Ryan & Jones, 2009).

Although technology is evolving at a rapid pace, it is just a small part of the digital marketing story: what is most exciting of a marketer is how technology is enabling people. Consumers are using digital media not just to enhance their relationship with brands and people, but also to get relevant information at the right point in their buying decision process.

There is no more denying the fact that Internet is the new voice of consumer. Earlier when not satisfied, consumers used to go to the consumer courts, but now they just have to go online and write a blog piece or post a video or simply comment on the discussion forums and get the (bad) word out. Word-of-mouth has become more and more powerful due to changed hands of power from the company to the consumer.The Internet's accessibility, reach, and transparency haveempowered marketers toinfluence, follow and monitor Word-of-mouth as never before(Kozinets, de Valck, Wojnicki, & Wilner, 2010).

FMCG firms traditionally have resorted to mass media advertising such as TV, radio and other media that can deliver. In recent years, there is increased focus on digital media as well. Internet is playing a key role, in terms of sales or as primary place for research about the product or service.

LITERATURE REVIEW

With the advent of Web 2.0 the marketing conditions have completely changed. Web 2.0 is not a revolution in technology; it is the evolution in people's behaviour. It is about accessing the power of internet via connecting; communicating and collaborating with other like-minded people online(Ryan & Jones, 2009). Web 2.0 has made internet a two-way communication channel between consumers and firms/ brands and changed the rules of the game.

By offering better product information, easy layouts, convenient payment methods and improved customer service, Internet marketing has helped increase online purchase frequency and money spent(Wu, 2002).

According to a research by Interactive Advertising Bureau (IAB) and Pricewaterhouse Coopers (PwC) in 2008, CPG (consumer packaged goods) companies in US spend only 6% of their marketing budget on online advertising. A research from Nielsen Catalina Solutions (NCS)[1], CPGbrands can experience a return of almost three dollars in incremental sales for every dollar spent in online advertising. This NCS research also found that in 2011 the online spend by CPG firms was approximately 13.6%, which is increasing over the years(Interactive Advertising Bureau, 2009).

Although, Internet advertising is on rise, its effectiveness in driving in-store and online sales is still a matter of debate. Web sites hosting online adsmostly push for exposure based metrics, such as "impressions" served, but advertisers, which prefer to pay on the basis of the performance of their advertisements, push for heuristic metrics of performance, such as "click-through," which indicates no. of clicks on the advertiser's URL from the banner ad(Chintagunta, Manchanda, Dubé, & Goh, 2006).

INTERNET AS CHANNEL FOR COMMUNICATION AND SALES

CPG firms have historically been hesitant to move from traditional to digital media, arguing that it doesn't make sense to advertise online when the majority of CPG products are purchased in brick-and-mortar retail stores.In recent years this thinking has changed as it is justified more often now that the Internet is much more than a direct response channel. Internet marketing has proven to have a strong branding impact and a significant ability to drive in-store sales. Furthermore, with the advent of e-retailers and brick-and-mortar retailers also using Internet as sales channel, CPG firms are increasingly adopting digital media.

Internet as Sales Channel

Internet serves as an important sales channel as consumers are increasingly using Internet or mobile for purchasing goods. India's biggest retailer Big Bazaar has started delivering assortment of goods at home, also Wal-Mart the biggest retailer of world now sells online.Moreover, many e-tailing websites have come up that sell FMCG goods online such as purplle.com.

Online advertising has impacted in-store sales as well. According to a study conducted by Accenture, comScore and dunnhumbyUSA in 2010-11 found that visitors to CPG brand websites spend 37 per cent more than non-visitors on the brand in retail stores and brand website visitors are heavier buyers within a brand's product category, spending 53 per cent more than non-visitors on the category in retail stores in US.

Internet as Communication Channel

Television is losing audience minutes/ viewership to internet. Some of the key challenges being faced by mass media such as television are increased programming costs, increased proliferation of cable and pay channels and increasing adoption of digital video recorders which allow viewers to skip through advertisements.

CPG brands are increasing their online footprint. Big CPG companies like P&G, Unilever, Kraft, Coca-Cola and Nestle pay digital marketing agencies huge sum to get their brands visible online. Advertisers seek to create and maintain brands, to provide information about new products and services, to advertise sales and price promotions, and to direct consumers to the proper retail outlet for their products.

There are wide variety of online advertising and targeting methods. Firms must ensure the use of most effective and appropriate method based on the campaign goals. Various online advertising methods are: Keyword Search (pay-per-click advertising), Classifieds, Display Ads, Affiliate Marketing, Rich media, Email etc.

Apart from advertising, marketers maintain website and presence on social media channels; these are the most important tool for online consumer engagement. Marketers use search engine optimization (SEO) techniques to further improve the brand's online presence as it is reflected in the organic searches.

Social media technologies take various forms and brands must be present in all the forms where target audience is present in huge number.

---

[1] Nielsen and Catalina established Nielsen Catalina Solutions as a joint venture in 2009; the firm deals in research specific to CPG industry and Online Media.

Different Forms of Social Media are

- Social Bookmarking -> save bookmarks of favourite sites and categorize them under tags e.g. stumbleupon.com
- Social Media submission sites -> where users submit contents that they think the community will like and as more people like and vote for the submitted content, its rating improves and reflects in searches, for example reddit.com and digg.com
- Forums and discussion sites ->Users discuss about products, services, brands or other relevant topics at these kinds of websites.
- Media sharing sites ->Users are increasingly sharing content of various media types be it videos, audio, photos etc. exampleFlickr, Pinterest, YouTube etc.
- A reviews and ratings site -> Internet is being used for basic information and search about products and services by people,for examplenaaptol.comis a website for comparing prices and specifications of variety of products.
- Blogs -> short for "web log" is a powerful medium for communication and self-expression. Surprisingly, corporates have also begun to use blogs to bring in personalization, individuality and personality to the otherwise non-human corporate entity.
- Podcasts -> is a rich media conceptually similar to blogs as it is digital media files (can be audio or video) that is distributed over internet to people.
- Social network sites ->Users connect and share personal and professional information on networking sites such as Facebook, LinkedIn etc.
- Micro blogging -> similar to blogs but shorter in size. In a way it serves as short message broadcast service. Twitter and Tumblr are the famous micro blogging websites.
- Wikis -> serve as mass collaboration space of knowledge, information and expertise online. These web pages are open to all and can be added, edited, discussed and commented upon by anyone. It is for the people, by the people such as Wikipedia.

Strategies and Tools Implemented by CPG Firms

Consumer goods marketers have embarked upon the online way long back, but now the spending on the digital medium as proportion of total marketing expenditure is increasing. FMCG giant HUL currently spends approximately 5-10% of its marketing budget on digital medium.

Engagement Methods Used by FMCG Firms

Social Media is all about giving power in the hands of your consumers, having them voice out their views openly and get insights from these views. Brands like Nestle have successfully run twitter campaigns such as the Parenting campaign where online ads with 'How do you stimulate your child's mind?' as question were posted on various sites and users who are logged onto twitter can post their answers directly, and the comments will appear on both online ads and the Nestle twitter feed. This was also a good example of an integrated social media campaign, as users who clicked on the ads instead of replying with a tweet, were taken to a YouTube channel containing promotional videos with parenting advice courtesy of Nestle.

Social Media help brands enter into the lives of its consumers and understand the real person behind. Heineken introduced the app "BeerFriender"[2] where users can gift a BeerTender and get one in return too. People like to present gifts to near and dear ones, and this FaceBook campaign elicits that part of human emotion.

Internet is increasingly used by brands to portray the human side or personality of brands and as a medium to connect with consumers to generate conversation. The Being Girl online community developed by P&G was targeted towards teenage girl audience and focussed on general issues that teenage girls face in their day to day life. P&G, a leading manufacturer of female hygiene products, found that teen girls want accurate and complete information on feminine issues and are usually embarrassed to discuss with family or at school. Being Girl (www.beinggirl.com) was developed to deliver specific content to these teen girls looking for answers and was also used as a medium to promote brands Tampax, Always and Whisper, Always and Whisper. Initially P&G guided and facilitated discussion online and now 100% content posted are by the users.In June 2007 alone there were 436,000 unique visitors to the website according to a Forrester[3] study. It shows that customer's experience of digital content is influenced by all stakeholders in the creation & delivery process as well as the customer's participation in the learning and co-creation of the experience(Rowley, 2008).

Engaging with consumers in various innovative ways and strong content marketing across digital channels is very rewarding. Best example of an integrated digital strategy would be Red Bull which engages audience in multitude of formats at various touch points. Red Bull Media House which is the media and content arm of Red Bull GmbH runs more than 900 domains in 36 languages under the name of redbull.com and has digital presence in all types of channels web TV, web radio, apps, online games and social networking. Ithas created an iPad app of its global monthly print magazine *The Red Bulletin*(http://redbulletin.com/) to offer its audience more interactive content and all the time access based on membership. As Red Bull has consistently associated its brand with sports, it has lot of games hosted on RedBull.com or on its social media channels for download. Red Bull has very close partnership with YouTube and it is noted that till date more than 300 million YouTube views has been generated by Red Bull content. Red Bull network community has more than 35 million followers across all its social channels.

Efforts by big brands are also on all time high to find newer and varied means on internet to connect with its target audience. Coca-Cola has launched in December 2011 a new Tumblr page "*Happiness Is*" to share happy content with teen bloggers. Coca-Cola plans to integrate

---

[2] BeerTender is home beer-tap appliance from Heineken

[3] Forrester Research is an independent market research company headquartered at Cambridge, MA

and share content that would appeal to teenagers such as sports, pop culture and music. More than 11 million teen bloggers spend an average of 37 minutes on Tumblr, Coke wants to be part of conversation of those teen bloggers by providing content appealing to teen audience and sharing happiness.

Measure the ROI of Internet Marketing

One of the key strengths of digital marketing is the fact that it is accountable and measurable. It is important to choose the right metrics for the campaign and to ensure that the measurement is meaningful and accurate. As the theory and practice of digital marketing is still evolving, any standardised measurement techniques are not in place. Firms use various known metrics or figure out some based on the type of campaign and the goal to be achieved.

Measuring Effectiveness of Online Campaignsby CPG firms is for estimating:web's contribution to branding objectives, impact of online campaigns on offline sales and impact on online sales.

Measuring the Impact of Online Campaigns on Brand

Advertisers carry out specific analyses or post-test studies to measure the impact on branding imperatives such as awareness, recognition, loyalty and purchase intent. Advertisers measure exposure to figure out the visibility of an ad and average amount of time users are exposed to that ad. By measuring interaction and browsing behaviour of users advertisers get an idea about correlation between these behaviours and brand image and reputation(PwC, 2012).

Measuring the Impact of Online Campaigns on In-store Sales

In general, advertisers use basic method of measurement by cross-checking sales data against media campaign strategies to calculate the impact. Sales are observed for a fixed period before and after running a campaign and results obtained provide empirical measurement.

Measuring the Impact of Online Campaigns on Online Sales

Websites are *conversion engine* for the traffic that flow in as a result of various campaigns and everything in the website should be designed to ultimately achieve the conversion goals(Ryan & Jones, 2009).A conversion funnel is the steps after the website's landing page that are required to complete a conversion and firms nowadays concentrate on optimizing the conversion funnel. Conversion goals can be anything such as an online sale (transaction), lead generation or opt-in for newsletter subscription or any other step important for business(Ryan & Jones, 2009).

There are five levels of measuring online campaigns with increasing importance:

1. Display – no. of impressions

2. Exposure – no. of advertisements viewed, exposure time
3. Interaction – length of interaction on one activity
4. Browsing – no. of visits, revisits, time, length
5. Engagement – no. of activities performed

Click through rate which is no. of clicks by no. of impressions is mostly used to determine the success of banner ads and other online ads.

Managerial Implications

Marketers for consumer packaged goods (CPG) brands are using diverse strategies to engage with today's consumers. Online coupons, social media ads and rich media are among the techniques that are being employed in CPG marketing.

CPG Marketers need an integrated social media strategy tailored to their product offerings and target audience, as social is the top online activity. Brands must keep in mind the fact that content is at the heart of all campaigns, it is very important to deliver cutting-edge, relevantand appealing content to one's audience, otherwise irrespective of delivery method the campaign won't run for long. And finally success of any campaign is limited by achievement of two goals: Return on Investment and increased Customer engagement.Hence Marketers should design their campaigns keeping the success metrics in mind.

REFERENCES

[1] Chintagunta, P. K., Manchanda, P., Dubé, J.-P., & Goh, K. Y. (2006). The Effect of Banner Advertising on Internet. *Journal of Marketing Research*, Vol. XLIII, pp. 98–108.

[2] Choudhary, V. (2012, 09). *HUL to spend more on digital advertising*. Retrieved 10 08, 2012, from Live Mint.

[3] Interactive Advertising Bureau. (2009, 12). *CPGs and Social Media*. Retrieved 10 05, 2012, from http://www.iab.net

[4] Kozinets, R. V., de Valck, K., Wojnicki, A. C., & Wilner, S. J. (2010). Understanding Word-of-Mouth Marketing in Online Communities. *Journal of Marketing*, Vol. 74, 71–89.

[5] PwC. (2012). *Measuring the effectiveness of Online Advertising*. Retrieved October 15, 2012, from Study conducted by PwC for IAB France and the SRI: www.pwc.com

[6] Rowley, J. (2008). Understanding digital content marketing. *Journal of Marketing Management*, Vol. 24, No. 5-6, pp. 517-540.

[7] Ryan, D., & Jones, C. (2009). *Understanding Digital Marketing*. Kogan Page Limited.

[8] Wu, S.-I. (2002). Internet Marketing Involvement and Consumer Behavior. *Asia Pacific Journal of Marketing and Logistics*, Vol. 14 Iss: 4 pp. 36 - 53.

The Role of the Satisfied Employee and its Impact on Customer Satisfaction

Matauddin Peerzada, J.K. Tandon and Lokesh Arora

Jaipur National University, Jaipur

ABSTRACT

It's a proven fact that virtually no business can exist without having customers.Within a very competitive marketplace where business organizations compete for customers, customer satisfaction is observed as key differentiator and increasingly has developed into primary factor of business strategy, at the same time it is equally important to find out the link between Employee Satisfaction and Customer Satisfaction, The overall purpose of this article is to develop a conceptual foundation for investigating the customer retention process. The article involves association of customer relationshipwith employee satisfaction the satisfaction and retention relationship, and the development of a more comprehensive view of the relationship of both.

INTRODUCTION

It has been observed that there was a cause-and-effect relationship between the Job Satisfaction and Customer Satisfaction, it is normally impossible to maintain a loyal customer base without a base of loyal employees and that the best employees prefer to work for companies that deliver the kind of superior value that builds customer loyalty,

Building loyalty has in fact become the acid test of leadership." Frederick Reichheld, The Loyalty Effect and Loyalty Rules

For most organizations, the goal of improving customer service levels is an article of faith. And so it should be, because there's an overwhelming body of research to show that building customer loyalty has a major impact on profitability. In fact, according to one study - based on 46,000 business-to-business surveys - a "totally satisfied" customer contributes 2.6 times as much revenue as a "somewhat satisfied" customer.

Virtually no organization can obtain its objectives if it doesn't supported by the right set of employees. The staff within a business mostly determines the success of the company. This is usually the factor why businesses invest enormous efforts in selecting candidates for their company. It can be observed many times, abilities and knowledge of the employee is viewed as to determine her or his performance within the company. One aspect which is certainly being overlooked by nearly all of the company owners is employee satisfaction.

In the process of improving customer satisfaction, normally it has happened that employers forget to pay attention to employees needs, for any competitive economic environment this may lead to a serious problem for employer if this kind of concern in neglected.

Studies in past have shown that customer satisfaction plays an important role in the health and future success of any company. When customers are satisfied, they keep coming back to the same place and invite many new potential customer as well but this can only be possible when customers are actually happy and satisfied, it has also happened that along with the product or services, an attitude of the employee is equally important to satisfy the customers.

Employee Attitudes and Customer Attitudes are related with each other, in other word it can be termed as Customer Attitude is depending upon the attitude of Employee, and finally as a part of outcome these two factors will have an impact on Business Results. It can be said that better relationship of Customer and Employee will lead to better Business Results.

A study from the University of Missouri has found that companies that attend to employee satisfaction can improve internal moral, prevent turnover, and enhance customer satisfaction, including repurchase intentions.

It not sufficient only to pay the attention to the customers, by providing them according to the requirement, along with the same, it has been observed that keeping your employees satisfied with their work experience and providing them with challenges and allowing them to have a sense of ownership in the business can have a tremendous effect on customer satisfaction and loyalty," said Christopher Groening.

The actual link between customer satisfaction and customer loyalty is almost twice as strong when you have high employee satisfaction compared to when they are not satisfied with their jobs. This double-positive finding stands in contrast to the idea that a firm can neglect to satisfy their employees as long as they pursue customer satisfaction.

While Groening and coauthors studied a large franchise, they believe the results would be comparable with a business of any size. In their study, the research team reviewed a European retail franchise system that has approximately 300 outlets with 933 employees and more than 20,700 customers.

Satisfaction data was obtained from employees and customers regarding either working for or buying from the business. The study was published in the Journal of Service Research.

This is not a one-way street where companies implement policies and can expect to experience gains solely through customer service," Groening said.

The relationships among the CEO, the employees and the customers are all linked. It's important for CEOs to know that they can have a large impact on customer service without ever talking with a customer or implementing a new customer service policy."

Following his study, Groening recommends the following actions, based on answers from the employee survey questions, to increase employee satisfaction:

- Train and empower employees so they have the tools to make decisions. This allows them to make decisions that are beneficial for the company and each individual customer – instead of following a simple flowchart and possibly upsetting a customer with the final outcome.
- Hire managers who serve as examples and also can be mentors with employees. If a company policy is established, it should be honored by managers as well as employees. Additionally, managers should help employees know what is expected in order to advance in the company.
- Create good working atmospheres. Offer incentives or intangible benefits, such as flexible working hours, if possible.

While many of these actions might seem like common sense, they can be very difficult to maintain, it is also very important to hire the right people in management positions who will take part in these activities – for example, serving as mentors or employers might have difficulty meeting their goals.

Researchers have indicated that customer satisfaction plays a vital part in wellness and future success of a business. Whenever customers are pleased, they keep coming back again to the same business and invite their close friends to try to do the same. Employee satisfaction can greatly improve internal moral. Trying to keep your staff enthusiastic about their work experience, supplying them with challenges and enabling the actual sense of ownership within the business may have an exceptional effect on customer satisfaction as well as loyalty.

Taking a business from good to great customer satisfaction basically is depending upon those who offer that service or product. This can only arise involving the desire, or to deliver beyond what exactly is required. Being ordinary to extraordinary performance takes place via discretionary efforts associated with frontline employee picking to help make the huge number of efforts, for every single approach to a client the business in-person, by telephone, or electronically, they handle each and every as positively as they can. This determination, loyalty, or faithfulness cannot be pushed on individuals. It simply takes place by just a "culture of concern to commitment,"

A business exterior customer satisfaction should be only as strong as the business's internal management, and the culture of dedication that this leader builds.

Vilares and Cohelo (2000) establish that perceived employee satisfaction, perceived employee loyalty, and perceived employee commitment had an enormous influence on perceived product standard as well as on perceived service quality (see model below).

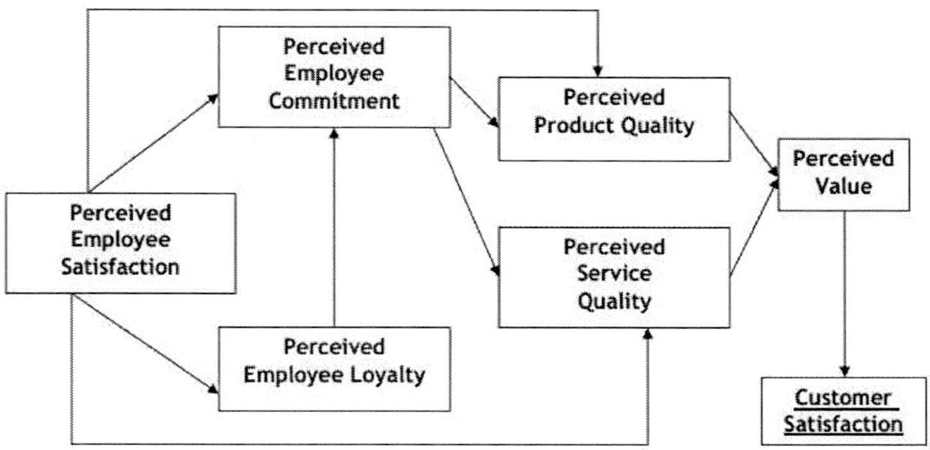

Overview about the Connection between Employee Satisfaction and Customer Happiness

The document provides many facts regarding the reason why employee happiness influences potential buyers happiness:

1. Staff which communicates with existing buyers come to a situation where he communicates directly with the customer and after understanding the queriesreply is given based on theobjectives and requirements.

2. Staff which is passionate and satisfied with the organizationwill have the motivation to provide sufficient hard work and other aspects to business.

Literature Review

Studies such as Frederick Reichheld's "The Loyalty Effect," (1996) and James Heskett,W. Early Sasser, and Leonard Schlesinger's "The Service Profit Chain" (1997) producedthe first sets of hard data quantifying these links. Both studies conclude that there aredirect and quantifiable links between customer service variables (such as satisfactionand loyalty), employee variables (such as satisfaction, enthusiasm, loyalty, commitment,capability, and internal service quality), and financial results.

In 1997, Development Dimensions International (DDI) conducted focus groups,customer interviews, literature reviews, and surveys to determine drivers of an effectiveservice environment. DDI found evidence of a circular relationship between employeesatisfaction and retention, and customer satisfaction and loyalty, and increases incompany profitability. In addition, employee satisfaction was strongly related toemployee commitment and loyalty, and both measures have proven relationships toretention and productivity.

In "The Service Profit Chain" (1997), the authors proposed a model that workforcecapability, satisfaction, and loyalty would lead to customers' perceptions of value.Value perception would lead to customer satisfaction and loyalty, which would lead toprofits and growth. The study found that employees' perceptions of their capabilities,satisfaction, and length-of-service were correlated with customer satisfaction.

Dr. Thomas Rollins of the Hay Group developed a model linking employee opinionsurvey results directly with business performance metrics while excluding customersatisfaction measures. Main findings include the following

- This model holds that company-wide employee satisfaction results affect business unitemployee satisfaction results, which affect business unit financial results, which in turn affectcompany-wide financial metrics.
- However, the model also holds that the company-wide financial metrics may also affectcompany-wide employee satisfaction results, allowing the model to demonstrate correlationbut not causation between the different areas considered.

The link between satisfaction and the long-term retention of customersis typically formulated by marketing practitioners and scholarsin a rather categorical way, and is therefore treated as the startingpoint, rather than the core question of the analysis (see, for the practitioners'side, e.g., Naumann&Giel, 1995; Quartapelle& Larsen, 1994, and for the academics, e.g.,Engel, Blackwell, &Miniard, 1993; Kotler, 1994;Woodruff, 1993).

LaBarbera and Mazursky point out - the assumption that satisfaction/dissatisfaction meaningfully influences repurchase behavior underlies most of the research in this area of inquiry,(1983, p. 400). Consequently, only a few researchers have investigated the nature and extent of the relation between satisfaction andretention itself (Bloemer&Poiesz, 1989).

Satisfied employees will much more involved, dedicated, have better organizational dedication, a lot more loyal and productive towards customer requirements, therefore improving client satisfaction, the ideal focus of companies today (Naeem,2010; Yee 2008; Kim, 2004; Lings, 1999; Heskett, 1997). Harter et al. (2002) come across that employee satisfaction lead in enhanced productivity and decrease in turnover rate. Dabholkar, (2008) posits that decrease in turnover rate result in profits resulting from the cost savings in not needing to regularly hire and train new staff members.

CONCLUSION

The research demonstrates that employee empowerment, employee compensation, team-work and also management leadership are considerably positive predictors of employee satisfaction and its relationship in the context of organization. The study also offers proof that employee loyalty is made through employee satisfaction.Employee satisfaction can also be termed key to customer satisfaction, as both these aspects are closely related with each other.Satisfied Employees are Loyal, Devoted and Productive, and at the same time the same will help to the great extent in achieving the Customer satisfaction and Customer Retention.

Above mentioned explanation also indicates the criticality with regards to the rapport between Employee attitudes and Customer comfort. Exactly how customer satisfaction awareness, and customer oriented work behavior have a influence on most of their work experience as well as on concrete business results including Customer satisfaction, revenues, and also income.

REFERENCES

[1] Consumer Behavior by Leon G.Schiffman, Prentice-Hall India

[2] C.B.Mamoria, (2002), Personnel Management, Himalaya Publications.

[3] C.R.Kothari, Research Methodology, New Age International Publishers.

[4] D.S.Saini,(2000), Human Resource Management: Perspective for the New Era, New Delhi.

[5] Human Resource Management, (2006),ICFAI Press, Hyderabad.

[6] K. Aswathappa,(2005), Human Resource Management & Personnel Management,Tata McGraw- Hill Publication.

[7] N.P.Podsakoff,(2007), "Differential Challenges with Job Attitudes, Turn over ad Withdrawal Behavior, A journal of Applied Psychology,p.883-891.

[8] N.W.Van,(2003), "Fatigued and Dissatisfied or Fatigue and satisfied", Academy of Management Journal,p.339-348.

[9] PHILIP KOTLER (2009) Marketing Management Prentice Hall Pvt. Ltd, New Delhi, Millennium edition.

[10] Robin Stiphen/ SeemaSanghvi,(2006), Organizational Behavior, Pearson Education.

[11] Slocum / Hellriegel , Fundamentals of organizational behavior,Cengage India Private Ltd.

[12] Strategic Human Resource Management,ICFAICenter for management research.

[13] T.V.Rao,(1999), HRD Audit: Evaluating the Human Resource Function for Business Improvement, New Delhi.

To Study the Impact of Internet Advertising as a Push on Indian Consumer's Demand in Delhi – NCR Region

Eshwarya Pathak, Dhiraj Jain, Dharmil Sheth and Richa Sikka

Institute of Management Technology, Ghaziabad

ABSTRACT

As per primary findings(IAMAI,Feb,2012), the Indian Digital Advertising Industry has risen from INR 785 Crores in March 2010 to INR 1,160 Crores by March 2011and is expected to continue growing at a healthy 19% in FY2012 to reach INR 1,355 Crores. Advertising on Portals / Vortals comprised about 30% or INR 316 Crores of the Indian Online advertising sector. This excludes Mobile or Tablet advertisements (INR 90 Crores). The dynamic market trend shows that online advertising has now established itself as an indispensable element of a comprehensive target group appeal. It is generally agreed that the effect of advertising and other promotions results in pushing up the aggregate consumption, but to what extent it effects consumption is a highly debatable issue. Advertising can help stimulate demand of new products by way of communicating relevant information and facts to the prospective end users. This is also true that every consumer do not have the same taste or preference for products and services thus marketers attempt to differentiate their offers in terms of price, features, benefits or psychological factors to woo the customers. Advertising offers consumers a right to choose. In this process, the brands that deliver more satisfaction to consumers become the most preferred one but interestingly the moment some other firm launches a new product with more effective advertising technique, the preferred products or brands lose their position, making way for newer better products. Advertising can have a range of impacts on consumer demand for a product or service. Depending on the message one sends with the advertising, he can target what type of demand the business will realize. This study aims to explore the factors that signify the impact of internet advertising on consumer demand by taking the perception of internet users in Delhi NCR Region.

INTRODUCTION

Interactive advertising is defined by the editors of the *Journal of Interactive Advertising* as "the paid and unpaid presentation and promotion of products, services and ideas by an identified sponsor, through mediated means involving mutual action between consumers and producers" (Leckenby and Li, 2000).Online advertising maybe defined as a form of marketing communication on the Internet intended to persuade an Internet user (viewers, readers or listeners) to purchase or take an action based on content displayed on a website (or webpage). This communication may be in relation to products, ideals or services. In economies such as India which are not regulated or dominated by monopolies, the market is open to fierce competition among several players who would use all the latest advertising tools available and have whatever advantage they can get over their competitors. However, conventional tri-media advertising channels are expensive and affordable only to large corporations. Internet advertising provides a versatile, effective and more affordable advertising medium that many businesses in India can utilize.

INTERNET USAGE AND SCOPE OF ONLINE ADVERTISING

The Internet, arguably the most exciting medium of the modern generation is witnessing appreciable growth in India since the turn of the century. The number of Active Internet Users has now touched 70 Million by September 2011 (Source: ICube 2011). This represents a growth of almost 20% as compared to September 2010, when the number of Active Internet Users was 59 Million. In terms of the number of Claimed Internet Users, the numbers have risen from 78 Million in 2010 to 88 Million over the same period. This represents a growth of about 13% in the last year. For a similar time frame, the number of PC Literates also exhibited a 12.5% increase with the total number of PC literates going up from 106 Million to 119 Million. In simpler words, once an individual is exposed to the Internet, it is quite likely that he or she would continue using it like any other media as television, newspapers or radio. Thus internet advertising has become a primary tool for firms to affect the performance of their products, especially in markets for consumer goods such as cars, computers, cell phones, and digital cameras. Such markets are characterized by the continuous turnover of multiple relatively close substitute products. Therefore, advertising becomes crucial in making consumers aware of the existence and characteristics of new products. Marketing literature therefore acknowledges how advertising influences consumers, beyond the traditional effects on their preferences. That is, a second channel is important in as much as it changes the consumer awareness of a product. This awareness determines consumers' choice sets; among the large number of products in the market.

The total online advertising spend can be subdivided among the following categories -

- Search
- Portals / Vortals
- Social Media
- Email
- Video

Among all, Search advertising constitutes about 47% of the total online advertising spend or about INR 499 Crores. The rest i.e. 53% of the total online advertising spend comprises of advertising done on Portals/Vortals (INR 316 Crores), Social Media (INR 80 Crores), Email (INR 123 Crores) and Video (INR 51 Crores).

INCREASING INTERNET ADVERTISING TRENDS IN VARIOUS INDUSTRIES

- The Automotive sector exhibited one of the highest increases in online advertisement spends in FY2011. Automotive display advertising almost doubled in FY2011 to reach INR 76 Crores, representing growth of 95%. Comparatively, the estimated growth in FY2012 is expected to be 22%. On the other hand, the growth in search advertising for the two financial years is also charted above. It has been 61% in FY2011 and is estimated to be 17% for FY2012. Clearly, the automotive sector therefore continues to invest a far greater amount to display advertising as compared to Search.
- The Consumer Durables vertical encompasses goods like Air Conditioners, Refrigerators, TV and Audio Systems. It excludes IT and Mobile products. For the segment, online display advertising forms the bulk of online advertising. The vertical is expected to exhibit steady growth of 15% in display ad spends in FY2012.
- The education sector's share in the overall Display + Search online advertising types hovers around 5% in FY2011. Other sectors are expected to grow faster in FY2012; the share of education to the overall pie therefore is expected to reduce to 4%. However more institutions are expected to invest in the online medium through display as well as Search advertising. In absolute numbers, Display Ad spend is expected to reach INR 31 Crores in FY2012 as compared to INR 26 Crores in FY2011. Relatively, for this vertical online Search advertising is expected to witness very limited growth with spend estimated to reach INR 20 Crores in FY2012, as compared to INR 19 Crores in FY2011.
- Information Technology as a vertical includes companies selling packaged / customized software applications or solutions, or computer hardware products like PCs, Laptops, Servers, PC accessories like Keyboard, Mice etc. As per the findings, online Search advertising observed a higher growth in FY2011 as compared to FY2010 when spend on Search as well as Display Ads was INR 33 Crores each. FY2012 expects the online Search ad spend to increase from INR 49 Crores to INR 56 Crores. Online Display advertising is expected to grow slightly faster and reach INR 56 Crores in the same period.
- Telecom encompasses online advertising done for telecom related products and services including Pre-Paid cards, Mobile Services, Landline Services, Mobile Phones and PDAs etc. The 2011 financial year saw further investments in the telecom space, with advertisers increasing online spends. Online Display advertising spend increased to INR 67 Crores

in FY2011 and is estimated to reach INR 85 Crores in FY2012. Online Search advertising spend almost doubled to reach INR 45 Crores in FY2011 and is estimated to reach INR 57 Crores in FY2012.

- The Travel sector is by far the leading online advertiser among various verticals. The total online ad spend in FY2011 was INR 214 Crores. This is expected to rise 20% and reach INR 258 Crores in FY2012. The vertical includes online advertising done by various travel companies. With the Indian economy doing reasonably well, people are spending a greater amount on travel than ever before. The increase in the number of air travelers as well as rail passengers has been very appreciable. Online ticketing which usually offers a host of discounts (and options) to travelers has in turn resulted in greater online advertising spends by various travel companies. In addition, with the convenience of the online medium, travelers who might not even own a personal computer are using the Internet to book air and rail tickets.

RESEARCH METHODOLOGY

The Study – The current study aims to explore the factors that signify the impact of internet advertising on consumer demand by taking the perception of internet users. In the study, the perception of the respondents was compared on basis of various demographic variables like age, gender, occupation and income. These demographic variables were independent variables. The depended variable was consumer demand.

The Sample- The external validity and generalize ability of a psychometric measure depends on the subjects on which the study is conducted. Keeping this in view, a sample of Internet users was chosen. The sample size was 400 Internet users belonging to NCR Region. The respondents were chosen on the convenience basis.

The final sample represented the population with respect to socio economic dimensions i.e. age, gender, income and occupation. The respondents were 200 male and 200 female internet users of different age groups ranging from 18 to 52 with an average of 30.546 years. Basically, respondents were from business as well as service class and some of them were management students.

Area of Study- The Area for the Study was NCR Region

For data collection- The tool for data collection was a questionnaire. After ensuring the content validity of the items selected, the reliability was determined by split half method corrected for full length by applying Spearman Brown Prophecy formula on the data collected from the sample of 400 subjects. The reliability coefficient was .9007. Since, no scale was available for the present study, thus the validity was taken equivalent to reliability index i.e. 09601.

Data Collection- The collected data was analyzed in three stages with the help of (SPSS). In the stage once, to ensure internal consistency, item total correlation was carried out to eliminate insignificant items, which resulted into dropping of three non-significant items. In the stage two, the data was subjected to factor analysis and five factors emerged signifying the impact of Internet advertising on consumer demand. In the next stage i.e. third stage different group were compared on the factors emerged in the second stage using z-test. These groups were formed on the basis of variables age, gender, occupation and income.

Details of Results

As a result of factor analysis, five factors were emerged signifying the impact of internet advertising on consumer demand is as follows:

Factor 1: Strengthens Consumer Loyalty

This factor implies that internet advertising leads to active participation of consumers by sending a clear message to consumers. It also turns potential consumers in to actual consumers by promoting materialism and stimulating consumer needs. (Variance=9.387)

Factor 2: Enhances consumer Awareness

This factor signifies the impact of internet advertising on consumer demand as it gives recognition to advertised products by shifting consumer attention from weak to strong side of product and conveys information to consumers. Advertising provides competitive edge to consumers as it adds value to the advertised products by communicating USP of products to consumers (Variance=8.902)

Factor3: Impact of Internet Advertisng

This factor signifies the impact of internet advertising on consumer demand as it places a specific brand in the mind of consumer as well as it enlarges the category of occasions for consuming the goods. Internet advertising converts price sensitive consumers into willingness consumers as it creates a match between consumers taste and attitudes of chosen brand. (Variance=8.608)

Factor 4: Responsive mode to consumers

It is the fastest way of advertising product in huge market as its responses can be traced immediately. It is highly selective for consumers and can easily target its consumers. (Variance=7.303)

Factor 5: Flexibility for product differentiation

The factor shows the internet advertising gives new look to product and offers unique opportunities, which are not possible with conventional media. It also provides anytime anywhere flexibility to consumers and creates open product differentiation. (Variance= 6.377)

Comparison was made on the basis of Demographic variables under five problems for each above mentioned factors.

Problem I: Does the perception of business and service class internet users differ regarding the impact of internet advertising on consumer demand?

Problem II: Does the perception of male and female internet users differ regarding the impact of internet advertising on consumer demand.

Problem III: Does the perception of internet users having age below 30 years and above 30 years differ regarding the impact of internet advertising on consumer demand.

Problem IV: Does the perception of internet users earning annual income below 2 lacs and above 2 lacs differ regarding the impact of internet advertising on consumer demand.

FINDINGS

Problem1

Factor 1: The result shows that Business class internet users perceive that internet Advertising Strengthen consumer loyalty, where as service class don't think so.

Factor 2: Result shows that there is no significant difference in the perception of business and service class internet users regarding the second factor enhances consumer awareness.

Factor 3: Result shows that there is no significant difference in the perception of business and service class internet users regarding the third factor control consumer preferences.

Factor 4: Result shows that there is no significant difference in the perception of business and service class internet users regarding the fourth factor Responsive mode to Consumers.

Factor 5: Result shows that there is no significant difference in the perception of business and service class internet users regarding the fifth factor Flexibility for product differentiation

Problem 2

Factor 1: Result shows that there is no significant difference in the perception of male and female internet users regarding the first factor strengthens consumer loyalty.

Factor 2: Result shows that there is no significant difference in the perception of male and female internet users regarding the second factor enhances consumer awareness.

Factor 3: Result shows that there is no significant difference in the perception of male and female internet users regarding the third factor control consumer preferences.

Factor 4: Result shows that there is no significant difference in the perception of male and female internet users regarding the fourth factor Responsive mode to Consumers.

Factor 5: Result shows that there is no significant difference in the perception of male and female internet users regarding the fifth factor Flexibility for product differentiation

Problem 3

Factor 1: Result shows that there is a significant difference in the perception of internet users having age below 30 years and above 30 years regarding the first factor strengthens consumer loyalty. Internet users having age below 30 years perceive that internet advertising strengthens consumer loyalty.

Factor 2: Result shows that there is a significant difference in the perception of internet users having age below 30 years and above 30 years regarding the second factor enhances consumer awareness. Internet users having age below 30 years perceive that internet advertising enhances consumer awareness.

Factor 3: There is a significant difference in the perception of internet users having age below 30 years and above 30 years regarding the third factor control consumer preferences. Internet users having age below 30 years perceive that internet advertising control consumer preferences.

Factor 4: Result shows that there is a significant difference in the perception of internet users having age below 30 years and above 30 years regarding the fourth factor Responsive mode to Consumers. Internet users having age below 30 years perceive that internet advertising is the fastest way of advertising product in huge market.

Factor 5: Result shows that there is no significant difference in the perception of internet users having age below 30 years and above 30 years regarding the fifth factor Flexibility for product differentiation.

Problem 4

Factor One, Two and Three: Result shows that there is no significant difference in the perception of internet users regarding factors one, two and three under Problem:4

Factor 4: Result shows that there is a significant difference in the perception of internet users earning annual income below 2 lacs and above 2 lacs regarding the forth factor Responsive mode to Consumers. Internet users earning annual income above 2 lacs perceive that internet advertising provides Responsive mode to Consumers

Factor 5: Result shows that there is a significant difference in the perception of internet users earning annual income below 2 lacs and above 2 lacs regarding the Flexibility for product differentiation Internet users earning annual income above 2 lacs perceive that internet advertising provides Flexibility for product differentiation.

CONCLUSION

Internet have becomes an increasingly important tool during the purchasing process, more marketers are seeing the advantages too. Advertisers are investing more into online advertising today because it is faster and less expensive to conduct direct marketing campaigns compared with traditional printing and direct-mail costs. Targeted, allowing you to pinpoint using geography, contextual relevance, and other useful parameters to reach a very specifically defined audience. Continuously available, letting you give away whitepapers or free webinars to gather good sources of leads over time. Cost-effective, in the long run by adjusting your paid search campaigns to find which ads work best for different keywords, you reduce your ad spend and online efforts over time while maintaining or increasing the number of leads or purchases gained. Going social, as more people share information among peers on websites like Facebook and LinkedIn, for business purposes. A recommendation from your friend or peer can go a long way towards closing a sale. The discussion in the previous sections has covered a wide range of topics, but several key areas have emerged where research on the Internet and other online media can add knowledge to the Marketing discipline. Despite of the fact there are the challenges, which need to be addressed at various levels: supply or provisioning, content as well as better targeting. A major hindrance in accessing the digital medium is the lack of infrastructure in terms of broadband connectivity. Accessibility and availability of the medium remains a challenge that the stakeholders need to address. Connectivity is largely governed by the regulations; as of now, the governments at various levels are still initiating policies (National Telecommunications Policy, being one of them) to provide a fillip to the broadband dissemination among rural as well as urban areas. The effects of such regulations are yet to be seen.

REFERENCES

[1] Adamic, L., & Huberman, B. A. (1999). The Nature of Markets in the World Wide Web. Working Paper, Xerox Palo Alto Research Center, 1-10.

[2] Anderson, D. (2000). Creating and Nurturing a Premier E-Business. Journal of Interactive Marketing, 14(3 (Summer)), 67-73.

[3] Bhargava, H., Choudhary, V., & Krishnan, R. (2000). Pricing and Product Design: Intermediary Strategies in an Electronic Market. Working Paper, MIT Ecommerce Forum, 1-20.

[4] Cara Garretson, "ISPs turning guns on newer breed of spam", Journal: Network World Volume 23, Issue 5, Pages 22 ,Provider Proquest, Year 2006

[5] Dutta, S., Kwan, S., & Segev, A. (1998). Business Transformation in Electronic Commerce: A Study of Sectoral and Regional Trends. European Management Journal, 16(5(October)), 540-551.

[5] George Joey F," Influences on the intent to make Internet purchases", Journal: Internet Research, Issn 10662243, Volume 12, Issue 2, Pages 165-180, Provider: Proquest, Year 2002.

[7] Yuan, Y., Caulkins, J. P., & Roehrig, S. (1998). The Relationship Between Advertising and Content Provision on the Internet. European Journal of Marketing, 32(7/8), 677-687.

Understanding the Role of Common Service Centres in Development of Village Level Entrepreneurs: A Case of Mandi District of Himachal Pradesh

Kaushik Dutta, Neeraj Awasthy, Shilpi Pachauri, Chandan Kumar Singh and Dheeram Meher Ramya

Institute of Management Technology, Ghaziabad

ABSTRACT

India, being the seventh most populous country in the world has almost 3/4ths of its population living in rural areas. As a developing nation India is trying to change itself constantly and adapt to the ever dynamic world of innovation and technology but the relevance of these innovation for the rural community is still a debatable with majority of its population being from rural area. India's strength lies in its rural population, Inclusive development of India can happen only when people living in these rural areas are empowered with information and technology relevant for development.

Information, infrastructure and services are the three essential resources required for rural development. Access to information, with relevant infrastructure, end-to-end services enables rural population to enhance their quality of life. Realizing this, the Government of India has under its National e-Governance plan, committed to setting up Common Service Centres (CSCs) in rural India. The main purpose of these centres is to provide a physical facility for delivery of e-Services of the Government of India to the rural and remote locations where availability of computers and Internet is currently negligible or mostly absent.

CSCs are run by Village Level Entrepreneurs (VLE) who are responsible for the kiosk operations. CSC has come up as a key source of employment; this paper presents an analysis of what roles has CSC played in the development of Village Level Entrepreneurs, whether this has led to the improvement the quality of life for individuals, families and communities and to sustain a healthy economy and environment. The paper talks about a case of the role played by common service centres in the development of village level entrepreneurs specifically in the Mandi district of Himachal Pradesh.

OVERVIEW OF CSC

CSC Scheme is a nationwide initiative of Government of India to provide support for establishing 1 lakh centres in 6 lakh villages of India. CSC scheme started in 2006 and is meant to be a low cost vehicle for Government institutions to deliver eGovernance services to the rural population of India in a cost-effective manner. They are the physical front-end for delivery of e-Government Services to citizens and accepting requests for government services from the private citizen via e-Forms. They would also be used for delivery of services and interaction with private service providers [(1)].

The CSC Scheme is being implemented in a public private partnership (PPP) framework with a focus on rural entrepreneurship & market mechanisms. The CSCs has been set up by private entities called as Service Centre Agencies (SCA), who are appointed by the State Governments. The CSCs are run by the VLEs who are appointed by the SCAs to run and manage the CSCs at pre-defined locations. [(13)]

As on 30th June 2011, 95710 Common Services Centers have been set up across the country, covering 31 States/UTs out of the targeted 100,000 centers to be set up - one per every six villages. The CSCs are being set up in the Public Private Partnership (PPP) mode. [(28)]

As envisaged under the Scheme, a National level Special Purpose Vehicle (SPV) has been formed as a permanent entity to provide ongoing support to the CSCs and to catalyze services to be channelized through the network. The name of the CSC SPV is CSC E-Governance Services India Ltd. [(5)]

It is also now proposed to reposition CSCs as a network of Bharat Nirman CSCs to be set up in each Gram Panchayat as a delivery point of public services for rural areas. Accordingly, additional 150,000 Bharat Nirman CSCs are proposed to set up for the uncovered Panchayats. [(29)]

The various services being offered from these CSCs comprise of several Government-to-Citizen (G2C) and Business-to-Consumer (B2C) services. G2C services include providing caste certificate, 'Nakal' (copies of various government documents), domicile certificate, income certificate, application collection and submission for subsidy on housing schemes, 'Laadli' scheme for the girl child (Ladli referring to 'dear one') and Indira Gandhi 'VivahShagunYojna' ('Marriage gift scheme)'. B2C services such as computer education, mobile top-ups, railway/air ticket booking, Internet surfing and downloads of various applications/forms used for government services are being delivered through these centres. [(36)]

The CSC was envisaged to offer different kinds of functions, some of its objectives are: [(2)]

- Providing e-governance services within easy reach and thereby save consumer's costs on distant and repeated travel
- Providing critical information on available government developmental programmes, beneficiary criteria and present beneficiary list to bring in transparency and efficiency in the programmes and an opportunity for development of the marginalized sections of the community

- Providing information and opportunities for income enhancement/generation
- Providing the platform for e-communication
- Providing avenues for e-marketing and e-shopping

Rural Entrepreneurship The Village Level Entrepreneur (VLE)

Defining entrepreneurship is not an easy task. There are almost as many definitions of entrepreneurship as there are scholar books on the subjects (Byrd W.A., 1987, p. 3). To some, entrepreneurship means primarily innovation, to others it means risk-taking? To others a market stabilising force and to others still it means starting, owning and managing a small business. Accordingly, the entrepreneur is then viewed as a person who either creates new combinations of production factors such as new methods of production, new products, new markets, finds new sources of supply and new organizational forms; or as a person who is willing to take risks; or a person who, by exploiting market opportunities, eliminates disequilibrium between aggregate supply and aggregate demand, or as one who owns and operates a business [(39)].

To choose the definition of entrepreneurship most appropriate for the rural area context, it is important to bear in mind the entrepreneurial skills that will be needed to improve the quality of life for individuals, families and communities and to sustain a healthy economy and environment. Taking this into consideration, we will find that each of the traditional definitions has its own weakness [(39)]. The first definition leaves little room for innovations that are not on the technological or organizational cutting edge, such as, adaptation of older technologies to a developing-country context, or entering into export markets already tapped by other firms. Defining entrepreneurship as risk-taking neglects other major elements of what we usually think of as entrepreneurship, such as a well-developed ability to recognise unexploited market opportunities. Entrepreneurship as a stabilising force limits entrepreneurship to reading markets disequilibria, while entrepreneurship defined as owning and operating a business, denies the possibility of entrepreneurial behaviour by non-owners, employees and managers who have no equity stake in the business. Therefore, the most appropriate definition of entrepreneurship that would fit into the rural development context, argued here, is the broader one, the one which defines entrepreneurship as: *"a force that mobilises other resources to meet unmet market demand", "the ability to create and build something from practically nothing", "the process of creating value by pulling together a unique package of resources to exploit an opportunity"*[(2)].

Rural entrepreneurs are those who carry out entrepreneurial activities by establishing industrial and business units in the rural sector of the economy. In other words, establishing industrial and business units in the rural areas refers to rural entrepreneurship. In simple words, rural entrepreneurship implies entrepreneurship emerging in rural areas. Or, say, rural entrepreneurship implies rural industrialization. Thus, we can say, entrepreneurship precedes industrialization [(16)].

Rural Entrepreneur Has the Following Essential Characteristics

1. **Labor Intensive**: Rural industries are labor intensive because they give more employment of labor than machines. Rural entrepreneurs are generally labor intensive because they give much stress on human capital.
2. **Use of traditional Skill**: Rural entrepreneurs give much emphasis on use of traditional skill during the course of production. They have no capacity to apply modern skill and technology in their industry.
3. **Less Capital**: Rural entrepreneurs generally invest less capital to produce goods and commodities in their industry. As they have no capacity to afford for much capital investment, they emphasize on less capital investment.
4. **Decentralized Production**: As rural industries are scattered and operated in a small scale, it encourages decentralized production.
5. **Use of Local Raw Materials**: Rural entrepreneurs make better use of local raw materials during the course of production. They usually make better and effective use of local raw materials because its transportation cost is less. (38)

VLE is the key to the success of the CSC operations. While content and services are important, it is the VLE's entrepreneurial ability that would ensure CSC sustainability.(37) A good VLE is expected to have some financial strength, entrepreneurial ability, strong social commitment as well as respect within the community. The quality of service at the CSCs would depend a great deal on the quality of VLEs. Selection and proper training of the VLE therefore would play a vital role in making the CSC Scheme a success.(19) Apart from facilitating the development of rural communities, CSC scheme will generate employment opportunities for rural folks in the state since they could work as VLE and establish themselves as good entrepreneurs.(8)

VLEs are very important in the entire structure of the CSCs as they were the ones entrusted with the job of running the centres and interacting with the people. Being placed at a vital position if the VLEs fail to perform efficiently the whole concept of CSC and the benefits it offers to a common man are at stake. But there are also cases where the VLEs are efficient but the program is still a failure. Many factors contribute to it (18).

Some of the key factors inhibiting the roll of CSC efficiently in an area include Geographical location because some of the villages are located in such inaccessible locations that it is impossible to set up a Centre in that area. Poor connectivity, poor power supply, poor IT infrastructure of the states along with a poor governance mechanism and lack of a proper institutional framework for ensuring successful rollout are also major contributing factors. The presence of insurgent groups like the Naxalites and the Maoists proves to be challenging for the officials. Lack of cooperation from government officials, especially at lower levels, lack of proper training to VLEs, inadequate content in regional languages, lack of capacity building, challenges like suitable place selection for CSC, appropriate population in the catchment area, lack of credibility of VLEs, proper maintenance of computers in remote areas are some of the important factors which are inhibiting the success of roll out. In spite of having all the prerequisites some CSCs were not functional because of VLEs who were demotivated due to the lack of G2C services. (27)

SERVICES OFFERED BY CSCs

CSCs would offer a multitude of services ranging in the areas of e-Government, education, health, agriculture, retail, etc. It is to be noted that delivery of Government services would be mandatory for CSCs. To that effect, some of the possible service areas are listed b in Table 1.(4)

Most preferred services with maximum citizen coverage are:

Issuance of certificates Record of Rights (RoR), Birth, Character, Death, etc. with over 10 Million (+) services being delivered till date throughout the country.

Service through which maximum revenue has been earned:

Issuance of Certificates (RoR, Birth, Character, Death, etc.) with over Rs.90crore revenue generated so far. (14)

Table 1. Summary of Services Offered by CSC

Land Records	*Digital Photos*	*Agriculture-inputs*
Registration of vehicles	Web surfing	Astrology
Issue of certificates/ Government schemes	Photocopy	Matrimonial
Employment exchange	DTP	Shopping
Ration cards	Email/Chats	Resumes
Electoral services	CD Burning	Advertising & Promotion Services
Pension schemes	Typing	Space marketing of CSC
Road transport	Printing	Promotions
Public grievance	Games	Data Collection Services
Utility/ Telephone Bills (Government undertakings)	Forms downloads/Estimates	Research Data collection
Railway Tickets	Utility/Telephone Bills (private enterprises)	Data Entry

Business to Citizen (B2C) denotes online communication between business entities and consumers/individuals. CSCs offering B2C services cater and cover large population base at the rural level. By integrating these services into CSC bouquet, rural villagers get access to such services in their vicinity, for which they might have to travel to nearby town and incur cost/face middlemen etc. This also resulted in income generating opportunities for VLEs apart from G2C services. As an assumption for CSC Scheme business model, G2C services could only form the 1/3rd of the total revenue (as most are at nominal fee). Hence there is a dire need to offer B2C services at such level. (12)

Number of CSC's Established in Various States Across India

The Government had set a target of establishing 100,000 CSC's by June 2011.As on 31st August 2012, a total of 93,523 CSCs are operational in thirty three States/ UTs. 100% CSCs have been rolled out in 11 States which include Arunachal Pradesh, Chandigarh, Gujarat, Kerala, Madhya Pradesh, Manipur, Meghalaya, Mizoram, Pondicherry, Sikkim & Tripura. More than 70% of the rollout has been completed in 8 States namely Assam, Bihar, Chhattisgarh, Himachal Pradesh, Maharashtra, Punjab, Uttaranchal and West Bengal. In about 7 States which include Andhra Pradesh, Jammu & Kashmir, Jharkhand, Lakshadweep, Orissa, Rajasthan and Uttar Pradesh implementation of CSCs have crossed half way mark. (45)

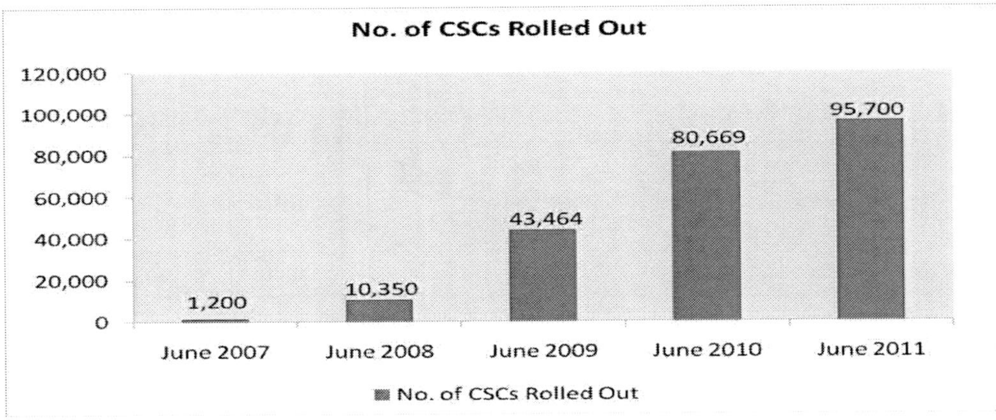

Fig. 1. Roll of CSC in India
Source: www.csc-india.org

Table 2 gives the status of the CSC rollouts across various states for the years 2008 (for five sample states for which the data is available) and 2009, and till June 2010. The table shows that most of the states had not been able to meet the rollout deadline. At the start of this project it was stipulated that SCAs should achieve the 100 percent rollout status within 18-24 months after signing the Masters Service Agreement (MSA) with the respective state governments. However, when the rollout status report was taken on June 2009 it was seen that except Haryana, Jharkhand and Sikkim, none of the states were even close to the 100 percent rollout mark. This forced the government to revise the deadline. (35)

Table 2. State Wise roll out of CSCs in India

States	*Area*	*Plan*	*Operation*	*% roll out*
Chandigarh	North	13	25	192%
Kerala	South	2200	2235	102%
Madhya Pradesh	Central	9232	9270	100%
Arunachal Pradesh	East	200	200	100%
Gujarat	North	13685	13685	100%
Manipur	East	399	399	100%
Meghalaya	East	225	225	100%
Mizoram	East	136	136	100%
Sikkim	East	45	45	100%
Tripura	East	145	144	99%
Puducherry	South	66	65	98%
Maharashtra	West	10846	10372	96%
West Bengal	East	6797	6119	90%
Assam	East	4375	3881	89%
Himachal Pradesh	North	3366	2803	83%
Uttarakhand	North	2804	2329	83%
Bihar	Central	8463	6608	78%
Punjab	North	2112	1600	76%
Chhattisgarh	Central	3385	2460	73%
Lakshadweep	South	18	12	67%
Andhra Pradesh	South	4687	3043	65%
Jammu & Kashmir	North	1109	714	64%
Jharkhand	Central	4562	2937	64%
Uttar Pradesh	North	18745	12021	64%
Orissa	Central	8558	5286	62%
Rajasthan	North	6626	3385	51%
Tamil Nadu	South	5440	2683	49%
Andaman Nicobar	South	45	12	27%
Goa	West	160	29	18%
Karnataka	South	5713	800	14%
Delhi	North	520	0	0%
Haryana	North	1159	0	0%
Nagaland	North	220	0	0%
Total		126056	93523	74%

Though the deadline was re-adjusted after the June 2009 review, very few states had been able to achieve 100 percent rollout status. [50]Even in June 2009 when the status of rollout was reviewed there were 17 states that had not been able to rollout even 50 percent of their allotted centres.[33] Gujarat showed an almost two times increase in the number of centres rolled out as on 31st May, 2010 because the Government of Gujarat had amalgamated its e-gram centres with the Common Service Centre Project making the rollout successful under careful supervision. [22]Also, given that the background planning and the selection of the agencies had been carefully done, itperhaps points to the fact that there have been critical problems in the setting up of the Centres. [4]

Over all there is 74% roll out of CSCs by August 2012, it can be inferred from Figure 2 that the roll out of CSCs have been distinctly different region, highest roll out of CSC is highest in the Eastern region followed by Central, North and South and Western region is lagging behind with less than 57% roll out . The reasons of such trend it can be attributed to both supply and demand side. Southern States are more developed as compared to states of other region so their need for CSCs is lesser, on the other hand for the least developed north eastern states, where there is need for CSCs there might be certain supply constraints that inhibits the development of CSCs in the region. There is a need of understanding these dynamics so that the mismatch of the allocation of resources to areas of need can be minimized.

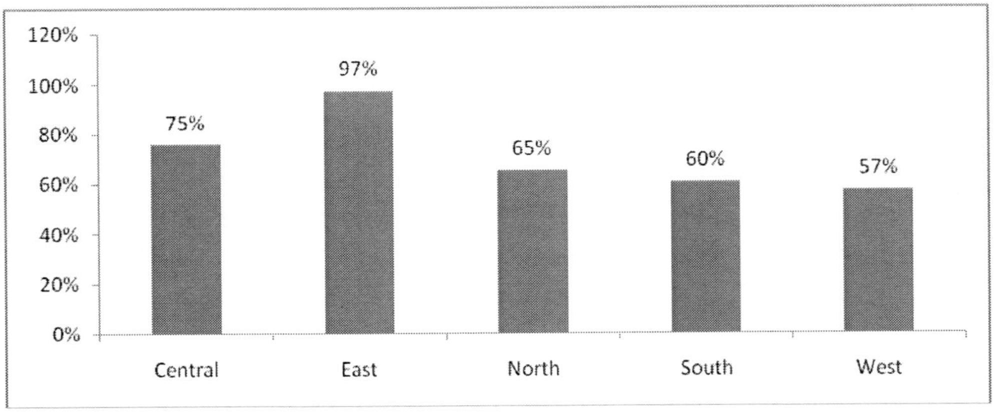

Fig. 2. Region Wise Roll Out CSCs vis-à-vis plan

CASE OF MANDI DISTRICT OF HIMACHAL PRADESH

In order to understand the role of CSCs in development of VLEs a district from a particular state is chosen and analyzed in the context of the paper and key points are collected and summarized in subsequent sections. The State of Himachal Pradesh was chosen for the study of awareness and acceptance of CSCs in rural areas as the state had initiated enthusiastic action in this direction. Another motivation for us had been that HP is primarily a Hindi speaking state, which being the mother tongue of the first author provided ample scope for free flow of conversations with the inhabitants of the village. The particular district of Mandi was chosen due to availability of some local contacts there and also because of convenience.

CSC IN HIMACHAL PRADESH

The CSC scheme is popularly known as Lokmitra Kendra project in Himachal Pradesh.(7) This aims to establish 3366 e-Governance centres at Panchayat level in the state. For implementation purpose the state has been divided into three divisions- Shimla division (Shimla, Solan, Kinnaur, Sirmaur), Kangradivision (Kangra, Chamba, Una), Mandidivision (Mandi, Bilaspur, Hamirpur, Kullu, LahaulSpiti). (5)

The services offered by Lokmitra Kendra are employment exchange services (Job Portal), land records (Unauthenticated copy), electoral services, public grievances (Lokvani / Lokmitra mode), HRTC / Railway Booking, registration for pension schemes, availability of all Government forms, all information related services hosted through web eg. Blood donors, Hotel directory, RTI, E-Kalyan scheme (for disbursal of pensions once banking services penetrate down to the level of Panchayats), issuance of Himachali Domicile, Caste and Agriculturist Certificates based on web based data, examinations results, AGRISNET Portal services, complaint / FIR registration with Police etc. (21)

Two private partners were selected as Service Centre Agencies (SCA) for implementing the scheme in Himachal Pradesh out of which M/s Zoom Developers Pvt. Ltd. operates in Kangra Division covering Kangra, Una and Chamba Districts and Consortium of M/s Terasoft Ltd. and M/s GNG trading Pvt. Ltd. operates in Shimla and Mandi Divisions. (25)

VILLAGE LEVEL ENTREPRENEURS IN MANDI DISTRICT OF HIMACHAL PRADESH

Mandi District consist has 9 Blocks with total number of VLE equal to 216. The number of VLE in each block varies from 37 to 17, highest number of VLE are there in MandiSadar followed by Balh and Golapur. Seraj and Sundernagar are having least number of VLE in the region. Refer Figure 3 for block wise number of VLE.

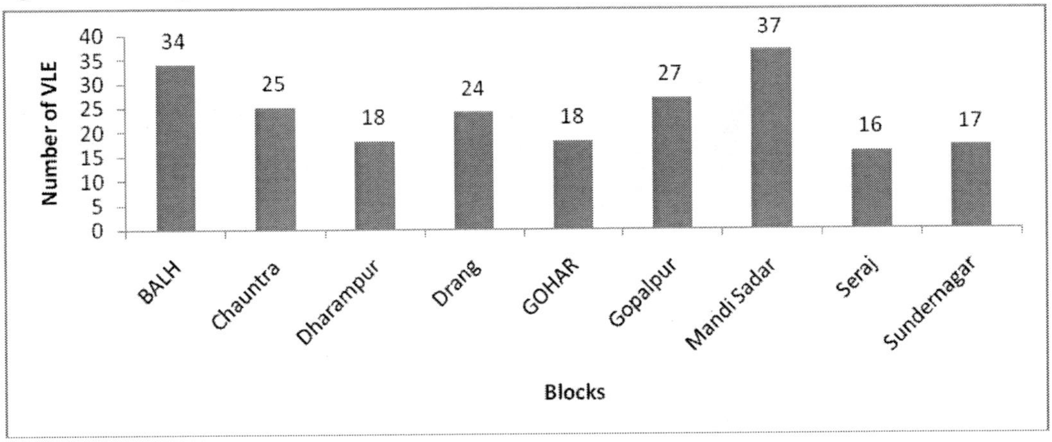

Fig. 3. Block Wise Number of VLE in Mandi District of HP

Most of the VLE in the Mandi district of HP have educational qualification of 10+2 which is 46% of all VLE in the region; this is followed by Graduates this can be attributed to the fact in village people not interested in going for higher education rather they are in search of opportunity to earn. Refer to Figure 4 for complete educational qualification profile of VLE in Mandi district of HP.

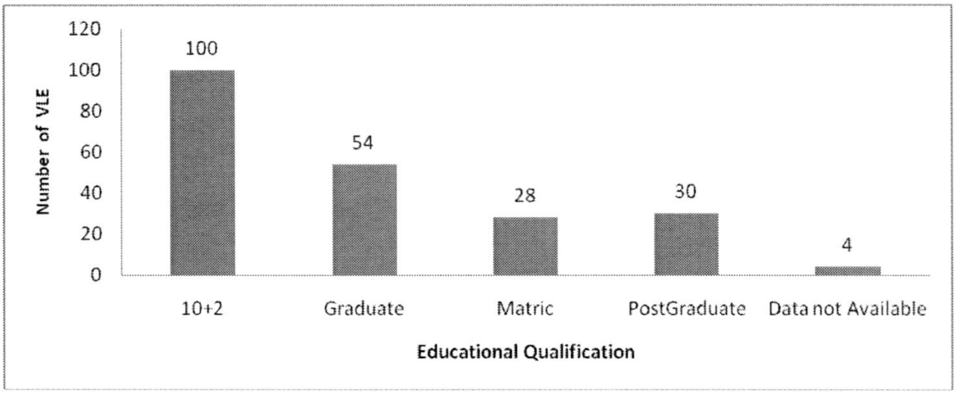

Fig. 4. Education Qualification Profile of VLE in Mandi District of HP

On observing the age profile of VLE in Mandi district it is clear that most of the VLE are from the age group 26-35 contributing more than 50% of total VLE in the region, the number of VLE decreased on either side of this age group. Refer to Figure 5 for detailed profiling of VLE of Mandi district based on age.

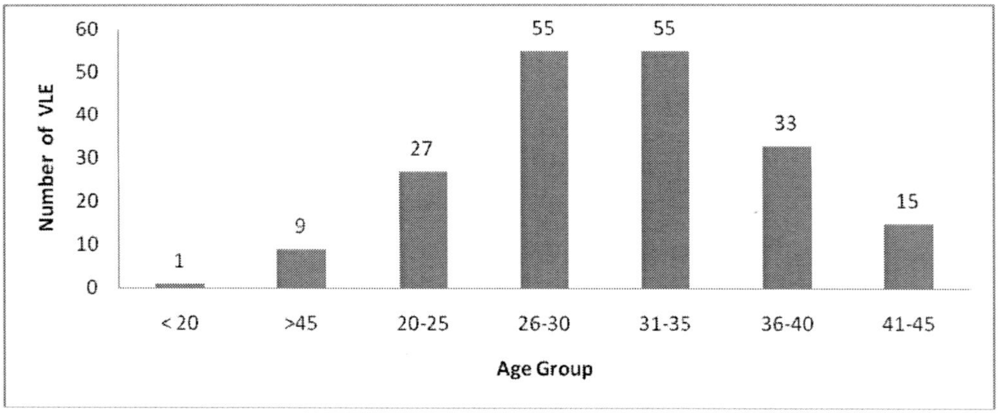

Fig. 5. Age Profile of VLE in Mandi District of HP

Medium of primary connectivity in Mandi District is Broadband which contributes to 67% of the connections followed by 2G and then 3G, which contributes only 13% and 7% of connections.

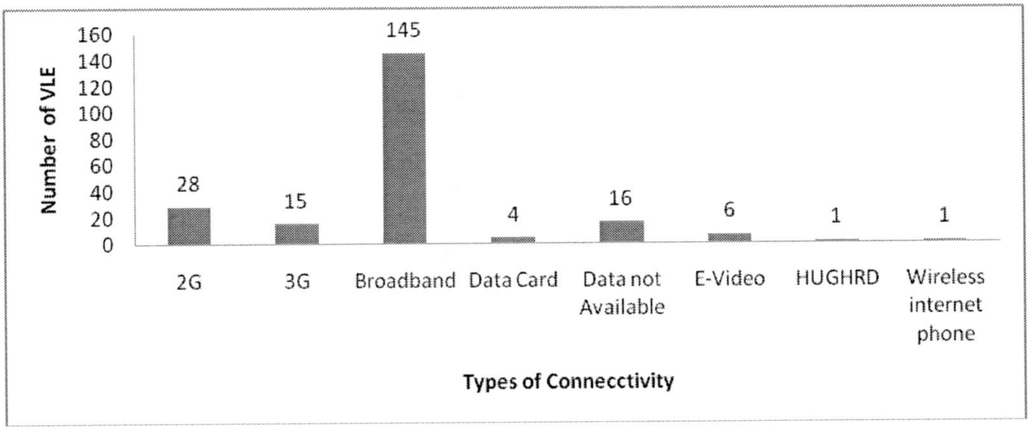

Fig. 6. Primary Connectivity Profile of VLE in Mandi District of HP

KEY CHALLENGES FACED BY CSCS AND VLES IN THE REGION

The biggest challenge is to make the CSC project financially feasible as well as viable to the VLEs in order to provide adequate income to the VLEs.The CSCs can only work efficiently and seamlessly if CSCs have reliable internet connectivity. Inconsistency in the connectivity and electricity comes up as a major challenge in implementation of CSCs effectively. It is important to ensure that the VLEs undergo training in delivering services to rural customers. Training should include technical as well as operating aspects of Services delivered. Further, VLEs need to be constantly motivated to proactively build awareness within their community (including local government officials) about the services they offer. Lack of awareness and community sensitization of rural community emerges as an important factor that has inhibited CSCs in achieving its objectives. There is a need to take proactive steps to build awareness and sensitize citizens and local government leaders in rural areas. Lack of support from the Local Government Agencies and SCAs are adversely affecting the operations for CSCs, which in turn is affecting the VLEs.

CONCLUSION

The CSC is spirited effort by the Government of India in making government services more accessible to rural population and it also aims at introducing transparency in the entire delivery process. However, it has been four years since the project was sanctioned and still most of the States have not been able to complete the centre rollout. The government should now take urgent step in order to ensure that the SCAs are successful in achieving the target rollout as fast as possible.

Researchers observe that 'technology cannot thrive unless it is people centered, inclusive, participative, and equitable and improves the quality of life a majority E-Government initiatives are failing due to a lack of understanding of effective planning, development and deployment [6] and varied sustainability challenges.

Future research should be taken to evaluate has these CSCs able to achieve the objectives that they were envisaged for them or they are just manifested as a hogwash, a detailed study is needed to understand the implementation challenges and bottlenecks. There should also be an attempt to study the emerging business model for a social enterprise and also take learning from best practices from CSCs operations in different states and apply those learning across the country.

REFERENCES

[1] RajanishDass and AtashiBhattacherjee; Status of Common Service Center Program in India: Issues, Challenges and Emerging Practices for Rollout; W.P. No. 2011-02-03, February 2011; Indian Institute Of Management Ahmedabad-380 015, India

[2] www.csc-india.org

[3] http://deity.gov.in/content/common-services-centers

[4] http://www.mit.gov.in/content/mission-mode-projects

[5] http://hp.gov.in/csc/

[6] Aichholzer, G. (2008). "Scenarios of egovernment in2010 and implications of strategy design." Electronic journal of e-government 2(1): 1-10.

[7] Bailey, A. (2009). "Issues affecting the social sustainabilityoftelecenters in developing countries: A field study of sixteen telecenters in Jamaica " European Journal of Information Systems for Developing Countries 36(4): 1-18.

[8] Bailur, S. (2007a). The complexities of community participation in rural information systems projects: the case of "Our Voices" IFIP 9.4 Social Implications of Computers in Developing Countries , Taking Stock of E-Development, Sao Paulo Brasil

[9] Basu, S. (2004). "E-government and developing countries:an overview." International review of law.computers and technology 18(1): 109-132.

[10] Benjamin, P. (2001). "Does "Telecentre" mean the center is far away:Telecenter development in Sounth Africa and around the World." The southern african Journal of information and communication1(1).

[11] Heeks, R., & Davis, A. (1999), "Different approaches to information age reform", in Heeks R. (Ed.) Reinventing Government in the Information Age: IT-Enabled Public Sector Reform, London: Routledge.

[12] http://www.mit.gov.in/content/common-services-centres

[13] Bhatnagar, P. S. and P. T. P. R. Rao (2007). Impact Assessment Study Of E-Government Projects In India, Indian Institute of Management,Ahmedabad.

[14] Bhatnagar, S. (2000). "Social Implications of Information and Communication technology in developing countries:lessons from Asian Success Stories." The electronic journal of Information Systems in Developing Countries 1(4): 9.

[15] Caspary, G. (2002). "Information technologies to serve the poor:how rural areas can benefit from the communications revolution." Development and Cooperation 1: 4-5.

[16] Cecchini, S. and M. Raina (2005). "Electronic government and the rural poor:The case of Gyandoot." The Massachussets Institute of Technology Information technologies and International development 2(2): 11.

[17] Clift, S. (2002). Roadmap for E-government in the Developing World.

[18] Dagron, G. (2001). "Prometheus Riding a Cadillac? Telecentres as the promised flame of knowledge." Journal of Development Communication: Special IssueonTelecentres 12(1).

[19] Edwin Lau (2003). Challenges for e-government development. 5th global forum on reinventing government. O.f.E.C.-O. a. Development. Mexico.

[20] Ernberg, J. (1998). Universal Access for Rural Development from Action to Strategies. First International Conference on Rural Telecommunications. Washington, 30 November - 2 December, 1998.

[21] Girardet, G. (2001). Case for Public Access. G8 UK Dot Force. London. Gomez, R., P. Hunt, et al. (1999). Telecenter Evaluation and research:A global perspective. International development Research center. Ottawa,Canada.

[22] Grace, J., C. Kenny, et al. (2004). Information and Communication Technologies and Broad-Based Development: A Partial Review of the Evidence.W. Bank. Washington DC.

[23] Harris, R. W., A. Kumar, et al. "Sustainable Telecentres? Two Cases from India."

[24] Heeks, R. (2002). "Failure,success and improvisation of information systems projects in developing countries." The Information society 18(2): 101-112.

[25] http://www.aisectcsc.com/aboutAISECT.html

[26] http://www.nictcsc.com/aboutnict.html

[27] http://www.utlindia.com/utl/templates/corporate/about_us.jsp

[28] http://www.basixindia.com/

[29] Islam, M. S. and M. N. Hasan (2008). "Multipurpose community centers in Bangladesh:problems and prospects." Emerald group pubilshing limited 27(3): 537-553.

[30] Islam, M. S. and M. N. Hasan (2008). "Multipurpose communitytelecentres in Bangladesh:problems and prospects." The Electronic Library Emerald Group Publishing Limited 27(3): 537-553.

[31] Jaeger, P. T. and K. M. Thompson (2003). "E-Government around the world: lessons ,challenges and future direction." Government Information Quarterly 20: 389-394.

[32] Khelladi, Y. (2001). What Works: The InfocentrosTelecenter Model. W. r. Center.

[33] Kumar, R. and M. L. Best (2006). "Impact and sustainability of egovernment services in developing countries:Lessons learned from Tamil Nadu,India." The Information Society 22: 13.

[34] Madon, S. (2005). "Governance lessons from the experience of telecenters in Kerala." European journal of Information Systems 14: 401-406.

35] Mahmood, K. (2005). "Multipurpose community centersfor rural development in Pakistan." Emerald group pubilshing limited 23(2): 204-220.

[36] Mahmood, K. (2005). "Multipurpose community telecenters for rural development in Pakistan." The Electronic Library Emerald Group Publishing Limited 23(2): 204-220.

[37] Mofleh, S. and M. Wanous (2008). "Developing Countries and ICT Initiatives:Lessons Learnt from Jordan's Experience." European Journal of Information Systems for Developing Countries 34(5): 1-17.

[38] Mofleh, S., M. Wanous, et al. (2008). "Developing Countries and ICT initiatives:Lessons learnt from Jordan's experience." The electronic journal of Information Systems in Developing Countries 34: 17.

[39] Ndou, V. D. (2004). "E-Governance for develpingcountries:Opportunities and Challenges." The electronic journal of Information Systems in Developing Countries 18(1): 24.

[40] Ndou, V. D. (2004). "E – Government For Developing Countries: Opportunities And Challenges." European Journal of Information Systems for Developing Countries 18(1): 1-24.

[41] Odedra, M. and Straub (2003). ""E-Commerce and Development":Whose Development?" The electronic journal of Information Systems in Developing Countries 11(2): 5.

[42] R.Colle and R. Roman (2002). Handbook for telecenter staff. New York.

[43] Scharffenberger, G. (September 1999). Telecentre Evaluation Methods and Instruments: What Works and Why? . IDRC Workshop on Telecentre Evaluation: A Global Perspective Québec

[44] Smith, C. (1992). Motivation and personality: Handbook of thematic content analysis New York, Cambridge University Press.

[45] Wakelin, O. and B. Shadrach (2001). Impact Assessment of Appropriate and Innovative Technologies in Enterprise Development. Manchester: EDIAIS. Manchester.

[46] Wong, K., C. Fearon, et al. (2007). "Understanding e-government and e governance: Stakeholders, partnerships and CSR." International journal of quality and reliability management 24(9): 927-943.

[47] WorldBank (1998). World Development Report 1998. World Development Report. New York, The World Bank.

[48] T. Petrin; Entrepreneurship as an economic force in rural development; Seventh FAO/ REU International Rural Development Summer School, Herrsching, Germany, 8-14 September 1994.

[49] Tyson, L., T. Petrin and H. Rogers (1994). 'Promoting Entrepreneurship in Central and Eastern Europe', Small Business Economics 6, pp. 1-20.

[50] www.nic.in/nicportal/nicportal/informaticsjanuary2010

Author Index

G1151